Step into Xcode

Step into Xcode

Mac OS X Development

Fritz Anderson

✦Addison-Wesley

Upper Saddle River, NJ • Boston • Indianapolis • San Francisco
New York • Toronto • Montreal • London • Munich • Paris • Madrid
Capetown • Sydney • Tokyo • Singapore • Mexico City

Many of the designations used by manufacturers and sellers to distinguish their products are claimed as trademarks. Where those designations appear in this book, and the publisher was aware of a trademark claim, the designations have been printed with initial capital letters or in all capitals.

The author and publisher have taken care in the preparation of this book, but make no expressed or implied warranty of any kind and assume no responsibility for errors or omissions. No liability is assumed for incidental or consequential damages in connection with or arising out of the use of the information or programs contained herein.

The publisher offers excellent discounts on this book when ordered in quantity for bulk purchases or special sales, which may include electronic versions and/or custom covers and content particular to your business, training goals, marketing focus, and branding interests. For more information, please contact:

U. S. Corporate and Government Sales, (800) 382-3419, corpsales@pearsontechgroup.com

For sales outside the U. S., please contact:

International Sales, international@pearsoned.com

Visit us on the Web: www.awprofessional.com

This Book Is Safari Enabled

The Safari® Enabled icon on the cover of your favorite technology book means the book is available through Safari Bookshelf. When you buy this book, you get free access to the online edition for 45 days.

Safari Bookshelf is an electronic reference library that lets you easily search thousands of technical books, find code samples, download chapters, and access technical information whenever and wherever you need it.

To gain 45-day Safari Enabled access to this book:

- Go to http://www.awprofessional.com/safarienabled
- Complete the brief registration form
- Enter the coupon code IDML-RFIM-T1UD-F3M1-GLAW

If you have difficulty registering on Safari Bookshelf or accessing the online edition, please e-mail customer-service@safaribooksonline.com.

Library of Congress Cataloging-in-Publication Data

Anderson, Fritz.
  Step into Xcode : Mac OS X development / Fritz Anderson.
    p.   cm.
  Includes bibliographical references and index.
  ISBN 0-321-33422-1 (pbk. : alk. paper)
  1. Operating systems (Computers)-Software.   2. Macintosh
(Computer)-Software.   I. Title.
  QA76.76.O63
  005.4'465—dc22   2005029875

ISBN 0-321-33422-1
Text printed in the United States on recycled paper at Courier in Stoughton, Massachusetts.
First printing, January 2006

For Chrissl,
Nancy, Roger, and Sarah,
who all made this possible.

Contents

Preface

From the moment it first published Mac OS X, Apple Computer has made a complete suite of application-development tools available to every Macintosh user. Since Mac OS X version 10.3, those tools have been led by Xcode, the development environment that Apple's engineers use to develop system software and such applications as Safari, iTunes, Mail, and iChat. These same tools are in your hands.

- A solid text editor with syntax coloring and API-based code completion
- The industry-standard gcc compiler suite
- A graphical, interactive debugger based on the GNU debugger (gdb)
- A mature human interface (UI) layout and object-linkage editor for Carbon and Cocoa
- Tools for gaining detailed insights into optimizing performance

Audience

I wrote this book for three types of readers.

1. Newcomers curious about the world of Mac OS X development
2. Experienced UNIX-family operating systems users who want an introduction to the Mac OS X tool set
3. Xcode users wanting to supplement their techniques

Step into Xcode will not attempt to teach programming, a programming language, or any of the Mac OS X programming frameworks; good books on those subjects have already been written. My aim is to focus squarely on using the Xcode tool set. Most of the book uses one example project—not as a showcase for the programming techniques involved but as a framework for how to do Mac development with these tools.

The CD-ROM accompanying this book provides the complete project directory—bugs and all!—for each chapter. Many of the examples in this book follow the progress of an application project that begins with a UNIX command line tool and progresses to a Core Data–based application with Spotlight support. As you follow along, you won't have to peck out every file and setting yourself. The CD-ROM directory, `Examples`, includes a copy of the project at every major stage of development—at least one version for each chapter. You can simply copy the current example project to your hard drive; the only errors are the ones I made deliberately.

Structure of the Book

Step into Xcode is divided into two parts. Part I introduces Xcode and Mac OS X development against the background of developing a simple application from a BSD command line tool to a Tiger-savvy Cocoa application taking advantage of Core Data and Spotlight.

- Chapter 1 introduces Xcode with the obligatory "Hello, World" demonstration.
- Chapter 2 demonstrates the typical Xcode workflow by building a command line tool that will form the heart of the application we'll be building throughout Part I.
- Chapter 3 moves from passive use of the Xcode debugger to active use, interrupting program flow to examine the workings of a flawed application.
- Chapter 4 shows what happens in compilation and linkage, both generally and in Mac OS X.
- Chapters 5, 6, and 7 wrap our command line tool in a Cocoa graphical interface. The Model-View-Controller design pattern is matched to the tools Xcode provides to implement it.
- Chapter 8 focuses on property lists, a must-know subject in Mac OS X development, and shows how to create text macros for Xcode.
- Chapter 9 moves our command line tool into a static library, showing how to build such a library and how to integrate a dependent target with Xcode's build system.
- Chapter 10 examines bundles and package directories. Most of the targets Xcode can produce are varieties of bundles. We look at the ubiquitous `Info.plist` file.

- Chapter 11 develops techniques for creating custom view classes for Cocoa and shows how the development tools support them.

- Chapter 12 extends the odyssey of our library from library to framework, showing how to package a dynamic library and its headers for sharing or for embedding in an application.

- Chapter 13 surveys the Xcode options in support of source code management systems. We set up a local CVS (concurrent versions system) repository and put our project under SCM (software configuration management) control.

- Chapter 14 covers two scenarios for cross-development: creating applications compatible with versions of Mac OS X earlier than your own and creating universal binaries to run on both Intel and PowerPC Macintoshes.

- Chapter 15 shows how to use the data modeling tool to generate a Core Data model for our application. After converting our application to use Core Data, many development tasks become a matter of using Interface Builder.

- Chapter 16 examines the techniques used to add Spotlight searchability to our data files.

- Chapter 17 finishes up our application with a localization and offers some thoughts on dead-code stripping.

Part II goes deeper into Xcode usage.

- Chapter 18 examines the Xcode human interface and explains how to use it to navigate projects.

- Chapter 19 considers Xcode from the point of view of a developer accustomed to using CodeWarrior, examining the stumbling blocks on the way to conversion and showing how to make the Xcode experience more familiar. At the end of the chapter, the notes on controlling the export of symbols may be useful to non-CodeWarriors.

- Chapter 20 looks at Xcode from the point of view of a developer accustomed to working with makefiles. This chapter describes the build system beneath the IDE (interactive development environment) and explains how you can customize and control it.

- Chapter 21 goes deeper into the debugging tools and techniques introduced in Part I.

- Chapter 22 shows how to make Xcode work faster.

Project Builder

Xcode 1.0 was released with Mac OS X version 10.3 (Panther) in September 2003 but has a much longer heritage. Xcode is a development of the Project Builder IDE used for Mac OS X through 10.2 and for NeXTStep and the NeXT operating system before that.

Xcode, the result of a rethinking of Project Builder, aimed at streamlining the work-flow of the typical programmer. Improvements centered on searching and managing large projects and speeding the edit-compile-link-debug cycle of development. Xcode added

- Code completion
- Distributed builds
- "Predictive" compilation, using idle CPU time to compile inactive source files in the background
- ZeroLink "lazy" linkage for fast launch times during development
- "Fix-and-continue" compilation for changing code while it is running in the debugger
- Version 3 (and now 4) of the gcc compiler
- A faster help system in a separate window, with its own search facilities
- Speed improvements

- Chapter 23 builds a simple AppleScript Studio application and considers Xcode's built-in support for unit testing.
- Chapter 24 shows how to use Xcode on a large open-source makefile-based project, and how to apply Xcode's debugger and the Shark performance measurement tool to it.
- Chapter 25 offers tips, traps, and observations that were left over from the rest of the book.

Finally, there are two appendixes:

- Appendix A reviews how to get the latest version of Xcode and how to install it.
- Appendix B lists the major settings variables used by the Xcode build system.

Xcode Versions Covered

This book is based on Xcode version 2.1, released in June 2005, although this version will probably vary from the one you will use, as Apple has not been timid about reworking Xcode substantially as performance and usability issues arise. The overall strategies and approach developed in this book—the Xcode workflow—will be the same across Xcode versions. For details, you may have to explore Xcode's menus, inspectors, and preferences; search its help system; or ask on Apple's mailing list for Xcode users: `http://lists.apple.com/mailman/listinfo/xcode-users`.

Most of the material in this book can also be applied to Xcode 1.5, the last version of Xcode for Mac OS X 10.3.

Typographical Conventions

In this book, code excerpts, symbols, and literal text inputs are set off in this `type-writer font`. In interactive text, such as at a terminal, the text you enter is shown in **`boldface typewriter font`**. Boldfacing is also used to emphasize changes to a program listing.

Human-interface elements, such as menu items and button names, are set in **boldface text font**. If elements are chained, such as hierarchical lists or menus, each level is set → off → by → arrows.

> Notes are set off in gray boxes.

Sidebars

Sidebars, which contain short digressions on subjects of interest, are set off by rules above and below.

Acknowledgments

This book was conceived by Ann Sellers at Addison-Wesley, and I hope I've lived up to her confidence in offering me the opportunity to write it. Greg Doench brought the book through editing and production. Lara Wysong was tireless in seeing the book into presentable shape; Evelyn Pyle's copy edits made me look much smarter.

I'd like to acknowledge the help given by David Gleason and Matthew Formica of Apple for responding to my questions. Matt nudged me into a couple of new directions, and although I couldn't completely follow his lead, his guidance improved this book.

Here in Chicago, Bob Frank and Jon Rentzsch offered helpful suggestions. And Kate, Bess, and Selena all showed faith.

PART I

The Life Cycle of a Mac OS X Application

Kicking the Tires

1.1 First Run

Xcode is installed, and it's time to see what it looks like. Find Xcode in /Developer/Applications and double-click its icon to launch it. If you're running Xcode for the first time, the New User Assistant window, as seen in Figure 1.1, will be presented.

The default settings in this window are best for most purposes. Simply click the **Next** button in each panel; in the last panel, click **Finish**. Every setting in the New

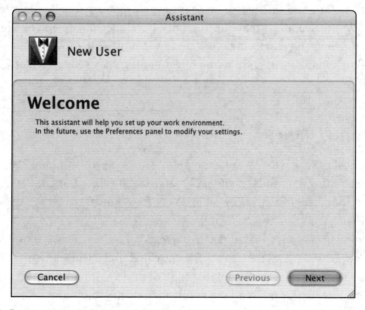

Figure 1.1 The New User Assistant. The dialog panels in this assistant capture your preferences the first time you run Xcode.

FileVault and Xcode

If you are using Mac OS X's FileVault feature to encrypt your home directory, the New User Assistant's default settings will slow the performance of Xcode significantly. Compiling and linking an application requires a lot of successive reads and writes to files, and if FileVault is on, each read and write will have to pass through the encryption engine. As compiler objects are unlikely to disclose significant secrets, this is wasted effort.

To avoid this problem, create new folders outside your home directory to hold intermediate and final build products. One possible location is in the /Users/Shared directory. In the second panel of the New User Assistant, select the radio buttons **Separate location for build products:** and **Separate location for intermediate build files:**, and use the **Choose . . .** buttons to designate the nonhome directories.

User Assistant is accessible through Xcode's Preferences window, so you won't be committing to anything.

If this is the first time you've run Xcode or this particular version, Xcode will automatically show you the release notes for the current version. Apple release notes are always worth reading—they are the only developer documentation written by Apple's engineers, and some subtleties are found only in the release notes—but for now, close the window. To return to the release notes, select **Show Release Notes** in the **Help** menu.

1.2 Hello, World

We want to get Xcode to do something for us, however minimal. By tradition, this means building a terminal command that prints `Hello, World`. Select the **New Project . . .** command from the **File** menu. Xcode presents the New Project Assistant, shown in Figure 1.2.

Xcode organizes your work around a *project,* a collection of files, tool settings, and *targets.* A target designates the project files used to build a particular product and the tool settings to apply. The most common kind of project, for building an application, has only one target—for building the application itself—but more complex projects may have several targets: for libraries, plug-ins, and small tools built ad hoc to test new components.

Figure 1.2 The New Project Assistant. Scroll down to **Standard Tool**, select it, and click Next.

> If you are coming to Xcode from CodeWarrior, the term *target* is used slightly differently. An Xcode target corresponds more closely to the CodeWarrior concept of a product. A CodeWarrior project typically has two targets—debug and final—for each product. Xcode has only one target—corresponding to the product—and any variant in building a target for debugging or release is a matter of *build configurations*.

Different target types require different tool settings and system libraries. Xcode eases the process of configuring a new project by offering you a choice of the most common target types for the first target in the project. We want to make a simple command line utility that runs in Mac OS X's BSD UNIX subsystem. Scroll down the list to **Command Line Utility** and the subitem **Standard Tool** (see Figure 1.2), select that item, and click **Next**.

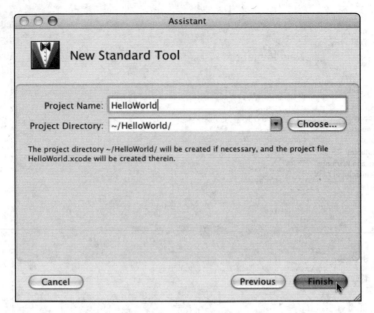

Figure 1.3   The New Standard Tool Assistant. To name a new project, type the name of the project. The assistant automatically names a new folder to enclose the project and its files.

. The next panel—New Standard Tool Assistant (Figure 1.3)—lets you name the project and place it on your disk hierarchy. For this exercise, type **HelloWorld** in the upper text field to name the project. The second field will echo what you type, designating ~/HelloWorld/ as the project directory. This means that the directory HelloWorld—which will be created if it isn't already there—will hold your *project file*, named HelloWorld.xcodeproj, as well as the other files needed to build your project's targets.

Click the **Finish** button. Xcode creates the HelloWorld directory, copies some files into it, and opens the project window (Figure 1.4). For a BSD command line tool, the project starts with a main.c file for the tool's main() function, a HelloWorld.1 template file for the man page, and the HelloWorld product, shown in red on the screen because Xcode can't find the file associated with it, which is natural enough, as we haven't built it yet.

These files are shown in the large *detail list* in the right-hand portion of the project window. The contents of the detail list are controlled by the selection in the Groups & Files column. Selecting the first item under this heading selects the project, filling

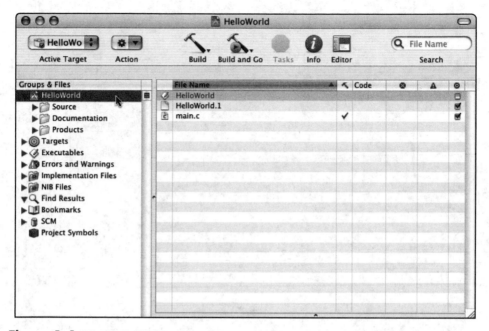

Figure 1.4 The HelloWorld project window. Names of files, arranged in groups, appear in the Groups & Files column at left. The list at right provides searchable details of whatever is selected in the Groups & Files column.

the detail list with every file included in the project. Below the project icon are folder icons, representing subgroups of files; clicking on a folder icon displays in the detail list only the files in that group.

To the left of the project and folder icons are the familiar disclosure triangles. Clicking on a disclosure triangle opens a container in a list. Expanding a file group folder shows the names of the individual files in the group.

If you've been exploring, click on the project icon at the top of the Groups & Files column to restore the list of all files in the detail list under File Name. Now double-click **main.c**. A window like the one in Figure 1.5 appears.

The placeholder for main() in the default main.c for a command line tool is Hello, World. This simplifies our first run of Xcode considerably. At the top of the window is a toolbar, the second item of which is labeled **Build and Go**. Click that button. A minute may pass—the first build of a target is always longer—but you are soon rewarded with an output window (Figure 1.6) saying Hello, World! Success.

Figure 1.5 An editor window, showing the default `main.c` from the Xcode command line tool template.

Quit Xcode (press **command-Q**, or select **Quit Xcode** in the **Xcode** application menu). There's nothing to save, so the project and editor windows disappear immediately.

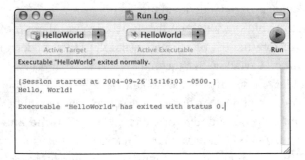

Figure 1.6 The `HelloWorld` output window.

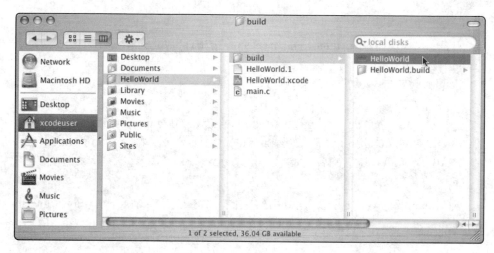

Figure 1.7 The HelloWorld project in the Finder. Creating and building a command line tool project in Xcode created a folder for the project, a project file, some template files, and a `build` directory containing the completed tool.

1.3 What Went Where

Switch to the Finder and examine the `HelloWorld` folder in your home directory (Figure 1.7). The `HelloWorld` directory is right where it was designated in the New Project Assistant and contains the files `HelloWorld.1` and `main.c` that came automatically with the new project. On the screen, the blue `HelloWorld.xcodeproj` icon is the project document file; double-clicking it opens Xcode and shows the HelloWorld project as you left it.

The `build` directory contains the `HelloWorld` tool and a folder named `HelloWorld.build`. This folder contains a dozen files or so, including the compiled object code from `main.c` and a number of files containing indexes to make it easier to navigate large projects and system libraries. You can ignore the `.build` directory; its use is strictly internal in Xcode.

The `HelloWorld` tool is a genuine UNIX executable, which you can demonstrate by using the command line terminal. Open the Terminal application in the `Utilities` subfolder of the `Applications` folder. Dragging the `HelloWorld` tool file's icon from the Finder into the Terminal window has the effect of "typing" into the terminal the full path of what you dropped. Press the **Return** key. The tool runs, prints `Hello,`

World!, and returns to the command line prompt:

```
xcodeuser$ /Users/xcodeuser/HelloWorld/build/Debug/HelloWorld
Hello, World!
xcodeuser$
```

Tools and applications built with the Debug build configuration, the default, are bound uniquely to the computer that built them and won't run on other computers. We'll get to this in Section 4.5.

At this point, we are done with the HelloWorld project. You can drag it and its files into the trash. Xcode will show no sign of having built or run HelloWorld.

1.4 Summary

In this chapter, we

- Ran Xcode and configured it for our use
- Created a project to build a command line tool
- Executed the tool from inside Xcode
- Saw what Xcode does when it creates a project directory and builds a product in it
- Verified that the tool we built will run from the command line
- Disposed of the project when we no longer needed it

2

Simple Workflow and Passive Debugging

2.1 Linear Regression

For most of this book, we'll be working on applications that do *linear regression*, a simple but informative statistic. Suppose that you have a series of data pairs, such as the quarterly sales figures for a particular department, shown in Table 2.1.

A *regression line* is the straight line that passes nearest all the data points (see Figure 2.1). The formula for such a line is $y = mx + b$, or the sales (y) for a given quarter (x) rise at a quarterly rate (m) from a base at "quarter zero" (b). We have the x and y values; we'd like to determine m and b.

The formulas for linear regression are as follows:

$$m = \frac{n \sum_{i=1}^{n} x_i y_i - \sum_{i=1}^{n} x_i \sum_{i=1}^{n} y_i}{n \sum_{i=1}^{n} x_i^2 - \left(\sum_{i=1}^{n} x_i\right)^2}$$

$$b = \frac{1}{n} \left(\sum_{i=1}^{n} y_i - m \sum_{i=1}^{n} x_i\right)$$

$$r = m \sqrt{\frac{n \sum_{i=1}^{n} x_i^2 - \left(\sum_{i=1}^{n} x_i\right)^2}{n \sum_{i=1}^{n} y_i^2 - \left(\sum_{i=1}^{n} y_i\right)^2}}$$

The value r is the *correlation coefficient*, a figure showing how well the regression line models the data. A value of 0 means that the x and y values have no detectable relation to each other; ± 1 indicates that the regression line fits the data perfectly.

Table 2.1 Quarterly Sales Figures for a Hypothetical Company (millions of dollars)

Quarter	Sales
1	107.5
2	110.3
3	114.5
4	116.0
5	119.3
6	122.4

Linear regression is used frequently in business and the physical and social sciences. When x represents time, lines derived from regressions are trends from which past and future values can be estimated. When x is volume of sales and y is costs, you can claim b as fixed cost and m as marginal cost. Correlation coefficients, good and bad, form the quantitative heart of serious arguments about marketing preferences and social injustice.

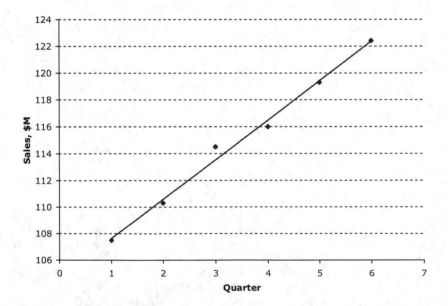

Figure 2.1 The sales figures from Table 2.1, plotted in a graph. The line drawn through the data points is the closest straight-line fit for the data.

The demands on a program for turning a series of x and y values into a slope, intercept, and correlation coefficient are not great: Keep a running total of x, x^2, y, y^2, and xy; keep note of the count (n); and run the formulas when all the data has been seen.

2.2 Plan of Action

If you're an experienced programmer for UNIX operating systems, the solution to this problem comes almost by impulse: Write a command line tool that reads data as pairs of floating-point numbers from standard input and writes m, b, and r to standard output.

Here's the first draft of such a tool:

```
#include <stdio.h>
#include <math.h>

int main (int argc, const char * argv[]) {
    int        nScanned;
    int        n;
    double     sumX, sumY;
    double     sumX2, sumY2;
    double     sumXY;

    n = 0;
    sumX = sumY = sumX2 = sumY2 = sumY = 0.0;

    do {
        double  x, y;
        int     nScanned = scanf("%lg %lg" x, y);
        if (nScanned == 2) {
            n++;
            sumX += x;
            sumX2 += x * x;
            sumY += y;
            sumY2 += y * y;
            sumXY += x * y;
        }
    } while (nScanned == 2);
```

```
double      slope, intercept;
slope = (n * sumXY - sumX * sumY)
        / (n * sumX2 - sumX * sumX);
intercept = (sumY - slope * sumX) / n;

double      correlation;
correlation = slope * sqrt((n * sumX2 - sumX * sumX)
                        / (n * sumY2 - sumY * sumY));

printf("%g\t%g\t%g\n", slope, intercept, correlation);

return 0;
}
```

Some veteran C programmers may be surprised to see declarations, such as double slope, intercept, interspersed with executable statements instead of being gathered at the top of the enclosing block. Declaring auto variables in the body of code is permitted by gcc version 3 and later and has been added to the C99 language standard.

Intermediate-level C programmers will see more than one error in this code. The errors are intentional.

2.3 A Command Line Tool

Let's put this plan into action. Start Xcode. As you did in the previous chapter, select **Command Line Utility** from the list of project types, and name the new project. We'll be calling the new tool Linrg, so it's most convenient to give the same name to the project.

Once again, Xcode will present you with a project window set up for a BSD UNIX command line utility. In Chapter 1, we double-clicked on the listing for the main.c file to bring up an editor window for that file. This time, try clicking once on the **main.c** file name and then on the **Editor** button in the project window's toolbar. The contents of the file appear in the right half of the project window (Figure 2.2). Selecting different file names in the Groups & Files column or in the detail list, display the contents of those files in the editor area.

Whether you work in a separate editor window or in an editor in the project window is completely up to you. The two views are equivalent. The detail listing that formerly

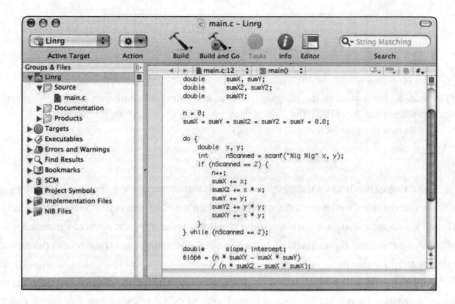

Figure 2.2 Editing the Linrg tool. Note that the small icon next to the file name main.c in the Groups & Files list and in the file name pop-up is darkened, indicating that the file has unsaved changes.

occupied the right half of the project window is still available. You can have it back by clicking the **Editor** toolbar icon again, or you can split the area between them by dragging the split bar that appears above the editor view or below the detail view. Xcode makes frequent use of completely closed split views, so be on the lookout for the telltale dimple in a thin bar at the edge of a view.

The content of main.c is, as before, the Hello, World program, which isn't nearly so useful to us this time. We substitute the source for our linear-regression tool, and click the **Build** button in the toolbar. If you hadn't saved the file before building, a dialog offers to do so before attempting the build; save the file. I've found that I always want to save changes before building; by visiting the Building panel of the Preferences window, you can set the **Unsaved Files:** pop-up to **Always Save**.

2.4 Build Errors

All has not gone well. The Xcode icon in the dock now has a red badge with a 1 in it. The status bar at the bottom of the project window says "Build failed for target 'Linrg' (1 error)." At the other end of the status bar is an error icon with the count

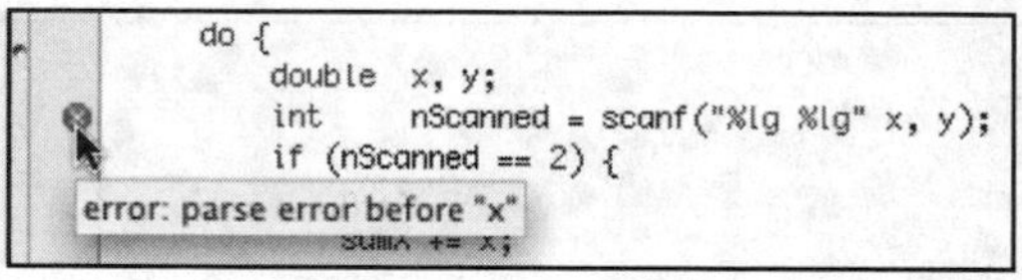

```
do {
    double   x, y;
    int      nScanned = scanf("%lg %lg" x, y);
    if (nScanned == 2) {
error: parse error before "x"
        sum += x;
```

Figure 2.3 Error icon in the margin, from the first attempt at building Linrg. When you point the mouse cursor at the icon, Xcode pops up a tooltip describing the error.

of 1. Looking at the text of the program, we see the same error icon at the left margin; holding the mouse cursor over the icon brings up a tooltip saying, "error: parse error before 'x'." Sure enough, as we examine the line marked by the icon (Figure 2.3), we find that we omitted the comma between the format string and the second parameter to the scanf() call.

Searching for errors by hand will not scale well to builds that span many errors among dozens, or even hundreds, of files. Even Xcode's trick of placing black marks in the scroll bar to mark the position of errors in the currently edited file only helps a little. Xcode provides a Build Results window for browsing error messages that arise in the course of building a project. You can see this window at any time by clicking the **Build Results** command in the **Build** menu or pressing **command-shift-B**. You can also open the Build Results window by clicking the error icons in the lower-right corner of any editor window.

Open the Build Results window now (Figure 2.4). The top half is taken up with an abbreviated transcript of the build process, with the single error, "error: parse error before 'x'," highlighted in red on the screen. Click the highlighted line. The editor view in the bottom half of the window fills with main.c, centered on the line at which the error was detected.

It is common for Xcode to present editors for the same file in multiple windows. Source code may be displayed in the Build Results window, the Project window, Editor windows, the Debugger window, and even the Source Control window. In each case, the view is a full-featured, writable—to the extent that the target file is writable—editor on the file in question. You can make a change to a file wherever the file appears; Xcode knows that all the views are on the same file, so there is no danger that the views will get out of sync.

With this in mind, use the editor in the Build Results window to insert a comma after the format string, and click **Build** again. Now we are rewarded with the message "Build succeeded for target 'Linrg'."

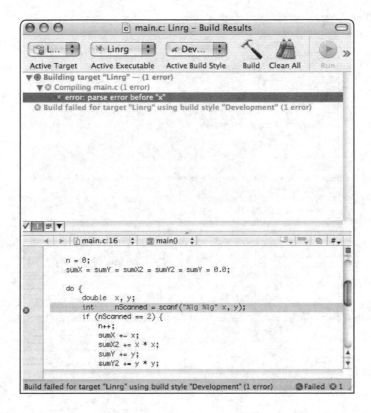

Figure 2.4 The Build Results window, showing an error in Linrg's main.c. Clicking the error line focuses the editor pane at the bottom on the line at which the error was detected. Any file in Xcode can have multiple editor panes open on it at one time.

Note the cluster of four icons at the lower left of the upper panel of the Build Results window. Clicking the icon that looks like a document with writing on it opens up the build transcript, which details the commands used to accomplish the last build and the messages returned by the tools. This transcript is worth looking at, first, for its value in showing how much goes on behind the scenes in response to a single command. Second, in the course of advanced tuning of the build process, this transcript is the only way to see what parameters are getting passed to the compilers, linkers, and other tools and in what sequence. Third, although it is usually very good at picking out the informative error messages from what its tools print out, Xcode isn't perfect. Sometimes, looking at the transcript for the full message is the only way to make sense of an error.

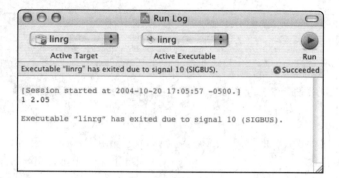

Figure 2.5 The first runable build of Linrg crashes with a bus-access error.

It's now time to run the Linrg tool. Hold the mouse button down on the **Build & Go** toolbar item, and select **Run** from the drop-down menu. Xcode opens a Run Log window and awaits our input.

For the first run, let's supply test data on the line $y = 2x$, adding a little bit of "noise" to make things more interesting. Type the following into the Run Log window, and press **Return**:

1.0 2.05

Once again, we have a problem (Figure 2.5). The console prints out the message "Executable 'Linrg' has exited due to signal 10 (SIGBUS)," and the program stops. Mac OS X raises signals 10 (bus error) and 11 (segmentation violation) when a program tries to access memory in a way that isn't permitted or that hasn't been allocated to its process. In a C program, this almost always means that a proper value has not been supplied for a pointer.

2.5 Simple Debugging

Although you may know what the problem with the Linrg tool is, let's prosecute this bug as though it were a mystery. It is time to start debugging.

Xcode's interactive debugger is a windowed user interface for gdb, the GNU project's interactive command line debugger. The command line interface to gdb is still available, through a console window, but most debugging—especially the simple kind we will do now—can be done entirely through the Xcode debugger window. The strategy here is simple: We'll run Linrg again, under the supervision of the debugger, and let it show us where the crash occurs.

To run usefully under gdb, an application has to be built with settings that preserve information that relates the binary in memory to the source code—the debugging flag, -g—and ensure that the binary being run works in the same sequence as laid out in the source: -00, the no-optimization flag. We don't have to do anything to bring these settings about; they are set, by default, in every new Xcode project.

If you've been following the Linrg example so far, the only thing you need to do is select **Debug Executable** from the menu that drops down from the **Build & Go** toolbar item. If you've made changes, select **Build and Debug** instead.

Xcode will take a few extra seconds to start gdb and display its Debug window before it has gdb execute Linrg. Matters will come to a rest when Linrg is running and looking for data on standard input.

> If you've been using CodeWarrior, you are used to the debugger's pausing before the first line of main(), waiting for your signal to proceed. Xcode sets no such automatic breakpoints; if you need to do set-up tasks at the start of execution, you'll have to set an early breakpoint yourself.

You will see that nothing new will be put into the Run Log window and that typing into that window will have no effect. For applications being debugged, Apple has chosen to conduct all standard input and output through a separate I/O window. Select **Standard I/O Log** from the **Debug** menu to display this window: It won't appear automatically, and there is no toolbar item available to make it visible.

Now, as before, type the following into the I/O window, and press **Return**:

1.0 2.05

This triggers the crash, but when crashing errors occur in a program being debugged, gdb stops the program at the site of the crash, and the Xcode debugger displays the state of the program. See Figure 2.6. The instruction that triggered the error is highlighted in red on the screen and has a red arrowhead in the margin next to it.

At first glance, the debugger seems to be doing us no favors: The offending line is highlighted, yes, but the code in question is in assembly language and appears to be in a system-supplied library. We were writing in C and were writing an application, not a system library.

Relief, however, is to be found in the panel at the upper left of the debugger window. This panel lists the chain of function calls that led to the present execution state of the program being debugged. The current function, _ _svfscanf, is at line 0.

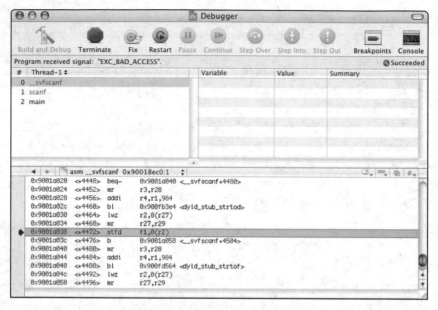

Figure 2.6 The Xcode Debugger window as it appears when the bus error in Linrg occurs. The machine instruction that caused the crash is highlighted; the chain of function calls that led to this instruction is listed in the upper-left panel.

This function was called by scanf (line 1), which in turn was called by main (line 2). This looks promising: We wrote a main function and called scanf inside it.

> CodeWarrior veterans will be used to the debugger's showing the call stack with the most recent function at the bottom. Under gdb and the Xcode debugger, it's at the top.

The Xcode debugger displays the first two function names in gray, but main is shown in black. The debugger displays all function names in the call stack, for which it has access to source code, in black. What happens if we click on main's item in the list?

The content of the Debugger window changes, most notably in the program listing at the bottom (Figure 2.7). We recognize this as the main function we wrote. Execution of the program was stopped inside the call to scanf, and the line containing that call is highlighted.

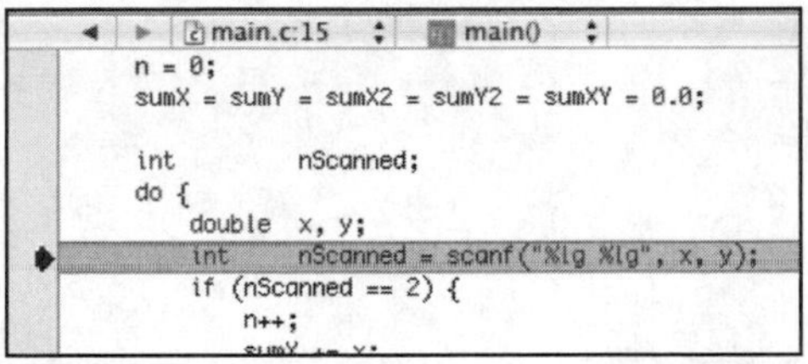

Figure 2.7 The Xcode debugger's lower, source code, display after selecting main in the stack trace. The line containing the call that led to the place where the program halted is highlighted.

At this point, we can allow at least one scale to fall from our eyes: The scanf function requires *pointers* to the variables it fills from standard input, not the *values* of those variables. As we have found our error, there is nothing more for the crashed Linrg to tell us. Dispose of its process by clicking the red **Terminate** item in the Debugger window's toolbar. Then edit the line

```
    int     nScanned = scanf("%lg %lg", x, y);
```

to read

```
    int     nScanned = scanf("%lg %lg", &x, &y);
```

Now this bug, at least, is killed.

2.6 Summary

In this chapter, we chose a problem to solve with a computer program and devised a strategy for solving that problem. We created a command line tool that does standard input and output. We ran into a compilation error, saw how to get information on the error, and corrected it. We saw how the Xcode debugger can be used passively to provide an instrument for examining the state of a program when it has crashed and used the resulting insight to fix a bug.

Simple Active Debugging

3.1 The Next Step

In Chapter 2, we got the `Linrg` command line tool to build without errors and used the Xcode debugger passively to track down and eliminate an early crashing bug. Let's run our tool again and see how it goes. Make sure that the project is built, and select **Debug Executable** from the **Build and Go** menu in the Project window's toolbar.

Once again, we select **Standard I/O Log** from the **Debug** menu, so we can interact with `Linrg`. Type some data:

```
1.0  2.05
nan nan nan
```

Well, after we enter two numbers and press **Return**, `Linrg` does not crash. It simply prints nan nan nan and quits. The status bar in the Debugger and Project windows says, "Debugging of Executable 'Linrg' ended normally."

Something else is wrong. An illegal floating-point operation—such as dividing 0 by 0, or square-rooting a negative number—took place somewhere in our calculations, resulting in a NaN (not a number), the special float value that signals an illegal operation. This need have happened only once; any arithmetic done with a NaN results in a NaN, so a single illegal operation early in the process could propagate the invalid-result marker through all subsequent calculations.

It makes sense that `Linrg` should report indeterminate results: Apparently, it tried to compute the regression line after reading only one point, which is not enough to determine a line. We suspect that this problem, then, is not in the computations but in the early exit from the input loop.

The time-honored way to track down a bug like this is to put a `printf()` call after every calculation, so that the problem code shows the state of the program at each significant step. If the right things are printed at the right time, you can see where the application went off the rails.

There is no need to instrument a step-by-step picture of Linrg's state, however, because we have a computer to take care of that for us. The Xcode debugger will do everything we need.

3.2 Active Debugging

In our previous encounter with the debugger, it took control over Linrg when a fatal error occurred. This time, we want the debugger to take control at a time of our choosing. By setting a breakpoint at a particular line in Linrg, we tell the debugger to halt execution of the application at that line, so that the contents of variables can be examined and execution resumed under our control.

The easiest way to set a breakpoint is to click in the broad gutter area at the left margin of the application source code in one of Xcode's editors. Select **main.c** in the Groups & Files list of the main Project window to bring that file into the editing area. Scroll down to the first line of the main() function if it isn't visible, and click in the gutter next to the line containing the command n = 0 (Figure 3.1). On the screen, a long, dark-blue arrowhead appears in the gutter to show that a breakpoint is set there. You can remove the breakpoint by dragging the arrowhead to the side, out of the gutter; you can move the breakpoint by dragging it up or down the gutter.

> Clicking the breakpoint turns it pale gray and deactivates it without clearing it, which is useful when more complex behaviors are attached to breakpoints. Control-clicking the breakpoint—or right-clicking if you're using a two-button mouse—brings up a menu that allows you to remove, edit, or disable the breakpoint or to attach one of several useful breakpoint actions. Breakpoint actions are discussed in Section 21.4.

```
double      sumX2, sumY2;
double      sumXY;

n = 0;
sumX = sumY = sumX2 = sumY2 = sumY = 0.0;

do {
    double  x, y;
    int     nScanned = scanf("%lg %lg", &x, &y);
    if (nScanned == 2) {
```

Figure 3.1 Clicking in the gutter at the left margin of an editor area to set a breakpoint at the adjacent line of code.

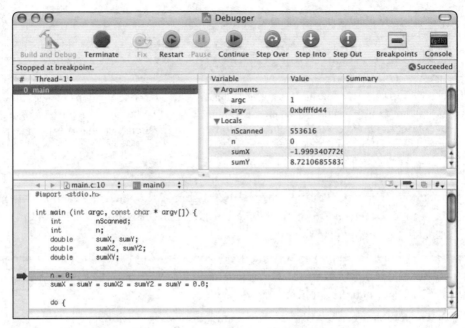

Figure 3.2 The Debugger window as `Linrg` stops for a breakpoint at the start of `main()`. The line at which execution paused is highlighted in red on the sceen, and the current values of function arguments and local variables are in the Value panel.

Select **Build and Debug** from the **Build and Go** toolbar item in the main Project window, or select **Build and Debug** (**command-Y**) from the **Build** menu. As before, Xcode performs any tasks needed to bring the `Linrg` tool up-to-date, and starts running it. This time, however, the Debugger window almost immediately shows that `Linrg` has halted at the breakpoint we set (Figure 3.2).

Now we can take control. The top of the Debugger window consists of a toolbar (Figure 3.3) that affords precise control over the execution of the program. The buttons and their actions are as follows:

- **Build and Debug**, available when the target application is not running, is a convenient way to return to debugging after editing application source in the Debugger window's editor pane.
- **Terminate** halts the target application and ends debugging. When no program is running, this button label is **Debug** and launches the current target under the debugger.

Figure 3.3 The toolbar of the Xcode Debugger window. The controls in the toolbar allow you to start and pause execution of the program being debugged or to step through the program line by line. Specialized commands allow you to step into functions and methods or to step out of the current function to its caller.

- **Fix** allows you to make some changes in programs while they are running under the Xcode debugger. This button compiles the file in the editor pane and attempts to patch the file into the running process.
- **Restart** halts the application being debugged and restarts it immediately under the debugger. This saves time over terminating the application and restarting both the debugger and the application.
- **Pause** breaks execution of the target application wherever it happens to be.
- **Continue** lets the target application continue running uninterrupted to the end or until it encounters a breakpoint or an error condition.
- **Step Over** lets the target application continue running until the next line in the function currently executing, stepping over any function calls. If the current line is the last line of the function, execution advances to the caller of the current function.
- **Step Into** lets the target application run until the next line, whether it is in the current function or in a function called in the current line. The debugger will step into function calls.
- **Step Out** lets the target application run until the current function returns.
- **Breakpoints** opens a window listing all the breakpoints set in the current project. You can add breakpoints by double-clicking in the label of the last, empty entry in the table and typing the location for the new breakpoint.
- **Console** opens a window that affords access to the command line features of the gdb debugger, which underlies the Xcode debugger. This is the only way to access some features of the debugger.

Now we can step through Linrg one line at a time. To get a sense of this, scroll the variable display—at the upper right of the Debugger window—down so that the values of the sum . . . variables are visible.

Now click the **Step Over** button a couple of times. The red highlight indicating the currently executing line moves down the display of main.c in the Debugger window's editor; as you pass the corresponding line, you see the values for sumX, sumY, and so on, change to 0.0. Whenever an entry in the variable display changes in value, the new value is shown in red.

But wait. We see sumX, sumY, sumX2, and sumY2 get set to 0, but sumXY still displays in black the junk value it had at the start. Did it get set? Will it? A quick examination of main.c in the editor pane shows that we don't initialize sumXY. The line that should zero it out initializes sumY twice instead.

Let's resolve to do something about that later. For now, we can force sumXY into good order by double-clicking its value, typing **0.0**, and pressing **Return**. The Xcode debugger and gdb, on which it is based, allow you to set variable contents on the fly.

Another click of **Step Over** takes us to the line

```
int      nScanned = scanf("%lg %lg", &x, &y);
```

We click **Step Over** at this line and find that **Step Over** is disabled. What's happening? This line can't complete execution until the input of two floating-point numbers either succeeds or fails. Awaiting input, scanf() blocks. To supply some, open the I/O log (**Debug → Standard I/O Log**), and again enter

1.0   2.05

Press **Return**. The application is no longer blocked waiting for input; scanf() returns, and the debugger can now honor our **Step Over** instruction by stopping at the next line.

Stepping slowly through the lines that follow, we see the progress of Linrg reflected in the changing values in the Variable pane:

nScanned ⇐ 2

sumX ⇐ 1.0

sumX2 ⇐ 1.0

sumY ⇐ 2.05

sumY2 ⇐ 4.2025

sumXY ⇐ 2.05

The next step takes us to the test for the do . . . while loop. Click **Step Over**; control goes not to the first line of the loop but to the first line after. The loop test failed.

Check the reason: Look in the Variable pane for nScanned. It isn't 2, so the loop test fails. It was 2 in the body of the loop; why isn't it now? Did it change? A review of the lines before the current one confirms that we didn't change it. There is no assignment and no possibility of pointer aliasing, all the way back to where nScanned is assigned.

Assigned—and declared—inside the loop. With a livelier eye, we now see two nScanned lines in the Variable pane, one of the lines labeled "out of scope." Sure enough, nScanned is declared inside the loop and separately as a local variable for the main() function. The outer variable, with its original garbage value, got tested in the loop condition; the loop-defined nScanned masked it from being updated.

How embarrassing. There's no point in continuing this run of Linrg, so click the **Terminate** button.

Let's turn the declaration of nScanned at the beginning of the loop:

```
int     nScanned = scanf("%lg %lg", &x, &y);
```

into a plain assignment:

```
nScanned = scanf("%lg %lg", &x, &y);
```

We can make the changes in the editor pane of the Debugger window. Click **Build and Debug**. When the Debugger stops at the old breakpoint, click **Continue** and let the program run:

```
1.0  2.05
```

No crash; no early exit. Excellent.

Enter some more data to flesh out an approximate line of $y = 2x$:

```
2.01  4
3  5.987
4  8.1
5  10.0
```

Now what? Like many UNIX tools, Linrg is meant to read standard input until it runs out. One signals the end of input at a terminal by typing the end-of-file character, control-D. Typing control-D into the I/O Log window seems to have no effect. The Standard I/O Log window is an imperfect mimic of a terminal.

We are saved by the fact that the read loop ends when the scanf call returns something other than 2—that is, when a nonempty line comes in that doesn't contain two floating-point numbers. So we simply type

```
X
```

Fix and Continue

You can't fix everything.

- You can't make a change that increases the number of local variables currently on the stack. Stack space has already been committed on the basis of the original, smaller demand, and Xcode has no good way of performing all the memory fixes that moving existing stack variables would require.

- For the same reason, you can't change the number of arguments a function on the stack takes.

- You can't change the name or return type of a function on the stack.

- You can't add an Objective-C class. New C++ classes are OK so long as they are not new specializations of template classes.

- You can't make a structural change to an Objective-C object: You can't add or remove methods or instance variables and expect the change to have effect on instances created before or after the change. The Objective-C runtime constructs its method-dispatch tables early in the life of an application, and the runtime is simply not designed for unloading and reloading class definitions.

Note also that if you fix a file that defines globals, they will be reinitialized.

Do a full-text search on "Restrictions on Using the Fix Command" in the Xcode documentation for complete details.

Now scanf() returns 0, no further additions are made to the statistics, and the loop exits.

At last, Linrg responds with actual numbers:

```
1.80163        0.618914       0.899816
```

But something's wrong: $y = 1.8x + 0.62$ is an implausible result, given that our data never strayed more than 0.1 from $y = 2x$. And although a 0.90 correlation coefficient isn't bad, it doesn't reflect how close the data is to a straight line.

We have to step through Linrg again, line by line, looking for what went wrong. Make sure that the breakpoint at the beginning of main() is still set, and click the **Debug** button in the Debugger window toolbar. Once again, we step through, watching the change in variables and deciding whether the changes make sense. Clicking **Step**

Variable	Value	Summary
▼ Locals		
nScanned	553604	
n	0	
sumX	0	
sumY	0	
sumX2	0	
sumY2	0	
sumXY	−1.999340057:	

Figure 3.4 The sum. . . variables after the execution of line 11 in main.c of Linrg. On the screen, all the variables show 0, indicating that they have been changed to that value. Only sumXY remains at its uninitialized value.

Over once initializes n. Clicking the button again initializes the sum. . . variables (Figure 3.4).

Oh, yes. Back when we were first stepping through Linrg, we meant to correct the failure to initialize sumXY, and we haven't done that yet. We'll do so now. Don't click **Terminate**. Instead, edit the second sumY in the line we just executed into sumXY. Then click **Fix**; if you have not set builds to save files automatically, you should accept Xcode's offer to save your change to main.c. Almost immediately, the status bar in the Debugger window should indicate that the build succeeded and that the fix was incorporated into Linrg.

Now drag the red arrowhead in the left margin of the Debugger window's editor up to line 11 (Figure 3.5). This resets Linrg's program counter so that line 11 will once again be the next line to be executed. Clicking **Step Over** executes the line, and we see by the Variable pane that sumXY is now initialized to 0.

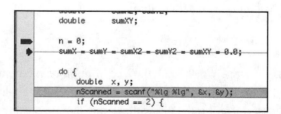

Figure 3.5 On the screen, dragging the arrowhead in the margin of the editor pane of the Debugger window, sets the next line to be executed. Here, we move the pointer to execute our change that initializes sumXY.

Now click the **Continue** button, and enter the test data:

```
1.0   2.05
2.01  4
3   5.987
4   8.1
5   10.0
X
2.00196      0.0175146      0.999871
```

We can believe $y = 2x + 0.018$, and a correlation as close to 1.0 as makes no difference.

3.3 Summary

In Chapter 2, we were led straight to a crashing bug when the debugger intervened at the crash. In this chapter, we used the Xcode debugger to take charge of how Linrg executes. We saw how to examine variables as they change value and how to change them directly from the Debugger window. We also saw how to fix minor bugs in a program without having to quit the program to edit, recompile, and relink. We even moved the program counter back so that our fix would be executed.

This chapter has completed our first pass through the life cycle—edit, compile, link, execute, and debug—of software development. In Chapter 4, we step back and consider the elements of that life cycle.

4

Compilation: The Basics

Before continuing, let's review how computer programs get made. If you're coming to Xcode from long experience with GNU Make or another development environment, this discussion will be extremely familiar to you.

Programmers use *source code* to specify what a program does; source code files contain a notation that, although technical and sometimes cryptic, is recognizably the product of a human, intended in part for humans to read and understand. Even the most precise human communication leaves to allusion and implication things that a computer has to have spelled out. When the Linrg tool refers to the local variable slope, for example we cared only that the name slope should consistently refer to the result of a particular calculation; the central processor of a computer running Linrg, however, cares about the amount of memory allocated to slope, the format by which it is interpreted, how memory is reserved for the use of slope and later released, that the memory should be aligned on the proper address boundary, that no conflicting use be made of that memory, and, finally, precisely how the address of slope is to be determined when data is to be stored or retrieved there. The same issues have to be resolved for each and every named thing in a program.

4.1 Compiling

Fortunately, we have a computer to keep track of such things. A *compiler* is a program that takes source files and generates the corresponding streams of machine-level instructions. Consider the following lines from Linrg:

```
int         nScanned;
do {
    double  x, y;
    nScanned = scanf("%lg %lg", &x, &y);
```

```
        if (nScanned == 2) {
            n++;
            sumX += x;
            sumX2 += x * x;
            sumY += y;
            sumY2 += y * y;
            sumXY += x * y;
        }
    } while (nScanned == 2);
```

These 13 lines translate into 21 lines of *assembly code,* a notation in which each line is a separate instruction to the processor:

```
LC0:
    .ascii "%lg %lg\0"  ; Reserve and initialize string constant
    .
    .
    .
L2:                                         ; Top of loop
    addis   r3,r31,ha16(LC0-"L00000000001$pb")
    addi    r4,r1,80                        ; x is at r1 + 80
    addi    r5,r1,88                        ; y is at r1 + 88
    la      r3,lo16(LC0-"L00000000001$pb")(r3) ; point to format
    bl      L_scanf$stub                    ; call scanf()
    cmpwi   cr7,r3,2                        ; Is result 2?
    bne-    cr7,L7                          ; No: jump to L7
    lfd     f0,80(r1)                       ; Yes: Fetch x.
    addi    r30,r30,1                       ; Add 1 to n
    lfd     f13,88(r1)                      ; Fetch y.
    fadd    f30,f30,f0                      ; sumX += x
    fmadd   f26,f0,f13,f26                  ; sumXY += x * y
    fmadd   f28,f0,f0,f28                   ; sumX2 += x * x
    fadd    f29,f29,f13                     ; sumY += y
    fmadd   f27,f13,f13,f27                 ; sumY2 += y * y
    b       L2                              ; Loop back again
L7:                                         ; Exit of loop
```

When imagining the tasks a compiler must perform in producing executable machine instructions from human-readable source, the first thing that comes to mind is the choice of machine instructions: the translation of floating-point add operations into `fadd` instructions or expressing the `while` loop in terms of `cmpwi`, `bne`, and `b`. Another important task is the management of *symbols*. Each C function and every variable has to be expressed in machine code in terms of regions of memory, with addresses and extents. A compiler has to keep strict account of every symbol, assigning an address—or at least a way of getting an address—for it and making sure that no two symbols get overlapping sections of memory.

In its analysis of `main()`, the compiler budgeted a certain amount of memory in RAM (random access memory) for local variables and assigned general-purpose register `r1` to keep track of that block. The 8-byte floating-point number `x` was assigned to the memory beginning 80 bytes into that block ($80 + r1$, or $80(r1)$ in the assembler's address notation); `y` was assigned to the eight bytes beginning at $88(r1)$. The compiler made sure not to use that memory for any other purpose.

The sums for the regression don't even get stored in memory but are computed in the processor's floating-point registers and used from there. Register `f30`, for instance, holds the value of the `sumX` variable. Once again, the compiler makes sure that each symbol gets associated with a particular piece of storage.

Why don't the calculations in the compiled code from `Linrg` follow the order specified in the source code? For instance, the sum of products of `x` and `y` is calculated second in the compiled code, although the statement `sumXY += x * y` appeared last in `Linrg`'s read loop. The compiled code shown here was generated with optimization turned on, which among other things lets the compiler change the order of operations for efficiency, so long as the changes do not change the overall effect of the code. This reordering is why you generally shouldn't turn optimization on if you intend to observe execution in the debugger: Control will appear to jump discontinuously through the source statements, which is very confusing.

In an Xcode project, files that are to be compiled are found under the target to which they belong, in the Compile Sources build phase. Open the **Targets** group by clicking on its disclosure triangle, and then open the application target's disclosure

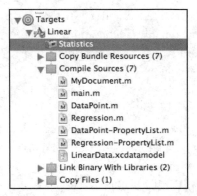

Figure 4.1 The build phases in the **Linear** target, with **Compile Sources** expanded to show the source files that go into the application. This listing is quite separate from the file listing in the upper part of the Groups & Files list. The upper listing determines whether the project contains a reference to a file; the file's presence in a build phase determines what Xcode will do with the file.

triangle when it appears. The build phases for that target will appear and can themselves be opened for inspection or editing. See Figure 4.1.

4.2 Linking

The accounting task does not end there. Five lines after L2 comes the instruction

```
    bl      L_scanf$stub
```

This line is the translation of the call to the scanf() function. What sort of symbol is L_scanf$stub? This symbol refers to a short code segment produced behind the scenes by the compiler:

```
L_scanf$stub:
    .indirect_symbol    _scanf
    mflr    r0
    bcl     20,31,L2$_scanf
L2$_scanf:
    mflr    r11
    addis   r11,r11,ha16(L_scanf$lazy_ptr-L2$_scanf)
    mtlr    r0
    lwzu    r12,lo16(L_scanf$lazy_ptr-L2$_scanf)(r11)
```

```
    mtctr   r12
    bctr
.data
.lazy_symbol_pointer
L_scanf$lazy_ptr:
    .indirect_symbol _scanf
    .long dyld_stub_binding_helper
    .subsections_via_symbols
```

This code segment is a bit convoluted but amounts to loading the address stored at L_scanf$lazy_ptr and continuing execution at that address. The next question is: What is stored at L_scanf$lazy_ptr? The code says that it is the address _scanf. And there the trail goes cold because the compiled code for main() does not assign any memory to a code block—or anything else—named _scanf.

And a good thing, too, as scanf() is a component of the standard C library. We don't want to define it ourselves: We want to use the code that comes in the library. But the compiler, which works with only one .c file at a time, doesn't have any way of referring directly to the starting address of scanf(). The compiler has to leave that address as a blank to be filled in later; therefore, in building a program, there has to be an additional step for filling in such blanks.

The product of the compiler, an *object file*, contains the machine code generated from a source file, along with directories detailing what symbols are defined in that file and what symbols still need definitions filled in. Under Xcode's gcc compiler, as with many others, C source files have the suffix .c; object files have the same name, with the .c removed and .o (for object) substituted. Libraries are single files that collect object files supplying useful definitions for commonly used symbols. In the simplest case, a library has a name beginning with lib and suffixed with .a.

The process of back-filling unresolved addresses in compiled code is called *linkage editing*, or simply *linking*. You present the linker with a set of object files and libraries, and, you hope, the linker finds among them a definition for every unresolved symbol your application uses. Every address that had been left blank for later will then be filled in. The result is an executable file containing all the code that gets used in the application. See Figure 4.2.

This process corresponds to the **Link Binary With Libraries** build phase in the application's target listing. This phase lists all the libraries and frameworks against which the application is to be linked.

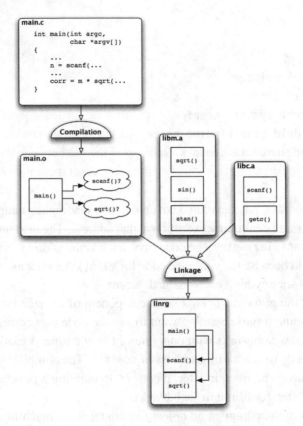

Figure 4.2 The greatly simplified process of building `Linrg`. Function `main()` in `main.c` refers to `scanf()` and `sqrt()`, but `main.c` provides no definitions; compiling `main.c` produces a `main.o` object file with unresolved references. Definitions are to be found in `libc.a` and `libm.a`. The linkage phase of building `Linrg` produces an executable file that contains both `main()` and the functions it refers to.

4.3 Dynamic Loading

In fact, it's one step more complicated than that. Standard routines, such as `scanf()`, will be used by many—possibly hundreds—of applications on a given system. Copying the machine code that implements `scanf()` into each application is a pointless waste of disk space. The solution is *dynamic loading,* referred to in the preceding assembly snippets by the abbreviation `dyld`. The application leaves the addresses of common library functions unresolved even in the final executable file, providing the partial executable code along with a dictionary of symbols to be resolved and the system libraries to find them in. The operating system then fetches the missing code and links it into the executable when the application runs.

Dynamic loading doesn't save only disk space but can also save RAM and execution time. Dynamic libraries—collections of object files set up for dynamic linking and having the prefix `lib` and the suffix `.dylib`—are loaded as read-only memory-mapped files. If two or more applications load the same dynamic library, the Mac OS X kernel will share the same in-RAM copy of the file between them. The second and subsequent users of a dynamic library therefore don't incur memory or load-time costs.

For these reasons, dynamic linkage is much preferred in Mac OS X's tool set over static linking, or the merging of library components directly into the executable file. When you specify library names and search directories for linkage to an application, the linker will look for `.dylib` files for dynamic linkage first and will use static linkage with `.a` files only if there is no `.dylib`.

> To force the linker to use a static library, pass the library's full pathname in a `-l` option to the linker. This technique also works for libraries not named according to the `lib*.a` or `lib*.dylib` convention.

If dynamic libraries don't literally get linked with the application's executable code until runtime, why do they figure in the linkage phase of the build process at all? There are two reasons. First, the linker can verify that all the unresolved symbols in your application are defined somewhere and can issue an error message if you specified a misspelled or absent function. Second, the linker-built tables in the dynamically linked executable code specify not only the symbols that need resolving but also what libraries the needed definitions are to be found in. With files specified, the dynamic loader does not have to search all the system's libraries for each symbol, and the application can specify private dynamic libraries that would not be in any general search path.

4.4 Prebinding

In the early releases of Mac OS X, true dynamic loading—determining that a library is needed, staking out a stretch of RAM for it, and stitching together all the references to its contents—was not an efficient process. Assigning memory regions among the pieces of dynamically linked applications was slow enough to impose significant delays on the process of launching a Mac OS X application.

The solution to this problem was *prebinding*. A library is said to be prebound if it specifies an address at which it prefers to be loaded. The author of the library chooses an address that does not collide with any other prebound library, and the linker, when building the prebound .dylib, prefills any pointers in the library, on the assumption that the library is loaded at its prebound address. A prebound application is built exclusively from prebound libraries and has almost all the address arithmetic necessary to load it already done.

As no author can know the prebound address claims of every other library on every user's system, collisions are inevitable; the command line tool fix_prebinding is provided to repair the prebinding hints of applications that are found to have lost prebinding because of such conflicts. The long phase at the end of most Apple installations, signaled in the installer by "Optimizing System Performance," is the application of fix_prebinding to all applications, in case the installation spoiled existing prebinding addresses.

This arrangement no doubt bemuses the experienced reader, who might have thought that hand assigning load addresses went out with 16-bit address spaces. Apple has worked hard to alleviate this problem. By applying the Shark performance analysis tool to the dynamic loader, Apple engineers have found ways to bind library addresses, at runtime, that are at least as fast as prebinding. As of Mac OS X version 10.3.4, prebinding of applications is no longer necessary.

Prebinding will still cut 10 percent to 30 percent from your application load times on earlier versions of Mac OS X, so you should know how to apply it. See Section 12.6 for details.

4.5 ZeroLink

You'll have gathered by now that the task of linking and loading a complex application is tedious and time consuming. Indeed, with most development systems, the linker adds a significant delay between changing source code and running the results. This delay weighs particularly heavy in the edit-compile-link-run-debug work cycle most developers spend most of their days pursuing.

One of Apple's goals in designing Xcode was to make that development cycle as quick and fluid as possible. One important insight was that more than in normal use, a program that is being debugged is idled waiting for user interaction and restricted to a small subset of its working code. In that particular, constrained circumstance, why link and load all the program, when only part will be exercised? And why not use the extra idle time at runtime to do linking as it is needed?

The result of this line of thinking is ZeroLink. An application built with ZeroLink will be launched with only the barest minimum of its code loaded—typically, the `main()` function and the runtime library. Code from other modules will be loaded only on demand.

Like a mythical hero granted special powers, a ZeroLinked application has tragic limitations. It is bound irrevocably to the dynamically loadable object files generated on your computer especially for ZeroLink and cannot be executed on another machine. To avoid a very common pitfall of Xcode development, do not distribute applications built with ZeroLink. (This caution would include any application built with the Debug build configuration—the Development build style in pre-2.1 releases of Xcode.) Such applications won't run, which is the ultimate failure to pass the embarrassment test.

A ZeroLinked application will be launched without the completeness checks afforded by traditional linking. Under a traditional linker, if you misspell `scanf` as `ssanf` and ignore the warning about an unprototyped function, the linker will refuse to produce an executable file, instead emitting the error message that the symbol `_ssanf`, referenced in such-and-such an object file, could not be resolved. Under ZeroLink, no attempt is made to resolve such symbols before running; the whole point is to save the time spent in resolving them. You won't know that anything is wrong until your application tries to call `ssanf()` and is halted by the ZeroLink loader because the symbol could not be resolved. If your application goes through many iterations under ZeroLink, it may be a good idea to switch the build configuration to Release or otherwise disable ZeroLink and rebuild to check for possible link errors.

Objective-C applications are subject to an insidious side effect of ZeroLink's permissiveness. If the implementation of a class—call it `AClass`—is included in the project—`AClass.m` and `AClass.h` appear in the Groups & Files list—but is not included in the application target—the box in the detail view next to `AClass.m` is not checked—attempts to create an instance of `AClass` will fail *silently*. The message `[AClass alloc]` will return `nil` without raising any error, and because Objective-C permits messages to `nil`—they return `nil` or integer zero or floating-point garbage— the application can execute for quite a long time before the error becomes apparent.

Finally, when you debug your application, be aware that at the first pass through your program, the code for functions and methods in other files will not have been loaded. The **Step Into** command is implemented by setting a temporary breakpoint at the beginning of the function being called; if the function hasn't been loaded into memory yet, there is no place to put the breakpoint! Instead of taking you into a function, **Step Into** will step you to the first line after the function call. Subsequent uses of **Step Into** on the same function, once it is loaded, work as expected. The workaround is to find the target function yourself and to set a breakpoint at the first line by hand.

These are the major points to attend to. The Xcode documentation goes into much deeper and more current detail. Select **Documentation** in the **Help** menu, select **Full-Text Search** in the search field's menu, and search on **ZeroLink Caveats** for full information.

4.6 Summary

In this chapter, we reviewed the process of compiling and linking an application, with particular reference to Mac OS X. The big task in the entire process is the management of symbols. We covered dynamic loading, how prebinding was once a solution to problems with it, and how ZeroLink is used to shorten the development loop. We learned enough about ZeroLink to pick up on some of the traps it leaves for developers.

5

Starting a Cocoa Application

In this chapter, we make the Linrg tool the heart of an application using the Mac OS X graphical human interface. Our framework for the application will be Cocoa, the application toolkit developed from NeXTStep and OpenStep; the language will be Objective-C.

5.1 Plan of Action

5.1.1 Program Tasks

We'll use Linrg unchanged for the computational part of the program. Our front-end program will therefore have the tasks of

- Storing a list of x and y data pairs
- Allowing the user to enter and edit the data-pair list
- Passing the data-pair list to Linrg
- Reading the results from Linrg and displaying them to the user

> Keeping Linrg as a separate executable is admittedly a strange decision: The code is so simple, it would be easier to fold it into the main application. We're doing it this way in order to illustrate a few additional points. If Linrg were a large-address-space application, using a 64-bit address space under Mac OS X 10.4 or later, it might make sense to build it as a 64-bit utility, with a 32-bit application running its human interface.

5.1.2 Model-View-Controller

Cocoa applications are built around the design pattern called Model-View-Controller (MVC). The pattern asserts that three kinds of things comprise an interactive program.

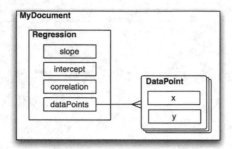

Figure 5.1 The minimal data model for a program that manages linear regressions. The document contains a list of data points and the results of the regression done on them. The regression refers to the list of data points.

1. *Model objects* embody the data and logic of a particular problem domain. Models tend to be unique to each application.

2. *View objects* handle user interaction, presenting information and enabling the user to manipulate data or otherwise influence the behavior of the program. Views are usually drawn from a repertoire of standard elements, such as buttons, tables, scrollers, and text areas. Views tend to have no intelligence about any particular problem domain: A button can display itself and report button clicks without having to know what clicking would mean in your application.

3. *Controller objects* mediate between the pure logic of the model and the pure mechanics of the views. A controller object decides how model content will be displayed by the views and how user actions translate into model events.

The Model

It seems plain that the first task of our program—storing a list of data pairs—is the sort of task a model object performs. Similarly, the task of calculating the linear regression is purely a function of the data we present to the calculation and would be the same no matter how we managed the data points beforehand or presented the results afterward.

What we want, then, is a document containing a set of data points and the results of calculating a linear regression on them. This simple design is shown in Figure 5.1.

We will be working in Objective-C, which provides the easiest access to Cocoa. From the figure, it's natural to imagine the interface for a DataPoint object:

```
@interface DataPoint : NSObject <NSCoding> {
    double      x;
    double      y;
}


- (id) init;
- (id) initWithX: (double) xValue Y: (double) yValue;

- (double) x;
- (void) setX: (double) newValue;
- (double) y;
- (void) setY: (double) newValue;
@end
```

This code segment declares DataPoint to be a subclass of the basic NSObject class, promises that DataPoint will be able to read and write itself in data streams according to the NSCoding protocol, and says that its data consists of two double-precision numbers: x and y. The code then declares a default initializer (init) and an initializer that sets the instance values (initWithX:Y:). After that come accessors for reading and setting the x and y values. Simple.

The interface for the Regression class is mostly the same concept, applied to the four data members instead of two:

```
@interface Regression : NSObject <NSCoding> {
    NSMutableArray *    dataPoints;
    double              slope;
    double              intercept;
    double              correlation;

    NSTask *            linrgTask;
}

- (id) init;

- (double) slope;
- (void) setSlope: (double) aSlope;
```

```
- (double) intercept;
- (void) setIntercept: (double) anIntercept;

- (double) correlation;
- (void) setCorrelation: (double) aCorrelation;

- (NSMutableArray *) dataPoints;
- (void) setDataPoints: (NSMutableArray *) aDataPoints;

- (BOOL) canCompute;
- (void) computeWithLinrg;
@end
```

Once again, we see the descent from NSObject, the promise of NSCoding, the four data members, and accessor methods for those members. We make dataPoints an NSMutableArray, which is a Cocoa class that keeps ordered lists of objects. There are two additional public methods.

1. The method canCompute returns YES—the Objective-C equivalent of true—only if at least two data points are available. This isn't a comprehensive test for whether the regression would be valid, but it's a start.
2. The method computeWithLinrg calculates the slope, intercept, and correlation coefficient.

One data member, linrgTask, didn't figure in our sketch model. This data member is an NSTask, an object used for running command line tools from Cocoa applications. We'll be using an NSTask to run Linrg on our data points.

The Controller

The controller object we create will be an instance of MyDocument, a subclass of Cocoa's NSDocument. Xcode's template for a new Cocoa document-based application automatically includes a MyDocument class with skeleton code in the project.

NSDocuments are automatically placed in the command-response chain of the application and bring with them the basics of loading and storing a document's contents in the file system. We can expect our documents to be told to load and store themselves, to compute the linear regression, and to add, edit, and remove data points. Therefore, we will want to provide methods for loading and storing and for

Accessorizer

Note that for every property named *propertyName* of type *type* in a class, the key-value coding (KVC) protocol has us writing a pair of methods:

- (*type*) *propertyName*;
- (void) set*PropertyName*: (*type*) aValue;

The individual methods are not difficult to write—they are almost identical—but they are tedious. Can't we automate the task of generating property accessors?

We can. The first resort is to Xcode's **Script** menu—it appears in the menu bar as a scroll—in the **Code** submenu. Select the four lines that declare Regression's instance variables, and select **Script → Code → Place Accessor Decls on Clipboard**. You can now paste declarations for setter and getter methods for each of the three instance variables into the header. Reselect the instance-variable declarations, and select **Place Accessor Defs on Clipboard** so you can paste the complete methods into the implementation file.

Kevin Callahan's Accessorizer application is a more comprehensive tool for generating accessors and many other kinds of boilerplate code for Cocoa. (Visit his site at http://www.kevincallahan.org/software/accessorizer.html) The application can be configured extensively to fit almost any style of code layout and philosophy of architecture for accessors. If you do a lot of Cocoa programming, Accessorizer will make your life easier and be worth the donation the author asks.

---

computing. These tasks can be done through Regression, our top-level model object, so we conclude that MyDocument need add a data member only for a Regression object.

Strangely, we won't be providing any methods for managing the data points. More on this later.

```
@class Regression;

@interface MyDocument : NSDocument
{
    Regression *    model;
}

- (IBAction) compute: (id) sender;
@end
```

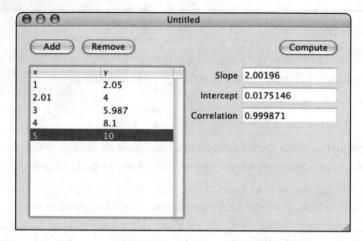

Figure 5.2 Planned layout of the main window of our linear-regression program. The **Add** and **Remove** buttons insert and delete points in the data set, which can be edited directly in the table at left. The **Compute** button passes the points to Linrg and causes the results to be displayed in the read-only fields below it.

By the vagaries of the Objective-C language, it is not necessary to declare in the interface every method a class implements. One method we do need to declare is compute:, the method that triggers calculation of the regression. As a method that responds to commands from the application's human interface, compute: follows a strict signature—taking one anonymous object (type id), the sender of the command, and returning IBAction, which is #defined as void but serves to inform Interface Builder that this command may be issued to this class by the human interface.

The View(s)

The view layer of our program is best specified by how we want it to look and behave. Figure 5.2 shows what we're aiming for.

5.2 Starting a New Project

We start by selecting **New Project** . . . from the **File** menu (or pressing **command-shift-N**). Once again, Xcode presents a choice of project templates; pick **Application → Cocoa Document-based Application**. We'll name the project Linear.

Now we're going to embed the Linrg tool in our application. We want the build process for Linear to copy a completely built Linrg into the application bundle; if a completely built Linrg isn't available, we want one built. You can include the products of other projects in an Xcode project, with one restriction: Those other products have to be in the same directory as the one used by your main project.

There are two ways to do this. One way is to double-click on the project (top) icon in the Groups & Files list in each of the projects concerned and then in the **General** tab of the resulting Get Info panel to select **Place Build Products In:** → **Custom location**. Choose the same folder each time. That way, all projects will put their products in the same directory, satisfying the restriction.

The other way is to put both projects into the same directory. In that case, they will both use the same subdirectory, build, as their products directory. This also satisfies the restriction.

We'll go the second way. In the project-naming panel, click the **Choose** button, and use the resulting open-file dialog to select the directory containing your Linrg project. Click **OK**. The path in the project-naming panel will now end in /Linrg/Linear, putting the new project in a subdirectory of Linrg, not the same directory. Delete /Linear from the path, and click **OK**.

The skeleton of the Linear project, built from Xcode's template, now appears in a new project window. This skeleton consists of a main.m file, which you won't be editing, and a MyDocument.m file, which will host the principal controller code. The project is linked to the Cocoa framework, and other frameworks are included, but not linked, for ready reference. A credits.rtf file provides content for an automatically generated About box for the application. Nib files specify human-interface appearance and behavior.

We mean to include the results of Linrg, so let's do that now. From the **Project** menu, select **Add to Project...** (**command-option-A**). Find and select the **Linrg.xcodeproj** project document in the same directory as the Linear project, and click **Add**. Click **Add** again for the options sheet that appears next; we don't need to copy the file for local use, and we have only one target it could apply to. An Xcode project icon labeled **Linrg.xcodeproj** can now be found in the **Resources** group under the project icon.

We could also have added the **Linrg.xcodeproj** document by dragging it from the Finder into the Groups & Files list.

Opening the **Targets** group in the Groups & Files list reveals the only target this project has: Double-click the application **Linear** to open the Get Info window

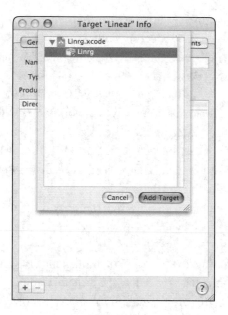

Figure 5.3 The Target Info window for Linear.app, showing the sheet for adding a dependency. Only one Xcode project is inside the Linear project and only one product of that project. Selecting it and clicking **Add Target** ensure that Linrg will always be up-to-date when it is included among Linear's resources.

for the target. The first panel of the window, General, includes a listing for **Direct Dependencies**. Click the + button below the list; in the sheet that emerges, select the **Linrg** product of Linrg.xcodeproj. See Figure 5.3. Then click **Add Target** and close the window. Now the process of building Linear will include a build, if necessary, of Linrg and will copy Linrg to Linear's Resources directory inside its bundle.

5.3 Implementation: Model

Now it's time to bring our design to reality. We'll start by creating source files for our model classes: DataPoint and Regression.

5.3.1 DataPoint

Select **New . . .** from the **File** menu or press **command-N**. Xcode will present you with a list of file templates and give you the choice of creating a blank file. Following

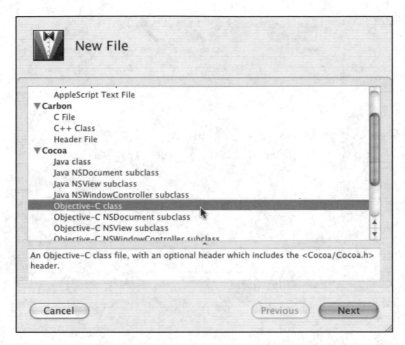

Figure 5.4 The New File Assistant, showing the option of creating a pair of new files containing a template for a subclass of NSObject.

the example of Figure 5.4, choose **Objective-C class** in the **Cocoa** category, and click **Next**.

You will then be asked to name your file and the class it defines; type **DataPoint**, leaving the .m suffix in the name field (Objective-C implementation files use the .m suffix). Make sure to check the checkbox offering to create a corresponding interface (.h) file. Xcode will now present you with a new file, named DataPoint.h, containing the skeleton of DataPoint as a class derived from NSObject.

We already know the contents of DataPoint.h, having specified it in our design sketch. Fill it out, and then press **command-option-up arrow**, which should make the counterpart—.c, .cpp, or .m file for .h, or vice versa—file for DataPoint.h visible. Here's the start of what should go in it—a reference to the interface file and the initialization and accessor methods:

```
#import "DataPoint.h"

@implementation DataPoint
```

```
//  Default initializer. Sets x and y to 0.0.
- (id) init
{
    return [self initWithX: 0.0 Y: 0.0];
}


//  Designated initializer (all initializers lead to this one).
- (id) initWithX: (double) xValue Y: (double) yValue
{
    x = xValue;
    y = yValue;
    return self;
}


#pragma mark Key-Value Coding
//  Getters and setters for the x and y attributes.

- (double) x { return x; }
- (void) setX: (double) newValue { x = newValue; }
- (double) y { return y; }
- (void) setY: (double) newValue { y = newValue; }
```

Instances of DataPoint have two attributes, x and y, which in this simple case correspond directly to the instance variables of the same name. We provide getter and setter methods for each.

In this book, we'll provide getter and setter methods—accessors—for every attribute of a class on which we will use the binding layer. The KVC protocol, which the binding layer uses to monitor and set object values, specifies that for every attribute named *name* of an object, there should be a getter of the same name and a setter with a selector of the form set*Name*: (note the capital letter after set). Strictly speaking, accessor methods aren't needed in the case of attributes that are implemented simply as instance variables, but in practice, it's cleaner to have the accessor methods.

MyCompanyName

The comment header of this file, and of all files Xcode creates, includes a copyright notice in the name of __MyCompanyName__. How annoying.

You could edit the copyright notice whenever you generate it, or you could do a cross-file search-and-replace when you've accumulated several. It's better, however, to have your name, or your company's, there in the first place.

Xcode does not provide a graphical preference for setting this string. The setting is, however, settable through defaults, the command line tool for editing system and application preferences. Open the Terminal application and type

```
defaults write com.apple.xcode \
    PBXCustomTemplateMacroDefinitions \
    '{ ORGANIZATIONNAME = "Joan Smith"; }'
```

It is useful to put #pragma mark lines wherever they make sense in source files. The compiler ignores them, but the pop-up menu of function names immediately above the editor pane will show the mark text in boldface, making navigation much easier.

We continue with a couple of methods required to fulfill the class interface's promise that DataPoint follows the NSCoding protocol—encodeWithCoder: and initWithCoder:. These methods simply transfer the x and y instance variables to and from an NSCoder data stream:

```
#pragma mark NSCoding
// Methods required by the NSCoding protocol.
// This class will require a keyed archiver; it makes life
// easier, even though it restricts us to 10.2 and later.

- (void) encodeWithCoder: (NSCoder *) coder
{
    [coder encodeDouble: x forKey: @"x"];
    [coder encodeDouble: y forKey: @"y"];
}
```

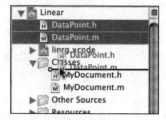

Figure 5.5 Dragging the `DataPoint` definition files into the **Classes** group. Command- or shift-click to select both files, and drag them so that an insertion bar appears below, and indented from, the **Classes** group folder.

```
- (id) initWithCoder: (NSCoder *) coder
{
    [self setX: [coder decodeDoubleForKey: @"x"]];
    [self setY: [coder decodeDoubleForKey: @"y"]];
    return self;
}


@end
```

Now that we've finished `DataPoint`, have a look at the Groups & Files list. Chances are that **DataPoint.h** and **DataPoint.m** appear at the top of the list, outside any of the folders below the project icon. It's helpful to keep project files organized as you go along; these files really should be inside the **Classes** group. To select both files, click on one of them and command-click on the other. Then drag the pair inside the **Classes** group. (See Figure 5.5.) This has no effect on the placement of these files on your disk but allows you to manage the clutter in the file list.

5.3.2 Regression **Model Class**

Now we can repeat the process for `Regression.m` and `Regression.h`. Create a new text file, make it for an Objective-C class, and include a header. Fill in `Regression.h` from the design, and then move on to `Regression.m`.

There isn't much new in the initialization and accessor methods of `Regression`, including the `NSCoding` methods; if you are stumped, you can find the full text of `Regression.m` in the CD-ROM directory for this chapter. What is new are the methods `canCompute` and `computeWithLinrg`:

```
+ (void) initialize
{
    [self setKeys: [NSArray arrayWithObject: @"dataPoints"]
     triggerChangeNotificationsForDependentKey: @"canCompute"];
}


- (BOOL) canCompute
{
    return [dataPoints count] > 1;
}
```

Unlike DataPoint, Regression has a property, *canCompute*, that is not implemented as an instance variable and can't be directly set but must be computed by counting the number of points in the regression data. The canCompute method delivers the value of this property. Objects that monitor the state of *canCompute* will want to know when that state changes. Without a direct setter for the property, the change can't be detected directly, but in the Regression class-initialization method initialize, we use the class method setKeys: triggerChangeNotificationsForDependentKey: to tell the key-value observing system that any time dataPoints changes, canCompute may have changed as well.

The method computeWithLinrg passes data off to Linrg and makes our program ready to receive the results. This method is longer than the others we've seen, but the length owes more to tedium than to complexity:

```
- (void) computeWithLinrg
{
    if (! [self canCompute]) {
        //  Regression not possible; zero out and give up.
        slope = intercept = correlation = 0.0;
        return;
    }

    //  With the Linrg tool...
    NSBundle *  myBundle = [NSBundle mainBundle];
    NSString *  linrgPath = [myBundle pathForResource: @"Linrg"
                                               ofType: @""];
    linrgTask = [[NSTask alloc] init];
    [linrgTask setLaunchPath: linrgPath];
```

```objc
// ...hook into stdin...
NSPipe *        inputPipe = [[NSPipe alloc] init];
NSFileHandle *  inputForData =
                    [inputPipe fileHandleForWriting];
[linrgTask setStandardInput: inputPipe];
[inputPipe release];


// ...hook into stdout...
NSPipe *        outputPipe = [[NSPipe alloc] init];
NSFileHandle *  outputForResults =
                    [outputPipe fileHandleForReading];
[linrgTask setStandardOutput: outputPipe];
[outputPipe release];


// ...await output in the dataRead: method...
[[NSNotificationCenter defaultCenter]
                    addObserver: self
                        selector: @selector(dataRead:)
                            name:
        NSFileHandleReadToEndOfFileCompletionNotification
                            object: outputForResults];
[outputForResults readToEndOfFileInBackgroundAndNotify];


// ...and run Linrg.
[linrgTask launch];


// For each DataPoint...
NSEnumerator *  iter = [dataPoints objectEnumerator];
DataPoint *     curr;
while (curr = [iter nextObject]) {
    NSString * currAsString;
    // ... format point as string...
    currAsString = [NSString stringWithFormat: @"%g  %g\n",
                        [curr x], [curr y]];
    // ... reduce string to ASCII data...
    NSData *    currAsData = [currAsString dataUsingEncoding:
                                NSASCIIStringEncoding];
```

```
        //  ... put data into stdin...
        [inputForData writeData: currAsData];
    }


    //  ... then terminate stdin.
    [inputForData closeFile];
}
```

ComputeWithLinrg sets up Linrg as an external task and establishes pipes for communications with its standard input and output. The method runs Linrg and sends the data points, line by line, down the input pipe, until they run out. Then the method closes the pipe and returns. When it set up the output pipe, the method designated dataRead: as the method to handle the output:

```
- (void) dataRead: (NSNotification *) aNotice
{
    //  When data arrives on stdout...
    NSDictionary *  info = [aNotice userInfo];
    NSData *        theData =
        [info objectForKey: NSFileHandleNotificationDataItem];
    //  ...convert the data to a string...
    NSString *      stringResult =
        [[NSString alloc] initWithData: theData
                             encoding: NSASCIIStringEncoding];
    NSScanner *     scanner =
                [NSScanner scannerWithString: stringResult];
    double          scratch;

    //  ...and step through, collecting slope...
    [scanner scanDouble: &scratch];
    [self setSlope: scratch];

    //  ...intercept...
    [scanner scanDouble: &scratch];
    [self setIntercept: scratch];

    //  ...and correlation.
    [scanner scanDouble: &scratch];
```

```
    [self setCorrelation: scratch];
    [stringResult release];

    //  Done with Linrg.
    [linrgTask release];
    linrgTask = nil;
}
```

Note the two lines

```
    NSBundle *  myBundle = [NSBundle mainBundle];
    NSString *  linrgPath = [myBundle pathForResource: @"Linrg"
                                               ofType: @""];
```

They reflect part of the structure of our application. The NSBundle class in Cocoa—and the CFBundle interfaces in Core Foundation—allow for programmatic access to structured directory trees, known as *bundles*. The application itself is a bundle, which can be accessed through the NSBundle object returned by [NSBundle mainBundle]. The method pathForResource: ofType: asks a bundle for the full POSIX-style path-name of a file within the bundle's Resources subdirectory, with the given name and extension.

This means that in the Finder, our program can appear as though it were a single file, Linear. In reality—and in command line listings—the application would be a directory, Linear.app, containing a cluster of files needed for Linear to run, including, at Linear.app/Contents/Resources/Linrg, the Linrg command line tool. See Chapter 10 for a detailed discussion.

5.3.3 Model: Done

This finishes our model. Note how abstract the model classes are from the application we're trying to build: They don't do anything about displaying themselves, configuring editors, or responding to user input. The model classes simply hold data and compute the regression statistics.

Nothing in our model classes would be out of place in an application that had no graphical user interface. That's how we know that our model has been properly factored out of the rest of the application.

Objective-C

This book focuses on the workflow of Mac OS X programming rather than on the specific techniques of a given language. A good tutorial and reference on Objective-C can be found in the ADC Reference Library; search for "Introduction to the Objective-C Programming Language." However, we'll be seeing a lot of Objective-C in this book, so a reading knowledge of the language might be helpful.

The first thing to know about Objective-C is that it is a proper superset of C. Any legal C program is legal Objective-C, which is a smaller superset of C than is C++. Objective-C introduces only one new expression type, the *message invocation*. A message invocation is delimited by brackets, begins with an object pointer, and continues with the name of a message and the message's parameters. For example, [foo retain] sends the retain message to the object pointed to by foo. A more complex invocation might be

```
NSSize      unitSize = { 1.0, 1.0 };
unitSize = [myView convertSize: unitSize
                    fromView: nil];
```

Here, an NSSize struct is sent, along with nil, in the message convertSize: fromView: to myView. The returned value, another NSSize struct, is assigned to unitSize. Parameters to messages are interspersed with the message name, which usually documents each parameter. The colons, indicating the need for a parameter, are a part of the message name; aMessage and aMessage: would be two different messages.

The variable at the beginning of a message invocation is an object pointer. There are no static or stack-based objects in Objective-C. Objective-C adds a type, id, for a generic pointer to an object (like a void * that can accept messages), or you can get some compile-time type checking by specifying an explicit type pointer, like NSView *, or DataPoint *.

Classes are objects and can have methods. Class methods are declared and defined with a leading "+", whereas instance methods are declared and defined with a leading "-". It's common to refer to methods by a plus or minus to indicate their domain, followed by the class and signature in brackets, such as -[NSView convertSize:fromView:] or +[NSObject alloc].

(continued)

Objective-C *(continued)*

Method invocation is not as tightly bound to types in Objective-C as member-function calls are in C++. The same message can be sent to objects in different classes even if they have no common ancestor; the only thing that matters is the message selector (its name). It is therefore common in Objective-C programs to establish "informal protocols," groups of methods that objects can implement to participate in the workings of a package. Objective-C also has formal protocols, whereby the compiler ensures that the class adopting the protocol implements all protocol methods, and assures the runtime that member objects conform.

5.4 Summary

In this chapter, we worked out a general design for a graphical program for doing linear regressions and analyzed it in light of the Model-View-Controller design pattern commonly used in Cocoa programming. We isolated the model tasks of managing the underlying data structures and produced Objective-C classes that did what we needed.

In terms of Xcode skills, we created a document-based Cocoa application and added classes to it, keeping the Groups & Files list organized along the way. We leveraged our work on the command line tool Linrg by using the tool as the computational engine for the application and made the application depend on keeping Linrg up-to-date.

6

A Cocoa Application: Views

Now that the model is taken care of, we turn to the other end of the application: the views. Our design for the application relies on standard elements in the Mac OS X Aqua interface.

Interface Builder (IB) is the indispensible tool for laying out human interfaces for Mac OS X applications. It edits *Nib files*, which are archives of human-interface objects that are reconstituted by your application when the files are loaded. All Cocoa application have a main Nib file, which the Xcode application template names Main-Menu.nib. This file contains at least the main menu bar for the application and may contain other applicationwide windows and views.

An application can have more than one Nib, and a Nib can be loaded and its contents instantiated more than once. For instance, the Xcode template for a document-based Cocoa application includes a MyDocument.nib file. The file contains a trivial window for documents of the MyDocument class, and the template for the MyDocument class implementation specifies MyDocument.nib as the Nib to load when creating a new document.

Because our design calls for a window that displays the data points and regression statistics for each document, we want to edit the window in MyDocument.nib to match our design. In the Groups & Files list, click the triangle next to **Resources** to open that group. You should see **MyDocument.nib**, with the gold icon of a Nib file, in that group. Double-clicking this item launches Interface Builder and opens MyDocument.nib for editing.

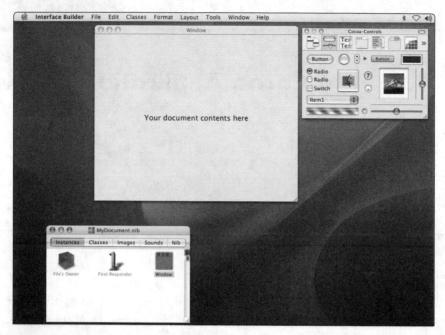

Figure 6.1 Interface Builder on opening MyDocument.nib. The window that represents the Nib is at lower left; above it is the simple window, with some filler text, that comes in MyDocument.nib as provided in the template. To the right is the palette containing standard Aqua controls that can be dragged into windows.

6.1 Interface Builder

The newly opened Interface Builder will show you three windows (Figure 6.1). (Use **Hide Others** in the **Interface Builder** application menu to reduce the clutter.) The largest, named Window, contains a text element saying "Your document contents here" in the middle. Close this window.

The window at the lower left, MyDocument.nib, shows the Nib file as a file opened by Interface Builder (Figure 6.2). It shows three icons. The first two—**File's Owner** and **First Responder**—are placeholders for certain objects outside the Nib. Any other icons are for objects in the Nib—in this case, a window named Window.

Double-click the **Window** icon. The window we're building for the MyDocument class opens again.

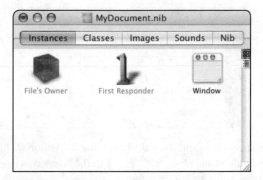

Figure 6.2 The window for the MyDocument.nib file contains icons for **File's Owner** and **First Responder**, which are placeholders for objects outside the Nib, along with an icon for every top-level object in the Nib. In this case, MyDocument.nib contains only a window, named Window.

> I'll have to be careful with my terminology here. At the bottom of your screen is the window for the MyDocument.nib file. You opened that file with Interface Builder, you're editing the file, and you'll save it when you're done. Above it is a window you're building for the use of the MyDocument class. In a sense, you're opening, editing, saving, and closing it, too, but the window is *inside* the MyDocument.nib file. I'll try to be as explicit as posssible in distinguishing the Nib window from the prototype document window, but you may have to watch out for the distinction.

The third window, to the right, is a utility window embodying a series of palettes containing objects you can add to a Nib file. We'll be using this window a lot.

6.2 Layout

First, we will use Interface Builder as a pure layout tool for our human interface. We'll start by getting rid of that "Your document contents here" placard. Click it, and press the **Delete** key. It's gone.

Next, let's add the buttons. If the palette window doesn't show "Cocoa – Controls" as its title, click the second toolbar icon—the one that shows a button and a slider. At the top left of the palette is a regular Aqua-style button labeled **Button**. Drag this

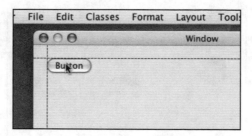

Figure 6.3 Placing a button in Interface Builder. Drag the button from the Cocoa–Controls palette to the window being built. Lines will appear in the window when the button is placed properly according to the Aqua human-interface guidelines.

button from the palette into the window we're building for MyDocument (Figure 6.3). As you drag the button into the upper-left corner of the target window, blue lines appear at the window's margins. The Aqua human-interface guidelines specify certain margins between controls and within windows, and Interface Builder puts up guides to help you place your elements properly.

Button is not an especially informative title for a control. Our design calls for this button to be named **Add**. The easiest way to change the label is to double-click the button, making the text editable, and replace the title. Instead, we'll take this opportunity to have our first look at Interface Builder's Inspector. Select **Show Info** from the **Tools** menu. A new utility window opens, offering a number of options for configuring the current selection—in this case, the button we just dragged in (Figure 6.4). The field at the top of the inspector is labeled Title: and shows the current value, **Button**. Edit this to say Add, and press **Tab** or **Enter** to complete the edit. The button is now named **Add**.

Leave the Inspector window open. It will change to keep up with the currently selected element in the Nib, and we'll be needing it later.

Repeat the button-dragging twice more, for the **Remove** and **Compute** buttons. Name the new buttons accordingly.

Next, we add the table of data to the window. Click the fifth icon at the top of the palette to reveal Interface Builder's repertoire of data-display views. The table view (NSTableView) is in the lower-left of the Cocoa–Data palette. Drag this view into the window we're building. Lines will appear that allow you to place the table view a short distance below the buttons and just off the left edge of the window. Small blue knobs appear at the edges and corners of the view to let you resize it. Make the view wide

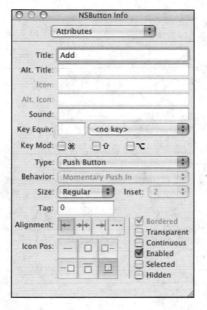

Figure 6.4 The Interface Builder Inspector, as a simple push button is selected. The default label for the button (**Button**) is replaced by **Add**.

enough to display two columns of numbers comfortably and deep enough to trigger a line at the bottom of the window.

What you've added to your document window is much more than simply an NSTableView. Look at the main Nib MyDocument window, which should be at the lower left of your screen if you haven't moved it. Make sure that the **Instances** tab is selected. At the top of the scroll bar at the right edge of window are two small buttons. The upper one, with four small boxes in it, is now highlighted; click the other one, with horizontal lines, to highlight it.

The Instances view changes to a hierarchical display of the Nib contents. **MyDocument** and **First Responder** come first, followed by an **NSWindow** with a disclosure triangle next to it. Clicking the disclosure triangle shows that a Cocoa window contains one **NSView**, the content view, which, because it contains other views, also has a disclosure triangle. If we open all the disclosure triangles we see, we end up with something like Figure 6.5. What we last dragged into the window was in fact an NSScrollView, containing an NSTableView, which in turn contained two NSTableColumns.

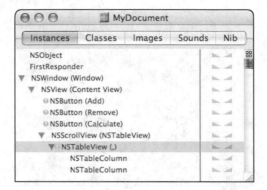

Figure 6.5 The hierarchical view of the MyDocument Nib in progress. You reach this view by selecting the **Instances** tab and then the list-view button just above the scroll bar at the right edge of the window. It can sometimes be easier to select views in this list than in the window display. The yellow caution badges on the screen indicate that "outlets"—links to other objects—in the flagged views have not yet been filled.

Select the header of the first column of the table. Using your mouse, click once to select the scroll view, double-click to get inside to the table view, double-click again to get down to the header view, and click once more to bring up the text field editor. Alternatively, simply keep clicking rapidly on the header until it turns white and a blinking insertion point appears. Type **x**. In the second header, type **y**. Putting the mouse between the headers will allow you to drag the boundary between them, so you can resize the columns to equal size.

The last element we'll put in the window is an NSForm, a simple array of labeled text fields that we'll use for the results of the regression. Find the form element in the third panel of the IB palette (Cocoa–Text), at bottom center. Drag it into the right half of the window you're building, under the **Compute** button. As supplied, the form has two big defects: It's too narrow, and it shows only two items. The width problem is easy to solve: Drag the handles on the sides of the form until they hit the spacing guidelines.

Dragging the handles on the top and bottom, however, gets you a taller form with two entries (**Undo** is your friend here). NSForm turns out to be a subclass of NSMatrix, a Cocoa class that manages an array of controls. You can add rows or columns to an NSMatrix in Interface Builder by dragging a resize handle *while holding the **Option** key down.* An **Option**-drag downward on the bottom handle of the form gets us our third row.

Click repeatedly on the labels in the form until they become editable, and change them to Slope:, Intercept:, and Correlation:. You'll probably have to resize the form when you're done.

6.3 Sizing

At this point, the layout of the window is almost done. Why "almost"? Pull down the **File** menu and select **Test Interface** (or press **command-R**). Your window now "goes live," using the components you put into it. There's nothing behind them, but you can click the buttons and work the other controls.

Now try resizing the window. The contents of the window ride the lower-left corner, sliding into and out of view as the window resizes (Figure 6.6). This is not what we want. Near the right end of your menu bar is an icon resembling an old-fashioned double-throw electrical switch. Click this icon to exit the interface-testing mode. None of the changes you made during testing are permanent.

Cocoa views can be set to resize or simply to stay put as their containers change size and shape. Click the **Add** button in the window we're constructing to select it. If

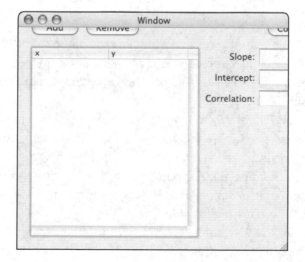

Figure 6.6 As supplied, Cocoa controls do not automatically size and position themselves in a window as the window resizes. You have to specify sizing and positioning behavior yourself.

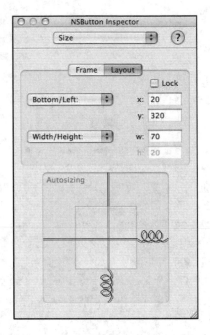

Figure 6.7 The Size Inspector for a view that should stay put, relative to the top left of its enclosing view. The inside struts are all straight, meaning that it never resizes. The outside struts below and to the right are springy, meaning that they don't influence the view's placement.

the Inspector panel is not showing, select **Show Inspector** (or press **command-shift-I**) from the **Tools** menu. In the pop-up menu at the top of the Inspector window, select the third item, **Size**. (Note that you can bring the Inspector forward with the Size panel visible by pressing **command-3**.)

The Size panel (Figure 6.7) is dominated by a diagram showing the behavior of the selected view when its enclosing view is resized. The square inside the diagram represents the view itself. The various lines in the diagram switch between "struts" (straight lines) and "springs" (curling lines) when you click them. A view whose inner box contains rigid struts in both directions does not resize; if it has a spring in either direction or both, it can resize in that direction.

When the outer lines are struts, the view will try to maintain the same distance from the corresponding edge of the container. (If both lines are struts and the view isn't resizable, lower and left wins over upper and right, which is why the contents of our window "rode" the lower-left corner out of sight when you resized the window.)

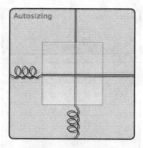

Figure 6.8 This view maintains its position relative to the top *right* of its enclosing view. The outside struts to the top and right are rigid.

If an outer line is a spring and the view is not resizable in that direction, the view will ignore the movement of that edge of the container. If the view is resizable and an outer line is a spring, the view will resize to a degree proportional to its position in the window. Two side-by-side views that obey this rule will maintain their respective shares of the window when it is resized and will not run into each other.

We reexamine the views in the window with an eye to how they should behave when the window resizes. The buttons should never resize and should stay where they are relative to the nearest corner—top left for **Add** and **Remove**, top right for **Compute**. Select each in turn, making Size Inspector for the **Add** and **Remove** buttons look like the one in Figure 6.7 and for the **Compute** button, like Figure 6.8.

How do we want the form at the right of the window to behave? We certainly don't want it to shrink or stretch vertically with the window, but we wouldn't mind its growing if the window were to get wider. So the vertical internal strut should be rigid, and the horizontal strut should be springy. We want it to keep its position near the right edge of the window, so the right strut remains rigid. We also want it to stay an inch or so below the title bar, so the top strut is rigid. The bottom strut becomes a spring, allowing the form to float free of that edge. The left strut also becomes a spring, indicating that the form will expand to take a share of the window rather than maintain a rigid margin from the left edge. See Figure 6.9.

The data table should be freest of all, widening with the window and also growing vertically to show more points if the window grows. Both internal struts should be turned into springs. We anchor the view to the top left of the window by leaving those outer struts rigid; we also leave the bottom strut rigid. That way, when the window gets taller or shorter, the table will keep a constant distance of 20 pixels from the bottom

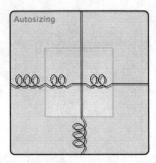

Figure 6.9 The resizing specification for the form at the right side of the window. We don't want it to stretch vertically, so the inside vertical strut is straight. It would be nice if this view could take advantage of more room horizontally, so its inside horizontal strut is springy, allowing resizing in that direction. It is strictly bound to the top and the right side of the surrounding view. Being resizable horizontally and loosely bound to the left, this view will resize itself proportionately as the window resizes.

of the window. The right-horizontal strut is made springy, so the table view will grow horizontally only to maintain its share of the horizontal space. See Figure 6.10.

Now press **command-R** to try out the window. Now resizing does not shove views out the window. You may want to experiment with other sizing options and see their effects. Remember, you can exit the interface test mode by clicking the switch icon in the menu bar.

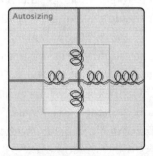

Figure 6.10 The resizing specification for the scroll view enclosing the data table. It resizes in both directions along with the window. It is strictly bound to the top, left, and bottom edges of its enclosing view, so it will resize to maintain its present distance from those edges; it is loosely bound to the right, so it will take only a proportionate share of growth in that direction.

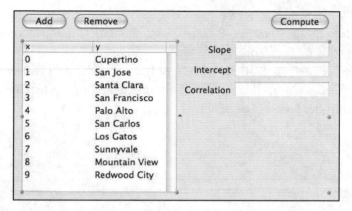

Figure 6.11 Adding a split view. Selecting two side-by-side views, and using the menu command **Layout → Make subviews of → Split View** encloses the views in an NSSplitView, with the splitter between them.

6.4 A Split View

Our idea of how much space to allocate between the table of data points and the form containing the output statistics might not be the one that should control. The user may have other ideas. It would be better to put the two views inside a split view so the user can drag the border between them back and forth.

Interface Builder does not provide an NSSplitView or an NSScrollView in its palettes, except for the ones prebuilt around other views. To get a split view, select the views you want to be in the split view—in this case, the scroll view containing the data table and the NSForm for the results. Then select the menu item **Layout → Make subviews of → Split View** to wrap the views in a split view big enough to contain them and oriented so the split comes between them. See Figure 6.11.

Try out the new view by pressing **command-R**. The halves of the split view should resize as you drag the dimpled bar between them. The new split view comes with no automatic resizing, so when you return Interface Builder to its normal editing mode, you'll want to set the split view's internal struts to springs so it can resize with the window.

6.5 Summary

This chapter introduced Interface Builder, a tool no less important to Cocoa development than Xcode itself. We used IB as a straightforward tool for laying out windows and views. We saw how to set the many options for automatic sizing of embedded views and how to use Interface Builder's own simulation mode to verify that our layout and sizing choices work.

This does *not* end our work with Interface Builder. Because it is a constructor for networks of Cocoa objects, Interface Builder will have a big role to play as we move on to the controller layer of our design.

A Cocoa Application: Controllers

7.1 Still in Interface Builder

We've drawn and configured our views and are ready to work on the Controller layer of our application. Surprisingly, we'll still be working with Interface Builder for much of this phase of development. Interface Builder is a powerful tool for storing Cocoa objects and specifying links between them. You have seen that IB keeps a placeholder for **File's Owner** in the Nib window. We're going to tell Interface Builder that the owner of this particular kind of Nib will be an object of class MyDocument and what the structure of a MyDocument is. We'll also create additional objects to do most of the work in managing the data in our application.

Arrange the windows of Xcode and Interface Builder so that the main Nib window and Xcode's Groups & Files list are visible. In the Groups & Files list, find MyDocument.h and drag it by the icon into the Nib window. You'll know you've succeeded when the Nib window changes to the **Class** browser tab, showing MyDocument as a subclass of NSDocument.

For the purposes of this Nib, Interface Builder now knows what a MyDocument is. Now we'll tell it why it cares. Switch the Nib back to the **Instances** tab, and select the **File's Owner** icon. Press **command-5** to bring up the Inspector with the Custom Class panel showing. It now shows the owner's class as NSObject; scroll to the top of the list and select **MyDocument**. Now IB knows that the owner of the file is a MyDocument.

We will now make the first link in our Nib file. While holding down the **Control** key, drag from the **File's Owner** icon to the **Window** icon. Release when the **Window** icon highlights (see Figure 7.1). The Inspector window pops up, displaying its Connections panel, listing all the possible connections that **File's Owner** could have to **Window**; in this case, there is only one, *window*. Click the **Connect** button at the bottom of the Inspector, and the link is made.

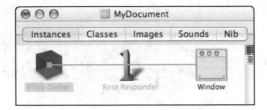

Figure 7.1 The result of control-dragging from the **File's Owner** icon to the **Window** icon in the Nib window. A link is created, as indicated by the line (blue on the screen) between the objects. Simultaneously, the Connections panel of the Inspector appears, showing the possible connections that **File's Owner** can make to **Window** and offering a button to complete the connection.

What did we just do? The contents of a Nib file get instantiated when an object—an owner—decides to load that Nib. The loading process consists of unarchiving and initializing all the objects stored in the Nib and initializing all the references made between objects in the Nib and between the owner and the object in the Nib. So when MyDocument loads MyDocument.nib, the instance variable window in the MyDocument object will be set to point to the **Window** object loaded from the Nib.

At the right end of the index bar at the top of Interface Builder's palettes window is a double arrowhead, indicating that more icons are in the bar than will fit in the initial size of the window. Widen the window so that the arrowhead disappears (Figure 7.2). We are interested in the Controllers pane, indicated in the index bar by a blue cube. Click the blue cube to reveal the Controller objects available for use in our Nib.

These objects are represented as cubes or variants on cubes and plainly aren't meant to represent anything that goes into a window. The icons in this panel represent instances of NSController subclasses, which can be used as building blocks for the Controller layer of our application. Drag three of these subclasses—two of the simple green cube, representing NSObjectControllers, and one with the three green cubes in a line, representing an NSArrayController—into the main small Nib window (with the icons, not the user interface window we've been building).

Select the first NSObjectController, and press **Return** to make the label of the icon editable. Let's call this icon **Document**. Edit the label of the second Controller to read **Model**. Rename the NSArrayController to **DataPoints**. These names will help us remember what kinds of data the Controller objects are managing.

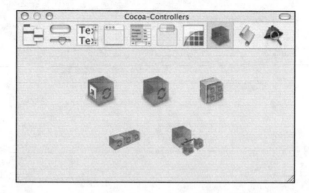

Figure 7.2 The Interface Builder objects palette made wider so that all the standard panels are visible: Menus, Controls, Text, Windows, Data, Containers, Graphics, Controllers, AppleScript, and Sherlock. The Controllers panel shown here contains five subclasses of NSObjectController for adding to the Nib container.

7.2 NSObjectController: Document

We will now weave the controller objects, our document, and our user interface elements into a mutually supporting web. Figure 7.3 maps the many steps to this process.

First, we tell the Document NSObjectController about the MyDocument instance it will be communicating with. The NSController data member content designates the object the controller is concerned with. This object is declared as an IBOutlet in the header for NSController, so control-dragging can be used to establish a link between the Document NSObjectController's content pointer and the MyDocument that is the **File's Owner** of this Nib.

In short: Control-drag from the **Document** cube to **File's Owner** (Figure 7.4). The Inspector will offer to connect the content outlet; accept this by clicking the **Connect** button.

While we have the **Document** controller selected, press **command-1** to bring up the Attributes Inspector. By default, NSController objects assume that they will be dealing with instances of NSMutableDictionary, but that isn't the case here. In the field labeled Object Class Name:, type **MyDocument**. Also, to tell Interface Builder that MyDocument has one property of concern to it, model, click the **Add** button at the bottom of the Inspector and edit the resulting new line in the list to read **model**.

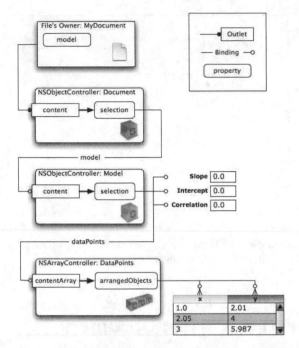

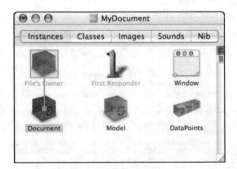

Figure 7.3 A road map to the links among the MyDocument object, the NSController objects, and the user interface objects in this chapter. The controller objects form a straight chain of references, so the NSArrayController is set to refer to the dataPoints property of the model (Regression) property of the document. The Document NSObjectController gets its content value by filling an IBOutlet with a control-drag; the Model NSDocumentController gets its content value by binding to the selection property of the Document controller.

Figure 7.4 Connecting the **Document** object controller to the **File's Owner**, which will be an external instance of MyDocument. Use the Inspector window to confirm the connection to the controller's content outlet.

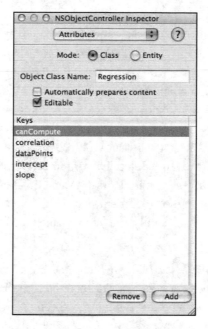

Figure 7.5 Setting up the second NSObjectController to manage Regression objects

7.3 NSObjectController: **Model**

As you may have guessed by now, this controller does whatever it does with the model property of MyDocument. Click the **Model NSObjectController**, and use the Attributes Inspector (**command-1**) to specify that the controlled class name is Regression and that its attributes are **slope**, **intercept**, **correlation**, **canCompute**, and **dataPoints**. The Inspector should look like Figure 7.5.

> Adding attribute names to an NSController in Interface Builder is simply a convenience, building a list for you to pick from later. Adding or omitting items has no effect on the state or behavior of the final application.

How will the Model NSObjectController get at its Regression object? No object in or introduced to the Nib represents the model member of the MyDocument object. Instead, the Model controller will ask the Document controller for the value of its content object's model property.

Press **command-4** to bring up the Bindings Inspector. You want to bind the Model controller's content object to the model property of the Document controller's content. The Bindings Inspector shows all the properties of the selected objects that can be bound to—can share values with—properties of other objects. The contentObject property is the second bindable property in the Bindings Inspector for an NSObject-Controller. Click the disclosure triangle next to the **contentObject** label to open the relevant subpanel.

What object keeps track of the model object? It is the content object of our Document NSObjectController. Select **Document(NSObjectController)** from the **Bind to:** pop-up. Now examine the choices that drop down from the **Controller Key:** combo box. These are the **Document** NSObjectController properties that this relationship might observe. The only one you are interested in is **selection**; select it.

> In theory, a single NSController might shift focus among various objects as, for instance, the user clicks on various objects to bring them forward for editing. The NSController would track such changes by changing its selection property to always point at the selected object. In practice, in our application, a given Document NSObjectController will always refer to only one Regression object, so the flexibility implied by "whatever the controller currently selects" is a little misleading.

Next, what facet of the current selection of the Document NSObjectController does the Model NSObjectController want to track? It wants to track the model property of the selected object. In the combo box labeled Model Key Path:, select **model**. (**Model** is in the list because we told Interface Builder that the Document NSObjectController tracks objects that have a property named model.) The Bindings Inspector should now look like Figure 7.6.

7.4 NSArrayController: DataPoints

The DataPoints NSArrayController needs content, too. Select its icon in the Nib window, and open the disclosure triangle labeled **contentArray**. We want to make the DataPoints controller into something that knows about the DataPoint objects in the array that is the dataPoints property of the model property of MyDocument. We have already set up the Model NSObjectController to track, as its selection, the current

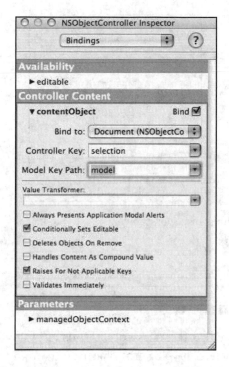

Figure 7.6 The Bindings Inspector showing how to set the Model `NSObjectController`
to track the Model object of the `MyDocument` tracked by the Document `NSObjectController`.

`Regression` model. We have also already told Interface Builder that `dataPoints` is
the name of one of the properties that the model has.

So we do the following:

- Select **Model (NSObjectController)** from the **Bind to:** pop-up.
- Select **selection** in the Controller Key: combo box.
- Select **dataPoints** in the Model Key Path: combo box.

Now all three of the `NSControllers` we dragged into the Nib have been made
"live." So long as a valid `MyDocument` exists as the owner of the Nib, the Document
object will identify with it and make its `model` property bindable; the Model object
will identify the `Regression` model object and make its properties bindable, including
the `dataPoints` array; and the DataPoints object will identify the `dataPoints` array
and make each `DataPoint` object within it bindable.

Figure 7.7 The Bindings Inspector, showing how to bind a cell of the results form to the slope of the model object.

7.5 Value Binding

All this binding is pointless if it does not move data. In the user interface window we've been building, click the **NSForm** object on the right; then double-click the top cell (**Slope:**). Press **command-4** to bring up the Bindings Inspector if it isn't already up, and note that the first available binding is **value**. Expand the item, and bind the value of this cell to **Model, selection,** and **slope** (Figure 7.7). Turn off the binding properties that would automatically make the form cell editable—there's not much sense in allowing user input of our results. While you're here, use the Attributes Inspector (**command-1**) to uncheck the **Editable** property of this cell.

Repeat this process—select the cell, bind to a corresponding value of **Model** and **selection,** make uneditable—for the other two cells of the form. The effect of this, combined with our having made all the properties involved comply with the key-value observing (KVO) protocol, is that whenever the slope, intercept, or correlation values of a MyDocument change, the display in this window will reflect the change.

Now we'll wire up the data entry table, in the left half of the window. Click repeatedly the first column of the table, until the column itself is selected. Press **command-4** to bring forward the Bindings Inspector. Interface Builder is moderately smart: It knows that table columns should be bound to multiples of data, so the Inspector appears with the arrangedObjects of the DataPoints NSArrayController already selected. All you have to do is select the **x** property in the Model Key Path: combo box.

Now select the second column and bind it to DataPoints, arrangedObjects, and y.

NSArrayController has a concept of an array of *arranged objects*, distinct from the content array that is its focus. The idea is that the content array may have constant membership and ordering, but the controller might sort it or filter subsets of it for presentation to the user. The current filtered and sorted subset of the content array constitutes the controller's arranged objects. When you want to operate on every user-visible member of an NSArrayController's array, you should ask for arrangedObjects.

We have now ensured that the contents of the NSTableView will reflect the data-Points of the current document and that any changes to the points will make their way back to the document. But all we've done is allow for display and editing of existing data. We have to do something about adding or computing new data.

7.6 Actions and Outlets

It is time to hook up the buttons to the objects that will respond to them. Control-drag from the **Add** button to the DataPoints NSArrayController. As you've come to expect, the Inspector pops up. But this time, it doesn't show a list of fields in its **Outlets** tab but rather a list of methods—you can tell, because they all end with colons—in its **Target/Action** tab.

What's going on here? As before, the control-drag from the **Add** button to Data-Points makes Interface Builder propose a link from the one to the other. In the case of an NSButton—or any other object derived from NSControl—IB does not offer to fill simply any outlet in the button, but instead offers to fill a pointer named target *and* an action field. When an NSControl is triggered, it sends its designated action to its designated target. So what you see is a list of all the action messages that Interface Builder knows that NSArrayController implements.

Action methods always have the signature - (IBAction) action: (id) sender;. IBAction is #defined as void and has two purposes. The first is to document the purpose of the method to human readers. The second is to signal to the header parser in Interface Builder that this method is to be added to the list of action methods supported by this class. By convention, the sender parameter is whatever control sent the action message. If you send an action message yourself, be sure that your parameter responds to reasonable NSControl-like messages; otherwise, pass nil.

NSArrayController provides an add: message that takes care of allocating, initializing, and inserting a new instance of the proper type of object into the array it manages. Having noticed the match in names, IB has already highlighted add:, so all you have to do is click the **Connect** button.

Control-drag from the **Remove** button to the DataPoints array controller, and accept the offer of the NSArrayController remove: action. Control-drag from the **Compute** button to the **File's Owner** icon. Because we've previously labeled MyDocument's compute: method as IBAction, dragged the header for MyDocument into our Nib, and designated **File's Owner** as a MyDocument, Interface Builder readily offers compute: as the action for this button. Connect it.

One last thing: It's illegal to do a linear regression on only one data point. It makes no sense to speak of the one straight line that "fits" one point, and with a single point, all three statistics involve the ratio 0/0. In class Regression, we have a simple-minded check on this condition, called canCompute, which is YES if at least two elements are in dataPoints. (It's simple-minded because it does not handle the case in which the data set consists of the same point repeated.)

We'd like our human interface to reflect this constraint. Select the **Compute** button, and look at the available bindings (press **command-4**). An **enabled** binding is available; bind it to **Model**, **selection** and **canCompute**.

Perhaps you remember that canCompute is a pure Objective-C method. No variable underlies it, and there is no way to set the property. That doesn't matter. So long as the canCompute property is accessible by a method of that name, you can bind to it.

This ends our work with Interface Builder. Make sure to save the Nib (press **command-S**), and return to Xcode.

7.7 MyDocument

We have come far in our controller work without writing any code. We have yet to touch the MyDocument.m skeleton that Xcode provided when we created our project. Now we make our changes:

```
- (id)init
{
    self = [super init];
    if (self) {
        // Allocate and initialize our model
        model = [[Regression alloc] init];
        if (!model) {
```

```
            [self release];
            self = nil;
        }
    }
    return self;
}


- (void) dealloc
{
    [model release];
    [super dealloc];
}
```

The only changes to the original are that we create a model object when the document is created and release it when the document is destroyed:

```
- (NSData *)dataRepresentationOfType:(NSString *)aType
{
    return [NSKeyedArchiver archivedDataWithRootObject: model];
}


- (BOOL)loadDataRepresentation:(NSData *)data
                        ofType:(NSString *)aType
{
    model = [NSKeyedUnarchiver unarchiveObjectWithData: data];
    [model retain];
    return YES;
}
```

Here, we respond to the Cocoa framework's calls for us to load or save our data. Most of the work was done in the Model object. All we have to do in the Controller is specify the facilities—NSKeyedArchiver and NSKeyedUnarchiver—that do the transformation between objects and data stream.

Finally, we add the command handler that glues the **Compute** button to the model:

```
- (IBAction) compute: (id) sender
{
    [model computeWithLinrg];
}
```

Once again, the model does most of the work.

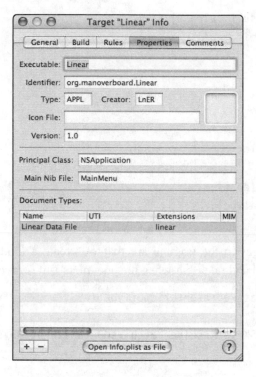

Figure 7.8 The Application Properties Info window. This window is used to set all the information that identifies the application and its documents to the Finder. This window is mainly an editor for the Info.plist file. Note that the table at the bottom—for information about document types—is much wider than the default size the panel allows.

7.8 Application Properties

The programming is done, but we need to take care of two more chores. First, we have to associate our data files with our application. In the Groups & Files list in the Project window, open the **Targets** group, and double-click **Linear**, the only target in the group. A Get Info window for the target will open. Click the **Properties** tab (Figure 7.8). This panel edits the Info.plist file of your application's package, which Launch Services uses to associate file types with your application. Some fields are already filled in with information from Xcode's template or the project name.

- Executable: The name of the file containing the compiled and linked binary code for your application. Xcode builds that file with the same name as the project.

Don't change this. If you ever change the name of your product, you must change both this field *and* the Product Name property under the Target Info window's **Build** tab, and *they must match*.

- Identifier: A string that uniquely identifies your application to the system. The convention is to use an inverted domain name followed by the name of the application. Xcode defaults this string to com.apple.myCocoaDocumentApp, but you'll want to change this.

- Type: Two four-character codes indicating the type of the file's contents and the application that created the file. Thus, the Macintosh, in 1984, could open a file with the correct application when you double-clicked its icon. Even though Mac OS X applications are no longer single files, the convention, dating from the beginning of the Mac OS, still holds that they have type and creator codes. The type of all applications is APPL. Leave this unchanged.

- Creator: The creator code to be set for this application and for all files created by it. By default, the agreed-on anonymous creator code is ????. Change this to LnER.

- Icon File: Skipped for now because we don't have one yet.

- Version: 1.0.

- Principal Class: The main() function which calls NSApplicationMain(), which in turn instantiates an application object, loads the main Nib, and runs the application. If you had a custom application class, you'd put its name here, and NSApplicationMain() would use that information in deciding what to run. Almost nobody needs a custom application class. Leave this as NSApplication.

- Main Nib File: The Nib file that contains at least the main menu bar and may contain other windows and views that might be common to the whole application. As Xcode provides a MainMenu.nib file with a standard menu bar in it, you can leave this as MainMenu.

A surprising number of people want to know whether they can put the main menu bar in another Nib file. The answer is no.

Next comes a table for all the documents that your application can create or at least read. As Xcode sets up the document-based application template to already have the MyDocument document class, the table has an entry for one document type. We can improve on the defaults.

- Name: A string used in the Finder to identify this file type. This string is also used as a parameter to the `NSDocument` methods you must implement for reading and writing document data. (The idea is that the same document class may handle more than one document type and would need the type name to identify which was desired.) We can do better than `DocumentType`; substitute `Linear Data File`.

- UTI and MIME Types: Initiatives for accurately classifying the format and content of files. As Mac OS X becomes more and more sophisticated in how it handles file metadata, this information, particularly UTI (uniform type identifiers), will gain importance. UTIs are used to distinguish file types for purposes of assigning Spotlight importers. You should search Xcode's documentation database on "UTI" for information on the interoperability of your file formats. Our application, however, will be using a file format that nobody else is expected to read; we can leave these blank.

- Extensions: The file name extension that will identify a file as being of this document type. We are not limited to three characters, and for most purposes, the extension will be hidden. Let's use `linear`—no period. We could specify more than one, if more than one extension is associated with this type, as with `htm` and `html`.

- OS Types: The type codes that, together with this application's creator code, identify this document type. Again, there could be more than one. Enter **linD**.

- Class: The class that handles the document type. When it gets a command to open or create a document, `NSDocumentController` determines—from the type name the user specified or from the extension or OS type code of the existing file—the document type. Here is where you specify that class. We have only one `NSDocument` class—`MyDocument`—so we leave this unchanged.

- Icon File: Blank because we don't yet have a document icon for our data files.

- Store Type: In this case, **binary** because we are storing our data as a stream of data bytes without indexing.

- Role: One of three roles an application can have with respect to a file. Editor for reading and writing files of this type; Viewer, for only reading files of this type; or None, for defining an icon for it—for instance for a configuration file. Our application reads and writes this file type: Editor.

- Package: A document saved not as a single file but as a structured directory tree. Once Launch Services "notices" this entry in your application's `Info.plist` file, the document will appear in the Finder to be a single file. Our document is in fact a single file, so we leave this unchecked.

7.9 Building

Our first iteration of Linear is complete. Try running it; run it under the debugger if you're cautious. Add lines to the data point table and fill them with data; note that the **Compute** button activates when the second point is added. Try removing a point. Click **Compute** and see whether the values displayed make sense. Close the document window and save it. Select **File → Open . . .** to open it up again.

Linear behaves like a real application—albeit one that is short on such important features as automatic calculation, undo, and dirty-document detection.

> Build configurations are covered in much more detail later in this book; for now, think of them as named groups of build system settings that make a product more suitable for debugging or for release. Recall that in Section 5.2, we added Linrg as a dependency of the Linear target. Whenever something in Linrg changes, Linear sees to it that Linrg is recompiled and the fresh version imported.
>
> But what settings are used to build Linrg in such circumstances? Are they the current compiler settings for Linear? The answer is no. Linrg will be built using the build configuration that has the same *name* as the active configuration of the project doing the building. If the same name isn't available, the configuration designated as default is used.
>
> It is important to make sure that your configuration names are consistent across projects. Xcode's templates take care of this, giving you Debug, Release, and Default configurations for every new project.

7.10 Summary

We continued our journey with Interface Builder in this chapter, into the Controller layer of our design. We saw how Interface Builder adds to Nib files objects and relationships that go far beyond the simple scope of interface layout. We linked objects to outlets, and controls to targets with actions. We bound controllers to our document class and to each other and saw how bindings can be used to make human-interface elements automatically track values in our model. Finally, we used the Target Info window to set the properties of our application.

8

Property Lists

Before continuing, we need to consider *property lists*. A property list is a simple, structured data format that is used throughout Mac OS X. Preference files, configuration files, the `Info.plist` files that specify bundle properties to the OS, and sometimes even application data files are all applications of the property list format. It's easy to use and powerful enough to serve as at least the first cut at most data storage problems and is the language of many OS services.

8.1 Data Types

A property list consists of one item of data, expressed in one of seven data types. Five property list types are scalar—number, Boolean, string, date, and data—and two are compound—ordered list and dictionary. An ordered list can contain zero or more objects of any property list type. A dictionary contains zero or more pairs, consisting of a string and an object of a property list type.

A property list can express most collections of data quite easily. A single data point from our linear-regression application could be represented as a dictionary of two numbers with the keys x and y; a data set would be a list of such dictionaries.

Both Core Foundation and Cocoa provide reference-counted object types that correspond to the property list types (see Table 8.1). In fact, you can pass a Cocoa property list pointer to a Core Foundation routine for the corresponding type; you can also use a `CFTypeRef` for a property list type as though it were a pointer to the corresponding Cocoa object.

> The dictionary data type in Cocoa requires only that the keys in a dictionary be objects of an immutable, copyable type; Core Foundation dictionaries can be even more permissive. However, if you want to use a Cocoa or Core Foundation dictionary in a property list, all keys have to be strings.

Table 8.1 Property List Types in Cocoa and Core Foundation

Data Type	Cocoa	Core Foundation	Markup
Number	NSNumber	CFNumber	`<integer>` `<float>`
Boolean	NSBoolean	CFBoolean	`<true/>` `<false/>`
Text	NSString NSMutableString	CFString CFMutableString	`<string>`
Date	NSDate	CFDate	`<date>`
Binary data	NSData NSMutableData	CFData CFMutableData	`<data>`
List	NSArray NSMutableArray	CFArray CFMutableArray	`<array>`
Associative array	NSDictionary NSMutableDictionary	CFDictionary CFMutableDictionary	`<dict>` `<key>` ... plist type ... `</dict>`

8.2 Property List Files

Let's investigate the property list file format by writing a .plist file of our own. Both Cocoa and Core Foundation provide methods for converting their property list values directly to the .plist format, so writing the file will be a simple matter of extending our model to provide a property list type; our views, to include a user action to trigger the writing of the file; and our controller, to link the two.

8.2.1 Writing a Property List
Model

Our first task is to add to Linear's data model the ability to express itself in property list types. We'll do this by adding categories to the Regression and DataPoint classes. *Categories* are an Objective-C mechanism for adding methods to a class—any class, even those supplied by Cocoa—without disturbing the core implementation of the class. (Realistically, there's no reason we shouldn't add our new methods directly to Regression and DataPoint. The original code is under our control, and nobody is relying on the old version.)

In Xcode, with the Linear project open, press **command-N** to bring up the New File Assistant. The variety of starter content Xcode offers for new files is extensive but doesn't cover category files. Select **Cocoa** → **Objective-C class**, and type **Regression-PropertyList** as the base file name. Make sure that the box is checked for generating a header file.

Xcode now presents you with a skeleton class declaration for an NSObject subclass called Regression_PropertyList. Edit the declaration to look like this:

```
#import "Regression.h"

@interface Regression (PropertyList)

- (NSDictionary *) asPropertyList;

@end
```

We declare an interface for an additional category, named PropertyList, on an existing class (Regression) containing the single method -asPropertyList.

To save yourself the trouble of retyping it, copy the line

```
- (NSDictionary *) asPropertyList;
```

Press **command-option-up arrow** to switch your view to the .m file. Once again, the template we're given has to be edited a bit, but it's close. Regression-PropertyList.m should look like this:

```
#import "Regression-PropertyList.h"
#import "DataPoint-PropertyList.h"

@implementation Regression (PropertyList)

- (NSDictionary *) asPropertyList
{
```

```
// Make an array to hold the property-list version of
//   the data points.
NSMutableArray *    pointArray = [NSMutableArray array];
NSEnumerator *      iter = [dataPoints objectEnumerator];
DataPoint *         curr;

// For each data point, add its property-list version
//   to the pointArray.
while (curr = [iter nextObject]) {
    [pointArray addObject: [curr asPropertyList]];
}

// Return a dictionary with the points
//   and the three statistics.
return [NSDictionary dictionaryWithObjectsAndKeys:
    pointArray,
    @"points",
    [NSNumber numberWithDouble: [self slope]],
    @"slope",
    [NSNumber numberWithDouble: [self intercept]],
    @"intercept",
    [NSNumber numberWithDouble: [self correlation]],
    @"correlation",
    nil];
}


@end
```

In the first part of the asPropertyList method, we build up an NSMutableArray containing the property list version of each data point. Then we build an NSDictionary with four keys—points, slope, intercept, and correlation—to identify the point list and the respective statistics. Note the use of NSNumber as the class embodying the simple number type for use in property lists.

The DataPoint-PropertyList.h header file uses the same principles:

```
#import "DataPoint.h"


@interface DataPoint (PropertyList)
```

```
- (NSDictionary *) asPropertyList;

@end
```

The same is true for the DataPoint-PropertyList.m implementation file:

```
#import "DataPoint-PropertyList.h"

@implementation DataPoint (PropertyList)

- (NSDictionary *) asPropertyList
{
    return [NSDictionary dictionaryWithObjectsAndKeys:
                [NSNumber numberWithDouble: x], @"abscissa",
                [NSNumber numberWithDouble: y], @"ordinate",
                nil];
}

@end
```

> Because all the objects created by the asPropertyList methods come
> from class convenience methods, not from methods with new, alloc, or
> copy in their names, we know that they are autoreleased, and we need not
> worry about releasing them ourselves.

View

Now that we have a way to get our model into property list form, we need a way to make use of it. The easiest way is to add a menu command that saves the active document as a property list. (The *right* way would be to add .plist as a supported document type for the Linear application and to add support for it to the dataRepresentationOfType: and loadDataRepresentation:ofType: methods in MyDocument, but for instructional purposes, we'll do it the easy way.) Open the MainMenu.nib Interface Builder file (Figure 8.1). The quickest way to do this is to click on the **Project** (top) icon in the Groups & Files list, then double-click **MainMenu.nib** as it appears in the detail list to the right.

MainMenu.nib contains only the application menu bar, which appears in a small window containing the menu titles as you'd see them in the application's menu bar

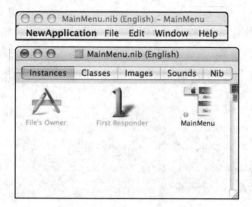

Figure 8.1 The MainMenu.nib file as it first opens. In a document-based application, the main menu Nib contains only the menu bar, represented by the small window at the top and the icon at the right of the Nib window. The other two icons are placeholders for objects outside the Nib.

(Figure 8.1). Clicking a title drops down a representation of that menu, identical except as hidden items are visible in the Interface Builder display (Figure 8.2).

We want to add a **Save as PList . . .** item to the **File** menu. (We include an ellipsis after the label because we'll be presenting a save-file dialog that will allow the user

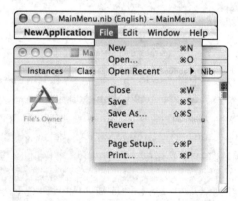

Figure 8.2 The **File** menu in **MainMenu.nib** expands when you click its title in the menu window. All items, including hidden ones, are visible in the menu as shown. Menu titles and key equivalents can be edited in place, and you can drag additional items into the menu from the Menus palette.

Detail Searches

The *className-categoryName* convention for naming category files can exploit the incremental search feature of the Project window's detail view. For an example, fill the detail view with all the files of the project by clicking the **Project** (top) icon in the Groups & Files list at the left. (If the detail view isn't visible, click the **Editor** icon in the Project window's toolbar.) Now type **Regression** in the search field in the toolbar. The detail view instantly narrows down to the four files that define the Regression class—Regression.m and .h and Regression-PropertyList.m and .h. If, instead, you type **Property**, the list narrows to Regression-PropertyList.m and .h and DataPoint-PropertyList.m and .h, the category files having to do with property lists. With the handful of classes in our application, this doesn't seem like much of a trick, but detail searches work as quickly on projects with hundreds of source files in dozens of group folders.

For another example, select the **Project Symbols** group toward the bottom of the Groups & Files list. The detail view fills with every method, class, and category defined in the project. Typing **Property** in the search field reduces the detail list to the definitions and implementations of the two PropertyList categories and the two asPropertyList methods.

---

to cancel.) Click the title of the **File** menu so it drops down, as shown in Figure 8.2. In the Interface Builder object palette at the upper right of your screen, select the first page, to show the available menus and menu items. Drag the object labeled **Item** from the palette to the opened **File** menu, and drop it just below the **Save As ...** item. (If you drop it somewhere else, it doesn't matter, but if it bothers you, you can drag it from where you dropped it to where you wanted it to go.)

With the item in place, double-click the title (**Item**) and type **Save as PList ...** as the new title. Press **Return** to end the edit.

Now we have a menu item. How do we make it do something? We know that Cocoa objects that send user commands keep two pieces of information: the action (what is to be done) and the target (what is to do it).

The action is the name of an Objective-C method taking one parameter: an identifier ending with a colon. We haven't written the action method yet, but we can make up a name for it: saveAsPList:.

What about the target? To what Cocoa object will we assign the task of responding to `saveAsPList:`? *I don't know*, says a stubborn part of our subconscious, *anything that wants to, I guess.*

This turns out not to be a stupid answer in Cocoa. Cocoa keeps a continually updated *responder chain*, a series of potential responders to user actions. The chain begins at the **First Responder**, which may be the selected view in the front window, and then proceeds to the front window, the window's document, and finally to the application itself. You have probably noticed that the second icon in an Interface Builder Nib window represents the **First Responder**. A user interface element can designate the **First Responder**, whatever it may be at the time, as the target of its action, and Cocoa will shop the action up the responder chain until it finds an object that can handle it.

> The responder chain is a little more complicated than that. For more information, consult Apple's documentation for `NSApplication`, `NSRe-sponder`, and the related Programming Topic articles.

If we tried control-dragging an action link from our new menu item to the **First Responder** icon, we'd quickly be balked. Interface Builder would present an Inspector for the link, asking us to designate the method selector for our desired action. The list it presents does not include **saveAsPList:**, because we just made that up. Before we make the link, we have to tell Interface Builder that **saveAsPList:** is a possible action.

Interface Builder allows you to do this by editing the **First Responder** as if it were a custom class. Click the **Class** tab in the MainMenu.nib window. Scroll the class list all the way to the left, and select **NSObject** in the first column. You will find **First Responder** listed among `NSObject`'s subclasses. Click **First Responder** (see Figure 8.3). You now want an Inspector on the **First Responder** "class." Select **Show Inspector** from the **Tools** menu. The Inspector window shows a tab for **Actions**, under which are listed all the known actions that `NSResponder` subclasses respond to. To add our new action, click the **Add** button, and type **saveAsPList:** in the new line that results. Press the **Return** key to make your edit final.

> Be sure to include the colon at the end of the selector `saveAsPList:`. Objective-C considers both `saveAsPList` and `saveAsPList:` to be legal, but completely different, method names. Forgetting the colon in action methods is one of the commonest errors Cocoa programmers make.

Figure 8.3 Finding the **First Responder** "class" in the Nib's class listing. Select **NSObject** in the leftmost column of the class browser, and click **First Responder** in the second column.

Now we can hook up our menu item. Click the **Instances** tab in the MainMenu.nib window to make the **First Responder** icon visible, and arrange the Nib window and the menu bar window so that you can see both the new item and the **First Responder** icon. When everything is in place, hold down the control key and drag from the new menu item to the **First Responder** icon. When the icon highlights, release the mouse button (Figure 8.4).

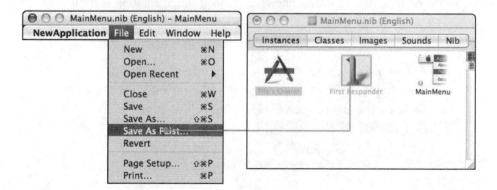

Figure 8.4 Linking a menu item to the **First Responder**. Control-drag from the new menu item to the **First Responder** icon. When the icon highlights, release the mouse button. The line between the two shows that the link has been made. The Inspector for the menu item appears, offering action methods for the link.

If it had been hidden before, the Inspector window now appears, showing a list of all the methods known for the responder chain. Our `saveAsPList:` method is in the list, because we added it; Interface Builder guesses that `saveAsPList:` is the right action for a menu item named **Save as PList . . .** and highlights that action, saving us the trouble of hunting for it. Click the **Connect** button at the bottom of the Inspector window, and the link is made.

Controller

When we pulled the name of the `saveAsPList:` method out of the air, we had no particular implementer in mind for it, but now we have to think about it.

- The implementer has to be on the responder chain; otherwise, it will never be offered `saveAsPList:` when it is shopped around.
- The implementer has to be associated with one, and only one, `Regression` set.
- The implementer should, preferably, be an existing class.

Fortunately, we have one such class: `MyDocument`. As a document class, it is on the responder chain. We've already made it the controller class associated with our `Regression` model. And, it exists.

We open `MyDocument.m` and add this line to the beginning:

```
#import "Regression-PropertyList.h"
```

We also add the following lines somewhere in the implementation section:

```
- (IBAction) saveAsPList: (id) sender
{
    // The response to the Save As PList... command.
    NSSavePanel *      savePanel = [NSSavePanel savePanel];
    // Take the shared save-file panel
    // and set it to save only plists.
    [savePanel setAllowedFileTypes:
               [NSArray arrayWithObject: @"plist"]];

    // Make a nice default name to present to the user.
    NSString *         defaultName;
    defaultName = [[self displayName]
            stringByAppendingPathExtension: @"plist"];
```

```
    // Present the save panel and designate a method
    // for receiving the result.
    [savePanel beginSheetForDirectory: NSHomeDirectory()
                              file: defaultName
                    modalForWindow: [self windowForSheet]
                    modalDelegate: self
                    didEndSelector:
            @selector(savePanelDidEnd:returnCode:contextInfo:)
                        contextInfo: NULL];
}


- (void) savePanelDidEnd: (NSSavePanel *) sheet
            returnCode: (int) returnCode
            contextInfo: (void *) contextInfo
{
    // The response to the Save-as-plist save panel.
    if (returnCode == NSOKButton) {
        // The user OK'ed the save.
        // Get the property-list representation...
        NSDictionary *     pList = [model asPropertyList];
        // ... and write it out.
        [pList writeToFile: [sheet filename]
                atomically: YES];
    }
}
```

Objective-C methods do not have to be declared in advance to be legal or usable by other objects.

With all this hooked up and compiled, we run Linear and fill the data table with the old familiar not-quite $y = 2x$:

```
1.0    2.05
2.01   4
3      5.987
4      8.1
5      10.0
```

We click the **Compute** button to update the statistics (2.00196, 0.0175146, and 0.999871, as before) and pull down the **File** menu to select our new **Save As PList . . .** command. A save-file sheet appears, most likely offering to save a file named Untitled in your home directory. You can change this if you like, but be sure that you put the file somewhere you can find it, because we will be inspecting its contents.

8.2.2 Examining Property Lists

As Text

When the save is done, we can quit Linear. Now go to the Finder and find the file you just saved. Drag its icon onto the Xcode icon in your dock. Xcode presents you with a text editor on the contents of the file, which looks something like this:

```
<?xml version="1.0" encoding="UTF-8"?>
<!DOCTYPE plist PUBLIC "-//Apple Computer//DTD PLIST 1.0//EN"
  "http://www.apple.com/DTDs/PropertyList-1.0.dtd">
<plist version="1.0">
<dict>
    <key>correlation</key>
    <real>0.99987099999999995</real>
    <key>intercept</key>
    <real>0.017514600000000002</real>
    <key>points</key>
    <array>
        <dict>
            <key>abscissa</key>
            <real>1</real>
            <key>ordinate</key>
            <real>2.0499999999999998</real>
        </dict>
        <dict>
            <key>abscissa</key>
            <real>2.0099999999999998</real>
            <key>ordinate</key>
            <real>4</real>
        </dict>
```

```
        <dict>
            <key>abscissa</key>
            <real>3</real>
            <key>ordinate</key>
            <real>5.9870000000000001</real>
        </dict>
        <dict>
            <key>abscissa</key>
            <real>4</real>
            <key>ordinate</key>
            <real>8.0999999999999996</real>
        </dict>
        <dict>
            <key>abscissa</key>
            <real>5</real>
            <key>ordinate</key>
            <real>10</real>
        </dict>
    </array>
    <key>slope</key>
    <real>2.00196</real>
</dict>
</plist>
```

You likely will be relieved to see that the property list file format is XML and that Cocoa's built-in writer for `.plist` files indents them fairly nicely. The top-level element is `<plist>`, which must contain one property list element—in this case, `<dict>`, for our Regression dictionary. A `<dict>` element's contents alternate between `<key>` string elements and property list value elements. One of the keys in the Regression dictionary, `points`, has an `<array>` value. An `<array>` may contain zero or more property list elements, of any type, though in this case, they are all `<dict>`s from our DataPoint objects.

The nice thing about XML is that it is standard: Correct XML will be accepted by any consumer of a document type definition, regardless of the source. A `.plist` file generated by Cocoa will be treated the same as one generated by a text editor.

The difficult thing about XML is that it must be correct. If you forget to close an element or miss the strict alternation of `<key>` and property list elements in `<dict>` lists, you will get nothing out of Apple's parser. There are three ways to cope with this restriction.

First, you can always start your own `.plist` files by editing a known good `.plist` file. It's difficult to omit the processing instruction or the `<plist>` skeleton if they are already in the file.

Second, you can use the macro or glossary facilities of your text editor to create a document skeleton and wrap your entries in proper tags. Bare Bones Software's BBEdit comes with a `.plist` glossary for just this purpose. Xcode 2.2, surprisingly, does not include property list macros. We'll be fixing that later in this chapter.

Third, you can use the Property List Editor application, found among the Xcode tools at `/Developer/Applications/Utilities` (Figure 8.5). The simplest use of Property List Editor is as a check on your text-edited file. Simply attempt to open your file with Property List Editor. If the file doesn't open, something's wrong. If the error isn't obvious, find a way to cut about half the list to the clipboard, leaving what, you hope, would still be a legal property list. Try opening the file with Property List Editor again. If the file opens, the error is in the part on the clipboard; if not, it's in the part still in the file. In either case, paste the missing lines back into the file, and cut half the elements out of the half of the file in which you isolated the problem in the previous pass. Repeat this process, reducing your search by halves, until you arrive at a stretch of XML small enough to proofread.

> One of the commonest errors is forgetting that the text portions of the property list XML are parsed character data, which means that < and & must be represented by `&lt;` and `&amp;`.

Property List Editor

Of course, you could simply use Property List Editor (PLE) to create your `.plist` files in the first place. Select **New** in the **File** menu (or press **command-N**) to open a window on a new, empty list. Add a root element to the list by clicking the **New Root** button. A line labeled **Root** appears under PropertyList with **Dictionary** listed under Class. **Dictionary** appears as a pop-up menu; clicking the mouse in the class cell shows the full range of choices of property list types.

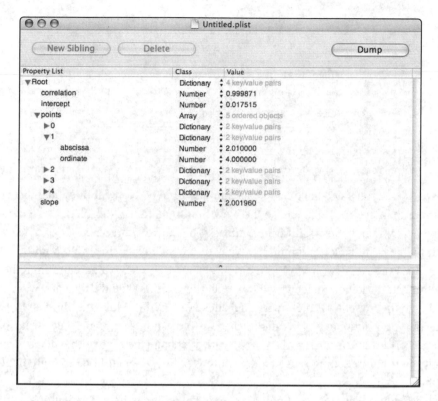

Figure 8.5 The Property List Editor application, found in the Utilities folder of the Developer Applications, presents the contents of property list files in a visual hierarchy that you may find easier to work with than the raw XML of the file itself. Trying to open a file with PLE is a good way to check whether the file contains a valid property list.

The button at the upper left of the window is the **New** button. Its meaning changes depending on what is selected in the list.

- When the property list is empty, the button is **New Root**. It puts one element in the file.

- When the selected line is an element inside a container—and is closed, if it is a container itself—the button is **New Sibling**. It adds one element to the same container as the selected element.

- When the selected line is an open container, the button is **New Child**. It adds one element to the selected container.

Table 8.2 The Remaining Ingredients in an Omelet

Key	Type of Value	Value
Mushrooms	Count	2
Salt	Pinch	1
Butter	Ounce	2

Because it is a container, a dictionary, the root element line can be opened. It is closed, so the rules say that the **New** operation should be **New Sibling**, but there can't be more than one root element, so the **New Sibling** button is disabled. Open the root element, and click **New Child** three times. This creates three new key/value pairs, with the keys in the left column, the types of the values (**String**) in the middle, and the values themselves (empty) in the right. Name these key/value pairs Ingredients, Material, and Method; make the first two dictionaries and the third an array.

Open the Ingredients dictionary, and click **New Child**. Make the child's key Eggs and its type **Dictionary**. This dictionary, in turn, should have the key/string pairs $unit \rightarrow count$ and $quantity \rightarrow 3$. Take care to change the type of the quantity value to **Number** before setting it. Add more siblings to Eggs—or children to Ingredients— as shown in Table 8.2.

The Material dictionary should be simple key/string pairs, as shown in Table 8.3. The Method array should contain strings, as shown in Table 8.4.

If you followed along with this exercise (see Figure 8.6), you've probably been persuaded that the Property List Editor has its advantages and disadvantages. On the plus side, it always generates correct property lists, and no matter how complex your

Table 8.3 Materials for Making an Omelet

Key	String
Bowl	Small
Fork	Table fork or small whisk
Crêpe Pan	10" nonstick
Spatula	Silicone, high-heat
Egg Slicer	Optional, for slicing mushrooms

Table 8.4 Making an Omelet

Instructions
Heat pan to medium (so butter foams but doesn't burn)
Warm eggs to room temperature
Slice mushrooms
Sauté until limp in 1/4 of the butter and set aside
Break eggs into bowl, add salt
Whisk eggs until color begins to change
Coat pan with 1/2 the butter
Pour eggs into pan and tilt to spread uniformly
When edges set, use spatula to separate from pan, then tilt liquid into gaps
Leave undisturbed for 30 seconds
Loosen from pan, and flip (using spatula to help) 1/3 over
Top with mushrooms
Slide onto plate, flipping remaining 1/3 over
Spread remaining butter on top

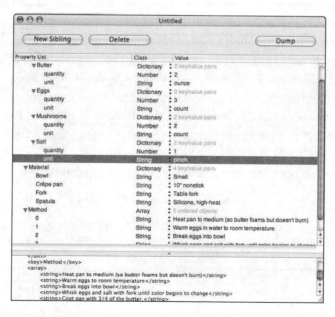

Figure 8.6 Construction of the Omelet Property List

property list structure becomes, PLE makes it easy to navigate. On the minus side, PLE was never meant for creating large, repetitious lists. By the third ingredient, you were probably wishing you could duplicate the quantity/number–unit/string dictionary pattern. Instead, you were forced to use the keyboard, the **New** button, and the Class pop-up. That PLE keeps dictionary keys in alphabetical order at all times is handy when you're browsing a property list, but it's a misfeature when you change a key and the line you are working on moves elsewhere on the screen.

8.3 Other Formats

8.3.1 ASCII Property Lists

Property lists came to Cocoa's architecture from its ancestor framework, OpenStep. In OpenStep, property lists were encoded in an ASCII format that Apple characterizes as a legacy technique, but is used often enough that you should be familiar with it. For instance, `defaults`, the command line interface to the preferences system, and many of the internal Xcode configuration files, use the ASCII format.

ASCII property lists have only two primitive types: string and data (Table 8.5). Strings are surrounded by double-quote characters, which may be omitted if there is no space in the string. Number, date, and Boolean values must be stored as string representations. The convention for Boolean values is to use the strings YES and NO.

Data elements are delimited by angle brackets and contain pairs of hexadecimal digits, representing the bytes in the data. Any spaces in the digit stream will be ignored.

Arrays are surrounded by parentheses, and the elements are separated by commas. Dictionaries are surrounded by braces, and the elements are *followed by* semicolons, which means that the last element must be closed off with a semicolon.

The Property List Editor reads ASCII-format property lists and its **Save As...** dialog presents an option to save a property list in ASCII format.

Table 8.5 Encoding for ASCII-Style Property Lists

Type	Coding
String	`"Two or more words"` *or* `oneWord`
Data	`< 466f6f 626172 >`
List	`(Shirley, "Goodness and Mercy", 1066 )`
Associative array	`{ key = value; "key 2" = < 332e3134313539 >; }`

8.3.2 Binary Property Lists

In Mac OS X version 10.2, Apple introduced a binary property list format. In the binary format, `plists` are smaller than in XML or ASCII format and load more quickly. As of Mac OS X version 10.4, application preference files are written as binary property lists. Property lists can be converted between XML and binary format in place using the `plutil` command line utility in the form

    plutil -convert *format pathToFile*

where *format* is either `binary1`, for conversion to the binary format, or `xml1` for the XML format; and *pathToFile* is the path to the file to convert.

8.4 Text Macros

Xcode 2.0 introduced text macros to its editor. A macro inserts previously prepared, commonly used text into the text being edited. Xcode may make simple substitutions as it inserts the macro, such as the current date, or the text that was selected when the macro command was issued.

Xcode comes with a set of macros for C, C++, HTML, Java, Objective-C, and the text-macro specification language itself. Surprisingly, there is no set for XML property lists. We'll be adding one in this section.

To insert a macro while you're editing a file, choose the macro from its language submenu of the **Insert Text Macro** item of the **Edit** menu. Some macros that may have more than one useful variant, such as the `if-then-else` variant of the C family's `if` statement, will rotate through the variants if you invoke them repeatedly.

It's obvious that a command three menus deep is difficult to invoke once, let alone repeatedly. Apple's intention is that you should use the Key Bindings panel of the Preferences window to assign special key combinations to the macros you use most. Then stepping through the variations of the `if` statement is as easy as repeatedly pressing, say, **control-option-I**.

Apple doesn't provide a way to extend or edit the macro sets except through writing your own macro-specification files. Xcode's root specifications can be found in the resource directory of the Text-Macro plug-in in the Xcode application bundle. The installation process may create additional, systemwide specification files at `/Library/Application Support/Apple/Developer Tools/Specifications`, and you can keep macro specifications for your own use in the equivalent subdirectory of the `Library` directory in your home folder.

Apple's release notes recommend examining the existing macro-specification files and developing your own from a copy of one that most nearly matches your needs. The nearest thing to an XML `.plist` file is HTML, so let's start from that.

In examining `HTML.xctxtmacro`, the important thing is not to panic. First, it's just a property list file, in the old, ASCII format. Second, it's merely a list of some fairly simple dictionaries, of three types: a header dictionary with the key `IsMenu` = YES, leaf dictionaries with `IsMenuItem` = YES, and category dictionaries with no menu characteristics at all. Every dictionary has an `Identifier`, with a dotted hierarchical name, such as `html`, `html.formatter`, or `html.formatter.bold`. The idea is that a menu item selects a leaf, and the leaf, together with its hierarchical ancestors, defines a `TextString` property that will be the text the macro inserts.

With that in mind, we can start with the root of the macro tree for property lists:

```
(
{
    Identifier = plist;
    Name = "Property List";
    IsMenu = YES;
    ComputerLanguages = ( plist );
},
```

Next, we see a leaf macro for the skeleton of an XML property list file:

```
{
    Identifier = plist.skeleton;
    BasedOn = plist;
    TextString = "<?xml version=\"1.0\" encoding=\"UTF-8\"?>\n
        <!DOCTYPE plist PUBLIC \
        "-//Apple Computer//DTD PLIST 1.0//EN\"\n
      \t\"http://www.apple.com/DTDs/PropertyList-1.0.dtd\">\n
        <plist version=\"1.0\">\n\t<#!text!#>\n</plist>";
    Name = "File Skeleton";
    IsMenuItem = YES;
},
```

Unfortunately, the string value of `TextString` had to be broken into several lines to fit on this page; to work properly, the string value must be in one line. Note that quotation marks in the string have to be escaped with backslashes and that newlines and tabs can be inserted with the familiar \n and \t sequences. The \t sequence does not mean a literal tab; instead, it means "tabbed one more level than the line the macro started at."

Now, we want the Boolean elements <true/> and <false/>. This suggests a simple application of a category node in the specification—the two tags are identical except for the names, so they can share some of the layout. We can define the TextString for both in the category, leaving the tag text to be specified by the leaf nodes:

```
{   Identifier = plist.boolean;
    BasedOn = plist;
    TextString = "<$(Tag) />"; %$
},
    {
        Identifier = plist.boolean.true;
        BasedOn = plist.boolean;
        Name = "True";
        IsMenuItem = YES;
        Tag = "true";
    },
    {
        Identifier = plist.boolean.false;
        BasedOn = plist.boolean;
        Name = "False";
        IsMenuItem = YES;
        Tag = "false";
    },
```

So plist.boolean.false is a menu item (IsMenuItem = YES), with title **False** (Name = "False") and inserts <false /> (because TextString = "< $(Tag) />", plus Tag = "false", yields <false />).

Now we move on to the elements that contain character data:

```
{
    Identifier = plist.element;
    BasedOn = plist;
    TextString = "<$(Tag)><#!text!#></$(Tag)>";
},
```

```
{
    Identifier = plist.element.string;
    BasedOn = plist.element;
    Name = "String";
    IsMenuItem = YES;
    Tag = "string";
},
{
    Identifier = plist.element.date;
    BasedOn = plist.element;
    Name = "Date";
    IsMenuItem = YES;
    Tag = "date";
},
{
    Identifier = plist.element.data;
    BasedOn = plist.element;
    Name = "Data";
    IsMenuItem = YES;
    Tag = "data";
},
{
    Identifier = plist.element.key;
    BasedOn = plist.element;
    Name = "Key";
    IsMenuItem = YES;
    Tag = "key";
},
```

This time, the common `TextString` for these elements includes the string `<#!text!#>`. This string is a placeholder for whatever text is selected when the macro was invoked. If, for instance, the string

```
we shall prevail
```

was selected and the **String** macro was selected, the selection would be replaced with

```
<string>we shall prevail</string>
```

Just for fun, let's have a cycling tag:

```
{
    Identifier = plist.element.number;
    BasedOn = plist.element;
    Name = "Integer";
    IsMenuItem = YES;
    Tag = "integer";
    CycleList = (
        plist.element.number,
        plist.element.number.real
    );
},
    {
        Identifier = plist.element.number.real;
        BasedOn = plist.element.number;
        Name = "Real";
        IsMenuItem = YES;
        Tag = "real";
    },
```

These add two menu items, **Integer** and **Real**, which are like other plist.element nodes in inserting <integer> and markup, respectively. We've added an element to plist.element.number, CycleList, which specifies that the first time the **Integer** command is invoked, it executes plist.element.number, but the next time, plist.element.number.real, and so on alternately. So if the current selection were:

1984

the **Integer** command would substitute

<integer>1984</integer>

the first time it is invoked, but

1984

the next time. Repeatedly issuing the same command would repeat the cycle.

We finish the specification with a category for the container classes:

```
{
    Identifier = plist.container;
    BasedOn = plist;
    TextString =
        "<$(Tag)>\n\t$(PreSel)<#!text!#>$(PostSel)\n</$(Tag)>";
    PreSel = "";
    PostSel = "";
},
    {
        Identifier = plist.container.array;
        BasedOn = plist.container;
        Name = "Array";
        Tag = "array";
        IsMenuItem = YES;
    },
    {
        Identifier = plist.container.dictionary;
        BasedOn = plist.container;
        Name = "Dictionary";
        Tag = "dict";
        IsMenuItem = YES;
        PreSel = "<key>";
        PostSel = "</key>\n\t";
    }
)
```

So the **Array** command makes the current selection the indented first item in
<array> markup, and **Dictionary** makes it the indented first key in <dict> markup.
Note how the PreSel and PostSel variables, which are empty in the case of an array,
carry the <key> tags and an extra line in the case of a dictionary.

Now all that remains is to install the specification. Save this file as plist.xctxt-
macro in the Specifications folder of the folder Library/Application Support/
Apple/Developer Tools in your home folder. Next, try opening the file with Property
List Editor—remember it's simply an ASCII-format property list, and it should check
out. If it doesn't, use the debugging strategy mentioned earlier in this chapter to track

down the problem. (*Hint:* What bit me was \-escaping all the quotes in the TextString of the plist.skeleton node.)

If Xcode is already running, you'll have to quit it and restart it for it to see the new specification file. It should appear as **Property List** in the **Insert Text Macro** menu.

8.5 Summary

This chapter introduced property lists, a ubiquitous data-storage format in Mac OS X. We've seen how to create them programmatically and how to use Property List Editor and text tools to manage them. We've even applied the ASCII property list format to create Xcode macros for XML property lists. By now, you should be pretty comfortable with the concept.

9

Libraries and Dependent Targets

Doing all the statistical work in Linrg has been fun, but it's time to bring that tool into the application. In this chapter, we'll create a C library for linear regressions as an additional target for the Linear project. We'll see how to make one target in a project depend on another, so our application target can always be assured of a current version of the library.

9.1 Adding a Target

We want our project to produce an additional product: a static library. Each product in a project is the result of a target. In the **Project** menu, select **New Target . . . .** The New Target Assistant appears (Figure 9.1), from which you should select **BSD →
Static Library**. Name the target Regression, and let it be added to project Linear.

A couple of things happen in the Groups & Files list. Under **Targets**, a new item, **Regression** appears, with an icon that looks like a toy building block. Above it, the **Linear** application target has a small green badge with a checkmark on it, indicating that it is the *active target*. All commands to build, run, or debug a target are sent to the active target, which you can select with a toolbar widget or in a submenu of the **Project** menu.

Also in Groups & Files, in the **Products** subgroup of the **Project** group, a new product, **libRegression.a**, has been added. (The name is in red on the screen because the file does not yet exist.) It is deeply ingrained in the GNU tool set that libraries have names with the prefix lib—the instruction to link this library to Linear will be -lRegression, and the linker will take that to mean libRegression.a. You *can* change the product name, but fighting the tools that way is inadvisable.

Change the active target to **Regression**, and note that the green checkmark badge in the **Targets** list moves to **Regression**'s icon. Press **command-N** to add a new text file to the project, a **BSD → C File**. The second panel of the New File Assistant

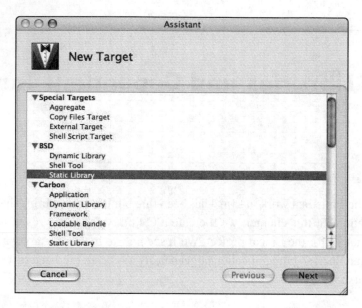

Figure 9.1 The New Target Assistant window. Select **BSD** → **Static Library** for this example, a C library for linear regressions.

takes on a new significance: Not only do we name the new file (libRegression.c) and opt for a matching header, but we also must assign the new file to a target in the current project. Even though **Regression** is the current target, **Linear** is checked, and **Regression** is unchecked. Turn that around, so that **Regression** is checked and **Linear** unchecked, as in Figure 9.2.

9.2 Library Design

Our specification is nothing special: Clients of our library should obtain an opaque pointer to the storage necessary to do a linear regression. The pointer is then presented to the library functions for any action related to that regression. The client should be able to add data points to the regression, and remove them. The regression should report on demand the regression statistics. To add interest, we'll add averages for x and y to the mix.

The public interface in libRegression.h follows naturally from the requirements:

```
#ifndef LIBREGRESSION_H_
#define LIBREGRESSION_H_
```

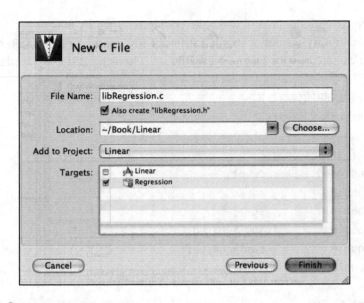

Figure 9.2 In a multitarget project, the New File Assistant presents options on which target the newly created file is to be assigned.

```
void *      RGCreate(void);
void        RGRelease(void * aRegression);

void        RGAddPoint(void * aRegression,
                            double inX, double inY);
void        RGDeletePoint(void * aRegression,
                                double inX, double inY);

unsigned    RGCount(void * aRegression);

double      RGMeanX(void * aRegression);
double      RGMeanY(void * aRegression);

double      RGSlope(void * aRegression);
double      RGIntercept(void * aRegression);
double      RGCorrelation(void * aRegression);

#endif
```

In keeping with the plan to make the cookie returned by RGCreate() opaque to clients of the library, we define its inner structure in a private header, libRPrivate.h, which you can create with **File → New File . . .** , choosing **BSD → Header File**:

```
#ifndef LIBRPRIVATE_H_
#define LIBRPRIVATE_H_

typedef struct Sums {
    unsigned        count;
    double          sumX;
    double          sumY;
    double          sumXSquared;
    double          sumYSquared;
    double          sumXY;

    int             dirty;
    double          slope;
    double          intercept;
    double          correlation;
}   Sums, *SumsPtr;

#endif
```

We'll split the workings of the library into two C files: one for the regression functions and the other for the distribution functions. Here is libRegression.c:

```
#include "libRegression.h"
#include "libRPrivate.h"
#include <stdlib.h>
#include <assert.h>
#include <math.h>

void *      RGCreate(void)
{
    SumsPtr     retval = calloc(1, sizeof(Sums));
    return retval;
}
```

```
void        RGRelease(void * aRegression)
{
    free(aRegression);
}


void        RGAddPoint(void * aRegression,
                            double inX,
                            double inY)
{
    SumsPtr     reg = (SumsPtr) aRegression;
    reg->count++;
    reg->sumX += inX;
    reg->sumY += inY;
    reg->sumXSquared += inX * inX;
    reg->sumYSquared += inY * inY;
    reg->sumXY += inX * inY;


    reg->dirty = 1;
}


void        RGDeletePoint(void * aRegression,
                            double inX,
                            double inY)
{
    SumsPtr     reg = (SumsPtr) aRegression;
    assert(reg->count > 0);

    reg->count--;
    reg->sumX -= inX;
    reg->sumY -= inY;
    reg->sumXSquared -= inX * inX;
    reg->sumYSquared -= inY * inY;
    reg->sumXY -= inX * inY;

    reg->dirty = 1;
}
```

```
static
void        CalculateRegression(SumsPtr aRegression)
{
    if (!aRegression->dirty || aRegression->count < 2)
        return;

    aRegression->slope =
        (aRegression->count * aRegression->sumXY
                    - aRegression->sumX * aRegression->sumY)
                        /
        (aRegression->count * aRegression->sumXSquared
                    - aRegression->sumX * aRegression->sumX);
    aRegression->intercept =
        (aRegression->sumY
                    - aRegression->slope * aRegression->sumX)
                        /
        aRegression->count;
    aRegression->correlation =
        aRegression->slope * sqrt(
                (aRegression->count * aRegression->sumXSquared
                    - aRegression->sumX * aRegression->sumX)
                        /
                (aRegression->count * aRegression->sumYSquared
                    - aRegression->sumY * aRegression->sumY)
                );

    aRegression->dirty = 0;
}

unsigned    RGCount(void * aRegression)
{ return ((SumsPtr)aRegression)->count; }

double      RGSlope(void * aRegression)
{
    CalculateRegression(((SumsPtr)aRegression));
    return ((SumsPtr)aRegression)->slope;
}
```

```
double      RGIntercept(void * aRegression)
{
    CalculateRegression(((SumsPtr)aRegression));
    return ((SumsPtr)aRegression)->intercept;
}

double      RGCorrelation(void * aRegression)
{
    CalculateRegression(((SumsPtr)aRegression));
    return ((SumsPtr)aRegression)->correlation;
}
```

And, finally, here is libRAverage.c (**New File ...**, **BSD** → **C File**, no header file):

```
#include "libRegression.h"
#include "libRPrivate.h"
#include <math.h>

double      RGMeanX(void * aRegression)
{
    return ((SumsPtr)aRegression)->sumX /
            ((SumsPtr)aRegression)->count;
}

double      RGMeanY(void * aRegression)
{
    return ((SumsPtr)aRegression)->sumY /
            ((SumsPtr)aRegression)->count;
}
```

9.3 Modifying Linear

In the application Linear, Regression remains the model object responsible for maintaining the list of data points and farming it out for computation of the regression statistics. That computation had been done in the computeWithLinrg method, which we'll leave untouched. We will add a new method, `computeFromLibrary`. Declare the new method in `Regression.h`:

```
- (void) computeFromLibrary;
```

Put the method itself in `Regression.m`:

```
#import "libRegression.h"

- (void) computeFromLibrary
{
    void *      reg = RGCreate();

    NSEnumerator * iter = [dataPoints objectEnumerator];
    DataPoint *     curr;
    while (curr = [iter nextObject])
        RGAddPoint(reg, [curr x], [curr y]);

    if (RGCount(reg) > 1) {
        [self setSlope: RGSlope(reg)];
        [self setIntercept: RGIntercept(reg)];
        [self setCorrelation: RGCorrelation(reg)];
    }
    RGRelease(reg);
}
```

> Why use the `set...` accessors instead of setting the instance variables directly? One way the key/value/observing protocol, on which the Controller-layer bindings are based, detects changes in observed properties is to intercept `set...` accessors. When we use the accessors, we notify the NSForm in the document window that the values have changed, and the display updates automatically.

Make sure that `MyDocument` uses the correct method; modify the `compute:` action method thus:

```
- (IBAction) compute: (id) sender
{
    [model computeFromLibrary];
}
```

9.4 A Dependent Target

Finally, make sure that whenever any part of the `libRegression` library changes, `Linear.app` will be rebuilt with the new library. Open the **Targets** group in the Groups & Files list in the project window, and double-click the **Linear.app** target. (It's easy to miss the target group and double-click the **Linear** application in the **Products** group under the project icon. If Linear started up when you double-clicked the item, you got the wrong one.)

A Get Info window for the **Linear.app** target appears. Under the first tab, **General**, is a large space for listing *dependencies*, targets that must be built before this target and incorporated into it. The list is currently empty. Click the + button, and a sheet (Figure 9.3) appears, offering the only other target known to this project, **Regression**. Select it, and click the **Add Target** button. **Regression** now appears in the Direct Dependencies list.

Make sure that the application Linear is the active target. (The pop-up in the toolbar is the easiest way, or you can use the **Set Active Target** submenu of the **Project**

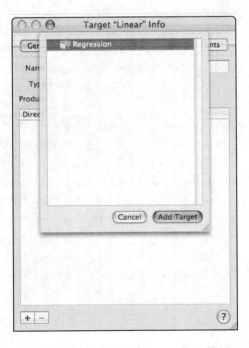

Figure 9.3 The Target Info window, **General** pane, after clicking the + button to add a dependency to the target. In this case, we want **Linear.app** to depend on the **Regression** target in this project.

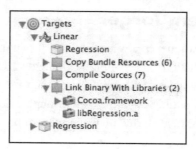

Figure 9.4 The build chain for **Linear**, showing **Regression** at the head of the chain, and **libRegression.a** as part of the linkage step. Unchecking **libRegression.a** in the detail listing would remove it from this phase.

menu.) Now select the project icon (the top icon) in the Groups & Files list. The detail view, to the right, will fill with all the files contained in the project. The last column of the detail view, contains checkboxes. This column indicates whether the file on that line generates code that should be linked into the target's final product. **AppKit.framework**, for instance, is not checked and should remain unchecked, because it is included in the project simply for reference to the headers it contains.

Switch the active target back and forth a bit to see what files get included in which target. In some cases, the checkbox for a file disappears, as with the Nib files, which cannot be included in a library product. When you're done, be sure to leave **Linear** as the active target.

Scroll down—or type in the search field in the toolbar—to find **libRegression.a**. Its box is unchecked, which is not what we want—we just changed the Regression class to use functions in that library. Check it. This will add the library to the build sequence for Linear. See for yourself: If you click the **Linear** target in the **Targets** group in the Groups & Files list, you will see a chain of build steps for **Linear** (Figure 9.4).

Open the **Link Binary With Libraries** build phase; if **libRegression.a** was checked in the detail listing, this phase includes libRegression.a. As you check and uncheck **libRegression.a**—you may have to reselect the top, project icon to get the checkboxes back—the library appears and disappears in the link-library build phase.

Now build. If you have a swift eye trained on the status bar at the bottom of the project window, you will see that even though libRegression.c is not a part of the active target, it nonetheless is compiled first, because it is needed to build libRegression.a, which we have specified as a prerequisite for our application.

While our attention is on the Groups & Files list, we should keep the list organized. Select **libRegression.c** and, using the **Shift** key, **libRegression.h**, **libRPrivate.h**, and **libRAverage.c**; then select the **Group** (**command-option-G**) command from the **File** menu, creating a new group folder, named **New Folder**, containing the files you selected. The name of the group is selected, so you can change it to something descriptive, such as **Regression Library**.

Groups, with tan folder icons, are solely a way to organize the Groups & Files list. They don't exist on disk and have no effect on the way your files are stored.

9.5 Examining the Library

Two BSD tools you can run from the Terminal application are useful in examining libraries and verifying their contents. The first tool, nm, examines the symbol tables of object files—applications, .o objects, and .a and .dylib libraries. Each of these file types includes a *symbol table*, a dictionary of entities the file defines and of entities that were left undefined but needed by objects in the file.

Start up the Terminal application, and set the working directory to the Linear project directory. (The easiest way to do this is to type **cd**; note the space after the **cd**—and then drag the folder containing the project file from the Finder into the Terminal window). Press **Return**. Type **nm build/libRegression.a**. The output should resemble this:

```
build/libRegression.a(libRegression.o):
00000108 t _CalculateRegression
00000010 T _RGAddPoint
00000234 T _RGCorrelation
000001cc T _RGCount
00000000 T _RGCreate
00000064 T _RGDeletePoint
00000204 T _RGIntercept
0000000c T _RGRelease
000001d4 T _RGSlope
         U ___eprintf
         U _calloc
         U _free
         U _sqrt
         U dyld_stub_binding_helper
```

```
build/libRegression.a(libRAverage.o):
00000000 T _RGMeanX
0000003c T _RGMeanY
```

This output shows libRegression.a to consist of two parts: libRegression.o and libRAverage.o. Both parts define various symbols in the text segment (the segment of an object file in which, by convention, Mach-O executable code is stored); for instance _RGAddPoint begins 16 (hexadecimal 10) bytes into the text segment of libRegression.o. The lowercase t in _CalculateRegression's line reflects its status as a private symbol—CalculateRegression() was declared static.

Five symbols, including _calloc, _free, and _sqrt, are marked U, for undefined. You would have to link in libraries defining these symbols for a project including libRegression.o to be satisfied.

The otool command gets into more detailed dissection of a library or object file. The various options for otool direct it to different parts of the archive or library file format. For instance, otool -av build/libRegression.a dumps the archive header in verbose (symbolic) format:

```
Archive : build/libRegression.a
-rw-r--r--501/501   364 Fri Mar  4 13:23:29 2005 __.SYMDEF SORTED
-rw-r--r--501/501  2452 Fri Mar  4 13:23:23 2005 libRegression.o
-rw-r--r--501/501   660 Fri Mar  4 13:23:24 2005 LibRAverage.o
```

Using the -Sv switch dumps the .SYMDEF pseudofile from the archive:

```
Archive : build/libRegression.a
Table of contents from: build/libRegression.a(__.SYMDEF SORTED)
size of ranlib structures: 80 (number 10)
size of strings: 112
object          symbol name
libRegression.o _RGAddPoint
libRegression.o _RGCorrelation
libRegression.o _RGCount
libRegression.o _RGCreate
libRegression.o _RGDeletePoint
libRegression.o _RGIntercept
libRAverage.o   _RGMeanX
libRAverage.o   _RGMeanY
libRegression.o _RGRelease
libRegression.o _RGSlope
```

The -t option would display the text segments of the archive as hex dumps; adding the -v verbosity option makes it a disassembly:

```
Archive : build/libRegression.a
build/libRegression.a(libRegression.o):
(__TEXT,__text) section
_RGCreate:
00000000  li   r3,0x1
00000004  li   r4,0x48
00000008  b    0x2e0
_RGRelease:
0000000c  b    0x2c0
_RGAddPoint:
00000010  lfd  f0,0x4(r3)
00000014  lfd  f13,0xc(r3)
00000018  lfd  f12,0x14(r3)
0000001c  lfd  f10,0x1c(r3)
00000020  lfd  f11,0x24(r3)
00000024  lwz  r2,0x0(r3)
       .
       .
       .
```

Both nm and otool offer much more than can be covered here. Be sure to run man nm and man otool for full documentation of what they make available to you.

9.6 Running the Library

The real proof of the new library, of course, is not in prodding it with command line tools but in running it. So issue the **Build and Run** command (press **command-R**, or use the toolbar), and see how it works.

Figure 9.5 shows the results of loading the old familiar data set and clicking the **Compute** button. We can see that there has been a change in that the statistics are now reported to twice as many digits' precision. In the previous version of Linear, all our data passed to and from the regression calculator through a printf() or equivalent function, which limited the precision the calculator could receive or report. We should have fixed this bug in the previous version of Linrg. Now, however, the data for the statistical calculations are taken and reported as binary data, without reformatting or truncation.

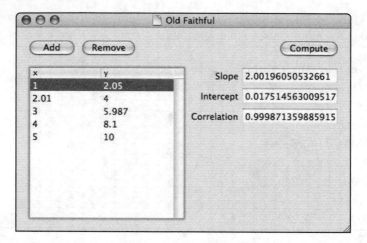

Figure 9.5 Linear, using the libRegression library. Because the data no longer passes through formatting steps on the way to and from the regression engine, we are given more digits of precision.

9.7 Summary

In this chapter, we've seen how to gather functionality into a static library. We've made our project generate that library as an additional product and made sure that our main product, the Linear application, is always provided with an up-to-date version of the library. We've also touched on some tools for examining libraries and other object files to see, among other things, what objects they define and what objects they need other entities to define.

We've also done a little project management: We've seen how to allocate files in a project among its targets and how doing so affects a target's build order. We've also organized our files related to our new library into a separate file group.

10

File Packages and Bundles

Many of Xcode's products take the form of *packages*, directory trees that the Finder presents as single files. Let's pause now to consider the problem of resources. Resources are the sorts of data that were historically put into Resource Manager resources: strings, lookup tables, images, human-interface layouts, sounds, and the like. One of the innovations of the classic Macintosh software architecture was the separation of such constant or parameterized data from the executable code of applications.

Before Mac OS X, the customary vehicle for aggregating packets of data into a single file system entity was the *resource file*. Resource files kept their structured data in the *resource fork,* a data store that HFS, the Macintosh file system, associates with files in addition to the traditional unstructured data stream. The resource fork cataloged its contents by type, integer identifier, and name, and applications accessed resources by those keys through the Resource Manager.

The problem with the Resource Manager is that it does not scale well to sets of many, large, or changeable resources. The catalog written into each resource file was notoriously fragile, and any corruption resulted in the loss of every resource in the file. With the multiplicity of large resources—images, sounds, human-interface layouts, lookup tables—needed to support modern applications, the tasks involved in managing them become indistinguishable from the tasks of a file system. File systems are a solved problem; they do their work as efficiently and robustly as decades of experience can make them. Why not use the file system for storing and retrieving resources?

One reason to avoid shipping application resources as separate files is that an application that relies on them becomes a swarm of files and directories, all more or less critical to the correct working of the application and exposed to relocation, deletion, and general abuse by the application's user. The user, in the meantime, who simply wants one thing that does the application's work, is presented with a swarm of files and directories.

Mac OS X provides a way to have the flexibility of separating resources into their own files while steering clear of the swarming problem. The Finder can treat directories, called *packages*, as though they were single documents.

10.1 A Simple Package: RTFD

A package can be as simple as a directory with a handful of files in it. The application that creates and reads the package determines how it is structured: what files are required, the names of the content files, what sort of subdirectory structure is used.

A common example of an application-defined package is the RTFD, or rich text file directory. The Apple-supplied application TextEdit, in its standard `Info.plist` file, specifies what kinds of documents TextEdit can handle; among these is `NSRTFDP-boardType`, which is listed as having suffix `rtfd` and is designated as a package file type. When it catalogs TextEdit, the Mac OS X Finder notes that directories with the `.rtfd` extension are supposed to be packages and so treats them as if they were single files, not ordinarily displaying the files within.

It is sometimes useful to look inside a package, however, and the Finder provides a way to do that. Control-clicking on a package file produces a pop-up menu containing the command **Show Package Contents** (Figure 10.1). Selecting that command opens a new window showing the contents of the package directory, which can be further navigated as in a normal Finder window (Figure 10.2).

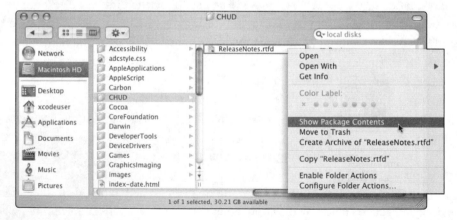

Figure 10.1 The **Show Package Contents** command is available in a pop-up contextual menu for any apparent file that is a package directory.

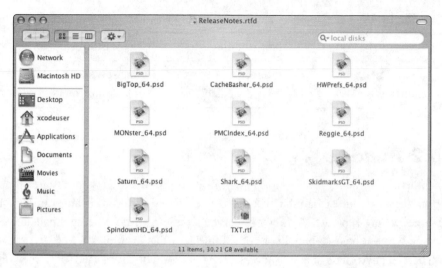

Figure 10.2 The contents of an RTFD package, in this case the release notes for the CHUD performance tools. The contents are simply a rich text format (RTF) file with a standard name, along with graphics files with names referred to in custom tags in the RTF file.

In the case of RTFD, the package directory contains one plain RTF file, TXT.rtf. The RTF file incorporates custom markup, such as

{{\NeXTGraphic Shark_64.psd \width1280 \height1280}}

Here, the markup refers to graphics files—in this case, Shark_64.psd—that are also in the RTFD directory.

> The Cocoa application framework provides support for package-directory documents. NSDocument subclasses handle package reading and writing by overriding readFromFile:ofType: and writeToFile:ofType:. The NS-FileWrapper class provides methods that assist in creating and managing complex file packages.

Having a name extension registered by a handling application as a file package is not the only way for a directory to be treated as a package. Directories are also treated as packages if they have the HFS "bundle" bit set, but this is not a useful variation.

Table 10.1 Examples of Directories that Are Bundles or Packages or Both

	Not Bundle	**Bundle**
Not Package	Other directories	Frameworks (versioned)
Package	Complex documents	Applications (modern)

10.2 Bundles

A bundle is a particular kind of *structured* directory tree. Often, bundles are shipped as packages—the most familiar type of bundle, the application, is an example—but the concepts are separate. A directory can be a bundle without being a package or a package without being a bundle or both. Table 10.1 has examples.

There are two kinds of bundles: *versioned bundles*, which are used for frameworks, and *modern bundles*, which are used for applications and most other executable products. Versioned bundles are covered in Chapter 12, where we build a framework.

At the minimum, a modern bundle encloses one directory, named `Contents`, which in turn contains all the directories and files comprising the bundle. The `Contents` directory contains an `Info.plist` file, which specifies how the bundle is to be displayed in the Finder and, depending on the type of the bundle, may provide configuration data for loading and running the bundle's contents. Beyond that, what the `Contents` folder contains depends on the type of the bundle.

10.3 Application Bundles

Applications are the most common type of bundle (see Figure 10.3). An application directory has a name with the suffix `.app`. The `.app` directory is a file package; even though it is a directory, the Finder treats it as a single entity. This allows the author of the application to place auxiliary files for the application in a known place—inside the application bundle itself—with little fear that such files will be misplaced or deleted.

The `Contents` directory of an application bundle contains

- `Info.plist`, an XML property list file that describes such application details as the principal class, the document types handled, and the application version. More on this file in Section 10.4.

- `Resources`, a directory containing the application icon file, images, sounds, human interface (UI) layouts, and other parameterized content for the application.

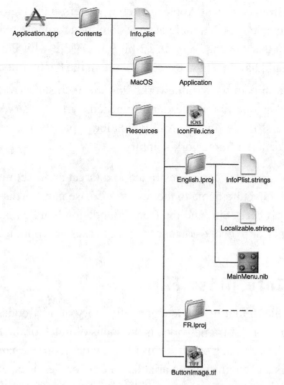

Figure 10.3   The structure of a typical application bundle. The executable file is at `Contents/MacOS/Application`. The application's human interface for English-speaking users is specified in `Contents/Resources/English.lproj/MainMenu.nib`; presumably, a French version of `MainMenu.nib` is inside `Contents/Resources/FR.lproj`. The custom image for a button, `ButtonImage.tif`, is common to all languages and therefore appears directly in the `Resources` directory.

This directory may be further organized into subdirectories, according to your convenience. In addition, there may be localization subdirectories, which have the `.lproj` suffix. When an application seeks a resource, the Cocoa or Core Foundation bundle managers will look first in the `.lproj` directory that corresponds to the current language and locale.

- `MacOS`, a directory containing the executable binary for the application, along with any other executables used by the application. A bundle may be *fat*, containing executable directories for all the supported target architectures, but for now, only `MacOS` and `MacOSClassic` (for Mac OS 9) are supported. (This fat bundle is to be distinguished from fat—or as Apple marketing prefers, universal—binaries, single Mach-O executable files that include code compiled for more than one processor. An application that runs natively on 32-bit PowerPC, 64-bit PowerPC, and Intel processors would have a single executable file in the MacOS folder.)

- Frameworks, a directory of frameworks that are themselves versioned bundles, containing a dynamic library, resources needed by the library, and header files needed by users of the library. An application typically includes a framework because it links to the framework's library.

Individual resource files can be restricted to a target architecture by appending a hyphen and the architecture name to the resource's base name. This way, an application may ask for picture.tif, and the Core Foundation bundle manager will return picture-macos.tif or picture-macosclassic.tif, as appropriate.

10.4 The Info.plist File

The Info.plist file, found in the Contents directory of any modern bundle and in the Resources directory of frameworks, is the locus of much of the information Mac OS X needs to make sense of a bundle. This file provides icon and naming information to the Finder, flags and environment variables to Launch Services, and specifications for the basic structure of applications and plug-ins.

In almost every case, you can put together an Info.plist file by using the editor presented by the **Properties** tab of the Get Info box of an Xcode target. This will allow you to set CFBundleExecutable, CFBundleIdentifier, CFBundlePackageType, CFBundleSignature, CFBundleIconFile, CFBundleShortVersionString, NSPrincipalClass, NSMainNibFile, and the CFBundleDocumentTypes array.

Some of these keys are localizable. A file named InfoPlist.strings should be in the .lproj directory for each localization of your application. Localizable keys can then be assigned per locale values. For instance, InfoPlist.strings in the English.lproj directory might include the pair

```
CFBundleName = "Linear";
CFBundleDisplayName = "Linear";
```

The same file in the fr.lproj directory might include

```
CFBundleName = "Linéaire";
CFBundleDisplayName = "Linéaire";
```

For users whose language preferences place French above English, the **Linear** icon in the Finder will be labeled **Linéaire**. The name of the bundle directory, however, will still be Linear.app.

10.4.1 Keys for All Bundles

The keys in this section apply to almost any kind of bundle, including applications.

Info

- CFBundleGetInfoString, a string containing a version and copyright notice, for display in Get Info boxes in the Finder. See also CFBundleShortVersionString. This key may be localized in InfoPlist.strings, but Apple no longer recommends it.

- CFBundleIconFile, the name of the .icns file, in the Resources directory, containing the bundle's custom icon.

- CFBundleIdentifier, a unique identifier string for the bundle, in the form of a Java-style reverse domain package name, such as com.apple.TextEdit. This identifier is used, among other places, by the preferences system to identify preference sets with the applications they relate to. Applications must specify this key.

- CFBundleInfoDictionaryVersion, a compatibility-check version number for the Info.plist format. Xcode injects this version number automatically when it builds bundles. All Info.plist files should include this key.

- CFBundlePackageType, the four-character type code for the bundle. Applications are type APPL, frameworks are FMWK, plug-ins are BNDL or a code of your choosing. See also CFBundleSignature. Applications must specify this key.

- CFBundleShortVersionString, a short string with the product version, such as 10.2.8, of the bundle, suitable for display in an About box. See also CFBundle-GetInfoString. This key may be localized in InfoPlist.strings. Applications must specify this key.

- CFBundleSignature, the four-character creator code associated with the bundle. Applications must specify this key.

- CFBundleVersion, the build version of the bundle's executable, which may identify versions within a release cycle, such as betas: 2.1b3, for instance. The build version is displayed in parentheses in the About box. See also CFBundleShort-VersionString.

Localization

- CFBundleDevelopmentRegion, the native human language of the bundle. If the user's preferred language is not available as a localization, this is the language that will be used.

Structure

- CFBundleExecutable, the name of the executable file, which may be an application binary, a library, or plug-in code. Applications must specify this key.
- CSResourcesFileMapped, if YES or <true/>, Core Foundation will memory-map the bundle resources rather than read the files into memory.
- NSPrincipalClass, the name of the bundle's main class. In a Cocoa application, this would normally be NSApplication.

10.4.2 Keys for Applications

These keys apply only to applications and cover launch configurations, help facilities, and information on the kinds of documents and URLs the application handles.

Documents and URLs

- CFBundleDocumentTypes, an array of dictionaries specifying every document type associated with the application. Use the **Properties** panel of the application target's Get Info window to manage this array and its contents. See Section 7.8 for details.
- CFBundleURLTypes, an array of dictionaries defining URL schemes, such as http: or ftp:, for which the application is a handler. See Apple's documentation for details.

Help

- CFAppleHelpAnchor, the base name, without extension, of the initial help file for the application.
- CFBundleHelpBookFolder, the folder—in either the Resources subdirectory or a localization subdirectory—containing the application's help book.
- CFBundleHelpBookName, the name of the application's help book. This name should match the name set in a <meta> tag in the help book's root file.

Info

- CFBundleDisplayName, the name for the Finder to display for this bundle. The value in Info.plist should be identical to the name of the application bundle;

localized names can then be put in InfoPlist.strings files for various languages. See also CFBundleName. Applications must specify this key.

- CFBundleName, the short—16-character maximum—name for the application, to be shown in the About box and the **Application** menu. See also CFBundleDisplayName. This key may be localized in InfoPlist.strings. Applications must specify this key.

- LSHasLocalizedDisplayName, the hint, if <true/> or nonzero, to the Finder that this application has localized versions of its display name (CFBundleDisplayName). Applications must specify this key.

- NSHumanReadableCopyright, a copyright string suitable for display in an About box. This key may be localized in InfoPlist.strings. Applications must specify this key.

Launch Behavior

- LSBackgroundOnly, indicating that, if the string 1, the application will be run in the background only and will not be visible to the user.

- LSEnvironment, a dictionary, the keys of which are environment variables and the values of their values, which are defined when Launch Services launches the application.

- LSGetAppDiedEvents, indicating that, if YES or <true/>, the application will get the kAEApplicationDied Apple event when any of its child processes terminate.

- LSMinimumSystemVersion, a string in the form 10.x.x, specifying the earliest version of Mac OS X this application will run under. However, this key appears to be ignored in Mac OS X version 10.1. Under 10.2, this key is enforced, and an explanatory alert is displayed. Running an application on a revision of Mac OS X version 10.3 earlier than LSMinimumSystemVersion will fail to run the application, without any notice to the user.

- LSMultipleInstancesProhibited, indicating that, if <true/>, only one copy of this application can be run at a time. Different users, for instance, would not be able to use the application simultaneously.

- LSPrefersCarbon and LSPrefersClassic, only one of which or LSRequiresCarbon or LSRequiresClassic may be assigned the string value 1. If set, the Finder's Get Info panel for this application will include the checkbox labeled **Open in the Classic environment**, which is set (or not) by default, depending on which option is used.

- `LSRequiresCarbon` and `LSRequiresClassic`, which when one is set one to 1 restricts execution of this application to Carbon or the Classic environment, respectively.

- `LSUIElement`, which if set to the string 1 identifies this application as an *agent application*, a background application that has no presence in the dock but that can present user interface elements, if necessary.

- `LSUIPresentationMode`, an integer between 0 and 4, representing progressively greater amounts of the system UI—dock and menu bar—to be hidden when the application is running. See Apple's documentation for details.

- `LSVisibleInClassic`, if set to the string 1, makes this background-only, or agent, application visible to the Classic Process Manager as a background-only application.

Localization

- `CFBundleLocalizations`, an array populated with codes for languages and regions in an application that handles localization programmatically instead of through localized resources.

Structure

- `NSAppleScriptEnabled`, indicating that, if YES or `<true/>`, this application is scriptable. Applications must specify this key.

- `NSMainNibFile`, the base name of the application's main Nib file.

- `NSServices`, an array of dictionaries declaring the Mac OS X services this application performs. The dictionaries specify the pasteboard input and output formats, the name of the service, and the name of the method that implements the service. See Apple's documentation for details.

10.4.3 Keys for Plug-Ins

These tags provide information on how a plug-in bundle is to be accessed and configured.

- `CFPlugInDynamicRegistration`, indicating that, if YES (`<true/>`), the plug-in in this bundle is to be registered dynamically.

- `CFPlugInDynamicRegistrationFunction`, the name of the dynamic registration function for this plug-in, if it is not `CFPlugInDynamicRegister`.

- CFPlugInFactories, a dictionary used for static plug-in registration. See Apple's documentation on plug-in registration for more details.

- CFPluginTypes, a dictionary identifying groups of entry points for plug-in registration. See Apple's documentation on plug-in registration for more details.

- CFPlugInUnloadFunction, the name of a function to call when the plug-in in this bundle is to be unloaded from memory.

10.4.4 Keys for Java

Cocoa Java applications must request a Java virtual machine (VM) and specify class paths. These tags do that.

- NSJavaNeeded, indicating that, if YES or <true/>, the Java VM will be started before loading the bundle. This is needed for Cocoa-Java applications but *not* for 100% Pure Java.

- NSJavaPath, an array of paths to Java class files, either absolute or relative to NSJavaRoot. Xcode maintains this array automatically.

- NSJavaRoot, a string containing the path to the root of the Java class tree.

10.4.5 Keys for Preference Panes

Panes for the System Preferences application specify the icons and labels used in the application's display window with these tags.

- NSPrefPaneIconFile, the name of the image file you provide in Resources as an icon for this preference pane in System Preferences. The picture should be 32 pixels by 32 pixels in size. Lacking this image, the bundle icon will be used.

- NSPrefPaneIconLabel, the name of this preference pane, as shown beneath its icon in System Preferences. You can break the string into lines with the newline (\n) character. Lacking this string, the CFBundleName will be used.

10.4.6 Keys for Dashboard Widgets

Dashboard widgets have their own set of keys, specifying their component files, security model, and basic layout. A widget Info.plist must also contain the keys CFBundleIdentifier, CFBundleName, and CFBundleDisplayName and should include other general-purpose keys, such as CFBundleShortVersionString or CFBundleVersion, as you see fit.

Layout

- `CloseBoxInsetX`, specifies how far right from the leftmost possible position to place the close box.
- `CloseBoxInsetY`, specifies how far down from the uppermost possible position to place the close box.
- `Height`, the height, in pixels, of the widget.
- `Width`, the width, in pixels, of the widget.

Security

- `AllowFullAccess`, indicating that, if `<true/>`, the widget is given full access to the file system, network assets, command line utilities, Java applets, and Web Kit facilities.
- `AllowInternetPlugins`, indicating that, if `<true/>`, the widget is allowed to use Web Kit to access browser plug-ins.
- `AllowJava`, indicating that, if `<true/>`, the widget is allowed to use Java applets.
- `AllowNetworkAccess`, indicating that, if `<true/>`, the widget is allowed to use network or other non-file-based resources.
- `AllowSystem`, indicating that, if `<true/>`, the widget is allowed to use command line utilities.

Structure

- `Font`, an array of strings naming fonts included in the widget bundle. Widget fonts are placed in the *root* of the bundle, not in a `Resources` directory.
- `MainHTML`, a required key: a path, relative to the bundle's root, to the main HTML (Hypertext Markup Language) file for the widget.
- `Plugin`, the name of a plug-in used by the widget.

10.5 Summary

This chapter explored bundles and package directories, important concepts in Mac OS X development. Most of Xcode's product types are bundles. We reviewed the structure of simple packages and application bundles and examined the `Info.plist` file, which communicates a bundle's metadata to the operating system.

Creating a Custom View

The three statistics—slope, intercept, and correlation—tell the whole story of our data set and its relation to the best line through it, but pictures are easier to understand. In this chapter, we'll add a window with a custom view that generates a simple graph of the points in the data set and the regression line.

11.1 Controller

Let's start thinking about this new window by imagining how it should make its appearance. The user would issue a command, either by selecting a menu item or by clicking a button, for the window to appear. Commands are issued *to* objects in the Mac OS human interface; what would the target of the command be? Plainly, it should be the same MyDocument instance that manages the Regression model. The command would be that a graph window be opened on a particular regression line and data set.

We'll do this in the simplest possible way, amending MyDocument so that it is the owner of the new window and manager of our new custom view. This view will respond to commands to show the window. The interface for MyDocument then becomes

```
@class  DataPoint;
@class  Regression;
@class  LinearGraph;

@interface MyDocument : NSDocument
{
    Regression *            model;

    IBOutlet LinearGraph *   graphView;
    IBOutlet NSWindow *      graphWindow;
}
```

```
- (IBAction) compute: (id) sender;
- (IBAction) showGraphWindow: (id) sender;

@end
```

LinearGraph is a name we made up for the new subclass of NSView we will create for displaying graphs. Both the new view (graphView) and its window (graphWindow) are declared as IBOutlets. IBOutlet is #defined as an empty string so far as the Objective-C language is concerned; when it reads this header, Interface Builder will identify graphView and graphWindow as potential outlets for connection to other objects.

Here is the code to add to MyDocument.m:

```
#import "LinearGraph.h"

- (IBAction) showGraphWindow: (id) sender
{
    if (! graphWindow) {
        //  If the graphWindow hasn't been loaded yet, load it.
        [NSBundle loadNibNamed: @"GraphWindow" owner: self];
    }
    //  Make the graphWindow visible.
    [graphWindow makeKeyAndOrderFront: sender];
    //  Make the graphView reload its data.
    [graphView refreshData];
}
```

You should also make the following change to MyDocument's dealloc:

```
- (void) dealloc
{
    [model release];
    [graphWindow release];
    [super dealloc];
}
```

Why release the graphWindow instance variable when we never retain it? In a Nib file, all top-level objects, such as windows, are instantiated with a retain count of 1. There is no need to retain it an additional time, and it is the responsibility of the file's owner to release it.

The Model-View-Controller (MVC) design pattern also leads us to believe that MyDocument should mediate the flow of data between the Regression model and the LinearGraph view. We can come back to that when we know more about Linear-Graph's requirements.

11.2 View

In Cocoa, most drawing is done by subclasses of NSView, a class that maintains a position and size within an enclosing view and provides a coordinate space and drawing state for graphics inside its area. We could create our LinearGraph class files in Xcode—Xcode even provides a special new-file template for NSView subclasses. Instead, we will use Interface Builder to do at least the rough work.

Start Interface Builder and from the Starting Point window, select **Cocoa** → **Window**. This sets up a new Nib with an empty NSWindow in it. Select the window, and use the Attributes Inspector (press **command-1**) to name it Graph.

Save the Nib file now. Name it GraphWindow, place it in the English.lproj subdirectory of the Linear project directory, and accept Interface Builder's offer to attach the Nib to the Linear project (Figure 11.1). Having a Nib file associated with a project early confers some advantages, as Interface Builder and Xcode are tightly integrated.

MyDocument will be the owner of this file, so we had better tell Interface Builder about it. In either Xcode or the Finder, find the icon **MyDocument.h** and drag it onto the GraphWindow Nib file window. The window will acknowledge the drop by showing MyDocument in its place in the class hierarchy; switch back to the **Instances** view. Select **File's Owner** and use the Custom Class (**command-5**) Inspector to change the owner's class to MyDocument. **File's Owner** now has the actions and outlets we need for running the Graph window. We can control-drag from **File's Owner** to the **Window** icon, select the graphWindow outlet in the resulting Inspector, and click **Connect**.

Now we will fill the window with a LinearGraph. Select the **Containers** palette; its icon is the sixth in the bar at the top of the palette window. Drag a **CustomView**

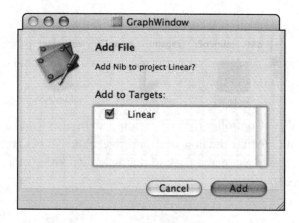

Figure 11.1 Adding a Nib to an Xcode target. If Xcode is running and has a project open, Interface Builder will offer you a choice of targets to which the Nib should be added. This happens the first time you save the Nib.

from the palette into the Graph window. Resize the **CustomView** until it fills the window, and use the Size Inspector (press **command-3**) to make the view resizable in both axes and fixed to all edges.

LinearGraph is still undefined, so we will define it for the first time in Interface Builder. Switch the GraphWindow Nib window to the **Classes** view. We're going to create a subclass of NSView; navigate in the browser **NSObject** → **NSResponder** → **NSView**. In the **Classes** menu, select **Subclass NSView** (**command-option-S**—you can find the same command by control-clicking the class name). Rename LinearGraph to the new class that appears in the next column, and press **Return**.

LinearGraph has one feature that Interface Builder cares about: an outlet for its delegate. With the **LinearGraph** class still selected, press **command-1** to show the class attributes. Switch the listing to the **Outlets** tab, and click the **Add** button. Type **delegate**, and press **Return**. See Figure 11.2.

And now for something neat: From the **Classes** menu, select **Create Files for LinearGraph** (or press **command-option-F**—this also is available in the context menu for the class). A modified save-file sheet emerges from the Nib window, offering to create, in our project directory, the files LinearGraph.h and LinearGraph.m and to add them to the Linear project. Click **Choose** to accept this.

If you like, you can make a side trip to Xcode now to see what Interface Builder has given you. You will find a header that declares LinearGraph as a subclass of NSView,

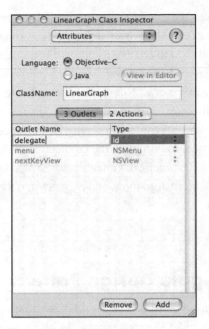

Figure 11.2 Adding an outlet to class LinearGraph in Interface Builder. Much of the programming interface of a new class can be built inside Interface Builder before any Objective-C or Java source files for the class are written.

with an IBOutlet named delegate, and an implementation file with skeletons for the initWithFrame: initializer and the drawRect: drawing method.

Note what is *not* in the generated files: "initialization code" setting up the view hierarchy, adjusting options, or linking pointers. Interface Builder doesn't generate code in the same sense that graphical interface tools for other frameworks do. It doesn't have to. Nib files are archives of the view and other objects in them, and loading a Nib consists simply of reconstituting the objects from the archive.

> An exception to the unarchiving rule is, ironically enough, the custom view. Most objects archived in a Nib are saved using the NSCoding protocol and are unarchived with NSCoding's initWithCoder: method. A custom view, however, may be an instance of a class that isn't linked into Interface Builder; if there's no class, there's no way to build an instance to archive. Custom views are therefore stored as specifications, and the Nib loader instantiates them with initWithFrame:.

Now we can return to the custom view we added to the Graph window. Newly placed custom views are of class NSView. Click on the custom view and use the Custom Class Inspector (**command-5**) to change its class to LinearGraph. The white label on the custom view changes to LinearGraph, and an alert badge appears next to the window icon in the GraphWindow Nib display, to indicate that one of the views it contains has an unfilled outlet. In fact, the unfilled outlet is the delegate outlet of LinearGraph. Fill the outlet by control-dragging from the custom view to the **File's Owner** icon. Click **Connect** to complete the connection.

This reminds us that MyDocument has an outlet for LinearGraph. Control-drag from the **File's Owner** icon to the custom view, and connect it to the document's graphView outlet.

11.3 The Delegate Design Pattern

What is LinearGraph supposed to do? It should draw a set of points and a line. How, then, should it get that data? One strategy would be to decide that LinearGraph is purely an object that renders Regression objects. A LinearGraph should be given a reference to a Regression; whenever it needs data, the view can pull it straight from the model.

This approach is simple, but in a more complex project, marrying LinearGraph so closely to the Regression API (application program interface) means that every time Regression changes, LinearGraph probably has to change, too. In a very complex project, it might even be impossible to test LinearGraph without a fully developed and tested Regression to drive it!

Let's choose a slightly different strategy. We will have LinearGraph take data from a *delegate*, an object whose implementation—even whose class—we don't care about, so long as it responds to certain messages.

Java programmers will recognize in this an analog to interfaces. Objective-C offers an even closer analog, *protocols*, for sets of methods a class guarantees, at compile time, it implements. In this case, we are simply declaring an *informal protocol*—a set of methods with no compile-time guarantee. Whether a method is implemented can be checked at runtime.

We'll define our informal protocol as a category on NSObject. The effect will be that the Objective-C compiler will assume that any untyped object—a pointer of type id—or descendant of NSObject implements these methods: whether they do or not:

```
@interface  NSObject (LinearGraphDelegate)
- (unsigned) countDataPoints;
- (void) dataPointAtIndex: (unsigned) index
                        x: (double *) outX
                        y: (double *) outY;
- (BOOL) definesLineOfSlope: (double *) outSlope
                  intercept: (double *) outIntercept;
@end
```

We can put this category declaration at the end of LinearGraph.h, so it will be seen in any .m file that deals with LinearGraph. To the declaration of the LinearGraph class itself, we add a pointer to the delegate object and the accessor methods:

```
@interface  LinearGraph : NSView {
    IBOutlet id     delegate;
}

- (void) refreshData;

- (id) delegate;
- (void) setDelegate: (id) newDelegate;

@end
```

The implementation is a little more complicated than we've seen before:

```
- (void) dealloc
{
    [delegate release];
    [super dealloc];
}
```

```
- (void) refreshData
{
    //  Force a redraw of the view, which means
    //   a reload of the data.
    [self setNeedsDisplay: YES];
}


- (id) delegate { return delegate; }

BOOL NotImpl(id object, SEL aSelector)
{
    //  Helper for setDelegate:
    //  Detects whether a proposed delegate fails to
    //   implement a method.  Allow nil also.
    return (object != nil) &&
            ![object respondsToSelector: aSelector];
}


- (void) setDelegate: (id) newDelegate
{
    if (delegate != newDelegate) {
        //  Check for compliance with (most of) the
        //   informal protocol.
        if (NotImpl(newDelegate, @selector(countDataPoints))
            || NotImpl(newDelegate,
                    @selector(dataPointAtIndex:x:y:)))
            [NSException raise: NSInvalidArgumentException
                format: @"%@ doesn't implement needed methods",
                    newDelegate];

        //  Proposed delegate is OK. Replace the old one.
        //  Retain the new one.
        [delegate release];
        delegate = [newDelegate retain];
    }
}
```

As with the setDataPoints: accessor in Regression, the setDelegate: accessor does the check against equality and the release-and-retain pair needed for memory management of Cocoa objects. Additionally, `setDelegate:` includes a local function to help test whether the object passed to `setDelegate:` implements two of the methods in the `LinearGraphDelegate` informal protocol; if the proposed delegate doesn't support them, an `NSException` is raised.

11.4 The Custom View

Our graph will draw different colors for the axes, the regression line, and the data points. We could hard-code the colors into `LinearGraph`, but let's be a little fancier and configure them from a property list file. Although it can't encode an `NSColor` object directly, the property list format can capture red, green, and blue values for each color:

```
<?xml version="1.0" encoding="UTF-8"?>
<!DOCTYPE plist PUBLIC "-//Apple Computer//DTD PLIST 1.0//EN"
    "http://www.apple.com/DTDs/PropertyList-1.0.dtd">
<plist version="1.0">
    <dict>
        <key>Axis</key>
        <!-- Light gray -->
        <dict>
            <key>r</key>
            <real>0.8</real>
            <key>g</key>
            <real>0.8</real>
            <key>b</key>
            <real>0.8</real>
        </dict>
        <key>Line</key>
        <!-- Black -->
        <dict>
            <key>r</key>
            <real>0</real>
            <key>g</key>
            <real>0</real>
            <key>b</key>
            <real>0</real>
        </dict>
```

```
        <key>Point</key>
        <!-- Medium green -->
        <dict>
            <key>r</key>
            <real>0.0</real>
            <key>g</key>
            <real>0.7</real>
            <key>b</key>
            <real>0.0</real>
        </dict>
    </dict>
</plist>
```

This file can be created by selecting **File → New File . . .** and choosing **Empty file in project** or by editing a new plist in the Property List Editor. Either way, save the file as GraphColors.plist, making sure that it is explicitly included as part of the Linear project. To keep your Groups & Files listing neat, you can drag GraphColors.plist so it falls into the **Resources** group.

GraphColors.plist need be read only once, to initialize classwide instances of NSColor. The class method initialize is sent to a class before any member of that class is used and is the usual place to put classwide initializations:

```
static NSColor *    sAxisColor = nil;
static NSColor *    sPointColor = nil;
static NSColor *    sLineColor = nil;

NSColor *   ColorFromDict(NSDictionary *    dict)
{
    //  Helper function for +initialize
    //  Read a dictionary with r, g, b numbers into an
    //  opaque NSColor.
    return [NSColor colorWithCalibratedRed:
                    [[dict objectForKey: @"r"] floatValue]
                                green:
                    [[dict objectForKey: @"g"] floatValue]
                                blue:
```

```objc
                        [[dict objectForKey: @"b"] floatValue]
                            alpha: 1.0];
}


+ (void) initialize
{
    if (! sAxisColor) {
        NSBundle *      mainBundle = [NSBundle mainBundle];

        // Find GraphColors.plist in the app's Resources:
        NSString *      dictPath =
                [mainBundle pathForResource: @"GraphColors"
                                    ofType: @"plist"];
        // Stop if we don't find it.
        NSAssert(dictPath, @"GraphColors.plist should exist.");

        // Read GraphColors.plist into a dictionary:
        NSDictionary * colorDict =
                [NSDictionary dictionaryWithContentsOfFile:
                                            dictPath];
        // Stop if the plist doesn't parse into a dictionary.
        NSAssert(colorDict, @"GraphColors should be valid.");

        NSDictionary *      curr;

        // Read the Axis dictionary into sAxisColor
        curr = [colorDict objectForKey: @"Axis"];
        sAxisColor = [ColorFromDict(curr) retain];

        // Read the Point dictionary into sPointColor
        curr = [colorDict objectForKey: @"Point"];
        sPointColor = [ColorFromDict(curr) retain];

        // Read the Line dictionary into sLineColor
        curr = [colorDict objectForKey: @"Line"];
        sLineColor = [ColorFromDict(curr) retain];
    }
}
```

The two uses of the NSAssert() macro are cheap insurance. The first will halt the program if dictPath is nil, which would happen if GraphColors.plist didn't make it into the application's Resources directory. This would mean that the application itself is malformed, and we can't proceed, so stopping is the right thing to do. Likewise, the second NSAssert() checks for a nil colorDict, which would happen if dictionaryWithContentsOfFile: could not parse GraphColors.plist as a property list containing a dictionary. Checking at this early moment is much easier than trying to puzzle out what went wrong from much later crashes or misbehaviors.

Now for the drawing. The Xcode template gave us a start on the drawing, but not much of one:

```
-(void)drawRect:(NSRect)rect {

}
```

We are more or less on our own. All we know is that rect is the portion of the view that needs redrawing, what we can learn from the methods of NSView, and what we can demand from our delegate. Offhand, we can be sure that we want to erase the view—set the current color to white and fill the target rectangle with it—and do nothing else if the view has no delegate. So now we have:

```
- (void) drawRect: (NSRect) rect
{
    [[NSColor whiteColor] set];
    NSRectFill(rect);

    if (delegate) {
    }
}
```

The question is, what happens inside the if (delegate) {} block? We should draw axes, a line, and some points. Where do we draw them? That is, if a point is at $\{x, y\}$, at what $\{u, v\}$ in the view's coordinates do we plot it?

Fortunately, we can make this very simple by telling the view to have a coordinate space that matches the extent of our data set. For the moment, suppose that LinearGraph has a method, dataExtent, that reports a rectangle that encloses the data set. We'll get to it later. We can then enlarge the rectangle slightly—for an aesthetic margin—and use the NSView method setBounds: to make the data's coordinate system our own:

```
if (delegate) {
    // What rect encloses all the points?
    NSRect      dataBounds = [self dataExtent];
    // Lower-left corner of the all-points rect
    NSPoint     origin = dataBounds.origin;
    float       margin;

    // Horizontal margin
    margin = dataBounds.size.width * 0.05;
    dataBounds.origin.x -= margin;
    dataBounds.size.width += 2.0 * margin;

    // Vertical margin
    margin = dataBounds.size.height * 0.05;
    dataBounds.origin.y -= margin;
    dataBounds.size.height += 2.0 * margin;

    // Make my coordinates == point coordinates
    [self setBounds: dataBounds];

    // Draw axes from the original minimum of dataBounds:
    [sAxisColor set];
    // vertical
    [NSBezierPath strokeLineFromPoint:
                NSMakePoint(origin.x, NSMinY(dataBounds))
                            toPoint:
                NSMakePoint(origin.x, NSMaxY(dataBounds))];
    // horizontal
    [NSBezierPath strokeLineFromPoint:
                NSMakePoint(NSMinX(dataBounds), origin.y)
                            toPoint:
                NSMakePoint(NSMaxX(dataBounds), origin.y)];

    // Draw regression line (if any):
    double      slope, intercept;
    if ([delegate definesLineOfSlope: &slope
                        intercept: &intercept]) {
```

```
            [sLineColor set];      //  Use the line color
            //  Y of regression line at the left.
            float   y0 = intercept + slope * NSMinX(dataBounds);
            //  Y of regression line at the right.
            float   yN = intercept + slope * NSMaxX(dataBounds);
            //  Draw the regression line across the view.
            [NSBezierPath strokeLineFromPoint:
                        NSMakePoint(NSMinX(dataBounds), y0)
                                    toPoint:
                        NSMakePoint(NSMaxX(dataBounds), yN)];
    }

    //  Draw points:
    [sPointColor set];        //  Use the point color
    unsigned    index, limit = [delegate countDataPoints];
    for (index = 0; index < limit; index++) {
        double    x, y;
        [delegate dataPointAtIndex: index
                            x: &x y: &y];
        //  Make a small rectangle around the point.
        NSRect  pointRect = NSMakeRect(x - 2.0,
                                       y - 2.0,
                                       4.0, 4.0);
        //  Fill the small rectangle with the point color.
        NSRectFill(pointRect);
    }
}
```

That should be it. We had put off the work of determining the smallest rectangle enclosing all the data points; let's do that now:

```
- (NSRect) dataExtent
{
    unsigned    index, limit = [delegate countDataPoints];

    //  Special case: No delegate or no points.
    //  Return empty rect as a signal value.
    if (limit == 0)
        return NSZeroRect;
```

```
double      x, y;
[delegate dataPointAtIndex: 0 x: &x y: &y];

// Special case: One point. Return tiny rect around it.
if (limit == 1)
    return NSMakeRect(x - 0.5, y - 0.5,
                        1.0, 1.0);

NSRect      retval = NSMakeRect(x, y,
                                0.0, 0.0);

for (index = 1; index < limit; index++) {
    [delegate dataPointAtIndex: index x: &x y: &y];
    NSPoint     currPoint = NSMakePoint(x, y);
    if (!NSPointInRect(currPoint, retval)) {
        // If a point in the list is outside the known
        // limits, expand the limits to include it.

        if (currPoint.x < NSMinX(retval)) {
            retval.size.width += NSMinX(retval) -currPoint.x;
            retval.origin.x = currPoint.x;
        }
        if (currPoint.x > NSMaxX(retval))
            retval.size.width += currPoint.x -NSMaxX(retval);

        if (currPoint.y < NSMinY(retval)) {
            retval.size.height += NSMinY(retval)-currPoint.y;
            retval.origin.y = currPoint.y;
        }
        if (currPoint.y > NSMaxY(retval))
            retval.size.height += currPoint.y-NSMaxY(retval);
    }
}

return retval;
}
```

Because it has not been declared in the header file, this method should appear in LinearGraph.m before drawRect:. Undeclared methods in Objective-C are assumed to return id, and the compiler will complain if an NSRect struct is initialized from an undeclared method call. Placing the method definition before drawRect: declares the return type to be NSRect from that point forward.

11.5 Showing the Window

We still have to do something about showing the Graph window. The simplest way is to add to the Regression window a button that makes the Graph window visible (Figure 11.3). To open Interface Builder on the Regression window, double-click

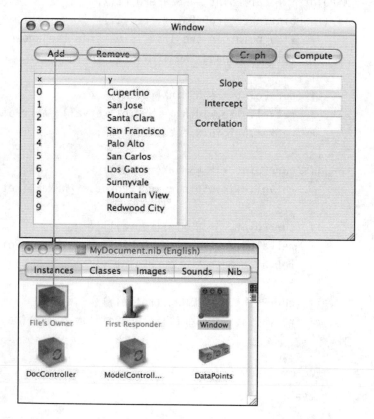

Figure 11.3 Adding a **Graph** button and linking its action to the MyDocument owner

MyDocument.nib, in either the Finder or the **Resources** group in the Groups & Files list in the Xcode Project window.

The MyDocument class has changed since the last time MyDocument.nib was saved, so the first order of business is to drop the current MyDocument.h—from Xcode or the Finder—into the MyDocument.nib window. Now Interface Builder knows about the new showGraphWindow: action method. With that done, we can control-drag a link from the **Graph** button to the **File's Owner** (MyDocument) icon and set the action for the link to showGraphWindow:.

Optionally, we might want to bind (**command-4**) the **Graph** button's enabled attribute to the canCompute property mediated by the Model NSObjectController. There's little sense in trying to plot fewer than two points.

11.6 Testing

It is time to see whether and how the new class works. Run Linear, and give it the old, familiar data set:

```
1.0    2.05
2.01   4
3      5.987
4      8.1
5      10.0
```

When you're done, click the **Compute** button to make sure that the statistics are loaded into the model; if you haven't yet saved this frequently used data set in its own file, maybe you should. Remember to press **Return** or **Tab** after you enter the last of the data: A Mac OS X text field doesn't take a new value until you end editing by pressing one of those keys or otherwise take focus out of the field. Next, click the **Graph** button.

No graph window appears. Instead, in the run log, we find a message much like this one:

```
2005-03-01 14:58:34.128 Linear[2154]
<NSKVONotifying_MyDocument: 0x33d4c0> doesn't implement needed
methods
```

This is our NSAssert message in -[LinearGraph setDelegate:], triggered by the fact that we forgot to implement LinearGraph's delegate protocol. Had the assertion not been there, we'd have been presented with a blank window and fewer clues.

The `setDelegate:` method was called in the course of loading the `GraphWin-dow.nib` file. This is important to remember: When the Nib loader fills in outlets, it looks for setter methods and uses them. Many is the programmer who named an outlet `temperature` and had a completely unrelated method named `setTemperature:` and wondered why the outlet variable was never set. (The Nib loader called `setTemper-ature:` in the false confidence that it was setting `temperature`.)

We add the delegate glue to `MyDocument`:

```
#pragma mark LinearGraphDelegate

#import "DataPoint.h"

- (unsigned) countDataPoints
{
    return [[model dataPoints] count];
}


- (void) dataPointAtIndex: (unsigned) index
                        x: (double *) outX
                        y: (double *) outY
{
    DataPoint *    item = [[model dataPoints]
                                objectAtIndex: index];
    *outX = [item x];
    *outY = [item y];
}


- (BOOL) definesLineOfSlope: (double *) outSlope
                 intercept: (double *) outIntercept
{
    if ([model canCompute]) {
        *outSlope = [model slope];
        *outIntercept = [model intercept];
        return YES;
    }
    else
        return NO;
}
```

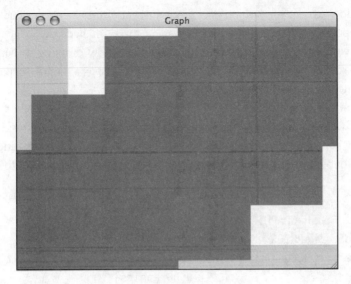

Figure 11.4 The first running example of LinearGraph is a disappointment.

Now we can run Linear and enter that data set again or, if we were provident, use **File → Open . . .** to load it all at once:

```
1.0    2.05
2.01   4
3      5.987
4      8.1
5      10.0
```

Click **Compute** to update the model and **Graph** for the test. This time, a Graph window appears; see Figure 11.4. The contents are all right, in an abstract-expressionist sort of way, but on the whole, we must call them a disappointment. We have some debugging to do.

11.7 Debugging a View

The natural thing to do is to set a breakpoint at the beginning of drawRect: and follow the progress of drawing the LinearGraph view step by step. However, we find that this doesn't help. The first time drawRect: is executed, the Graph window is not even on the screen. Moving, hiding, and exposing the window do not trigger redraws. Resizing the window does trigger a redraw, but as you step through drawRect:, nothing appears in the window except the striped background of an empty window. The completed drawing appears, all at once, only when drawRect: is finished.

You have probably guessed what is happening: View drawing in Mac OS X is done in off-screen buffers and is transferred to the screen as a complete, painted pixel map. Intermediate stages are not available.

They can be made available. The NSGraphicsContext class embodies the graphical state of whatever medium your view is currently drawing into. By sending flush-Graphics to the current NSGraphicsContext after every drawing operation, we can see what is happening as we step through drawRect:. Before the drawRect: method, we put

```
#define FLUSH_GRAPHICS  1
#if FLUSH_GRAPHICS
    #define DEBUG_FLUSH [[NSGraphicsContext currentContext] \
                            flushGraphics];
#else
    #define DEBUG_FLUSH
#endif
```

And after every drawing operation, we add DEBUG_FLUSH:

```
        .
        .
        .

        [NSBezierPath strokeLineFromPoint:
                    NSMakePoint(NSMinX(dataBounds), y0)
                            toPoint:
                    NSMakePoint(NSMaxX(dataBounds), yN)];
        DEBUG_FLUSH
    }

    //  Draw points:
    [sPointColor set];
    unsigned    index, limit = [delegate countDataPoints];
    for (index = 0; index < limit; index++) {
        double      x, y;
        [delegate dataPointAtIndex: index
                        x: &x y: &y];
```

```
        // Make a small rectangle around the point.
        NSRect  pointRect = NSMakeRect(x - 2.0,
                                       y - 2.0,
                                       4.0, 4.0);
        // Fill the small rectangle with the point color.
        NSRectFill(pointRect);
        DEBUG_FLUSH
}
```

Running this version, with FLUSH_GRAPHICS set to 1, we find that we still can't watch the first pass through the drawing code—it's to a window that isn't on screen yet. But a slight move of the resize box forces a redraw, and stepping through drawRect:— past the drawing of the axes and the line to the drawing of the first point—leaves us with a partially drawn view that looks like Figure 11.5.

That rectangle in the lower-left corner on the screen is supposed to be four-by-four units in size. It is very large. But wait: We redefined the units of measurement for this view when we called setBounds: with a rectangle made loosely around the data points. Looking at the variable summary, we see that dataBounds has an origin at {0.8, 1.6525} and a size of {4.4, 8.745}. So a rectangle "four units wide" would turn

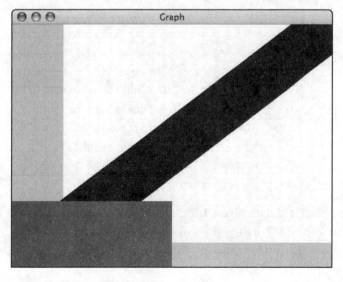

Figure 11.5 Using -[NSGraphicsContext flushGraphics] to get step-by-step access to our drawing gets us a clearer picture of what's wrong.

out to be most of the width of our view! This would explain why all the lines are so thick.

What we'd like to know is how big, in graph units, *one pixel* is. Fortunately, NSWindow is always sized in terms of pixels, and NSView provides a way of converting sizes—and points and rectangles—to and from the coordinate systems of other views and the window. Passing a size of {1, 1} to convertSize:fromView:, with nil (the window) as the source view, yields the size, in the graph's coordinates, of a rectangle 1 pixel by 1 pixel. We can then set the default width for all line drawing and express, in terms of that size, the rectangles for the data points:

```
[self setBounds: dataBounds];
NSSize      unitSize = {1.0, 1.0};
// Convert the window's one-pixel size
// to this view's coordinate dimensions.
unitSize = [self convertSize: unitSize fromView: nil];
[NSBezierPath setDefaultLineWidth: MIN(unitSize.height,
                                      unitSize.width)];
    .
    .
    .
for (index = 0; index < limit; index++) {
    double      x, y;
    [delegate dataPointAtIndex: index
                        x: &x y: &y];
    // Make a small rectangle around the point.
    NSRect  pointRect = NSMakeRect(
                x - 2.0 * unitSize.width,
                y - 2.0 * unitSize.height,
                4.0 *unitSize.width,
                4.0 *unitSize.height);
    // Fill the small rectangle with the point color.
    NSRectFill(pointRect);
```

Make this change and terminate Linear, if you haven't already quit it. Re-#define FLUSH_GRAPHICS to be 0, and build and debug Linear one more time. It feels like turning the crank: Load the data set, make sure the regression has been computed, and click **Graph** (Figure 11.6).

This time, it works. You can move the window, close it, and reopen it. Resize it, and the graph resizes so it always fills the window, assuming you set the sizing struts

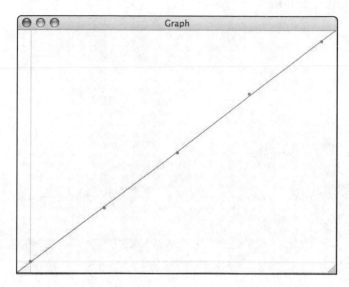

Figure 11.6 The Graph window, containing the `LinearGraph` view, working as designed

properly when you laid out the Graph window in Interface Builder. It uses the colors specified in the configuration file.

11.8 Summary

In this chapter, we took an `NSView` subclass from idea to reality. We used Interface Builder to create the initial shell for the class and to hook it up to its controller, My-Document, leaving virtually no initialization work to be done in code.

We saw how to configure class options from a property list file embedded in the application. We fleshed out the skeleton Interface Builder gave us into a working graphing class. We saw how to use `NSGraphicsContext` to debug the drawing of `NSView` subclasses.

`LinearGraph` is far, far from being a first-rate graphing class. At the very least, it should label its axes to give some context for what you're seeing. There should be options for colors and for the shapes of points. There should be a way to specify the range the axes span, instead of simply blowing the graph up to the region of the data set. But it's a start, and it adds a little life to what was a text-bound application.

12

Dynamic Libraries
and Frameworks

Let's do some more with our statistics package. We already have a static library that accumulates sums toward a linear regression. This library has some limitations, however.

- The statistics are limited. For instance, because the library doesn't keep individual data points, we can't calculate standard deviations.

- The header file is a separate entity from the library. By the standard means of distributing libraries and headers, users of our library will have to separate the header and the library into different directories, such as /usr/local/lib and /usr/local/include, and specify the additional directories at build time, an accident-prone process. One file or the other can get lost, deleted, or miss a revision to a new version.

- The problems of the associated header file are multiplied if the library has other kinds of associated files, such as configuration or image files. If we want to add features that could take advantage of such files, our library would become much more fragile.

The first limitation can be overcome by an enhancement to our existing design for our static library, adding to the library some means to access our data through either copying or a callback. The other limitations are inherent to a conventional library and are remedied by switching from a conventional library to a *framework*.

A framework is a bundle, a structured directory tree, containing a dynamic library, headers, and resources. When a framework is passed to the gcc that ships with Xcode, using the -framework option, gcc correctly searches the framework's subdirectories for the library and headers. Both Cocoa's NSBundle class and Core Foundation's CFBundle afford easy access to files inside frameworks.

12.1 Adding a Framework Target

We start with the Linear project and add a framework target by selecting from the **Project** menu **New Target . . .** and picking **Cocoa → Framework** from the list of target templates. Name the new target `Statistics`.

This new target could be the home of all our consumers of lists of points, so let's move `LinearGraph` out of the application and into the framework. Select the **Project** (top) icon in the Groups & Files list to make the target-membership checkboxes visible in the detail view. Make `Linear` the active target, using the pop-up in the toolbar or the submenu in the **Project** menu, and uncheck **LinearGraph.m** and **GraphColors.plist**. Switch the active target to `Statistics`, and add the implementation and header files for `LinearGraph` and `GraphColors.plist` to the target.

Why does `LinearGraph.h` have a checkbox for the `Statistics` target and not for the `Linear` target? Header files are *used* in the making of an application file, but they don't ship as a *part* of it. Frameworks, however, usually contain header files to afford access to the framework for its users. We'll be using Cocoa in this framework, so make sure that `Cocoa.framework` is checked in the `Statistics` listing.

For our statistical consumer of points, we define a new Objective-C class, `Point-Stat`:

```
#import <Cocoa/Cocoa.h>

@interface PointStat : NSObject {
    unsigned        count;
    double          sumX;
    double          sumY;
    double          sumXSquared;
    double          sumYSquared;
    double          sumXY;

    double          slope;

    double          sumSqFromMeanX;
    double          sumSqFromMeanY;

    BOOL            dirty;
    id              delegate;
}
```

```
- (id) init;

- (void) refreshData;

- (double) meanX;
- (double) meanY;
- (double) stdDeviationX;
- (double) stdDeviationY;

- (BOOL) regressionValid;
- (double) slope;
- (double) intercept;
- (double) correlation;

- (id) delegate;
- (void) setDelegate: (id) newDelegate;

@end
```

As with `LinearGraph`, `PointStat` does not define any storage for the individual data pairs it deals with but instead, like `LinearGraph`, relies on a delegate to store the points and report their number and content. In fact, `PointStat` will use the informal `LinearGraphDelegate` protocol for access to the data set.

`PointStat.m` implements what the header promises. No statistic is calculated until the client asks for one. A private method, `collectStatistics`, is then called, and the `dirty` flag is cleared to indicate that the sums don't have to be recalculated. When it changes its data set, the delegate is supposed to inform its `PointStat` by sending it `refreshData`, which does nothing more than set the `dirty` flag, forcing a recalculation the next time a statistic is asked for:

```
#import "PointStat.h"
#import "LinearGraph.h"
#import <math.h>

@implementation PointStat
```

```objc
- (id) init
{
    dirty = YES;
    return self;
}

- (void) dealloc
{
    [delegate release];
    [super dealloc];
}

- (void) refreshData
{
    dirty = YES;
}

- (void) collectStatistics
{
    if (! delegate || ! dirty)
        return;

    unsigned    index;
    count = [delegate countDataPoints];
    sumX = sumY = sumXSquared = sumYSquared = sumXY = 0.0;

    double      x, y;

    for (index = 0; index < count; index++) {
        [delegate dataPointAtIndex: index x: &x y: &y];
        sumX += x;
        sumXSquared += x * x;
        sumY += y;
        sumYSquared += y * y;
        sumXY += x * y;
    }
```

```
        sumSqFromMeanX = sumSqFromMeanY = 0.0;
        if (count > 0) {
            double      meanX = sumX / count;
            double      meanY = sumY / count;
            for (index = 0; index < count; index++) {
                [delegate dataPointAtIndex: index x: &x y: &y];
                double      term = x - meanX;
                sumSqFromMeanX += term * term;
                term = y - meanY;
                sumSqFromMeanY += term * term;
            }
        }

        if (count > 1) {
            slope = (count * sumXY - sumX * sumY)
                    /
                    (count * sumXSquared - sumX * sumX);
        }

        dirty = NO;
}

- (double) meanX
{
    [self collectStatistics];
    return sumX / count;
}

- (double) meanY
{
    [self collectStatistics];
    return sumY / count;
}

- (double) stdDeviationX
{
    [self collectStatistics];
```

```
        return sqrt(sumSqFromMeanX) / count;
}


- (double) stdDeviationY
{
    [self collectStatistics];
    return sqrt(sumSqFromMeanY) / count;
}


- (BOOL) regressionValid
{
    return delegate && [delegate countDataPoints] > 1;
}


- (double) slope
{
    [self collectStatistics];
    return slope;
}


- (double) intercept
{
    [self collectStatistics];
    return (sumY - slope * sumX) / count;
}


- (double) correlation
{
    [self collectStatistics];
    return slope * sqrt((count * sumXSquared - sumX * sumX)
                        /
                        (count * sumYSquared - sumY * sumY)
                        );
}
```

PointStat also has delegate and setDelegate: methods. They are exactly the same as for LinearGraph, however, so aren't reproduced here.

Edits are needed to complete the transition. We've removed GraphColors.plist from the main bundle and put it into our framework, so LinearGraph's initialize class method has to be amended:

```
if (! sAxisColor) {
    NSBundle *     mainBundle =
                    [NSBundle bundleForClass: self];

    // Find GraphColors.plist in the app's Resources:
    NSString *     dictPath =
                [mainBundle pathForResource: @"GraphColors"
                                     ofType: @"plist"];
```

One last thing: In the Groups & Files list, open the **Targets** group, and select **Statistics**. The detail listing now shows every file included in the Statistics target, including the headers. The second column, Role, shows a pop-up menu for the headers, offering a choice of **public**, **private**, and **project**.

- A public framework header is built into the product framework's Headers directory and is intended for the use of clients of the framework.

- A private framework header is built into the framework's Private Headers directory. It is not intended that general users of the framework include such headers, but they may be needed by developers with privileged access to framework code.

- Project headers are used solely for building the framework and are not intended for distribution in the framework bundle.

Make sure that both LinearGraph.h and PointStat.h are set to **public**.

12.2 Framework Structure

Now issue the **Build** command to compile the Statistics library and marshal its framework directory. If you switch to the Finder and look in the build directory of your project folder, you will find Statistics.framework, a directory with a structure like that shown in Figure 12.1.

Statistics.framework contains an Info.plist file in the Resources directory for each version. (Most bundles put Info.plist in the root Contents directory, but frameworks can encompass more than one version of themselves, each of which must supply its own information.) The source for the file appears in the Groups & Files

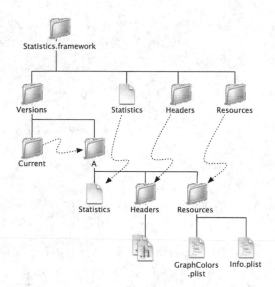

Figure 12.1 The layout of `Statistics.framework`. The top-level directory contains a `Versions` directory and links to the current versions of the `Statistics` library and the `Headers` and `Resources` directories. The `Versions` directory in turn contains all versions of the framework contents—only version A, in this case—and a link indicating which version is current. The A directory contains the library and its associated headers and resources. The `Headers` directory contains all project headers that were marked **public** in the detail listing of the `Statistics` target.

list as **Statistics-Info.plist** to distinguish it from the `Info.plist` for `Linear.app`, but Xcode provides an editing form when you double-click the **Statistics** target in Groups & Files and select the **Properties** tab of the resulting Get Info window.

This is the same properties display you see for an application, including document information, which doesn't apply to frameworks. The interesting fields are as follows:

- `Executable` (`CFBundleExecutable`), the name of the principal library file in the framework. You generally don't need to change this.

- `Identifier` (`CFBundleIdentifier`), an inverse domain-style string that will uniquely identify the framework. Xcode's template defaults this as `com.your-company.Statistics` for this target.

- `Type` (`CFBundlePackageType`), the HFS file type for the bundle; this is always `FMWK` for a framework.

- Creator (CFBundleSignature), a four-character code to serve as the HFS creator code for the framework bundle. You can leave this as ????; in our case, it makes sense to use LnER, the code for Linear.app.

- Version (CFBundleVersion), the marketing version number for the framework. Xcode starts you at 1.0. This version number is distinct from the compatibility versions, such as A, B, C, that may be built into the framework as it evolves.

The remaining parts of the panel aren't used with frameworks. There are, however, additional keys that may be used in Info.plist for a framework:

- NSHumanReadableCopyright, a copyright string for the framework

- CFBundleGetInfoString, an additional string to be displayed in the Finder's Get Info window

- CFBundleGetInfoHTML, the same as CFBundleGetInfoString but formatted in HTML

12.3 Using the Framework

Now let's switch Linear over to using the Statistics framework.

First, we have to figure out how to fit PointStat into our document model. MyDocument already implements the LinearGraphDelegate informal protocol, and the scope of the data that PointStat asks for and keeps is the same as the scope of the document. It follows that we should add a PointStat to the MyDocument data members:

```
@class  LinearGraph;
@class  PointStat;

@interface MyDocument : NSDocument
{
    Regression *          model;
    PointStat *           statEngine;
    .
    .
    .
```

Make sure that it gets initialized and released:

```
#import <Statistics/PointStat.h>
```

```
- (id)init
{
    self = [super init];
    if (self) {
        model = [[Regression alloc] init];
        statEngine = [[PointStat alloc] init];
        if (!model || ! statEngine) {
            [self release];
            self = nil;
        }

        [statEngine setDelegate: self];
    }
    return self;
}


- (void) dealloc
{
    [statEngine release];
    [model release];
    [graphWindow release];
    [super dealloc];
}
```

Finally, incorporate it into the compute: action method:

```
- (IBAction) compute: (id) sender
{
    [statEngine refreshData];
    [model setSlope: [statEngine slope]];
    [model setIntercept: [statEngine intercept]];
    [model setCorrelation: [statEngine correlation]];
}
```

Note that headers inside frameworks are always #imported or #included with a path prefix of the framework name. gcc will have been told of the framework name in a command line option and will identify an #include in this form as being from that framework.

A smarter design would observe model's dataPoints array, send refresh-Data to statEngine whenever it or any member changed, and update slope, intercept, and correlation accordingly. This would eliminate the **Compute** button and make Linear a more satisfactory interactive application. We're keeping it simple here.

Next, we have to switch Linear from depending on libRegression.a to Statistics.framework. Select the **Project** icon at the top of the Groups & Files list and make sure that Linear is the active target. You should check Statistics.framework. Finally, double-click **Linear** under the **Targets** group (or choose **Project** → **Edit Active Target "Linear"**—command-option-E), and in the **General** tab of the Get Info window, add a dependency on the Statistics target.

Set a breakpoint at the beginning of collectStatistics in PointStat.m, clicking in the gutter next to the first line. If the debugger stops execution at that breakpoint when we test this latest revision of Linear, we'll know that it is using the dynamic-library Statistics package, not our earlier code.

Select **Build and Debug** from the Project window's toolbar or from the **Build** menu. Linear should build cleanly and launch under the supervision of the Xcode debugger. Enter a data set and click **Compute**. Sure enough, the debugger breaks execution at the beginning of collectStatistics.

Note that there was no difficulty in setting a breakpoint in collectStatistics, even though it was a method defined in a dynamic library that was not the product of the active target. The debugger underlying Xcode, gdb, is pretty smart about such things.

12.4 Where Frameworks Go

The gcc build tools and the Mac OS X dynamic loader are set up to find framework libraries and headers automatically on no more basis than specifying the framework's name with the -framework option. So far, the magic has worked for us because of the simplest search rule: looking for frameworks in the same directory as the applications that call for them. As both Linear.app and Statistics.framework are built in the build directory of our project directory, finding the Statistics framework presents no problem.

This is not a good distribution strategy, however. The whole idea of bundled applications and frameworks is to *avoid* having user-visible dependencies on files in

System Frameworks

The other main provider of frameworks for your application is, of, course, Apple itself. Apple-provided frameworks are found at /System/Library/Frameworks. The ones most used, Cocoa.framework and Carbon.framework, are included in the new-project templates Xcode provides.

Many of Apple's frameworks are *umbrella frameworks* containing additional library and header packages that themselves are frameworks. For instance, Application-Services.framework contains a Frameworks directory that includes AE.framework (for Apple Events) and CoreGraphics.framework. This subdivision is for Apple's convenience in engineering and for yours in finding headers, but don't rely on it by trying to import a subframework of an umbrella framework.

If made part of an umbrella framework, a framework may rely on sister frameworks' being linked in order to work properly. Apple does not document such dependencies, beyond putting interdependent libraries into umbrella frameworks. Further, Apple reserves the right to refactor the contents of umbrella frameworks, so linking against a subframework is not guaranteed to be stable.

The rule is not to link against anything that doesn't appear in /System/Library/Frameworks. Some frameworks there are also contained in umbrella frameworks—for example, Foundation.framework, which is part of Cocoa.framework, can also be linked separately.

The Xcode tools do not support the creation of umbrella frameworks. Apparently, they require some hand tuning that Xcode does not automate.

---

a fixed directory relationship. The other place gcc and the dynamic loader search for frameworks is /Library/Frameworks. A framework installed here will be available to all users.

If a framework is to be installed anywhere else, the program that links to it has to know where to find it. The installation path is built into the library. When the client program is built, gcc copies the installation location into the instructions for the dynamic loader.

You set the installation path with the **Build** panel of the Get Info window for the framework target. Find **Statistics** under the **Targets** group in the Groups & Files list, and double-click it; then select **Build**. You find that scores of settings can influence the build of `Statistics.framework`. Fortunately, Xcode provides ways to sort through the mass of options.

You can narrow the list by functional group by making a selection from the **Collection:** pop-up menu at the top of the Get Info window. Selecting **Deployment** reduces the choices enough so that **Installation Directory** is easily found.

> If you are following along using Xcode 1.5, the collection pop-up is still there but more difficult to find. It is built into the header of the left-hand column of the **Build** panel's list of settings.

Another way to find an option is to use the search field in the upper-right corner of the window. With **All Settings** selected in the **Collection:** pop-up and `install` typed into the search field, you can once again readily find **Installation Directory**. Note, by the way, that not all the settings shown include "install" in their names; the search is done on the narrative explanations the **Build** panel displays when you select an option. See Figure 12.2.

In the Configuration: pop-up, select **All Configurations**. You want to affect the content of the framework regardless of whether it is built for debugging or release.

If we wanted to install `Statistics.framework` in `Library/Frameworks` in a user's home directory, we'd select that line of the build settings and edit the setting in the right-hand column to read **~/Library/Frameworks**. This line of the setting table appears in boldface, which is Xcode's way of showing that the setting is a change from the default value. If `Statistics.framework` was built with this setting, the dynamic loader will look for the framework first at the specified directory, then at `/Library/Frameworks`, and then at `/System/Library/Frameworks`.

Having a framework at an unusual location brings up a second consideration: where gcc will look for the headers at compile time and the library at link time. This issue is separate from setting the installation path for the framework, because before it can read that built-in installation path, gcc has to find the framework at build time.

If we were building Linear against a copy of `Statistics.framework` in the user frameworks library directory, we would edit the settings for the `Linear` target and type **frame** into the search field. This reveals the **Framework Search Paths** setting; clicking that line of the table and reading the explanation at the bottom of the Get Info window confirms that this setting tells gcc where to look for frameworks. The explanation ends with [FRAMEWORK_SEARCH_PATHS, -F], which means that if we want

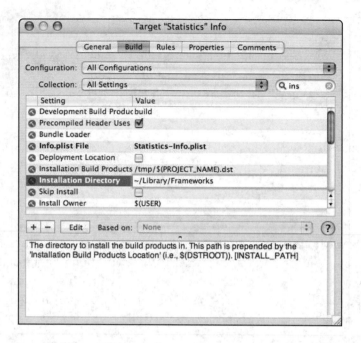

Figure 12.2 Specifying that `Statistics.framework` should be in the user's Library/Frameworks directory. Note that typing **ins** in the search field at the top of the window narrowed the multitude of settings in the window enough to make the installation setting visible. **Installation Directory** is shown in boldface, indicating that the setting has been changed from the default value. Because **All Configurations** has been selected, any value we enter will be set for the Debug, Release, and Default configurations simultaneously.

scripts or other settings to refer to this setting, we should use $(FRAMEWORK_SEARCH_PATHS) and that this setting affects the -F option to gcc.

We could edit this setting in place, but **Framework Search Paths** is a list option. I always find lists to be tricky in the limited space provided in the right-hand column of the **Build** settings editor. Xcode provides a nicer way to edit list options; select **Framework Search Paths** and click the **Edit** button immediately below the table. A sheet emerges (Figure 12.3) that makes it easy to manage list settings.

There is little reason to go to the trouble of installing a public framework anywhere but in /Library/Frameworks. If the package is to be accessible to only one user, it's difficult to imagine the need to package a library and associated headers and resources for sharing among applications. The major case in which a framework might

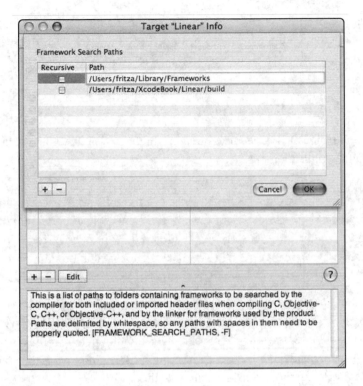

Figure 12.3 The list editor for build settings. In this case, we add the user framework library directory to the search paths for frameworks, allowing us to build Linear against frameworks installed in that directory.

be installed elsewhere is when it isn't a public framework at all but a private framework installed inside an application's bundle.

12.5 Private Frameworks

Suppose that our goals for Statistics.framework have changed, and we no longer want to make it available to all comers. We simply want to use it in our own application, Linear. We can install the framework inside the application bundle.

The first task is to set the dynamic-loader information so that when Linear runs, the loader will look in the right place for Statistics.framework. As Linear could be installed anywhere, an absolute path is not possible, but a special path notation is available for just this purpose. To edit the target settings for `Statistics`, make it the active target and press **command-option-E** or double-click **Statistics** under the **Targets** group. Type **install** in the search field. Next to **Installation Directory**, type

```
@executable_path/../Frameworks
```

In short, look inside the `Frameworks` directory in the parent directory of the directory containing the application binary.

> Beginning in Mac OS X 10.4, bundles that are not the principal executables of a process—plug-ins, for instance—can refer to load paths within the plug-in bundle. A framework installed in a plug-in bundle, for instance, can have `@loader_path/../Frameworks` as its installation directory.

You should also check **Skip Install**. A full, final build of an Xcode project will attempt to place all the products in their intended installation locations. We, however, have just specified a `Statistics.framework` installation path that makes no sense at the time it is being built and installed. Checking **Skip Install** avoids the confusion by keeping `Statistics.framework` in the `build` directory.

Now that the framework advertises its destination properly, we have to make sure that it gets there. To make it the active target, choose **Linear** in the toolbar pop-up or in the submenu of the **Project** menu, and select **Project** → **New Build Phase** → **New Copy Files Build Phase**. A Get Info window will appear; in the **Destination:** pop-up, select **Frameworks**.

We've now specified that something will be copied to `Linear.app`'s Frameworks subfolder whenever `Linear` is built. What? Obviously, `Statistics.framework`. Under the **Targets** group, use the disclosure triangles to open first the `Linear` target and then the **Copy Files** build phase. Drag **Statistics.framework** from the **Products** group above into the **Copy Files** phase. This specifies what gets copied to the `Frameworks` subfolder in the build process. See Figure 12.4.

Build the `Linear` target one more time; when that is done, control-click the completed application, in the `build` subdirectory of the project directory, in the Finder, and select **Show Package Contents**. Open the `Contents` folder and then the `Frameworks` folder inside, and you should see `Statistics.framework`.

You should also run the Linear application to verify that it works with the embedded framework.

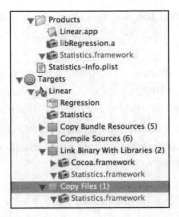

Figure 12.4   Putting `Statistics.framework` into a **Copy Files** phase in the build of Linear. We had previously added the phase with a command from the **Project** menu and specified that the target for the phase was the output package's `Frameworks` directory. Now we have dragged **Statistics.framework** from the **Products** category down to the **Copy Files** phase to specify that it is to be copied.

12.6 Prebinding

Xcode gave one warning in the build of Linear with `Statistics.framework`: "prebinding disabled because dependent library . . . Statistics is not prebound." We remember from Section 4.4 that prebinding entails picking out a loading address for a library in advance, so that applications that use it will not have to calculate the addresses of entities in the library when it is loaded.

Prebinding became unnecessary with Mac OS X version 10.3.4, so it might not be a good use of our time to specify a prebinding addess for `Statistics.framework`. Let's do it anyway, in case we need it for Mac OS X 10.2. In the **Target** group double-click the **Statistics** target, and select the **Build** tab in the resulting Get Info window. We will be setting two options for the linkage phase: `-prebind`, which tells the linker to attempt prebinding, and `-seg1addr`, which specifies a suggested load address for our library.

Select the **Linking** group from the **Collection** pop-up menu, resulting in a manageable handful of choices. The first thing is to check the **Prebinding** option, which will add the `-prebinding` flag to the link phase.

Because Xcode does not provide a table entry for it, `-seg1addr` is a little trickier. Select **Other Linker Flags** and click the **Edit** button below the table. This will give you a sheet for adding options without disturbing what's already there. Click the + button twice; then edit the first new line to contain -segladdr and the second 0xd3e00000. This tells the linker to prebind Statistics.framework at the base address of 0xd3e00000.

How did I choose that address? I pulled it more or less out of the air. Apple's online documentation on prebinding specifies certain address ranges as permissible for library code and others as reserved to applications or the system. The range 0xc0000000–0xebffffff is the prime real estate for third-party libraries; 0xb0000000–0xfdffffff and 0xffc00000–0xfffdffff are primarily for other uses but may be used for prebinding, if absolutely necessary.

Beyond that, you're on your own and must pick an address random enough that it is unlikely to collide with someone else's library. In the end, your loading address is subject to revision when someone—such as Apple's installer—runs update_prebinding to "optimize system performance."

You must also set prebinding on the Linear application itself, double-clicking on the **Linear** application target, finding the **Prebinding** setting in the **Build** panel, and setting the checkbox.

12.7 Summary

Frameworks are an essential part of the Mac OS X developer's repertoire. We reviewed the structure of the framework bundle and how to access framework contents. We built a framework and solved the problem of where to put it: first by placing it in a standard directory and then by embedding it in an application bundle. We also saw how to prebind our new framework in case we need good performance on older versions of Mac OS X.

13

Version Control

Change has been coming in a steady stream to our family of linear-regression tools, and for the most part, we've been able to accommodate the changes in a compatible fashion. When we had new features and implementations to deal with, most of the change involved adding modules, moving files between targets, and making only minor alterations to existing code.

The changes to come, however, are more extensive, and if you're like most programmers, you are conservative of the code you've written. An old method may no longer be required, but it may embody an understanding of the underlying problem. One solution might be simply to keep all the obsolete code in your active source files, possibly guarded by #if 0 blocks, but this bloats the file considerably and obscures the active core of the code. Once the revisions get more than one layer deep, it can be difficult to track which blocked-out stretch of code goes with which.

It's for these reasons that a *software configuration management system* is a good idea even for single-programmer projects. An SCM system is a database that keeps track of all the files in a module and allows you to register revisions of those files as they change. Revision control frees you to make extensive changes, secure in the knowledge that all the previous versions of each file are still available if you need to roll back your changes.

Xcode 2 supports revision control mediated by three SCM systems: CVS, Subversion, and Perforce.

- CVS (concurrent versions system) is the standard for open-source and enterprise version control in the UNIX/Linux world. CVS is open-source software itself, and version 1.11 shipped with Mac OS X 10.4 and Xcode 2.0. The Darwin project, which makes the Mac OS X kernel available as open source, is built on CVS archives.

- Subversion is an open-source SCM system built with the design goal of being a better CVS. Subversion embraces WebDAV access to the latest revision of modules, support for deleting or renaming versioned files, and "atomic" check-ins. (If you try to check in a group of files and one fails to check in, none are checked in, thus heading off an inconsistency in the archive.) Subversion keeps a local copy of the last version of every file you check out, so you don't have to be in touch with the server to review or roll back any changes you made.

- Perforce is a commercial SCM system from Perforce Software. Its advantages are speed and scalability to very large file bases. Licenses for open-source projects or for projects with at most two users and two workspaces are free; for other terms, see the Web site (`http://www.perforce.com/`).

If I were recommending an SCM system to a programmer who had no constraints and little fear of the command line, I'd recommend Subversion because it is helpful, reliable, and easy to use and understand. Its check-ins and checkouts are "atomic," meaning that they have no effect on the database or your directory unless *all* the files in the operation have been processed successfully; that, in turn, means that there's no need to "wrap" Nib and project documents, because there's no way to check them in or out in an inconsistent state. (This book was written on three different Macintoshes, kept in synch with a Subversion repository.)

The disadvantages of Subversion come from its not being as widespread, and therefore as supported, as CVS. Although you have CVS installed on your Mac right now, you will have to find a binary distribution of Subversion or download the source package and install it and its prerequisite packages, such as Berkeley DB, yourself.

> If you do set up a Subversion repository, consider using the file-system based "fsfs" repository structure instead of the original Berkeley database structure. On Mac OS X, at least, fsfs repositories seem to be much more reliable.

Perforce is a high-powered SCM system providing tools for central management of the code base. Its maker claims that it will perform well on code bases as large as hundreds of thousands of files while requiring little in the way of maintenance. Unlike the other two systems, which rely on the users to reconcile the changes they make to controlled files when they interact with the repository, Perforce enforces file consistency by permitting only one client at a time to check a file out as a writer. Perforce is free to try, but in late 2005 cost $800 per user for commercial development. Free licenses are available to open-source projects.

CVS is the "common language" of source control; concepts from CVS carry over to other systems. And, even if you choose another system for version control, chances are that you will have to deal with a CVS-controlled code base some day. This chapter will therefore concentrate on CVS.

13.1 Setting up a Repository

The heart of a revision-control system is its repository, the files or databases that constitute the history it keeps of the files in a module. All revision-control commands you issue relate to a repository. We're going to set up a local repository intended for access only from the computer on which it resides. Networked repositories are beyond the scope of this book; consult the documents for your SCM system for instructions and tutorials if you're interested.

Open the Terminal application, found at /Applications/Utilities. By convention, local repositories are kept at the path /usr/local/cvsroot. Direct your command line session to /usr, and determine whether the local subdirectory exists:

```
$ cd /usr
$ ls local
ls: local: No such file or directory
```

If, as here, there is no local directory, we'll have to create it. Do so by typing

```
$ sudo mkdir local
   .
   .   (A short lecture may appear here)
   .
Password:
```

The sudo command requests that the rest of the line be executed as though it came from the most privileged user on the system. Type your password at the prompt—it will not be shown as you type.

Now that we know /usr/local exists, move your session there, and use sudo again to create the cvsroot subdirectory:

```
$ cd local
$ sudo mkdir cvsroot
```

If you rerun sudo within a minute or two, it doesn't ask you for your password again. Now we tell CVS to initialize /usr/local/cvsroot as a repository:

```
$ sudo ocvs -d /usr/local/cvsroot init
```

Note well that we are using the command ocvs, not cvs. The cvs shipped with Mac OS X 10.4 is version 1.11; the version that shipped before, and that now appears as ocvs, was 1.10. Xcode uses the "old" CVS because version 1.11 dropped support for processing file package directories as they enter and leave repositories. Such packages are common in Mac OS X development—the .xcodeproj project document itself is a package—so Apple has split the difference: It uses ocvs, with its ability to wrap package directories, in Xcode, while providing a more current cvs for general use.

For you to use CVS as an ordinary user, you have to have write permission on certain files and directories in the repository. CVS's init command marks these as group-writable. For users of your machine, we could define a special group allowed to use CVS, but let's assume that you are an administrative user—a safe bet if your password has been working for sudo—and that you are content to allow all administrative users to use the CVS repository. We will therefore transfer group ownership of /usr/local/cvsroot and everything in it to group admin. We will also make the repository directory itself writable by members of the group so they can create new modules in it:

```
$ sudo chgrp -R admin /usr/local/cvsroot
$ sudo chmod g+w /usr/local/cvsroot
```

Our setup has one final step. CVS, like most SCM systems, is oriented toward storing text files, such as source code. Changes between versions may be saved as line-by-line differences rather than as whole-file saves, for instance. But strategies that work well for archiving text are poor for binary files, such as graphics. CVS has to be told what files should be treated as binary

Further, Xcode makes extensive use of file packages. It makes no sense to archive the component files of a Nib separately if any change to one component *must* be accompanied by the corresponding change in the others. CVS provides a way to process files and directories as they enter and leave the repository, so that packages can be archived in single "wrapper" files before they are stored.

The file that directs this behavior is a CVS wrapper file and is found in two places:

1. CVSROOT/cvswrappers, the default rule file for all clients making local use of the repository. You'll find a file empty but for comments at /usr/local/cvsroot/ CVSROOT/cvswrappers.

2. .cvswrappers, which may be stored in your home directory. This file controls wrapping behavior for archives that are not local.

The cvswrappers file created by the CVS init command is essentially empty, which is no good for our purposes. We'll have to edit it. We'll gain access to the CVSROOT/cvswrappers file by checking it out of the local repository, fill it in with Apple's recommended contents, and save the change by checking the file back in. We will not only get some work done but also get a first exposure to working with CVS.

Checking a module out of CVS will produce a directory containing all the files in the module. Pick a place in your home directory—perhaps your home directory itself—where you'd be comfortable having the checked-out copy of the CVSROOT directory. In the Terminal application, point your command line interface at that directory. Then tell CVS that you want to check out CVSROOT:

```
$ cd ~
$ ocvs -d /usr/local/cvsroot co CVSROOT
cvs checkout: Updating CVSROOT
U CVSROOT/checkoutlist
U CVSROOT/commitinfo
U CVSROOT/config
U CVSROOT/cvswrappers
    .
    .
    .
```

In SCM terms, a file is *updated* when a copy is transfered from the repository to your workspace.

Let's use Xcode to do the rest of the work. Create a new project (**File → New Project** . . .), and specify an empty project, named CVSROOT. Make sure that the project directory is the same ~/CVSROOT directory as was created by the CVS checkout command.

Next, add the files to the project, using the **Project → Add to Project** . . . (**command-option-A**) command. When the select-file sheet appears, hold down the **command** key and click on every file—except CVSROOT.xcodeproj—in the ~/CVS-ROOT directory; then click **Add**.

Turn on source code management (SCM) for this project. Select **Project → Edit Project Settings**, or double-click the project icon in the Groups & Files list. Make sure that the **General** tab is showing. Near the bottom is a pop-up menu labeled **SCM**

System:; set this to **CVS**. Setting a system activates the **Enable SCM** checkbox, so you can now check it. Dismiss the Project Info window.

We also want to monitor the SCM status of our files in the Groups & Files list. Click any item in the list to bring focus to it; then select **View** → **Groups & Files Columns** → **SCM**. This adds a column at the left of the list for single letters that indicate what files are part of the current module, which have been changed since the last update, which need updating, and so on.

Select **cvswrappers**. As you can see, the file contains about a screenful of documentation on how to use the file but no active content. Fortunately, Apple has supplied a recommended cvswrappers file. Open it with the **File** → **Open . . .** (**command-O**) command; navigate to /Developer/Tools/cvswrappers. (*Hint:* Typing **/Developer/Tools** will open a sheet allowing you to type the path in directly.) The Apple file, you see, is nearly a hundred lines long. Select the whole file (**command-A**), copy it (**command-C**), return to the cvswrappers in the CVSROOT project (**command-option-left arrow**), and replace the entire contents (**command-A**, **command-V**).

You'll know you've modified the correct file if the **cvswrappers** icon in the Groups & Files list turns gray. Save your changes (**command-S**). Note that an M appears to the left of cvswrappers in the SCM flag column of the Groups & Files list. This is Xcode's CVS support telling you that this file has been modified since you checked it out. (Code A is for files that have been marked for adding to the module but not yet checked in, and ? is for files that are not under revision control.)

Let's play with the SCM menu a little. Select **cvswrappers** in the Groups & Files list, and issue the command **SCM** → **Diff With** → **Latest**. Xcode presents you with the results of running the standard diff tool against the cvswrappers in your project directory and the one in the repository:

```
Index: cvswrappers
===================================================================
RCS file: /usr/local/cvsroot/CVSROOT/cvswrappers,v
retrieving revision 1.1
diff -r1.1 cvswrappers
1c1
< # This file affects handling of files based on their names.
---
> # This file describes wrappers and other binary files to CVS.
3,5c3,6
```

```
< # The -t/-f options allow one to treat directories of files
< # as a single file, or to transform a file in other ways on
< # its way in and out of CVS.
---
> # Wrappers are the concept where directories of files are to be
> # treated as a single file.  The intended use is to wrap up a
wrapper
> # into a single tar such that the tar archive can be treated as
a
> # single binary file in CVS.
 .
 .
 .
```

If you find diff listings difficult to visualize, you are not alone. Most people would rather view the differences by using the command **SCM → Compare With → Latest**. In response to this command, Xcode will present the current version of the file and the latest version in the repository to FileMerge, a /Developer/Applications/Utilities application that shows the two side by side, with the differences joined graphically in gray bands (see Figure 13.1). Differences within lines are set off in colored text. You could browse through the difference blocks and select which version—old or new—you wish to keep in your file.

BBEdit, the text editor from Bare Bones Software, also incorporates a fine file-difference tool, and Xcode will use it instead of FileMerge if you ask. The setting is in the **SCM** panel of the Preferences window.

It's time to put our edits into effect. With **cvswrappers** selected in the Groups & Files list, select **Commit Changes...** from the **SCM** menu. All revisions must be accompanied by a comment, so a sheet slides out for a description of the changes in this revision (Figure 13.2). Type something in, and click **Commit**.

Remember that we also want the contents of this file at .cvswrappers in our home directory. Select **File → Save a Copy As...**, select your home directory, and put a dot (.) in front of the cvswrappers name; then click **Save**. Xcode will complain that files with leading dots in their names are system files, so you will have to confirm that this is what you intend to do.

This concludes your setup of a local CVS repository. You no longer need the copy of CVSROOT you checked out; remember that the "real" copy is at /usr/cvsroot, not in your directory, and an authentic copy can be had at any time by checking it out again. Feel free to delete your scratch copy.

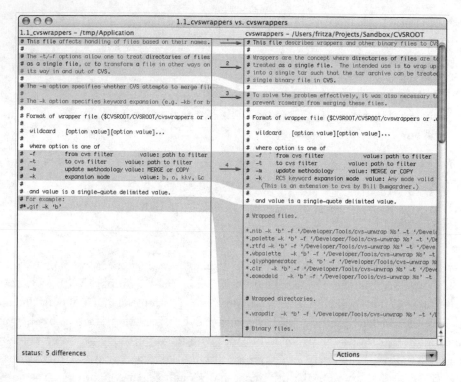

Figure 13.1 The FileMerge utility, showing the differences between the original cvswrappers file and as edited to Apple's recommended contents. Gray bands join areas of the files that have been changed. The pop-up menu at lower right can be used to choose which version—old or new—of each difference should be saved.

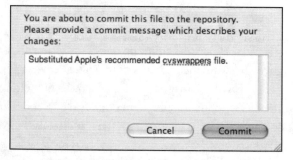

Figure 13.2 Sheet for entering a message on committing changes to CVS

13.2 Controlling Linear

Now that we have a working repository, we can open a store for Linear in it. Bringing the contents of a directory into a repository for the first time is called *importing*. We go to the directory that contains the Linear project:

```
$ cd ~/Linear
```

We're in a quandary right here. Issuing a CVS import command on this directory would create in the repository a new archive containing everything in the Linear directory: *everything*. That includes the multimegabyte build directory, which consists only of files that are the product of compiling the relatively smaller source files, and the backup MainMenu~.nib and MyDocument~.nib files. Both classes of files change continually, and neither adds value to the history of the project.

It doesn't have to be that bad, and even if we left matters alone, it wouldn't be. CVS automatically ignores files that obviously contain object code. We can add to the list of ignored files by saving the following text file under the name .cvsignore in our home directory:

```
*~.nib
build
.DS_Store
*.model *.pbxuser *.perspective
```

We remove all files—directories—they're file packages—that fit the pattern of backup Nibs, the entire build directory, the Finder's .DS_Store scratch files, and .model, .pbxuser, and .perspective files, which contain user-specific information, such as bookmarks and window positions inside .xcodeproj project file packages.

Next, we invoke ocvs, addressing the repository at /usr/local/cvsroot, telling it to import the current directory. All transactions must have a message, so we supply **Initial check-in**. We will call the new CVS module CVSLinear, the vendor of the project—which doesn't matter much in a single-developer project—SintoX, and the identifying tag for this initial state of the archive start:

```
$ ocvs -d /usr/local/cvsroot \
        import -m 'Initial checkin' CVSLinear SintoX start
I CVSLinear/.DS_Store
I CVSLinear/build
N CVSLinear/DataPoint-PropertyList.h
N CVSLinear/DataPoint-PropertyList.m
```

```
N CVSLinear/DataPoint.h
N CVSLinear/DataPoint.m
N CVSLinear/GraphColors.plist
N CVSLinear/Info.plist
   :
   :
```

CVS responds with a list of all the files it introduced to the repository, prefixed with N, to show that they were all new to the CVSLinear module. Right away, we're gratified to see the I before .DS_Store and build, indicating that they were ignored.

A CVS import is simply that—a transfer of file data from a directory to the repository. The repository is changed, but no change is made to the source directory. If you try to perform a CVS operation on files in Linear, it will fail, with the message that no revision information is present:

```
$ ocvs status
cvs status: No CVSROOT specified!  Please use the '-d' option
cvs [status aborted]: or set the CVSROOT environment variable.
$ ocvs -d /usr/local/cvsroot status
cvs status: in directory .:
cvs [status aborted]: there is no version here;
    run 'cvs checkout' first
$
```

If we want a revision-controlled version of Linear, we must check out an entire new copy of the directory. As we have seen, the checkout command will create a new directory with the same name as the module. We go to the parent directory of Linear and ask CVS, via the repository in /usr/local/cvsroot, to check out the CVSLinear module:

```
$ cd ..
$ ocvs -d /usr/local/cvsroot checkout CVSLinear
cvs checkout: Updating CVSLinear
U CVSLinear/DataPoint-PropertyList.h
U CVSLinear/DataPoint-PropertyList.m
U CVSLinear/DataPoint.h
U CVSLinear/DataPoint.m
```

```
U CVSLinear/GraphColors.plist
U CVSLinear/GraphWindow.nib
  .
  .
  .
```

CVS responds by creating a directory named CVSLinear and filling it with all the files in the CVSLinear module. The difference between the CVSLinear and Linear directories is that CVSLinear and all its subdirectories have an additional subdirectory named CVS, which marks the directory as being under revision control and contains files pointing to the repository and noting the status of all the checked-out files.

> If you find it tiresome to specify the repository with the -d option every time, you can set a default value in the environment variable CVSROOT. For example:
>
> ```
> export CVSROOT=/usr/local/cvsroot
> ```
>
> CVS will use that value unless another is specified with the -d option. However, now that the current directory has a CVS directory to point to the repository, the -d option is no longer necessary.

If the original Linear.xcodeproj is open in Xcode, close it. Open the Linear.xcodeproj in the CVSLinear directory. As you did with the CVSROOT module, open the project settings (**Project → Edit Project Settings**, or double-click the project icon in the Groups & Files list) and in the **General** tab, select **CVS** as the SCM system, and activate SCM.

Projector

Veteran Macintosh developers will remember Projector, the version-control system used with the Macintosh Programmer's Workshop. Projector put revision information into the resource fork of each controlled file. This information included a lock—Projector's concept of checkout permitted only one user with write privileges at a time. CVS, Subversion, and Perforce do not alter the controlled files in any way. They don't restrict any user's writing in a checked-out copy; the resulting conflicts are to be resolved by user-mediated file merges at update or check-in time.

13.3 Long Live Linear

Play around with the CVSLinear copy of Linear: Examine source files, open Nibs, and build, run, and debug the targets until you are satisfied that the copy is identical to the original. When you are satisfied, quit Xcode, put the original Linear directory in the Trash, and rename CVSLinear as Linear. From now on, the revision-controlled directory will be our workspace.

Now we are in a position to clean up the Linear project.

- In MyDocument.m, if the compute: method still has references to computeWith-Linrg or computeFromLibrary commented or #if 0'ed out, remove them.
- In Regression.m, remove computeWithLinrg, dataRead:, and computeWithLibrary.
- Remove computeWithLinrg and computeWithLibrary from Regression.h as well.
- Edit the Linear target, and remove the dependency on libRegression.

Build the newly slenderized Linear, and run it to assure yourself that it still works. When you're happy with it, return to Xcode, and select the menu command **SCM → Commit Entire Project**. Xcode will ask you for a comment on your changes; when you click **Commit**, it will copy all the files you changed to the repository. The repository now contains your current version of Linear, as well as Linear as it was before the changes.

We've made repeated use of Xcode's Get Info window, notably to set options for targets and the project. Xcode has a variant on the Info window, the Inspector. The Inspector is just like the Get Info window, but its content changes to reflect whatever is selected in the Groups & Files view. You can open an Inspector by clicking **command-option-I** or by holding down the **option** key while selecting **File → Show Inspector**.

The Inspector is particularly handy when you want to troll your project for a certain kind of information. Select the **SCM** tab in the Inspector, and select **Regression.m** or one of the other files we modified and checked in. The window shows a history of all the revisions of that file, with the details of the selected revision shown below. The following buttons allow you to perform various operations on the selected revision.

- **Compare** launches your designated file-comparison application—either File-Merge or BBEdit—so you can merge lines from an old revision back into the current one.

- **Diff** creates a new file documenting the differences between your copy of the file and the selected revision, in `diff` format.

- **Annotate** creates a new file that is the selected revision, with each line prefaced by the revision number at which that line was last changed and the login name of the person responsible for the change.

- **Update** is the most interesting of all. If you update to a selected revision, CVS will replace your copy of that file with the selected revision. This is how you can revert to an earlier revision of a file.

Another way to roll a file back is to select it in the Groups & Files list and select **SCM** → **Update to** → **Revision** . . . . Xcode will present a sheet containing the revision history of the selected file, from which you can make your choice and click the **Update** button. If you happen to know the specific update number or tag you want, you can use **SCM** → **Update to** → **Specific Revision** . . . instead.

13.4 Tagging

As now checked in, the Linear project may be considered a baseline, or release version—something we might want to return to. It would be helpful if there were some way to identify the set of revisions in the CVS repository that make up Linear as it is now. Using CVS's revision numbers won't do, because CVS advances these for each file as changes are checked in, so that even now, some of our files for this "release" are at revision 1.1, whereas others are at 1.2. CVS uses *tags* to identify the cross-section of revisions that make up a snapshot of the repository.

Establishing a tag from the command line is not difficult; simply point your terminal session at the base directory of the Linear project and tell CVS that you want a tag of a certain name attached to the files in this directory, but *don't do this*:

```
$ cd ~/Projects/Linear
$ ocvs tag Panther-1-0 .
T DataPoint-PropertyList.h
T DataPoint-PropertyList.m
T DataPoint.h
T DataPoint.m
  .
  .
  .
```

Why Are My Files Red?

As soon as you divorce a project from the directory in which it was created, you may find that some of the file names under the project group have turned red, indicating that Xcode can no longer find the file associated with that file reference. There are two causes.

First, the file may simply not be there. The copy of the original directory is incomplete, perhaps because not every essential file from the original was checked into the repository. The solution is to go back to the original copy and add the missing files with the SCM tool's add command or with Xcode's **SCM → Add to Repository**.

Second, the file may be there, but Xcode may have an absolute to it, that is, a reference specified as a full pathname on your hard drive. If the project is checked out or otherwise transferred to a machine that doesn't have access to the original file, the reference becomes vacant and is shown in red. You can resolve this problem by changing the absolute reference to a relative one, which is what it usually should have been in the first place.

Hold down the **command** key and click all the red files under the project group to select them. Press **command-I** to open an Info window for all the selected references. Change the **Path Type:** pop-up to **Relative to Enclosing Group** or **Relative to Project**. This will make Xcode search for the files relative to the directories associated with the groups the files are in or the project file, respectively.

In some cases, you may have to open an Info window on individual files and use the **Choose . . .** button to establish the path to a file.

The sheet presented when you add files to a project offers a choice of methods by which the project can refer to the added files. In general, it's wisest to avoid absolute paths for project-specific files.

Here, `Panther-1-0` is the name of the tag, in reference to this being release 1.0 of an application that relies on technology from Mac OS X Panther, and . is the conventional way of referring to the current directory.

The reason I asked you not to do it this way is that I wanted to touch on a helpful utility for users of CVS: Concurrent Versions Librarian (CVL), from Sen:te Software (`http://www.sente.ch/software/cvl/`). It's a simple download, and installation is a matter of dragging the application from the downloaded disk image to your

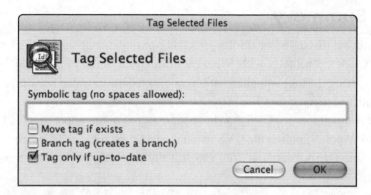

Figure 13.3 The CVL Tag dialog box. Entering a tag name (no spaces) and clicking **OK** will associate the tag with the current revision of all the selected files.

`Applications` folder. Run it, select **Work Area → Open . . . (command-O)**, and point it at the project directory for Linear.

What you'll see is not, at first glance, impressive: simply a browser either empty or showing only the `build` directory. To the left of the browser window is a filter drawer full of checkboxes whereby you can include and exclude files from the browser listing. If you check **Up-To-Date**, you'll see all the files that are checked into the Linear module. The other items in the drawer show you what kinds of files can be shown in the browser and how they are flagged.

If some files show up as **Locally Modified**, select them (command-click to select more than one), and issue the **Commit . . .** command (**command-shift-S**) from the **File** menu. A dialog appears, offering space to type in your comments. Enter them, and click **Commit**.

Now we'll use CVL to establish a tag for the current revision set. Select all the files and directories that are under CVS control. The easy way to do this is to set CVL's filters to show everything except items not in CVS, ignored, or unknown and to then press **command-A** to select all the items in the resulting list. Now select **File → Tag . . . .**

A dialog box appears (Figure 13.3), providing space to name your tag and options. Leave the options as is, enter the tag `Panther-1-0`, and click **OK**. The tag is then assigned.

13.5 Summary

This chapter has discussed what software-configuration management is and what SCM systems Xcode coordinates with. We went through the setup of a simple, local CVS repository, using the tools supplied with Xcode, and demonstrated how to get a project started under revision control.

There is much more to CVS than has been covered in this short chapter. Until Mac OS X 10.4, Apple supplied the CVS manual, also known as "the Cederqvist," a part of the installed documentation. You can still find it on the Web at `http://ximbiot` `.com/cvs/manual/`.

14

Cross-Development

Linear is working pretty well for us now, so it is time to throw a wrench into the works. The application makes use of `NSObjectController`, `NSArrayController`, and the attendant bindings architecture introduced with Mac OS X version 10.3. Let's decide that we want to serve a wider audience and make a version of Linear that is compatible with Mac OS X version 10.2.

14.1 Cross-Development SDKs

Apple has anticipated this need. Up to now, we've been compiling and linking against headers and libraries that "came with the system"—the libraries were the ones used in running the computers we compiled on, and the headers reflected them. An Xcode project can be directed away from a machine's installed development environment to use libraries and headers from earlier releases of Mac OS X.

> If you haven't put your code under source code management, as covered by Chapter 13, I recommend that you do so. If you didn't install the cross-development SDKs when you installed Xcode, rerun the installer and add them if you want to follow the example in this chapter.

Apple provides a cross-development software development kit (SDK) for the current version of Mac OS X and the last release of each of the previous two major versions. The choice of SDK is a projectwide option. Double-click the project (top) icon in the Groups & Files list (or select **Project** → **Edit Project Settings**), and select the **General** tab of the Get Info window. From the pop-up menu labeled **Cross-Develop Using Target SDK:**, select **MacOSX10.2.8**.

A sheet will appear, warning you that big things may happen to the project, as its build environment will change substantially. We know this; we seek it. Click **Change**.

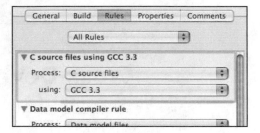

Figure 14.1   Adding a rule for using gcc 3.3 on C source files to the rules list in the Target Info window. The new rule is created when we try changing the existing system rule for C files; the system rule can't be changed, but Xcode offers to add a new rule. When the new rule appears at the top of the rules list, we select **GCC 3.3**.

We also need to change a target setting. Double-click the **Linear** target, and select the **Build** tab in the Get Info window. In the **Collection:** pop-up, select **Deployment**. Look for the setting **Mac OS X Deployment Target**, a pop-up menu which defaults to **Compiler Default**; select **Mac OS X 10.2** instead. Note that this line of the **Build** table becomes bold, to show that the setting represents a change from the default.

Finally, we have to change compilers. The gcc 4.0 compiler that Xcode uses by default links C-family code to runtime libraries that are present only in Mac OS X 10.3 and later—in the case of C++, it's 10.3.9 or later. The 3.3 version of gcc uses runtime libraries that are compatible back to 10.2. Select the compiler in the **Rules** tab of the Target Info window: Double-click the **Linear** icon under the **Targets** group in the Groups & Files list to open the info window.

The **Rules** pane associates a tool with each kind of source file that might be in your project. Near the top of the list is the **System C rule**, associating **C source files** with **GCC System Version (4.0)**. Change the tool pop-up to **GCC 3.3**; an alert sheet will appear offering to make a copy of the rule, as the system-level rule can't be changed. Click **Make a Copy** to create a new rule at the top of the list; set the tool pop-up to **GCC 3.3** (Figure 14.1).

The application binary interface (ABI) for C++ changed with each update of gcc from 3.1 to 3.3 and 4.0. Some of these changes were subtle, so code built with one compiler might link with code built with another but not function properly. Especially if you have C++ code in your project, make sure to do a **Clean All** whenever you change compilers. Xcode 2.1 is supposed to catch such dependencies, but it can't hurt to make sure.

Make the same changes to the **Rules** panel and the **Deployment Target** setting to the **Statistics** framework target.

Let's see how extensive the changes were in switching to the 10.2.8 SDK. Clean out all the previous build products by issuing a **Clean All** from the **Build** pop-up button in the Project window toolbar or selecting **Build → Clean All Targets**. Now build.

Already, we see signs of trouble. The build yields no errors, but the warnings include these:

```
warning: 'NSSavePanel' may not respond to '-setAllowedFileTypes:'
warning: 'MyDocument' may not respond to '-windowForSheet'
warning: 'Regression' may not respond to 'setKeys:
                    triggerChangeNotificationsForDependentKey:'
```

If we look at the headers for NSSavePanel, NSDocument, and NSObject, where those methods had been declared before, we find them absent in the headers for the 10.2.8 SDK or, if we look at current headers, marked as being for post-10.2 versions of Mac OS X. In fact, the current headers say that -windowForSheet became available in 10.1, but this may be a misprint.

So our first order of business is to remove our dependency on the newfangled methods. We can let windowForSheet go by brute force: We know that MyDocument has only one window, connected by only one NSWindowController. We can substitute the results of crawling that chain:

```
- (IBAction) saveAsPList: (id) sender
{
    // The response to the Save As PList... command
    NSSavePanel *      savePanel = [NSSavePanel savePanel];
    // Take the shared save-file panel and set it to save
    // only plists
    [savePanel setAllowedFileTypes:
                [NSArray arrayWithObject: @"plist"]];

    // Make a nice default name to present to the user
    NSString *        defaultName;
    defaultName = [[self displayName]
                stringByAppendingPathExtension: @"plist"];
```

```
NSWindowController *    controller1st;
controller1st = [[self windowControllers] objectAtIndex: 0];

// Present the save panel and designate a method for
// receiving the result.
[savePanel beginSheetForDirectory: NSHomeDirectory()
                             file: defaultName
                  modalForWindow:[controller1st window]
                   modalDelegate: self
                   didEndSelector:
        @selector(savePanelDidEnd:returnCode:contextInfo:)
                     contextInfo: NULL];
}
```

However, setAllowedFileTypes: is a different story. Having the **Save** panel restrict the saved file type is useful behavior, and we can't reliably duplicate it. If we can't have it, we'll have to live without it, but is there a way to have the benefit if it's there?

There is. It costs nothing but a negligible amount of time to ask a Cocoa object whether it implements a method. When we get our NSSavePanel, we send it responds-ToSelector: with the setAllowedFileTypes: selector. The reply will be NO on Mac OS X version 10.2.8 and below, and we must carry on without; it will be YES on 10.3 and later, and we can issue the message:

```
NSSavePanel *      savePanel = [NSSavePanel savePanel];
// Take the shared save-file panel and set it to save
// only plists
if ([savePanel respondsToSelector:
                    @selector(setAllowedFileTypes:)])
    [savePanel setAllowedFileTypes:
                [NSArray arrayWithObject: @"plist"]];
```

The third warning, about setKeys:triggerChangeNotificationsForDependent-Key:, is a symptom of a more pervasive problem—Linear's reliance on bindings and NSController objects. We can address the symptom by deleting the initialize class method from Regression.m, but the underlying reliance on the 10.3 Controller layer runs deeper. Recall that we created our controller objects and set up the bindings by using Interface Builder. It's time to revisit MyDocument.nib.

14.2 Nib Compatibility

In the **Resources** group under the **Project** icon, find **MyDocument.nib** in the Groups & Files list, and double-click that item to open it in Interface Builder. Select the **Nib** tab in the MyDocument.nib window, and set the **Oldest Target:** pop-up menu to **Mac OS X Version 10.2** (Figure 14.2).

The line below the pop-up says "Incompatibilities: 12." Click the **Show . . .** button next to it. A window appears (Figure 14.3) that lists each of the obstacles Interface Builder sees to opening our Nib under Mac OS X version 10.2. As you select an item on the list, the **Select Object** button becomes active; clicking it displays the object that has the incompatibility selected.

The first problems are with the NSController objects. That class was introduced in 10.3, and Interface Builder tells us that a Nib containing NSControllers won't load. So switch to the **Instances** tab of the Nib window, select each of the controller objects, and press the **Delete** key. With the controllers gone, click the **Refresh** button on the Compatibility Checking window.

We're clean. No further incompatibilities remain. The remaining incompatibilities are related to our use of bindings. All the bindings went through the controller objects and went away when the controllers were deleted. Now, as the remaining object in the Controller layer of our application, MyDocument will have to take over the task of joining Linear's views to its model.

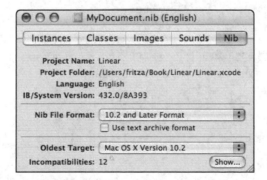

Figure 14.2 The **Nib** tab in Interface Builder. This panel shows general information about the Nib and its environment, including the file format and the oldest Mac OS X version the Nib is intended to be used on. Select the oldest target system with the lower pop-up menu. If the Nib includes features that are not available in the selected system, the incompatibilities will be flagged. The **Show . . .** button opens a browser on all the incompatibilities.

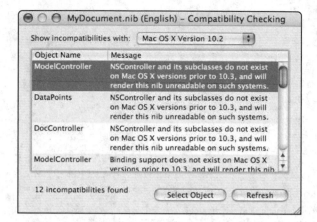

Figure 14.3 Interface Builder's compatibility browser. Each use in the current Nib of a feature that is not available in the target version of Mac OS X is listed and explained in this window. Select an item in the listing, and click **Select Object** to show the exact object that gave rise to the incompatibility.

Interface Builder will still be the tool we use to make the connections, but we have to add outlets for those connections to MyDocument. We go back to Xcode to edit MyDocument.h. We add four lines to the data members:

```
@interface MyDocument : NSDocument
{
    Regression *           model;
    PointStat *            statEngine;

    IBOutlet LinearGraph * graphView;
    IBOutlet NSWindow *    graphWindow;

    IBOutlet NSCell *      slopeCell;
    IBOutlet NSCell *      interceptCell;
    IBOutlet NSCell *      correlationCell;
}
```

Save the change to MyDocument.h, and drag its icon—from the Finder, the detail listing, or the Groups & Files list—into the MyDocument.nib window in Interface Builder. This tells Interface Builder that MyDocument has those three new outlets.

Now we can connect the result cells. Switch to Interface Builder, and double-click on the **Window** icon in the MyDocument.nib window to make sure that the prototype document window is visible. Control-drag from the **File's Owner** icon to the form cell labeled Slope:. The Connections Inspector appears; you can select **slopeCell** and click **Connect**. Similarly, connect **interceptCell** and **correlationCell**.

That takes care of the right half of the window; now for the table in the left half. We had been relying on NSArrayController to bind the columns of the NSTableView to the dataPoints array of our model. In the absence of bindings, NSTableView relies on a data source delegate to provide the contents it displays—much as our LinearGraph and PointStat classes rely on delegate methods to pull in the data they need. As with those classes, MyDocument will serve as the data source for the table.

Click on the table in the left half of the prototype document window. The title bar of the Inspector window likely says NSScrollView Inspector, because the first click will select the surrounding scroll view instead of the table view. Double-click on the table, and you should end up selecting the table view. Control-drag from the table view to the **File's Owner** icon, which represents our MyDocument instance, and make the connection to the table view's dataSource outlet.

The table data source methods work by telling the data source—MyDocument— what row and column of the table is being displayed or edited. The row is identified by number; the column is given as an instance of NSTableColumn. You can attach strings to NSTableColumns to help tell them apart, and that's what we'll do now.

Click on the header of the first column of the table, and use the Attributes Inspector (**command-1**) to set the Identifier: of the column to **xColumn**. Similarly, click on the second column, and set its identifier to **yColumn**. Save the Nib (**command-S**).

14.3 NSTableDataSource

We have committed ourselves to implementing the NSTableDataSource informal protocol in MyDocument. Under the protocol, the data source must report how many rows are in the table and what is in each row and column; receiving new values from editing the table is an optional part of the protocol, but we have to implement it for our application to work.

Being economical of effort, we write one line at the end of MyDocument.h:

```
#pragma mark NSTableDataSource
```

This line adds a marker to the function pop-up in the editor pane but allows us to hold down the command key and double-click on the word NSTableDataSource. Doing so takes us to the part of NSTableView.h that declares the NSTableDataSource informal protocol. We can then copy the declarations of the methods we need, return to `MyDoc-ument.h`, and be content with the saved effort and reduced chance of error. (We can navigate backward and forward in a sequence of files in an Xcode editor by using the arrowhead buttons at the top left of the editor view, or by pressing **command-option-left arrow** to go back or **command-option-right arrow** to go forward.)

```objc
- (int) numberOfRowsInTableView: (NSTableView *) tableView
{
    return [[model dataPoints] count];
}


- (id) tableView: (NSTableView *) tableView
objectValueForTableColumn: (NSTableColumn *) tableColumn
            row: (int) row
{
    // The table has a row and column, wants an
    // object value to display.
    // Here's the data for the row:
    DataPoint * item = [[model dataPoints]
                            objectAtIndex: row];
    NSString *  identifier = [tableColumn identifier];

    // Construct an NSNumber with data for the column:
    if ([identifier isEqualToString: @"xColumn"])
        return [NSNumber numberWithDouble: [item x]];
    else
        return [NSNumber numberWithDouble: [item y]];
}

- (void) tableView: (NSTableView *) tableView
    setObjectValue: (id) object
    forTableColumn: (NSTableColumn *) tableColumn
            row: (int )row
{
    // The table has an object value newly entered at
    // a row and column. We're supposed to propagate
    // it to the model.
    // This is the model for the row in question:
```

```
    DataPoint * item = [[model dataPoints]
                                objectAtIndex: row];
    NSString *  identifier = [tableColumn identifier];

    // Change the part of the model according to the column:
    if ([identifier isEqualToString: @"xColumn"])
        [item setX: [object doubleValue]];
    else
        [item setY: [object doubleValue]];
}
```

Let's not forget the output cells:

```
- (void) fillOutputCells
{
    // Fill in the output cells:
    [slopeCell setObjectValue:
        [NSNumber numberWithDouble: [model slope]]];
    [interceptCell setObjectValue:
        [NSNumber numberWithDouble: [model intercept]]];
    [correlationCell setObjectValue:
        [NSNumber numberWithDouble: [model correlation]]];
}


- (NSData *)dataRepresentationOfType:(NSString *)aType
{
    return [NSKeyedArchiver archivedDataWithRootObject: model];
}


- (BOOL)loadDataRepresentation:(NSData *)data
                        ofType:(NSString *)aType
{
    model = [NSKeyedUnarchiver unarchiveObjectWithData: data];
    [model retain];
    [self fillOutputCells];
    [dataPoints reloadData];
    return YES;
}
```

```
- (IBAction) compute: (id) sender
{
    [statEngine refreshData];
    [model setSlope: [statEngine slope]];
    [model setIntercept: [statEngine intercept]];
    [model setCorrelation: [statEngine correlation]];
    [self fillOutputCells];
}
```

14.4 Add, Remove, Compute, and Graph Buttons

What about the **Add** and **Remove** buttons? In our original Linear, those buttons were connected to an NSArrayController, but that has gone away in the conversion to 10.2 technology. MyDocument will have to take up the slack. Activate Interface Builder and edit the MyDocument class. The easiest way to do this is to select the **File's Owner** icon, which we have assigned the class MyDocument, and then click on the **Classes** tab and select **MyDocument**.

Press **command-1** to bring up the Attributes Inspector for MyDocument. Select the **Actions** tab, and click the **Add** button twice to add two new outlets. Edit them to the names **add:** and **remove:**.

Now hook up the buttons. Control-drag from the **Add** button to the **File's Owner** icon. In the resulting inspector, select **add:** action, and click **Connect**. (Remember that the connection isn't permanent until you click **Connect**!) Do the same for the **Remove** button, with the **remove:** action selector.

We've committed ourselves to adding two action methods to MyDocument. Switch back to Xcode, and edit MyDocument.h. (Note that we do not try repeating the **Create Files for MyDocument** command. That command generates mere skeleton files, and we're far beyond the skeleton phase.) Add declarations for the new IBActions:

```
- (IBAction) add: (id) sender;
- (IBAction) remove: (id) sender;
```

In MyDocument.m, we add implementations for the new methods. For add:, this entails creating a new instance of DataPoint and adding it to the dataPoints list of the model object; for remove:, finding the DataPoint object corresponding to the selected row and removing it from the model:

```
- (IBAction) add: (id) sender
{
    //  Create and initialize a new DataPoint
    DataPoint *     newPoint = [[DataPoint alloc] init];
    //  Add it to the model's data-point list
    [[model dataPoints] addObject: newPoint];
    //  Have the table view reflect the change
    [pointTable reloadData];

    [computeButton setEnabled: [model canCompute]];
    [graphButton setEnabled: [model canCompute]];
}


- (IBAction) remove: (id) sender
{
    //  What, if any, is the selected row?
    int     row = [pointTable selectedRow];
    //  Do nothing if no row is selected
    if (row == -1)
        return;
    //  Remove the point corresponding to the selected row
    [[model dataPoints] removeObjectAtIndex: row];
    //  Have the table view reflect the change
    [pointTable reloadData];

    [computeButton setEnabled: [model canCompute]];
    [graphButton setEnabled: [model canCompute]];
}

- (void) awakeFromNib
{
    [computeButton setEnabled: [model canCompute]];
    [graphButton setEnabled: [model canCompute]];
    [self fillOutputCells];
    [pointTable reloadData];
}
```

But in both cases, we have to tell the table of points to reload its data to match the change in the dataPoints list. We use the instance variable name pointTable to refer to the table, but we haven't declared or initialized it yet. We do the same thing with the **Compute** and **Graph** buttons, which we have to enable and disable in response to the **Add** and **Remove** buttons now that the bindings layer isn't there to track them automatically. We also have to initialize the state of those buttons in the newly added awakeFromNib method, which gets triggered whenever a Nib owned by a MyDocument is loaded.

Let's correct the lack of instance variables immediately: pointTable, compute-Button, and graphButton should be IBOutlets, so that Interface Builder can know about them and initialize them in the Nib. We edit MyDocument.h thus:

```
@interface MyDocument : NSDocument
{
    Regression *          model;
    PointStat *           statEngine;

    IBOutlet LinearGraph *  graphView;
    IBOutlet NSWindow *     graphWindow;
    IBOutlet NSTableView *  pointTable;
    IBOutlet NSButton *     computeButton;
    IBOutlet NSButton *     graphButton;


    IBOutlet NSCell *       slopeCell;
```

We now bring this change through to the Nib. Save MyDocument.h, and drag its icon—from the detail view, the Groups & Files list, or the Finder—into Interface Builder's MyDocument.nib window. This brings Interface Builder's model for My-Document up-to-date. You can now control-drag from the document (**File's Owner**) to the table view in the prototype document window. Interface Builder's Connections inspector appears, offering to connect the MyDocument's pointTable outlet. Click the **Connect** button to complete the connection. Do the same for the **Compute** and **Graph** buttons.

The amount of interconnection in Linear is extensive and can be confusing. Figure 14.4 shows how to make sense of it. At the upper-right corner of the Nib window in Interface Builder are two buttons to switch the window's view from an array of icons to a hierarchical list.

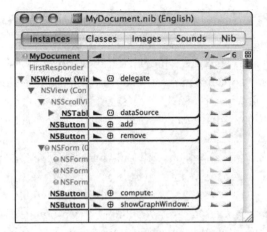

Figure 14.4 Clicking on the arrowhead that points toward the `MyDocument` instance at the top of the Nib listing shows all the objects that make connections to that instance. The "outlet" symbol next to the `NSWindow` instance shows that `MyDocument` is linked to the window's `delegate` outlet. The first `NSButton` in the list connects its `add` action to the `MyDocument` instance.

If you click the lower button, to switch to the list view, you'll find that each line has a pair of arrowheads next to it: one pointing away from the item, to show all the connections the item makes; the other, toward the item, showing all the connections made to the item. Clicking one of the arrowheads expands the list to show all the objects that connect in that direction and the names of the connections. This view allows you to browse all the connections in a Nib.

14.5 Run and Archive

We've had to do a lot of extra work, but it appears to be all done. All our buttons are hooked up, and we've found a way to activate them appropriately. We back the data table with a data source. We fill in the results form whenever a document is loaded or recalculated. Issue the **Build and Go** command—or **Build and Debug**, if you're cautious—and watch it work.

If you are keeping a CVS archive of the Linear project, this would be a good time to commit all the changed files in and establish a tag with a name like `jaguar-1-0` for the current revision set.

14.6 A More Sophisticated Approach

Our approach to cross-development for Mac OS X 10.2 on a 10.4 development machine has been simple: Write a throwback application that (almost) exclusively relies on 10.2 APIs. Xcode doesn't restrict us to writing throwback applications, and the approach we took with -[NSSavePanel setAllowedFileTypes:] shows the way: We can code so that we discover whether a feature is available and, if it is, take advantage.

If we had adopted this approach, we would have switched the target build setting for the deployment target OS version to 10.2 as before—we want a binary that will run on Mac OS X as early as that. We would also have switched over to the 10.2.8 SDK but *only for one build*. Our aim would not be to produce a 10.2 application but to identify the post-10.2 features in our code. We would then switch the SDK back to the current version setting.

The effect of combining a current SDK with a backward-compatible deployment target is to *weak-link* the parts of the system frameworks that came later than the deployment target. A weak-linked function behaves like any other if it is present and linkable. But if it is not present—if it's a 10.3 function and the application is being loaded on a 10.2 system, for instance—there won't be errors, but any pointers to the weak-linked function will be NULL. An application can take advantage of this by checking pointers to 10.3 functions, for example, before calling them: If the pointers are NULL, the application should substitute a workaround.

Similar techniques are available for Objective-C methods and classes. Section 14.1 showed how to check whether a method is available. To see whether a class is available, test whether you can get a class pointer from the class name:

```
Class   aClass = NSClassFromString(@"NSAlert");
if (aClass != NULL) {
    :
    :
    :
}
```

14.7 Producing a Universal Binary

The other use for an SDK in Xcode is in producing a *universal binary*, a single, linked executable file for the Mach-O linker that contains machine code for both the PowerPC and the Intel architecture.

Linear is an undemanding application and would probably run perfectly well under Rosetta, the PowerPC translation system for running PPC software on Intel Macintoshes. But pride, if nothing else, drives us to add the Intel code.

14.7.1 Auditing for Portability

In adding an Intel version to Linear, the first thing to do is examine the application for anything that would make it behave differently on an Intel processor, such as use of

- PowerPC assembly
- Altivec (Velocity Engine) instructions
- Binary numerics in a context that might be shared with other devices, such as a network, low-level file system structures, or Macintoshes of other architectures
- UTF-16 or UTF-32 encoding for Unicode text, without the use of a byte-order marker (BOM)
- Arrays of char in unions to examine the contents of other data types
- Bitfield struct or union members in cross-platform data
- bool, which is 32 bits in gcc on the PowerPC but 8-bits on Intel (and in Code-Warrior)

The first two points of incompatibility should be obvious: You can't run PowerPC standard or extended code on a processor with a different architecture. You can guard such code in C-family source code by checking for the target processor:

```
/*  Processor symbols begin and end with two underscores  */
#if __ppc__
    /*  Altivec or PPC assembly here  */
#end
#if __i386__
    /*  MMX/SSE2 or Pentium assembly here *  /
#end
```

I assume that you're using assembly for a good reason—you've measured the equivalent C code in Shark and discovered a bottleneck in exactly that place—so I'll spare you the reminder to consider using plain C code for both cases.

The next three categories of compatibility arise from the fact that the PowerPC stores numbers in memory so that the lowest-addressed memory gets the most-significant byte (big-endian), and Intel processors store numbers so that the lowest-addressed memory gets the least-significant byte (little-endian). Bit patterns that represent identical numbers on the two architectures are not identical when considered as a sequence of bytes.

Network numbers—addresses, port numbers—are big-endian, and Intel applications have to reverse any numbers that pass between net protocols and internal use. Numbers stored as binary images in files can be big- or little-endian, but a decision has to be made as to which, and the opposite platform has to convert at the read/write boundary.

Multibyte Unicode encodings, being strings of 2- or 4-byte integers, are simply a special case of the endianness problem. Writers of such files should write the byte-order mark character, 0xfeff (0x0000feff in UTF-32), at the beginning of the file to inform readers of endianness. If a Latin-text multibyte Unicode file comes out in Chinese when opened on a Macintosh with the opposite architecture, the BOM was either omitted or ignored.

14.7.2 Auditing Linear

When we examine Linear for Intel-porting issues, we find nothing much. There is no reliance on machine code or processor features. Linear does a lot of numeric computation internally, but internal use is not an issue. Similarly, passing the numbers to and from the user interface is not an issue: Although reading and displaying numeric strings involve an external interface, it's to a string format, not a binary format. The Macintosh frameworks themselves are of the same endianness as the machine they run on, so they're of the same endianness as our numerics; no byte-swapping issue there.

What about our storage formats? We have two. The plist format has no byte-swapping issues, because the numbers are translated into XML character data; it's not a binary format.

That leaves the reading and writing of .linear document files. We use NSKeyed-Archiver and NSKeyedUnarchiver to reduce our data to the file format. Apple assures us that anything that passes through the Cocoa archivers is byte-order safe. A .linear file written on a PPC Mac will be readable on an Intel Mac.

Just for illustration purposes, suppose that we did have a raw-binary file format for Linear data files. We would choose whether numerics should be stored in the file in big- or little-endian format. If our PowerPC application had a binary format in the first place, it probably saved its data as a direct binary image, so the choice of big-endian order is already made; the conversion task is simply to change the binary reading and writing so that it behaves well regardless of the architecture it runs on.

Let's imagine our binary-I/O code in more, though certainly not complete, detail:

```
#import <NSFoundation/NSByteOrder.h>

// All numerics in disk storage are big-endian

struct PointBinFmt {
    NSSwappedDouble     x;
    NSSwappedDouble     y;
};
typedef struct PointBinFmt PointBinFmt, *PointBinFmtPtr;

struct LinearBinaryFmt {
    NSSwappedDouble     slope;
    NSSwappedDouble     intercept;
    NSSwappedDouble     correlation;
    unsigned long       pointCount;
    PointBinFmt         points[0];
};
typedef struct LinearBinFmt LinearBinFmt, *LinearBinFmtPtr;

inline static unsigned
LinearBinFmtSize(LinearBinFmtPtr anLBF) {
    return sizeof(LinearBinFmt)
           + anLBF->pointCount * sizeof(PointBinFmt);
}

@interface DataPoint (BinaryFormat)
- (id) initWithBinary: (const PointBinFmtPtr) binary
{
    x = NSSwapBigDoubleToHost(binary->x);
    y = NSSwapBigDoubleToHost(binary->y);
    return self;
}
```

```
- (void) fillBinary: (PointBinFmtPtr) binary
{
    binary->x = NSSwapHostDoubleToBig(x);
    binary->y = NSSwapHostDoubleToBig(y);
}
@end

@interface Regression (BinaryFormat)

- (LinearBinFmtPtr) allocBinaryPtr
{
    LinearBinFmtPtr retval = malloc(sizeof(LinearBinFmt)
                               + [dataPoints count] *
                                    sizeof(PointBinFmt));
    retval->slope = NSSwapHostDoubleToBig(slope);
    .
    .
    .
    retval->pointCount = NSSwapHostLongToBig([dataPoints count]);
    .
    .
    .
}
```

We set up structs to lay out our file format and add a BinaryFormat category to both DataPoint and Regression to translate between those classes and the file format. The data format structs use NSSwappedDouble in place of double for floating-point values. Apple's documentation speaks of NSSwappedDouble and its partner NSSwappedFloat as "canonical representations" of real numbers; in practice, they are, respectively, long long and long ints containing the same bit pattern as a swapped or unswapped floating-point number. They are the recommended storage type for floats and doubles.

The Foundation header NSByteOrder.h contains in-line function definitions for swapping numeric data types between the processor's native format and either big- or little-endian format. Versions of these functions are guarded with #if __BIG_ENDIAN__ or #if __LITTLE_ENDIAN__ so that attempts to swap in the native ordering are replaced with simple assignments. The following statement is equivalent to x = binary->x; on the PowerPC but on Intel reverses the byte order of binary->x before the assignment:

```
x = NSSwapBigDoubleToHost(binary->x);
```

If you're using Core Foundation instead of Cocoa, the equivalent functions can be found in `CFByteOrder.h`; as with the `NS*` versions, these functions are optimized away at compile time if no swapping is necessary.

Making the `BinaryFormat` categories byte-order safe is a matter of identifying the places in the code where swappable data becomes shareable. In our case, it's when the data is committed to the file format. At that point, we interpose the appropriate swapping function. On writing, that would be a function that begins with `NSSwapHost` and ends `ToBig`, as we've decided that the file format will be big-endian. On reading, the swap-function names would begin with `NSSwapBig` and end with `ToHost`.

14.7.3 Building Universal

To produce a universal executable, you must tell the Xcode tools to compile and link Linear once for each target architecture. Then you have to link both images to Mac OS X frameworks.

Adding the second architecture is easy. Double-click the project icon at the top of the Groups & Files list. Switch to the **Build** tab of the Project Info window. In the top pop-up menu, select the **Release** configuration. Select **Architectures** in the second pop-up, or type **arch** in the search field until you see the Architectures setting. This should be, by default, $(NATIVE_ARCH), which means whatever processor Xcode is running on.

Click the **Edit** button below the settings list; a sheet appears with checkboxes for PowerPC and Intel. See Figure 14.5. Check both, and click **OK**. Now all future Release builds will include two compilation and linkage passes, one for each processor.

Figure 14.5 Setting the architecture for a project. Select the **Release** configuration in the Project Info window to ensure that all targets inherit the setting. Check each architecture you want to run on.

> Make the change only in the Release build configuration. You can't use the other architecture's debug output, so producing it is a waste of time. Do this on the *project* Release configuration, not on the target, so that both the targets that go into the Linear application—the application and the statistics framework—inherit the new setting.

The Release build of an application has to be linked against frameworks that supply its runtime library, Carbon, Cocoa, and every other service the system provides. The resident Mac OS X libraries you get when you compile without an SDK will not do; they don't have entry points for Intel code. Fortunately, we have, for the production of universal binaries, a Universal edition of the SDK for Mac OS X 10.4. This edition contains stub library entry points for both PowerPC and Intel.

So open the Project Info window again, if you've closed it. In the **General** tab, select cross-development, using **Mac OS X 10.4 (Universal)**. Now you will be able to build Linear without complaints from the linker about missing all kinds of fundamental symbols. Select **Project → Set Active Build Configuration → Release**, make sure that Linear is the current target, and build. The result should be a version of Linear that will run natively on both Intel and PowerPC.

14.7.4 Mixing SDKs

If you want your application to run on an Intel Macintosh, you are, in late 2005, committed to compiling it against an SDK for Mac OS X 10.4. There's no other choice. It may be that you want the PowerPC side of your application to target an earlier release of Mac OS X. This is possible.

When you select an SDK in the **General** tab of the Project Info window, you are setting the SDKROOT variable in Xcode's build system. The contents of this variable are prepended to the search paths for frameworks, headers, and libraries in the course of a build. Xcode also observes processor-specific SDKROOTs, SDKROOT_ppc, and SDKROOT_i386, if those are set.

Once again, open the Project Info window, select the **Build** tab, and choose the Release build configuration. Click the + button twice to add two custom settings, named SDKROOT_i386 and SDKROOT_ppc. Type in the path to the desired SDK in the right-hand column for each (for example, **/Developer/SDKs/MacOSX10.4u.sdk**; or, you could drag the SDK folder from the Finder into the right-hand column, and the

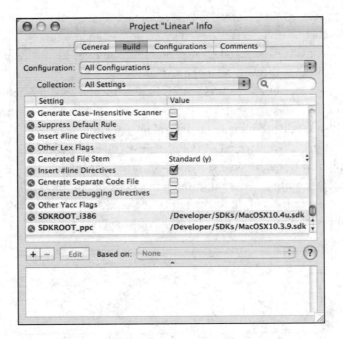

Figure 14.6 Setting separate SDKs for Intel and PowerPC builds. Add two settings, SDKROOT_i386 and SDKROOT_ppc, to the project Release configuration. The setting should be the path to the SDK's directory in /Developer/SDKs, and dragging the SDK folder from the Finder into the setting is a convenient way to enter the path.

correct path would appear. (See Figure 14.6.) Release builds from then on would target Mac OS X 10.4 on the Intel side but Mac OS X 10.3.9 on PowerPC.

Things get trickier if you want your PowerPC code to run on versions of Mac OS X earlier than 10.3.9. Those earlier versions lack runtime libraries required by applications built with gcc 4, but gcc 4 is required for Intel builds. Your best solution is to create a separate target for your PowerPC code, use the **Rules** tab of the target Info window to set the compiler to gcc 3.3, and build separate binaries for Intel and PowerPC. When you have the two binaries, you can combine them using the lipo command line tool, which is documented in a man page.

14.8 Summary

In this chapter, we've seen how to change the fundamental development environment for an Xcode project to ensure that its products will be compatible with a particular version of Mac OS X. We've practiced the back-and-forth workflow that is typical of active development with Cocoa and seen strategies for keeping Interface Builder and Xcode in sync. Finally, we looked at how combining an early deployment-target build setting with a current software development kit allows you to make applications that take advantage of Mac OS X features as they may be available on the target machines.

We also examined issues that arise in preparing an application designed on a PowerPC Macintosh for distribution as a universal binary, runnable on Intel processors as well as the PowerPC. We covered a brief checklist you can use to audit your applications and saw how to guard against byte-order problems, which are the commonest source of incompatibility. We went through the steps in building a universal edition of Linear and experimented with techniques for mixing a 10.4 Intel release with a PowerPC binary designed for earlier versions of Mac OS X.

15

Using the Data Modeling Tools

Having succeeded in making Linear compatible with Mac OS X version 10.2, Jaguar, let's go completely in the opposite direction and make use of features available only in Mac OS X version 10.4, Tiger. Tiger introduced Core Data, an object-persistence framework that can front for a binary file, a flat XML file, or an SQLite database. Core Data automates most tasks in storing, retrieving, and managing complex data models. In this chapter, we will make Linear a Core Data–based application.

If you followed the Chapter 13 suggestion, and set a CVS tag for `panther-1-0`, the version that used `NSController` objects to manage the controller layer of the application, you should revert to that version. Select the command **SCM → Update to → Specific Revision . . .** , and enter **panther-1-0** as the version to update to.

If you haven't been archiving Linear in CVS, you could simply copy the first project directory for this chapter from the CD-ROM.

15.1 Data Modeling

So far, we've been working with data to which we had some thread of reference. `Data-Points` contained x and y components and were themselves indexed components of a `Regression` object that was kept by the `MyDocument` instance. By contrast, Core Data works like a database, keeping a "soup" of objects—instances of `NSManagedObject` or classes descended from it—that exist independent of any reference to them, retrievable by evaluating a fetch request. All objects that are simultaneously accessible share an `NSManagedObjectContext`, which fronts for all the mechanisms that handle the storage, retrieval, and life cycle of the objects. The structure of an `NSManagedObject`— its attributes, relationships, default values—is specified by an `NSEntityDescription`, which is specified in an `NSManagedObjectModel`.

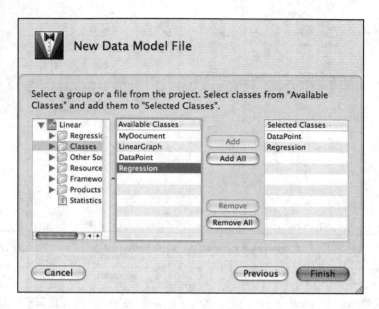

Figure 15.1 The New Data Model File Assistant. The list at left shows all the groups and files in the current project. Selecting a group (**Classes**) in this list fills the next list (Available Classes) with the names of all the classes defined in that group. You can then select classes to add to the Selected Classes list at right. Click **Finish** when done.

An NSManagedObjectModel, the blueprint for the object store, is specified in a managed-object model (.mom) file. The file, read at runtime to initialize the object store, is produced by compiling an Xcode data model (.xcdatamodel) file.

Our first concrete step will be to produce a data model file. Choose the **New File . . .** command from the **File** menu; in the New File Assistant, scroll down to select **Design → Data Model**. Click **Next**. Name the data model file Linear.xcdatamodel, and click **Next**.

Xcode can derive much of a data design from existing source code (see Figure 15.1). The Assistant presents a window for just that purpose. At the left is a truncated view of the Groups & Files list, from which you can select the files or groups that contain your model objects. In the case illustrated, the DataPoint and Regression objects, along with others, were defined in the **Classes** group. Selecting **Classes** filled the next list, Available Classes, with the names of the classes defined in that group. From this, we can select only the model classes and use the **Add** button to transfer them to the Selected Classes list. When the list on the right contains DataPoint and Regression, click the **Finish** button. We are rewarded with a sim-

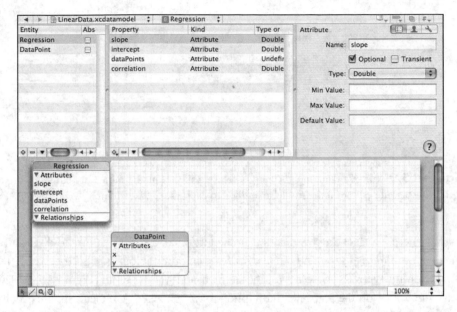

Figure 15.2 The "reverse-engineered" data model diagram for the model classes of Linear. The process for generating a new data model file reads the headers for the classes and detects the instance variables as attributes of the respective data entities. Slope, intercept, and correlation are correctly typed as Double.

ple diagram (Figure 15.2) that is not so very far from the data model we originally sketched (Figure 5.1).

Above the graphical model are tables for browsing and editing the model. At the left, we see that the model contains two *entities,* or kinds of storable objects: Regression and DataPoint. **Regression** is selected, so the middle table shows all its attributes: slope, intercept, dataPoints, and correlation. In this table, **slope** is selected, and we see at the right that it is set up in the model as optional—it may have no value at all—of type Double, and without minimum, maximum, or default values.

The model as set up automatically is not quite satisfactory. All the attributes are set to be optional, but the logic of our application is that it makes no sense for any of them to have no value. We might grumble as we resigned ourselves to clicking on each attribute in the two entities and clicked each Optional checkbox. We might grumble a little less if we noticed that by control-clicking in the header of the middle table, we get a contextual menu that can add the Optional checkbox to that table, saving us a step.

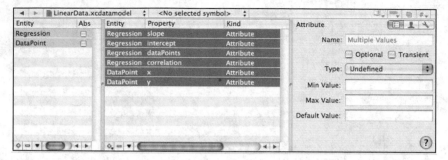

Figure 15.3 If more than one attribute is selected in the middle table, any edits you make with the Attribute editor on the right are applied to each selected attribute.

But there is something even better. In the left table, a sensible thing to do is shift-click on both `Regression` and `DataPoint`. The middle table fills with the properties of *both* entity types. Now select all the items in the middle table (Figure 15.3). The Attribute editor on the right has the Optional box checked. Uncheck it. This really does clear the Optional property in all the selected attributes.

Now unselect **dataPoints** by command-clicking it: It's the only attribute listed that is not a Double. Set a default value of 0 for all the `double`-valued attributes in the two entity types.

15.2 Revisiting the Model

Now that we have a new way of putting it into practice, it may be time to rethink our data design. Certainly, the implementation of the design has to change to suit the way Core Data works, but what about the design itself? Should the *shape* of the design change in light of what Core Data needs and what it makes possible?

One thing stands out. Our design says that a `MyDocument` has one `Regression`, which has an array of `DataPoint`s. Both the `Regression` and the `DataPoint`s are stored when the `MyDocument` is stored. But is the *has-a* relationship between `Regression` and `DataPoint` really necessary? It connects all the `DataPoint`s in the document to all the `Regression`s (one) in the document. Core Data's fetch requests give us a way to summon up all instances of an entity type in a context, so the relationship adds no information. There's nothing special about being a `DataPoint` in the `Regression`'s `dataPoints` array.

In the data model, select the `dataPoints` attribute of `Regression` in either the diagram or the middle table. It's no longer useful, so press the **Delete** key.

15.2.1 DataPoint

Now we can rework `DataPoint` to reflect what Core Data will do for it. `DataPoint` has been an `NSObject`, implementing the `NSCoding` protocol. Now, because we want Core Data to manage `DataPoint`, it must be a subclass of `NSManagedObject` instead. This is no loss, as `NSManagedObject` is a subclass of `NSObject`.

We've also promised ourselves that we can replace `Regression`'s list of all the `DataPoint`s in the document with one obtained from Core Data. Let's add a method that produces such a list. Also, you see that we've removed the instance variables, x and y. Our managed-object model already specifies that a `DataPoint` has two double-valued attributes of those names; that is enough for `NSManagedObject` to provide storage and persistence for them automatically:

```
@interface DataPoint : NSManagedObject {
}


+ (NSArray *) allDataPointsInContext:
                        (NSManagedObjectContext *) context;
```

The + at the beginning of the method declaration means that `allDataPointsIn-Context:` is a class method, to be sent to the `DataPoint` class itself, not to an instance of `DataPoint`. You must pass the method an instance of `NSManagedObjectContext` to identify the "soup" of objects from which you want to cull the `DataPoint`s. A `MyDocument` object would specify the document's own context, whereas a `Regression` or another `DataPoint` would specify the context it came from.

All DataPoints

The first thing we'd add to `DataPoints.m` is an implementation of `allDataPointsIn-Context:`. This consists of the most basic type of fetch request, one that specifies only an entity type—in this case, type `DataPoint`, which yields every object in the context of that type. The method constructs the request, executes it, and returns the result:

```
+ (NSArray *) allDataPointsInContext:
                        (NSManagedObjectContext *) context
{
    NSError *          error;
    NSArray *          retval;
    NSFetchRequest *   request = [[NSFetchRequest alloc] init];
```

```
[request setEntity:
            [NSEntityDescription entityForName: @"DataPoint"
                        inManagedObjectContext: context]];
    retval = [context executeFetchRequest: request
                                    error: &error];
    return retval;
}
```

Initializers

We look further into `DataPoint.m` and see that the `init` method is no longer needed. It initializes the instance variables to 0. We no longer have instance variables, and we have the managed-object model initialize the equivalent storage to 0 automatically.

What about `initWithX:Y:`, which covered arbitrary initialization? We could put together a substitute initializer, one that called through to `NSManagedObject`'s designated initializer, but first let's check whether this initializer is in fact used. Select **Find → Find in Project . . .** (**command-shift-F**) to search for `initWithX:`. Type the search string in, and select **In Project**—you aren't interested in finding the string in framework headers—**Textual**—you don't need a regular-expression search, and you need more than the definition—**Whole words**, and don't **Ignore case**. Click **Find**.

The list below the search-criterion pane fills with matches, but the only matches are from the definition and declaration of `initWithX:Y:`. You've verified that it isn't used. Out it goes.

Accessors

We now confront the accessor methods: `x`, `setX:`, `y`, and `setY:`. Obviously, our simple methods that front for instance variables are obsolete. Core Data guarantees that the key-value coding methods will always work for object attributes, so if we wanted to access the x attribute of `aPoint`, we might write

```
double    pi = 3.1415926;
// setter:
[aPoint setValue: [NSNumber numberWithDouble: pi]
          forKey: @"x"];
// getter:
pi = [[aPoint valueForKey: @"x"] doubleValue];
```

But this is awkward for us, at least in the getter case, because we make such extensive use of the x accessor in calculations. Because we never call them, we can live without `setX:` and `setY:` but not x and y.

The pattern for accessing attributes in a managed object is to first reserve the attribute by sending the object willAccessValueForKey:, then fetch the attribute by using primitiveValueForKey:, and, finally, relinquish the attribute by sending the object didAccessValueForKey:. The method primitiveValueForKey: simply moves the data without additional housekeeping; it is assumed that you have taken responsibility for that:

```
- (double) x
{
    [self willAccessValueForKey: @"x"];
    NSNumber *  xAsObject = [self primitiveValueForKey: @"x"];
    [self didAccessValueForKey: @"x"];
    return [xAsObject doubleValue];
}

- (double) y
{
    [self willAccessValueForKey: @"y"];
    NSNumber *  yAsObject = [self primitiveValueForKey: @"y"];
    [self didAccessValueForKey: @"y"];
    return [yAsObject doubleValue];
}
```

Delete setX: and setY:. We never called them directly, and Core Data takes care of key/value access to the setters automatically. Also, because Core Data handles storage and retrieval, delete encodeWithCoder: and initWithCoder:.

We also rewrite the asPropertyList method in DataPoint-PropertyList.m to access the x and y values of the DataPoint through the accessors instead of through the no-longer-existing instance variables:

```
- (NSDictionary *) asPropertyList
{
    return [NSDictionary dictionaryWithObjectsAndKeys:
            [NSNumber numberWithDouble: [self x]], @"abscissa",
            [NSNumber numberWithDouble: [self y]], @"ordinate",
            nil];
}
```

15.2.2 Regression

In Regression.h, once again, we must change the superclass from NSObject <NSCoding> to NSManagedObject and remove all the instance variables. True to our theory that it is no longer Regression's business to track DataPoints, remove the declarations of the accessor methods for dataPoints. We'll keep the rest of the accessors, however, because we use them elsewhere in our code.

Turning to Regression.m, examine the init method. It initializes the statistics variables to 0—our managed-object model does that anyway—and allocates the dataPoints array, which is obsolete. The init method does nothing we need, and dealloc serves only to release dataPoints. Delete both methods. The NSCoding methods, initWithCoder: and encodeWithCoder:, are no longer needed. Delete them, as well as the dataPoints accessor methods: dataPoints, setDataPoints:, and countOfDataPoints.

Replace canCompute. Previously, it counted the dataPoints array and returned YES if it had more than one member. Now it can ask the DataPoint class for an array of all DataPoints in the same context as itself and count that:

```
- (BOOL) canCompute
{
    NSArray *  allPoints = [DataPoint allDataPointsInContext:
                                      [self managedObjectContext]];
    return [allPoints count] > 1;
}
```

The accessors for slope, intercept, and correlation no longer front for simple instance variables. We'll have to use primitive accessors guarded with notifiers. Fortunately, you can save a lot of trouble in writing explicit accessors by selecting the attributes of interest in the data model diagram, control-clicking, and selecting **Copy Method Implementations to Clipboard**. None of the methods this command generates are mandatory—Core Data will perform the full range of services for your data without them—but they can be useful. In this case, we need setters and getters but not the validation methods.

Here are the generated getter and setter for slope; the other two pairs are substantially identical:

```
- (double)slope
{
    NSNumber *tmpValue;
```

```
    [self willAccessValueForKey: @"slope"];
    tmpValue = [self primitiveValueForKey: @"slope"];
    [self didAccessValueForKey: @"slope"];

    return (tmpValue!=nil) ? [tmpValue doubleValue] : 0.0;
}

- (void)setSlope:(double)value
{
    [self willChangeValueForKey: @"slope"];
    [self setPrimitiveValue: [NSNumber numberWithDouble: value]
                    forKey: @"slope"];
    [self didChangeValueForKey: @"slope"];
}
```

The asPropertyList method, in Regression-PropertyList.m, needs only one change:

```
- (NSDictionary *) asPropertyList
{
    //  Make an array to hold the property-list version of
    //  the data points.
    NSMutableArray *    pointArray = [NSMutableArray array];
    NSArray *           dataPoints = [DataPoint
            allDataPointsInContext: [self managedObjectContext]];
    NSEnumerator *      iter = [dataPoints objectEnumerator];
        .
        .
        .
```

Now, we redefine our data points set from "the array of DataPoints held by the model Regression," to "all the DataPoints in the current soup." By the same token, we are redefining our model object as "the only Regression object in the soup." This singleton definition has to be implemented by reference to the data store. We can define a new Regression class method that returns the one-and-only Regression object in an NSManagedObjectContext or creates one if there isn't one yet:

```
+ (Regression *) sharedRegressionInContext:
                                (NSManagedObjectContext *) aContext
{
    NSError *           error;
```

```
NSArray *           allRegressions;
NSFetchRequest *    request = [[NSFetchRequest alloc] init];
Regression *        retval = nil;

// Ask for all the Regressions, hoping there's only one
[request setEntity:
    [NSEntityDescription entityForName: @"Regression"
            inManagedObjectContext: aContext]];
allRegressions = [aContext executeFetchRequest: request
                                    error: &error];
[request release];

// Squawk if there is more than one
NSAssert([allRegressions count] <= 1,
        @"Should never be > 1 Regression object");
if ([allRegressions count] < 1) {
    // If there are none, make one
    retval = [NSEntityDescription
                insertNewObjectForEntityForName: @"Regression"
                    inManagedObjectContext: aContext];

    // This isn't a user action; don't allow it to be undone
    [aContext processPendingChanges];
    [[aContext undoManager] removeAllActions];
}
else    // If only one, return it.
    retval = [allRegressions objectAtIndex: 0];

return retval;
}
```

One last thing in Regression.m is the initialize class method. It tells the key-value observing mechanism to signal a change in the canCompute key whenever there is a change to dataPoints. There is no longer a dataPoints; how to replace this functionality? Core Data provides a notification whenever a managed-object context changes. We can make sure that every Regression object will get this notice and signal a possible change in canCompute when the count of DataPoints may have changed. The designated initializer method for NSManagedObject, Regression's new superclass, is `initWithEntity:insertIntoManagedObjectContext:`. We can provide an override that registers each new `Regression` for the notification. We make sure that `dealloc` ends the registration:

```
- (id) initWithEntity: (NSEntityDescription *) entity
insertIntoManagedObjectContext:(NSManagedObjectContext *) context
{
    self = [super initWithEntity: entity
  insertIntoManagedObjectContext: context];
    if (self) {
        [[NSNotificationCenter defaultCenter]
            addObserver: self
              selector: @selector(storeChanged:)
                  name:
              NSManagedObjectContextObjectsDidChangeNotification
                object: context];
    }
    return self;
}

- (void) dealloc
{
    [[NSNotificationCenter defaultCenter] removeObserver: self];
    [super dealloc];
}

- (void) storeChanged: (NSNotification *) notice
{
    NSSet *     inserted = [[notice userInfo]
                              objectForKey: NSInsertedObjectsKey];
    NSSet *     deleted = [[notice userInfo]
                              objectForKey: NSDeletedObjectsKey];

    if ([inserted count] > 0 || [deleted count] > 0) {
        [self willChangeValueForKey: @"canCompute"];
        [self didChangeValueForKey: @"canCompute"];
    }
}
```

The initializer registers `storeChanged:` as the message to send when the managed-object context changes. This message checks for object insertions or deletions and forces the key-value observing mechanism to register any change in the `canCompute` property.

15.2.3 MyDocument

In `MyDocument.h`, change the base class of `MyDocument` from `NSDocument` to `NSPersistentDocument`. This Core Data–supporting `NSDocument` subclass adds many automatic behaviors, including reading and writing the document file and maintaining the in-memory object-model store.

Reading and writing the file are now done by `NSPersistentDocument`, so `dataRepresentationOfType:` and `loadDataRepresentationOfType:` in MyDocument.m, are obsolete. Delete them both.

We have to do something about the `model` instance variable. We want the `model` variable to reflect a `Regression` object loaded from a `.linear` file when opening an existing document, and we want it to be a fresh `Regression` object when creating a new document. It has to point to a proper model after any saved model is loaded but before any data is displayed.

Fortunately, `NSDocument` provides a method that gets called at just the right moment. Cocoa sends a new document `windowControllerWillLoadNib:` after data arrives but before the contents of the document's Nib have been loaded and hooked up. We can use the `sharedRegressionInContext:` method to find an existing `Regression` if it is there or create one if there isn't one. We then use `setValue:forKey:` to set our own `model` instance variable. The use of `setValue:forKey:` is one way of making the change visible to the key-value-observing mechanism on which our user interface bindings depend:

```
- (void)windowControllerWillLoadNib:
                            (NSWindowController *) aController
{
    [super windowControllerWillLoadNib:aController];

    Regression *    myModel =
                [Regression sharedRegressionInContext:
                            [self managedObjectContext]];
    [self setValue: myModel forKey: @"model"];
}
```

Remove the allocation and initialization of model from MyDocument's init method. Keep the release of model in the dealloc method—the setValue:forKey: has the effect of retaining the shared Regression instance for the document.

Two of MyDocument's methods implementing the LinearGraphDelegate informal protocol drew from the Regression model object for a list of all DataPoints. Regression no longer knows about DataPoints. We change the methods so they pull the lists from the data store:

```
#pragma mark LinearGraphDelegate

- (unsigned) countDataPoints
{
    NSArray *   allPoints = [DataPoint allDataPointsInContext:
                                    [self managedObjectContext]];
    return [allPoints count];
}


- (void) dataPointAtIndex: (unsigned) index
                       x: (double *) outX
                       y: (double *) outY
{
    NSArray *   allPoints = [DataPoint allDataPointsInContext:
                                    [self managedObjectContext]];
    DataPoint * item = [allPoints objectAtIndex: index];
    *outX = [item x];
    *outY = [item y];
}
```

Core Data stores objects in one of three formats. Binary format is a fast, compact, serialized format that is not indexed. XML format is bulkier and slower but is readable by humans and other applications without much trouble. It is not indexed. SQL format is best for large collections of objects and for rapid searches. Double-click the **Linear** target icon to open its Get Info window, select its **Properties** tab, and in the Document Types list, switch **Store Type** from **Binary** to **XML**. Just for fun.

15.3 Interface Builder

Our use of the Cocoa Controller-layer classes will remain much the same. But there is a slight modification to make now that we are pulling our point list "out of the soup" and not from a list linked to the MyDocument through a Regression.

As a first step, let MyDocument.nib know about the changes in the MyDocument class, dragging the **MyDocument.h** file onto the Nib's window. Interface Builder will notice that the changes to MyDocument are extensive and ask how you want to handle the discrepancy; choose **Replace**.

In the Nib window for MyDocument.nib, select the **DataPoints** NSArrayController: In the Attributes Inspector (**command-1**), change the **Mode:** of the controller from **Class** to **Entity**, and set the **Entity Name:** to DataPoint. Also, make sure that the **Automatically prepares content** box is checked. Setting this ensures that the controller will perform the initial query to load the content set and will subscribe to notifications of changes in the managed-object context to keep the content current.

In Bindings (**command-4**), unbind the content array by opening the content array item and unchecking the **Bind** box. Bind the managedObjectContext property to **File's Owner / managedObjectContext** to ensure that the **DataPoints** controller will be working from the same data store as the MyDocument that owns this document window. The combination of specifying the DataPoint entity type, specifying the MyDocument managed-object context, and not making any further fetch specification in the first, Attribute pane is exactly analogous to the fetch done in the allDataPointsInContext: class method of DataPoint.

The other two controllers remain the same. The **ModelController** NSObjectController provides access to the slope, intercept, and correlation properties of the model Regression object, just as it did before it became a Core Data–managed object.

The NSTableView is bound to the **DataPoints** controller just the same as before, but there is a trick to using numeric values in the user interface with Core Data. Core Data wants numeric values to come as instances of NSNumber and nothing else. However, the contents of cells in an NSTableColumn are provided as NSStrings *unless* an NSFormatter intervenes to translate the string value to another object type. We need to add NSNumberFormatters to the columns of our point table.

Obtain an NSNumberFormatter, represented by an icon showing a dollar sign pointing into a text field, from the third panel of the object palette—the Cocoa–Text palette—at the bottom-left corner. Drag the formatter into the x column; repeat with the y column. You should see the sample contents of the columns change in response to the drop.

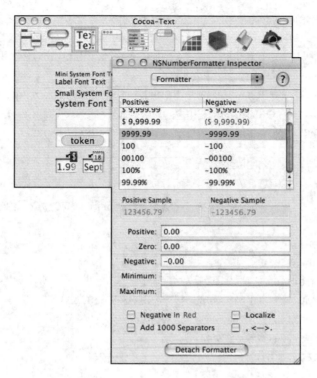

Figure 15.4 Configuring an NSNumberFormatter for an NSTableColumn. When a table column has a formatter associated with it, this panel is added to the pop-up menu at the top of Interface Builder's Inspector window. Add a formatter to a column by dragging one from the Cocoa–Text palette directly to the column. Formatter icons can be seen at the lower-left corner of the palette.

Adding a formatter to the columns adds a panel to the IB Inspector window for those columns. Repeatedly click on the x column until it is selected, pull down the menu at the top of the Inspector window, and select **Formatter**. (See Figure 15.4; the Formatter option does not have a command key equivalent.) The panel will offer a variety of prepared number formats, which you can use as is or as a basis for custom formats of your own.

15.4 Build and Run

Build Linear and run it. It should behave more or less as before. You won't be able to reload any previously saved .linear files, because we've specified an XML file format for this new version of Linear, and previous versions used a binary format produced by NSKeyedArchiver, and even if we chose a binary Core Data format, it would be unlikely to coincide. In general, Core Data data files are not compatible across any changes to the object schema.

Do save a .linear file in the new format, and drag its icon from the Finder onto Xcode's icon in the dock. Xcode will open it in a text editor, and you can verify that the file is, in fact, XML, and in a pretty easily understood format:

```xml
<?xml version="1.0"?>
<!DOCTYPE database SYSTEM
                    "file:///System/Library/DTDs/CoreData.dtd">

<database>
    <databaseInfo>
        <version>134481920</version>
        <UUID>57A8BE18-3D3C-4498-9831-EF62076DB168</UUID>
        <nextObjectID>104</nextObjectID>
        <metadata></metadata>
    </databaseInfo>
    <object type="DATAPOINT" id="102">
        <attribute name="x" type="double">2.05</attribute>
        <attribute name="y" type="double">4</attribute>
    </object>
    <object type="DATAPOINT" id="103">
        <attribute name="x" type="double">1</attribute>
        <attribute name="y" type="double">2.01</attribute>
    </object>
    <object type="REGRESSION" id="104">
        <attribute name="correlation" type="double">
                        0.9999999999999996</attribute>
        <attribute name="intercept" type="double">
                        0.114761904761906</attribute>
        <attribute name="slope" type="double">
                        1.895238095238095</attribute>
    </object>
</database>
```

15.5 Adding an Entity

15.5.1 Adding to the Data Model

Let's do one more thing just to see what Core Data and its associated programming tools can do. Suppose that our `DataPoint` data came from various sources and that it is important to keep track of which points come from which sources. We could imagine a `DataSource` entity, with the properties `title`, `author`, and `date`.

Bring up `LinearData.xcdatamodel`, and click the + button in the entity list at the top left of the data model browser. This creates a new entity, named `Entity`, which we rename `DataSource`. We will not be subclassing `NSManagedObject` for the `DataSource` entity but instead will be adding an entirely new data type with zero code!

With `DataSource` selected in the entities list, click the + button three times in its attributes list. Rename them, respectively, `title`, `author`, and `date`. Hold down the command key and click the attributes to select `title` and `author`; in the editor pane at the right, select the **String** type. Select the `title` attribute, and uncheck the **Optional** property. Select the `date` attribute and make it of type **Date**.

What's new about `DataSource` is that it does have a restrictive relationship with other entities—only certain `DataPoints` are associated with a given `DataSource`. We have to define the relationship between `DataSource` and `DataPoint`. One way to do this is to switch the middle browser to **Show Relationships**, using the drop-down menu at its lower edge, and then clicking the + button; another is to select the line-drawing tool at the bottom of the data model diagram and drag from the DataSource block to the DataPoint block. See Figure 15.5.

Use the drop-down menu at the bottom of the center browser pane, and select **Show Relationships**. Rename newRelationship to reportedData. Make it a to-many

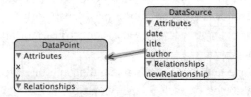

Figure 15.5 Creating a new relationship in the data model. By choosing the line-drawing tool at the bottom edge of the data model diagram and dragging from DataSource to DataPoint, we create a new relationship between the two entity types. Initially, the relationship is named newRelationship, as seen in `DataSource`'s block.

relationship—a single `DataSource` can report more than one `DataPoint`. The arrowhead of the relationship line from DataSource to DataPoint is doubled to reflect the multiplicity. Change the **Delete Rule:** to **Cascade**. (Deleting a source will delete all the associated data points.)

We'll also add an inverse relationship, from DataPoint to DataSource. Draw a line from the DataPoint block to DataSource, or add a relationship to the middle browser while **DataPoint** is selected in the left browser. Name the relationship `source`; let it not be optional; and set its **Inverse:** to **reportedData**.

The inverse relationship for the `DataSource-to-DataPoint` relationship, by the way, is set automatically.

15.5.2 Human Interface

Now that we have an additional data type to manage, we need some way to input and examine it. Open `MyDocument.nib` in Interface Builder. Make the prototype document window roughly double its original height. Place it on the screen so it can be visible at the same time as your data model window.

Bring your data model window, in Xcode, forward. Make sure that the large empty space in the document window in Interface Builder is visible. Hold down the **option** key and drag the DataSource block from the data model diagram to the empty space in the prototype document window.

Switch to Interface Builder, which is now seeking your attention for an alert window. IB asks whether you want to create a user interface for one or many data source objects. Click **Many Objects**. A rough-built list-and-detail interface for `DataSource` appears in the document window. See Figure 15.6.

You'll have to move it out of the way of the rest of the window contents and maybe resize the window further to accommodate the extra content. The link from Xcode to Interface Builder has done all the necessary work for making this human interface work. It has even added an `NSArrayController` for all the `DataSources` in the document's managed-object context.

What can't be done automatically is expanding the interface for `DataPoints` so we can set the `DataSource` of each point. Because we will have to widen the data points list to accommodate an extra column, widen the window and drag the results form to the right. If you enclosed the points list and output form in a split view, you'll find it easier to modify the table if you select the split view and issue the command **Layout → Unpack subviews**. Widen the list—select its surrounding `NSScrollView` and drag its right handle out by about a column's width—then double-click to select

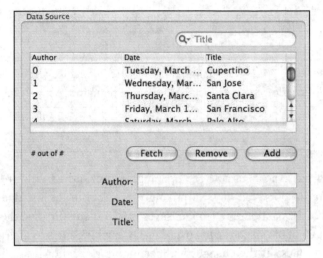

Figure 15.6 The automatically generated UI for DataSource. Option-dragging the DataSource block from the data model window in Xcode to a window being built in Interface Builder produces your choice of a single- or multiple-instance human interface for that entity type. The multiple-instance variant is shown in the bottom half of this window.

the **NSTableView**. In the Attributes Inspector (**command-1**), change the number of columns from two to three. You will probably have to drag the column boundary to make the third column visible.

We're trying to fill the new third column with pop-up lists, from which the user can choose the title of a data source. From the fifth pane of the IB palette (Cocoa–Data), take a pop-up cell—in the cluster at the upper-left corner of the pane—and drop it into the third column of the data point table.

To link the column to the Controller layer, click repeatedly in the header of the third column until the Inspector shows that an **NSTableColumn** is selected. Edit bindings (**command-4**). Make the following bindings:

- **content**: The choices—the things being chosen—should be bound from the **Data Source** NSArrayController → arrangedObjects.

- **contentValues**: The way the choices are displayed in the list. Again, this is taken from the **Data Source** NSArrayController → arrangedObjects → title.

- **selectedObject**: The choice made for this DataPoint. Bind it to the **DataPoint** NSArrayController → arrangedObjects → source.

Table 15.1 Sources for Budget Trend Lines

Author	Date	Title
OMB [Bush 43]	15-Jan-2004	Economic Report of the President
The Great Wizzardo	12-Oct-2003	Predictions

15.5.3 First Run

Build and run the `Linear` target. Try opening an old `.linear` file from a previous Core Data run, if you saved any. Surprisingly, the data in the file does load—it's a proper subset of the data our new model saves in a `.linear` file, and the XML format discloses enough of the structure to ensure that everything goes in the right place. We would not be so lucky if the changes had been more radical or if the file format had been SQL or binary.

This time, we'll create a new file by filling in the blank document `Linear` presents when it opens. Start by adding data sources, such as those in Table 15.1. Click the **Add** button under the data source table, and fill in the data, either in the form below the buttons or directly into the table. When you're finished, the search field is fully functional.

Then add `DataPoints` to the top table as before, using Table 15.2 as a guide. The third column is filled with pop-ups containing the titles of the source documents. Selecting a source assigns a point to the source.

You can graph and regress this data as you could before. Try selecting the Predictions of The Great Wizzardo in the data source table and clicking **Remove** below

Table 15.2 Data for Budget Trend Lines

x	y	Source
2000	472.5	Economic Report of the President
2001	490.0	Economic Report of the President
2002	525.3	Economic Report of the President
2003	530.9	Economic Report of the President
2004	529.0	Predictions
2005	538.0	Predictions

that table. Because the deletion rule for the DataSource-to-DataPoint relationship is **Cascade**, deleting the source also deletes the associated points.

Selecting **Edit** → **Undo** (**command-Z**) restores Wizzardo's place in the public debate. Again: You wrote no code to get Linear to do all this.

15.5.4 One More Table

When examining DataSources, it would be convenient to see what data comes from each source. Looking at the list of all DataPoints and attending only to the items from one source would get unwieldy with a large data set. We'd like another NSTableView, one that displays just the DataPoints belonging to the selected DataSource.

This is solely a job for Interface Builder. Enlarge the prototype document window enough to accommodate a two-column table next to the automatically generated interface for DataSources (Figure 15.7). Drop an **NSTableView** into the space from the Cocoa–Data palette, and adjust it to a reasonable size.

We will need something that gives the table access to the reportedData relationship of the selected DataSource. We already have an NSArrayController named Data Source that monitors the whole "soup" of DataSources, and one of the keys NSArrayController affords is selection—the selected DataSource. Because we're interested in more than one thing, all we need is an NSArrayController that sources from the Data Source NSArrayController, key selection, path reportedData.

From the Cocoa–Controllers palette, drag an NSArrayController into the MyDocument.nib window. Press **Return** to edit the label on the new controller, and name it **DS Points**. In the Attributes Inspector (**command-1**), make sure that the new controller's content type is the *entity* DataPoint and that **Automatically prepares content** is set. In the Bindings Inspector (**command-4**), bind contentSet—because the contents of a relationship form an unordered set, not an array—to Data Source → selection → reportedData.

Don't forget to bind the **DS Points** controller's managedObjectContext to **File's Owner's** managedObjectContext.

Drop NSNumberFormatters onto each column of the table, which you should label x and y, respectively. Bind the value of the first column of the table to DS Points → arrangedObjects → x, and the second to **DS Points** → arrangedObjects → y.

Save the Nib file; then build and run Linear. Reload a multiple-source document, or create one. Now selecting a row in the Data Source table will fill the table to the right with the data points provided by the selected DataSource.

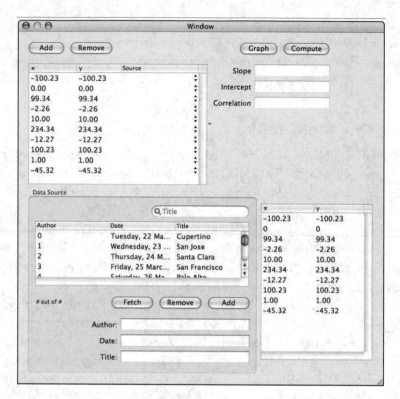

Figure 15.7 The last iteration of Linear's human interface in Interface Builder. This time, we add an `NSTableView` next to the automatically generated browser for `DataSources`. We create an `NSArrayController` linked to the `reportedData` relationship of the selection of the Data Source `NSArrayController`, and bind the x and y values of its `arrangedObjects` to the columns of the table.

15.6 Summary

In this chapter, we used Xcode's data-modeling tool to reverse-engineer Linear's data model and edited that model to produce a managed-object model (`.mom`) file to drive a Core Data–based version of Linear. We saw how to use the modeling tools to set attribute properties, such as default values and whether a property is optional. We saw how Interface Builder supports Core Data development by allowing us to set up object ccontrollers that focus on objects based on simple queries to the managed-object context.

16

Spotlight

Before our excursion into Core Data, there was not much worth sharing about Linear's data files. You may remember that when we laid out the data file type, I skipped the uniform type indicator (UTI) declaration, saying, "Our application . . . will be using a file format that nobody else is expected to read; we can leave [UTI] blank."

The expansion of Linear's data files to encompass data sources has changed this. Think only of the query "every file sourced from the Economic Report of the President," and you can see that Linear data files are now a natural for indexing in the Spotlight metadata system.

16.1 How Data Gets into Spotlight

Metadata is information that isn't necessarily *in* a file but is *about* the file. All file systems maintain modest amounts of metadata, such as file ownership, creation and modification dates, access privileges, and the like. With Mac OS X 10.4, Apple has added to the Macintosh file system a metadata database that can hold large amounts of almost arbitrary metadata in any category a developer chooses.

The `mdls` command line tool shows what metadata is associated with any file or package. Here is what came back when I typed **`mdls Xcode\ book\?.oo3`** to examine the OmniOutliner 3 file package that contains my notes for this book:

```
Xcode book?.oo3 -------------
com_omnigroup_OmniOutliner_CellCount                  = 272
com_omnigroup_OmniOutliner_CheckedItemCount           = 84
com_omnigroup_OmniOutliner_ColumnCount                = 2
com_omnigroup_OmniOutliner_ColumnTitles               = (Topic)
com_omnigroup_OmniOutliner_IndeterminateItemCount     = 15
com_omnigroup_OmniOutliner_ItemCount                  = 279
com_omnigroup_OmniOutliner_MaxItemDepth               = 6
```

```
com_omnigroup_OmniOutliner_NamedStyleCount        = 1
com_omnigroup_OmniOutliner_NamedStyles            = (pathname)
com_omnigroup_OmniOutliner_UncheckedItemCount     = 180
kMDItemAttributeChangeDate          = 2005-05-04 20:40:32 -0500
kMDItemContentCreationDate          = 2004-08-27 09:43:57 -0500
kMDItemContentModificationDate      = 2005-05-02 16:19:37 -0500
kMDItemContentType    = "com.omnigroup.omnioutliner.oo3-package"
kMDItemContentTypeTree              = (
    "com.omnigroup.omnioutliner.oo3-package",
    "public.composite-content",
    "public.content",
    "com.apple.package",
    "public.directory",
    "public.item"
)
kMDItemDisplayName                  = "Xcode book?"
kMDItemFSContentChangeDate          = 2005-05-09 00:24:41 -0500
kMDItemFSCreationDate               = 2004-08-27 09:43:57 -0500
kMDItemFSCreatorCode                = 0
kMDItemFSFinderFlags                = 16
kMDItemFSInvisible                  = 0
kMDItemFSLabel                      = 0
kMDItemFSName                       = "Xcode book?.oo3"
kMDItemFSNodeCount                  = 4
kMDItemFSOwnerGroupID               = 502
kMDItemFSOwnerUserID                = 502
kMDItemFSTypeCode                   = 0
kMDItemID                           = 3545686
kMDItemKind                         = "OmniOutliner 3"
kMDItemLastUsedDate                 = 2005-05-04 20:40:32 -0500
kMDItemTitle                        = ""
kMDItemUsedDates                    = (
    2005-05-02 16:19:37 -0500,
    2005-05-01 19:00:00 -0500,
    2005-05-04 19:00:00 -0500
)
```

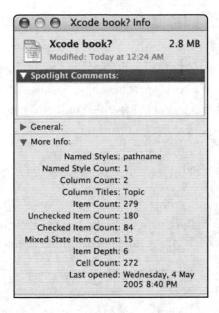

Figure 16.1 The Finder's Get Info window for an OmniOutliner 3 document. Because the Omni Group has provided a metadata importer for OO3 files and published the meanings of its custom metadata tags, applications like the Finder can show useful information about the content of OO3 files without having to understand the file format.

The metadata listing is a roster of tag/value pairs. We can recognize many of these, such as kMDItemFSCreationDate, as carryovers of common file system metadata. The operating system will keep this information current itself. More interesting are the tags that begin with com_omnigroup_OmniOutliner_ at the beginning of the listing. From these, we can see that it's an outline with 279 items: 84 checked, 180 unchecked, and 15 indeterminate. You could get this information by opening the file and doing the counts yourself, but with the metadata and its keys published from OmniOutliner 3, any application, such as the Finder's Get Info window (Figure 16.1), can say something useful about an OmniOutliner file without having to open the file and understand its format.

The final thing to attend to in the metadata listing are the tags kMDItemContentType and kMDItemContentTypeTree. The content type identifies the uniform type identifier (UTI) associated with this document. In this case, the identifier is in reverse domain name style—com.omnigroup.omnioutliner.oo3-package—for a private document type. The type tree identifies other, published UTIs that also describe OO3 outline documents:

- `public.item`, because anything is an item; the root UTI
- `public.directory` and `com.apple.package`, because it's not a single file but a directory and is handled by the Mac OS X Finder as a single-document package
- `public.content`, because the document contains its information rather than refers to it or serves as a flag
- `public.composite-content`, because an outline document may mix text, images, and media

This is live, actionable information for you. If you have the suffix oo3, you can obtain the UTI associated with that suffix and determine that it's a package document type:

```
CFStringRef     uti;
uti = UTTypeCreatePreferredIdentifierForTag(
                          kUTTagClassFilenameExtension,
                          CFSTR("oo3"), NULL);
Boolean         isPackage;
isPackage = UTTypeConformsTo(uti, CFSTR("com.apple.package"));
```

The UTI is the key by which Spotlight selects the importer for a file. A metadata importer is a piece of plug-in code that understands how to extract metadata from a particular type of file and enter it into the Spotlight database. The task of making a Spotlight-friendly application, then, consists of properly setting up UTIs for the application's documents and providing an importer for the metadata.

16.2 Uniform Type Identifiers

Obtaining a UTI for Linear data files is easy—we make it up: `org.manoverboard. linear.sourced`; the data from Linear that has source information in it. UTIs must not contain uppercase letters.

Add the UTI to the document type declaration in the `Info.plist`. This is most easily done by opening the target Info window—double-click the **Linear** icon under **Targets**—and selecting the **Properties** tab. **Linear Data File** should be the only entry in the document type list. Type **org.manoverboard.linear.sourced** into the second column, for the UTI.

This takes care of associating the UTI with Linear data files but does not fully declare the UTI to the system. To do this, you must add an array to the Info.plist with the key UTExportedTypeDeclarations:

```
<?xml version="1.0" encoding="UTF-8"?>
<!DOCTYPE plist PUBLIC "-//Apple Computer//DTD PLIST 1.0//EN"
                "http://www.apple.com/DTDs/PropertyList-1.0.dtd">
<plist version="1.0">
<dict>
    .
    .
    .
    <key>UTExportedTypeDeclarations</key>
    <array>
        <dict>
            <key>UTTypeIdentifier</key>
            <string>org.manoverboard.linear.sourced</string>
            <key>UTTypeReferenceURL</key>
            <string>http://www.manoverboard.org/</string>
            <key>UTTypeDescription</key>
            <string>Linear Data File</string>
            <key>UTTypeConformsTo</key>
            <array>
                <string>public.data</string>
                <string>public.content</string>
                <string>public.item</string>
            </array>
            <key>UTTypeTagSpecification</key>
            <dict>
                <key>com.apple.ostype</key>
                <string>linD</string>
                <key>public.filename-extension</key>
                <array>
                    <string>linear</string>
                </array>
            </dict>
        </dict>
    </array>
</dict>
</plist>
```

The UTExportedTypeDeclarations array contains one dictionary for each type declared. Here, we declare only one, org.manoverboard.linear.sourced. We give a URL for further information about the type and resolve to provide such information some day. The UTTypeDescription is a human-readable name for the type. For type conformance, we look at the system-declared UTIs in the *Uniform Type Identifiers Overview* document in the ADC Reference library and at the header UTCoreTypes.h. The file is necessarily a public.item and definitely a public.content; it's not clear whether a Core Data store qualifies as the "simple" byte stream envisioned for public.data, but we'll take it for contrast to packaged documents.

In fact, we could do more. We're using the XML format for Core Data storage, making the file eligible for classification as public.text and public.xml. If those types were listed and no importer for org.manoverboard.linear.sourced were available, Spotlight would run an XML or text importer whenever a Linear data file is saved. (Spotlight runs only one importer—the one for the most specific type—for each file.) This time through, we'll reserve our option to change the format by not publishing the fact that we're using XML for now.

The UTTypeTagSpecification dictionary tells the system how to identify a file as an org.manoverboard.linear.sourced. We provide the old-style Mac OS creator code linD and the linear suffix.

With this much done, build Linear, and if you have not done so already, save a Linear data file. Switch over to the Terminal application, point it at the directory in which you saved the data file, and tell the Spotlight importer to analyze the data file, with the debugging level set to 1:

```
$cd /Users/xcodeuser
$mdimport -d1 savedFile.linear
2005-05-09 12:38:05.439 mdimport[8807] Import '/Users/xcodeuser/
savedFile.linear' type 'org.manoverboard.linear.sourced'
no mdimporter
$
```

The response from mdimport should show that the saved file was correctly identified as being of the type org.manoverboard.linear.sourced but that no metadata importer plug-in was defined for the type. If instead it told you that the type was a long hashed string beginning with dyn., the sourced UTI is not yet known to the system, and it automatically generated a "dynamic" UTI for the nonce. Recheck your Info.plist file, and make sure that it parses and includes everything we covered.

16.3 The Metadata Plug-In

Xcode provides for metadata importers a project template that takes care of a world of detail you do not want to deal with. As a Core Foundation plug-in, it must supply a universally unique identification (UUID) string identifying the metadata plug-in API with which it complies. It must supply, in three places, a second UUID to uniquely identify itself. It must do certain set-up and tear-down chores and take care of reference counting from its host application. All of this is necessary, but none of it has anything directly to do with passing metadata from a file to Spotlight. The template generates files that do all the housekeeping automatically. Use the template.

Using the template, however, commits us to putting the importer in its own project. We might prefer to have the importer share its project with the main application, but there is no target template for metadata importers. Further, we find that if we try to put the importer project in the same directory as Linear, Xcode offers to overwrite various of the main application's files. We'll have to give the importer its own directory.

16.3.1 MetaLinear Project Files

Let's do it. Create a new project, choosing the template **Standard Apple Plug-ins → Metadata Importer**. Name the project MetaLinear, and put it in a directory of its own. The project comes populated with all the files it will ever need.

- Info.plist and InfoPlist.strings are old friends.
- schema.xml describes any metadata keys, beyond the Apple-defined ones, that we define for our documents.
- schema.strings provides plain-text equivalents for the custom metadata keys, for presentation to the user.
- GetMetadataForFile.c contains the single function we will write to transfer the metadata to Spotlight.
- main.c takes care of all the housekeeping details for the plug-in.

Info.plist

If you haven't written your UTI declaration already, the Info.plist provides a commented-out form for one, with the recommendation that you put the declaration in your application's Info.plist. Under CFBundleDocumentTypes, we see a placeholder, SUPPORTED_UTI_TYPE, for our UTI, org.manoverboard.linear.sourced; make that substitution. For the CFBundleIdentifier, enter something that distinguishes this bundle from all others, including the application bundle; I used org.manoverboard.linear.importer. The rest you can leave alone.

schema.xml

We are supposed to declare custom metadata keys, if any, in schema.xml, which gives rise to the question: What metadata are we going to export? Values for x and y in data tables are numerous and usually undistinctive, making them a poor choice for identifying documents. Characteristics of data sources are a better bet. Let's settle on the authors of the sources, the titles of the sources, and the number of sources.

Wherever possible, we should use existing metadata keys. Proliferating keys would overwhelm users with a huge list of search categories and would make search terms so restrictive as to be useless except for finding documents from the applications that defined those terms. So we search the *Spotlight Metadata Attributes Reference* in the ADC Reference Library for the closest match to what we want to publish.

For the authors of the sources, kMDItemAuthors would not be a good choice, as that plainly is meant for authorship of the file itself. Better is kMDItemContributors, for "entities responsible for making contributions to the content," which looks to be closest. By the same token, kMDItemTitle is a document title; kMDItemWhereFroms is a stretch but fits.

There is nothing close to a count-of-sources attribute. For this, we'll have to define a custom key, which by convention uses reverse-domain name formatting for uniqueness: org_manoverboard_Linear_SourceCount. Now that we know what we want, we can turn to schema.xml.

The schema.xml provided by the project template includes helpful instructions in the form of <note> elements, which you should eventually delete, and three instances of the placeholder com_Foo_YourAttrName. Replace the placeholders with org_manoverboard_Linear_SourceCount.

- In the first instance, the <attribute/> tag, you are declaring the attribute key to the system. The name attribute is the name of the key; the multivalued attribute is false in this case, because the count of sources is a single value and not an array; and `type` is the Core Foundation primitive type of the attribute, in this case `CFNumber`. Attributes can be only `CFString`, `CFNumber`, `CFBoolean`, or `CFDate` or `CFArrays` (`multivalued = true`) of these.

- The second instance is the `<allattrs>` element lists, one per line: all the custom attributes this importer transfers into Spotlight.

- The third instance is the `<displayattrs>` tag lists, one per line: all the custom attributes that will be shown in public displays of the document, as, for instance, in the Finder's Get Info window.

When you have edited the `schema.xml` file and saved it, open the Terminal application, set the working directory to the MetaLinear project directory, and test the schema with the `mdcheckschema` command:

```
$ cd Projects/Metalinear
$ mdcheckschema schema.xml
schema.xml : successfully parsed.
$
```

schema.strings

The `schema.strings` file governs how your custom metadata key is presented in the user interface—in the label in the Get Info window or the explanation in the list of searchable attributes. For each custom key, the short name is assigned in the form `"key" = "short name";`. The brief documentation is assigned in the form `"key.Description" = "brief documentation";`.

The relevant lines in `schema.strings`, rewrapped to fit this page, should be:

```
"org_manoverboard_Linear_SourceCount" = "Source count";
"org_manoverboard_Linear_SourceCount.Description"
               = "How many sources are cited in the document";
```

GetMetadataForFile.c

There remains nothing to write but the importer itself. The project template provides us with this shell of the import function:

```
Boolean GetMetadataForFile(void* thisInterface,
            CFMutableDictionaryRef attributes,
            CFStringRef contentTypeUTI,
            CFStringRef pathToFile)
```

```
{
      /* Pull any available metadata from the file at the
         specified path */
      /* Return the attribute keys and attribute values
         in the dict */
      /* Return TRUE if successful, FALSE if there was no
         data provided */

      #warning To complete your importer please implement the
               function GetMetadataForFile in GetMetadataForFile.c
      return FALSE;
}
```

We will be summarizing a Core Data–generated file and adding the summary to the attributes dictionary passed into the function. To do this with Core Data, we'll have to add Cocoa to the project, add our object model, initialize an NSManagedObjectModel with that, from there get an NSPersistentStoreCoordinator, create an NSManagedObjectContext, and point it at the NSPersistentStoreCoordinator.

This is beginning to look a little heavyweight. Metadata importers are not supposed to be heavyweight; they are run in the background, in stolen cycles. They are supposed to be quick and undemanding of memory. Initializing the whole Core Data stack for two short string lists and a number seems like overkill.

Anticipating just this quandary, Apple has provided API for Core Data applications to attach metadata to Core Data files. The originating application, which has the Core Data stack open anyway, does the extraction, and all the importer has to do is pick up the metadata and pass it on.

So we will need Core Data and Objective-C but not as much of it. Add the Cocoa framework to the project (**Project** → **Add to Project . . .**, and find Cocoa.framework in /System/Library/Frameworks). Option-click **GetMetadataForFile.c** in the Groups & Files list so you can change its suffix from c to m.

The function then becomes:

```
Boolean GetMetadataForFile(void* thisInterface,
             CFMutableDictionaryRef attributes,
             CFStringRef contentTypeUTI,
             CFStringRef pathToFile)
{
    // Turn the path to a URL
    NSURL *          url = [NSURL fileURLWithPath:
```

```
                                    (NSString *) pathToFile];
// Get the prepared metadata from the file
NSDictionary * metadata = [NSPersistentStoreCoordinator
                    metadataForPersistentStoreWithURL: url
                                        error: NULL];


if (metadata) {
    // If there was metadata, add it to the set given.
    [(NSMutableDictionary *) attributes
                    addEntriesFromDictionary: metadata];
    return YES;
}
else
    return NO;
}
```

The importer plug-in is now complete. Build it to make sure that everything is correct. If we were shipping the importer as a stand-alone product, we'd now install it in /Library/Spotlight, and we'd probably also uncomment the UTI declaration in its Info.plist. With an importer for the Linear data file UTI in the well-known place, even users without Linear would be able to search for Linear documents by source and see in Finder Info windows the number and titles of the sources. See Figure 16.2.

Figure 16.2 The Finder Get Info window for a Linear data file, showing the source count, which was declared in the displayattrs list of schema.xml, and the source titles.

16.3.2 Packaging the Plug-In

Our importer is not to be a stand-alone product but will be packaged as part of the Linear application. We should modify the build process for the application to make sure that the importer is included in the proper place.

Add the importer project to the Linear project. There is no need to add it to any target; we simply need to be able to refer to it and its product, the plug-in, in the next couple of steps.

The importer is part of the Linear product: Importers are typically delivered inside application packages in the `Contents/Library/Spotlight` directory. The importer, therefore, should be a dependency of Linear. This can work only if the two projects share a build directory. In the Groups & Files list of the importer project, double-click the top project directory; in the **General** panel, select **Place Build Products In: Custom location**, and click the **Choose...** button. Navigate to Linear's build directory, and select it.

A Copy Files build phase completes the packaging. With the Linear application the selected target, select **Project → New Build Phase → New Copy Files Build Phase**. For the new build phase, set the destination path to `Contents/Library/Spotlight` in the **Wrapper** destination. The build phase knows where to copy; now to tell it what. Find the importer project in the Groups & Files list, and open the disclosure triangle next to it to make the importer visible. Drag the importer icon to the new Copy Files build phase.

16.4 Core Data and Metadata

Core Data's ability to attach metadata to a file in an easily accessed packet made the writing of the importer very simple but shifted the responsibility for generating the metadata to Linear itself. The code shown here for attaching metadata to a Core Data persistent-store file is derived from the code provided in Apple's tutorial on `NSPersistentDocuments`.

In the life of an `NSPersistentDocument`, there are two moments at which metadata should be patched: when the persistent store, the file, is created and when the persistent store is saved. The bottlenecks are at the end of `configurePersistentStoreCoordinatorForURL:ofType:error:` and at the beginning of `writeToURL:ofType:forSaveOperation:originalContentsURL:error:`. In the first case, Apple seems to recommend checking the persistent store to see whether one's meta-

data has already been added. It isn't clear why this is so, but the code here follows
suit.

Both cases lead to a common method, setMetaDataForStoreAtURL:, which
searches the doument's Core Data store and uses the NSPersistentStoreCoordinator method setMetaData:forPersistentStore: to pack the metadata away in the
file:

```
@implementation MyDocument
  .
  .
  .
- (NSArray *) fetchUniqueColumn: (NSString *) columnName
                    ofEntity: (NSString *) entityName
{
    // Given a named property for a named entity, return an
    // array of the unique values for that property among all
    // instances of the entity in this document.

    // Get all instances of the entity.
    NSManagedObjectContext *  moc = [self managedObjectContext];
    NSFetchRequest *        fetch = [[NSFetchRequest alloc] init];
    [fetch setEntity: [NSEntityDescription entityForName:
                                            entityName
                       inManagedObjectContext: moc]];

    NSError *          anError;
    NSArray *          objects = [moc executeFetchRequest: fetch
                                        error: &anError];
    [fetch release];
    // Return nil if there are none; otherwise iterate over
    // the result.
    if (objects) {
        // Accumulating the properties into a set will suppress
        // duplicate values.
        NSMutableSet *      accum =
                [NSMutableSet setWithCapacity: [objects count]];
        NSEnumerator *     iter = [objects objectEnumerator];
        NSManagedObject *  curr;
```

```
        while (curr = [iter nextObject]) {
            [accum addObject: [curr valueForKey: columnName]];
        }

        // Return the set, converted to an array.
        return [accum allObjects];
    }
    else
        return nil;
}

- (BOOL) setMetadataForStoreAtURL: (NSURL *) aUrl
{
    NSManagedObjectContext *        moc =
                                [self managedObjectContext];
    NSPersistentStoreCoordinator *  sc =
                                [moc persistentStoreCoordinator];
    id                              store =
                                [sc persistentStoreForURL: aUrl];
    if (store) {
        // Start with existing metadata.
        NSMutableDictionary *   metadata =
            [[sc metadataForPersistentStore: store] mutableCopy];

        // Get author list and save as contributors.
        NSArray *               dataList;
        dataList = [self fetchUniqueColumn: @"author"
                            ofEntity: @"DataSource"];
        if (dataList)
            [metadata setObject: dataList
                    forKey: (NSString *) kMDItemContributors];

        // Get title list and save as where-froms.
        dataList = [self fetchUniqueColumn: @"title"
                            ofEntity: @"DataSource"];
        if (dataList)
            [metadata setObject: dataList
```

```
                          forKey: (NSString *) kMDItemWhereFroms];

        // Set Linear as the creator of the document.
        [metadata setObject: @"Linear"
                    forKey: (NSString *) kMDItemCreator];

        // Count the titles and save as source count.
        [metadata setObject: [NSNumber numberWithInt:
                                            [dataList count]]
                    forKey:
                        @"org_manoverboard_Linear_SourceCount"];
        // Set the file's metadata to the updated dictionary.
        [sc setMetadata: metadata forPersistentStore: store];
        return YES;
    }

    return NO;
}


- (BOOL) configurePersistentStoreCoordinatorForURL:
                                    (NSURL *) aURL
                         ofType: (NSString *) aType
                         error: (NSError **) anError
{
    // New persistent store. First do default setup.
    BOOL    retval =
        [super configurePersistentStoreCoordinatorForURL: aURL
                                    ofType: aType
                                    error: anError];

    if (retval) {
        // Verify that our metadata (e.g. source count) is not
        // already present, and then add our data to store.
        NSManagedObjectContext *      moc =
                                [self managedObjectContext];
        NSPersistentStoreCoordinator *  sc =
                        [moc persistentStoreCoordinator];
```

```
        id              store = [sc persistentStoreForURL: aURL];
        NSDictionary *  prevMetadata =
                        [sc metadataForPersistentStore: store];
        if (! [prevMetadata valueForKey:
                        @"org_manoverboard_Linear_SourceCount"])
            retval = [self setMetadataForStoreAtURL: aURL];
    }

    return retval;
}


- (BOOL) writeToURL: (NSURL *) destURL
             ofType: (NSString *) fileType
    forSaveOperation: (NSSaveOperationType) saveOperation
originalContentsURL: (NSURL *) originalURL
              error: (NSError **) anError
{
    // Existing persistent store. Update the store's metadata.
    if ([self fileURL])
        [self setMetadataForStoreAtURL: [self fileURL]];

    // Continue with the default behavior.
    return [super writeToURL: destURL
                      ofType: fileType
            forSaveOperation: saveOperation
         originalContentsURL: originalURL
                       error: anError];
}
   .
   .
   .
@end
```

16.5 The Proof of the Pudding

The first step in proving that a metadata importer works is determining whether Spotlight knows that the plug-in exists. You can get a listing of all the importers Spotlight knows about by passing the -L flag to the mdimport tool:

```
$ mdimport -L
2005-05-11 11:23:28.413 mdimport[732] Paths: id(502) (
    "/System/Library/Spotlight/Image.mdimporter",
    "/System/Library/Spotlight/Audio.mdimporter",
    "/System/Library/Spotlight/Font.mdimporter",
    .
    .
    .
    "/Users/xcodeuser/Projects/Linear/Linear.app/Contents/
              Library/Spotlight/MetaLinear.mdimporter",
    "/Library/Spotlight/Microsoft Office.mdimporter",
    "/System/Library/Spotlight/iPhoto.mdimporter",
    .
    .
    .
    "/System/Library/Spotlight/iCal.mdimporter"
)
$
```

(The output is wrapped to fit this page.)

We find `MetaLinear.mdimporter`, nestled in the contents of the Linear application, among the other importers registered with Spotlight. If MetaLinear does not show up for you, first try running Linear. If that does not fix it, verify that the `schema.xml` and `Info.plist` files are correct. Also, be certain that MetaLinear installs at `Contents/Library/Spotlight` in the `Linear.app` bundle; it's easy to treat it as a simple resource and load it into `Contents/Resources` instead.

The next step is to run Linear, with its new metadata-exporting code. At the very least, you should put breakpoints at the two bottleneck methods in order to assure yourself that you understand what they are doing and that the correct values are being added to the metadata dictionary. You will also generate a file or two to be entered in the Spotlight database.

It's trickier to watch the import in progress. Metadata importing is in the hands of a system daemon, running in the background on its own schedule. What you can do is use the `mdimport` tool to force an application of the indexing mechanism to a file. The `-d` flag governs how much debugging output the tool produces. Point your Terminal application session at the directory in which you saved the metadata-enabled files, and run `mdimport`:

```
$ cd
$ mdimport -d 3 Scattered.linear
```

```
2005-05-11 11:45:34.541 mdimport[736] Attributes of file
            '/Users/xcodeuser/Scattered.linear' before import: {
    "_kMDItemImporterCrashed" = <null>;
    "com_apple_metadata_modtime" = 137015745;
    kMDItemContentCreationDate = 2005-05-05 14:55:45 -0500;
    kMDItemContentModificationDate = 2005-05-05 14:55:45 -0500;
    kMDItemContentType = "org.manoverboard.linear.sourced";
    kMDItemContentTypeTree = (
        "org.manoverboard.linear.sourced",
        "public.data",
        "public.item",
        "public.content"
    );
    kMDItemDisplayName = {"" = Scattered; };
    kMDItemKind = {"" = "Linear Data File"; };
}
2005-05-11 11:45:34.542 mdimport[736] Import
                        '/Users/xcodeuser/Scattered.linear'
    type 'org.manoverboard.linear.sourced'
    using 'file://localhost/Users/xcodeuser/Projects/
                        Linear/Linear.app/Contents/Library/
                        Spotlight/MetaLinear.mdimporter/'
2005-05-11 11:45:34.596 mdimport[736] Sending attributes of
    '/Users/xcodeuser/Scattered.linear' to server.  Attributes: '{
    NSStoreType = XML;
    NSStoreUUID = "37BC8A89-8964-4D89-BE59-59C19DC41F47";
    "_kMDItemImporterCrashed" = <null>;
    "com_apple_metadata_modtime" = 137015745;
    kMDItemContentCreationDate = 2005-05-05 14:55:45 -0500;
    kMDItemContentModificationDate = 2005-05-05 14:55:45 -0500;
    kMDItemContentType = "org.manoverboard.linear.sourced";
    kMDItemContentTypeTree = (
        "org.manoverboard.linear.sourced",
        "public.data",
        "public.item",
        "public.content"
    );
```

```
    kMDItemContributors = ("OMB [Bush 43]","The Great Wizzardo");
    kMDItemCreator = Linear;
    kMDItemDisplayName = {"" = Scattered; };
    kMDItemKind = {"" = "Linear Data File"; };
    kMDItemWhereFroms = ("Economic Report of the President",
                                              Predictions); _
    "org_manoverboard_Linear_SourceCount" = 2;
}'
$
```

There are four debug levels. Level 4 adds a listing of all the importers the system loads and considers; at level 3, we learn the following.

- The system identifies `Scattered.linear` with the UTI `org.manoverboard.linear.sourced`, as we intend. This comes from Linear's `Info.plist`.

- Before the importer is run, the file starts with a handful of attributes, derived from the file and type systems.

- The system identifies the UTI `org.manoverboard.linear.sourced` with `Meta-Linear.mdimporter`. If it didn't, we'd know that something was wrong with MetaLinear's `Info.plist`.

- Running our importer did not add a diagnostic to the `_kMDItemImporterCrashed` key.

- Running our importer did add all the metadata attributes and values we expected. If it hadn't, we'd be in for a tricky bit of debugging.

Because of the environment in which it runs, debugging a Spotlight importer is a matter of carefully auditing the source files and placing statements that will print status messages to the system console.

16.6 Summary

This chapter took us through the building of a project that was separate from, but coordinate to, our main project. We reviewed how to add the product of such a project as a dependent target of our main project and saw how to route the plug-in to its proper place in the application package. With considerable help from Apple's project template, we saw what was involved in writing a standard CFBundle plug-in. We also added Spotlight visibility to our application, which is a good thing in itself.

Finishing Touches

17.1 Trimming the Menus

When we created the Linear project, the `MainMenu.nib` we got was generic for a document-based application. Most of the contents of the menu bar in that Nib do apply to Linear, but a few items will never be used, and a handful still refer to NewApplication. Now that we've settled on a final feature set, we can edit the menu bar to reflect what Linear does.

Double-click **MainMenu.nib** in either the Groups & Files list or the Finder. When the file opens, double-click the **MainMenu** icon in the Nib window to make sure that the prototype menu bar is visible.

- The **Application** menu is named **NewApplication** in the Nib. If you've been observant, you've seen that when Linear is running, this menu is named **Linear**. That's because Cocoa substitutes the localized `CFBundleName` from an application's `Info.plist` as the title of the application menu. So even though it doesn't change anything, double-click the menu title and change it to **Linear**.

  Three items in the application menu use the dummy name **NewApplication**: **About**, **Hide**, and **Quit**. (All three are handled automatically by `NSApplication`, by the way.) Edit each so that **NewApplication** becomes **Linear**. We don't have a Preferences panel, so delete the **Preferences...** item and one of the gray-line separator items to either side of it.

- In the **File** menu, `NSApplication`, `NSDocument`, and `NSPersistentDocument` handle almost every item. Alas, Linear doesn't print. Delete the last three items (**Print...**, **Page Setup...**, and the separator above them).

- In the **Edit** menu, to the extent that we use text fields, we support **Cut**, **Copy**, **Paste**, **Delete**, and **Select All**. Switching to Core Data gave us **Undo/Redo** support. Linear doesn't support finding text or checking spelling, however, so once again, delete the last three items in this menu.

- The **Window** menu is managed, and filled, automatically by Cocoa. No changes are needed.

- The **Help** menu can be deleted, as we don't have a help system.

Save `MainMenu.nib` and quit Interface Builder.

17.2 Avoiding Singularity

Linear does not check for having all data points the same. Having all-identical data points amounts to having only one, and a single point does not define a line. A well-behaved program should prevent this from happening and give notice of the condition rather than permit an undefined computation, which results in dividing 0 by 0.

`MyDocument` has an abstraction for getting at all the points in the document and access to a window to which to attach an alert sheet. It is the obvious place to put a check for a singular data set. We'd add a method, `pointsAllTheSame`, to detect the problem condition and change the `compute:` action method so that it puts up the alert sheet if the condition is detected:

```
- (BOOL) pointsAllTheSame
{
    double    x, y, x0, y0;
    unsigned  count = [self countDataPoints], i;

    if (count <= 1)
        return YES;

    [self dataPointAtIndex: 0 x: &x0 y: &y0];
    for (i = 1; i < count; i++) {
        [self dataPointAtIndex: i x: &x y: &y];
        if (x != x0 || y != y0)
            return NO;
    }
    return YES;
}

- (IBAction) compute: (id) sender
{
```

```
if ([self pointsAllTheSame]) {
    NSAlert *        alert = [[NSAlert alloc] init];
    [alert setMessageText: @"No distinct points"];
    [alert setInformativeText: @"There must be at least two "
                               @"distinct data points for a "
                               @"regression to be possible."];
    [alert addButtonWithTitle: @"OK"];
    [alert beginSheetModalForWindow: [self windowForSheet]
                      modalDelegate: nil
                     didEndSelector: NULL
                        contextInfo: NULL];
    [alert autorelease];
}
else {
    [statEngine refreshData];
    [model setSlope: [statEngine slope]];
    [model setIntercept: [statEngine intercept]];
    [model setCorrelation: [statEngine correlation]];
}
}
```

Now run Linear and enter a data set consisting of two or more points, all identical. Because there are at least two points, the **Compute** button activates but brings up the alert sheet, as seen in Figure 17.1.

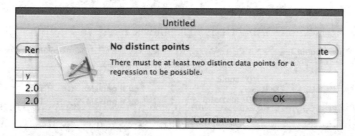

Figure 17.1 The no-distinct-points alert as it appears in Linear. The string set in the NSAlert instance method setMessageText: appears in boldface on the top line of the alert, and the rest of the text is supplied by the string passed to setInformativeText:.

17.3 Localization

We're pretty satisfied with Linear, but having it available in French would really make it perfect. Users of Mac OS X specify what languages they understand by setting a list of available languages in order of preference in the **Language** tab of the International panel of the System Preferences application. When a user's list sets French at a higher priority than English, we'd like Linear to present menus, alerts, and labels in the French language.

When they search for application resources, the `NSBundle` and `CFBundle` facilities first search the subdirectories of the application bundle's `Resources` directory, in the order of the user's preferences for language. Language subdirectories are given such names as `English.lproj`, `fr.lproj` or `en_GB.lproj`; plain-text language names are now deprecated, and it's preferred that you use ISO-standard language abbreviations, optionally suffixed with a code to identify a regional variant.

If we look in the Finder, we see that an `English.lproj` directory is associated with Linear and contains `Credits.rtf`, `InfoPlist.strings`, `MainMenu.nib`, and `My-Document.nib`, as well as Interface Builder's backup copies of Nibs.

Reviewing those files in Xcode's Groups & Files list, under the **Resources** group, we see that every file that appears in the `English.lproj` directory has a disclosure triangle next to it. Opening the disclosure triangle reveals the localized versions—in every case so far, English.

17.3.1 `Credits.rtf`

We haven't looked at `Credits.rtf` before. If a file by that name is available in `Resources` or a localized subdirectory, its contents will be displayed in a scrollable view in the application's About box. The file is filled with silly credits that are obviously intended to be replaced. We will not replace them but instead make them French.

Control-click the **Credits.rtf** line of the Groups & Files list and select Get Info from the menu that pops up. (Or, select the line and click the **Info** button in the toolbar, or press **command-I**.) The **General** tab for localized group **Credits.rtf** contains a list of localizations, with one item, English. Click the **Add Localization** button. A sheet will slide down, asking for a name for the localization, and the combo box for the name will include **French** in its choices, but enter **fr** instead. Click **Add**, and **fr** now appears in the list.

Go to the Finder and see what happened: A new directory, fr.lproj, has been added to the Linear project directory and includes a Credits.rtf file. Returning to Xcode and opening the disclosure triangle next to **Credits.rtf**, we see that the group now contains both **English** and **fr** and that both versions seem to be identical. The credits file becomes

Les ingénieurs: Certains gens

Conception d'interface humaine: D'autres gens

Test: On espère que ce n'est pas personne

Documentation: N'importe qui

Nous remercions particulièrement: Maman

17.3.2 MainMenu.nib

Select what we now know is the localized group for MainMenu.nib, and open the Info window for it. Click **Add Localization**, and enter **fr**. Once again, the English version of MainMenu.nib is copied into fr.lproj, and both versions appear under the **MainMenu.nib** group in Groups & Files.

To open it in Interface Builder, double-click the **fr** localization of **MainMenu.nib**. The goal is to translate every menu title and item into French. At this point, we have to decide what name Linear should have in French. We'll go with Linéaire. We proceed to edit the menus, using the terms found in Table 17.1.

17.3.3 MyDocument.nib

Using the same technique as before, make a fr-localized copy of MyDocument.nib, and open that copy with Interface Builder. Use the glossary in Table 17.2 to translate the items. The buttons and the form, you will notice, are made a little bit wider by the changes in the text; you'll have to adjust their placement to bring them back into Aqua standards. Localization can often make Nib elements much larger than they were in English, which is why there isn't any good way to automate the translation of Nibs.

One thing that might catch you in the translation of the Nib: The label text below and to the left of the Data Source table contains the dummy string "# out of #," but that isn't how the label will be filled when Linear runs. If you look at the bindings for the label (**command-4**), you will see that the label is bound to two values—the count of the selection and the count of all DataSources—formatted by the string %{value1}@ out of %{value2}@. It is here that you'll have to translate *out of* into *de*.

Table 17.1 Translation of Menu Titles and Items

English	French
Linear	Linéaire
About Linear	À propos de Linéaire
Services	Services
Hide Linear	Masquer Linéaire
Hide Others	Masquer les autres
Show All	Tout afficher
Quit Linear	Quitter Linéaire
File	Fichier
New	Nouveau
Open . . .	Ouvrir . . .
Open Recent	Ouvrir récent
Close	Fermer
Save	Enregistrer
Save As . . .	Enregistrer sous . . .
Save As PList . . .	Enregistrer sous format plist . . .
Revert	Revenir
Edit	Édition
Undo	Annuler
Redo	Rétablir
Cut	Couper
Copy	Copier
Paste	Coller
Delete	Supprimer
Select All	Tout sélectionner
Window	Fenêtre
Zoom	Réduire/agrandir
Minimize	Masquer
Bring All to Front	Mettre tous au premier plan

Table 17.2 French Equivalents for Linear's Document Display

English	French
# out of #	# de #
Add	Ajouter
All	Tous
Author	Auteur
Compute	Calculer
Correlation	Corrélation
Data Source	Source des données
Date	Date
Fetch	Chercher
Graph	Tracer
Intercept	Interception
Remove	Enlever
Slope	Pente
Source	Source
Title	Titre
Window	Fenêtre

Another trap lies in the `NSSearchField` in the upper-right corner of the Data Source (Source des données) box. It has placeholder text to be translated in its General (**command-1**) settings and a pop-up menu that describes what fields it filters on. The internal names of these fields don't change, of course, but the names displayed in the menu should be translated. Inspect the bindings (**command-4**) for the field, and translate the display name for each of the predicate bindings.

Save and close `MyDocument.nib`.

17.3.4 `GraphWindow.nib`

GraphWindow.nib, the next item in the **Resources** group, doesn't have any localized variants. Left as it is, it would be built directly into the application bundle's **Resources** directory, and that one file would be used regardless of the user's locale. Do we need to localize it? Yes: It has a title, Graph, or Trace in French, so in the Groups & Files list, select the **Nib** file, open its Info window (**command-I**), and click the button **Make File Localizable**.

This turns **GraphWindow.nib** in the Groups & Files list into a localized group, with the single English localization. In the Info window for the group, click **Add Localization**, and, as before, add `fr`.

Open the **fr**-localized **GraphWindow.nib**, select the window, and in its Attributes Inspector (**command-1**), change the title from Graph to Trace. Save and close the Nib.

17.3.5 InfoPlist.strings

The next item in the **Resources** group is **Info.plist**, but it is unique in that there is only one per bundle. If you want to localize strings in an `Info.plist`, you do so by editing the `InfoPlist.strings` file in the appropriate `.lproj` directory. So what we want to do is localize and extend the `InfoPlist.strings` file. Select it and add a **fr** localization. Select the **fr**-localized variant in the Groups & Files list.

Because a `.strings` file is a text file, the contents appear in the editor portion of the project window, if you have it open. You can edit the file directly in Xcode. The file consists of a list of *key* = *value* pairs, where the keys are in the `Info.plist` file, and the values are localized string values for those keys. Only certain keys are localizable; check Section 10.4 or Apple's documentation for which.

Here's the English version of `InfoPlist.strings`:

```
/* Localized versions of Info.plist keys */

CFBundleName = "Linear";
NSHumanReadableCopyright = "© Myself 2005. All rights reserved.";
```

And here's the translation:

```
/* Localized versions of Info.plist keys */

CFBundleName = "Linéaire";
NSHumanReadableCopyright = "© Moi 2005. Tous droits réservés.";
```

> In `.strings` files accented characters pose no problem, because they are supposed to be encoded in UTF-16 Unicode. By contrast, program source code is not guaranteed to be correct if it strays from 7-bit ASCII.

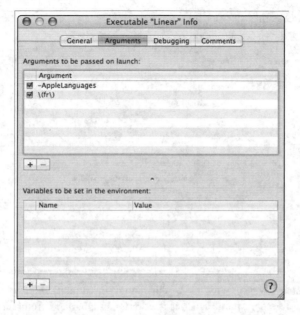

Figure 17.2 Passing an **AppleLanguages** preference list specially to Linear. Open the Info window for the Linear executable, and select the **Parameters** tab. Click the + button twice to add two parameters, and make the first **-AppleLanguages** and the second **\(fr\)**. (The parentheses must be escaped.)

17.3.6 Trying It Out

The obvious way to test all this localization is to shuffle your language preferences in the System Preferences application, launch Linear, and see whether it has become Linéaire. This would, however, also make any other application you launch use its French localization until you switch the preference back. This is inconvenient unless, of course, you prefer to work in French.

A command line option is available to change your language preference only for the application being launched. To the command that launches the application, simply append the flag -AppleLanguages and the value: in this case, (fr).

To accomplish this within Xcode, open the **Executables** group in the Groups & Files list, and select **Linear**. (Double-clicking it will run it.) Instead, bring up its Info window (**command-I**), and select the **Arguments** tab. Add two items to the upper list of arguments. Make the first **-AppleLanguages** and the second **\(fr\)**. (The parentheses have to be guarded with backslashes to protect them from being interpreted by the shell during handling.) See Figure 17.2.

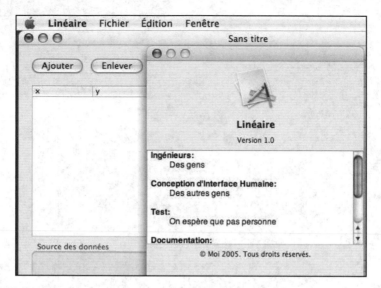

Figure 17.3 Linear working in French. The menus, document window, and About box of Linear all display in French when French is the dominant language preference.

We are rewarded by an application that presents its human interface in the French language, as in Figure 17.3. There is, however, one problem: If we present the application with a data set consisting of two or more identical points, the alert sheet we see is still in English.

17.3.7 Localizable.strings

A bundle, including an application bundle, can have one or more .strings files of its own. In Cocoa, the NSBundle method localizedStringForKey:value:table: returns the string from the named .strings table for the best current locale for a given key. The value: parameter is a default in case no value is found in a .strings file.

Most commonly, the localizedStringForKey:value:table: method is wrapped in one of a family of macros. These macros have two advantages. First, they provide convenient defaults for the bundle—the application main bundle—and the table file (Localizable.strings). Second, the genstrings command line utility can scan source code for these macros and generate .strings files automatically.

The simplest of these is NSLocalizedString, which takes a key string to identify the string and a comment string to clarify, in a comment in the .strings file, the purpose of the string. We can edit compute: to use NSLocalizedString:

```
if ([self pointsAllTheSame]) {
    NSAlert *       alert = [[NSAlert alloc] init];
    [alert setMessageText:
        NSLocalizedString(@"No distinct points",
                          @"Alert message for singularity")
        ];
    [alert setInformativeText:
        NSLocalizedString(@"There must be at least two "
                          @"distinct data points for a "
                          @"regression to be possible.",
                          @"Alert detail for singularity")
        ];
    [alert addButtonWithTitle:
        NSLocalizedString(@"OK",
                          @"Singularity alert dismissal")
        ];
```

We can then fire up the Terminal application, point the command line at the Linear project directory, and have genstrings produce a Localizable.strings file, working from MyDocument.m:

```
$cd ~/Projects/Linear
$genstrings MyDocument.m
```

Listing the Linear directory shows that a Localizable.strings file is now there. Go back to Xcode, and select **Project → Add to Project ...** (**command-option-A**). Browse for the new Localizable.strings file, and add it to the project.

Be careful! The added-file sheet that appears next will offer to interpret the text encoding of the new file as MacRoman, an 8-bit encoding. *This is not what you want.* Remember that .strings files are encoded as 16-bit UTF-16 Unicode. Select **UTF-16** from the encoding pop-up before accepting the file.

If by accident you accepted the file in an 8- or 7-bit encoding, Xcode will show most of its contents as characters interspersed with gray inverted question marks, signifying the zero bytes that lead UTF-16 characters coinciding with the ASCII character set. All is not lost. Select the problem file in the Groups & Files list, open the Info window on it, and select **Unicode (UTF-16)** from the **File Encoding:** pop-up. An alert will ask whether you mean to convert the file to UTF-16 or to reinterpret the file as UTF-16. Choose **Reinterpret**, and you're back in business.

For the sake of neatness, move **Localizable.strings** to the **Resources** group in Groups & Files. Now, as so many times before, open an Info window on **Localizable.strings**, make it localizable, and add a **fr** localization. This gives you a copy of Localizable.strings in the fr.lproj directory, ready to receive our translations (line-broken here in the interest of space):

```
/* Alert message for singularity */
"No distinct points" = "Les points ne sont pas distincts";

/* Singularity alert dismissal */
"OK" = "OK";

/* Alert detail for singularity */
"There must be at least two distinct data points
for a regression to be possible." = "Il doit y avoir au moins
deux points distincts pour qu'une régression soit possible.";
```

Apple makes AppleGlot glossaries for much of its software available at http://developer.apple.com/intl/localization. These glossaries provide a base of precedents you can draw on in translating resources into the more common languages.

17.4 Checking Memory Usage

We are confident about our discipline in handling Cocoa memory, but the fact remains that handling Cocoa memory—or the reference-counted objects of Core Foundation—is a discipline. You have to take care to do it right. To see whether we slipped, let's run Linear under the supervision of the MallocDebug application. Select **Debug → Launch using Performance Tool → MallocDebug** to launch MallocDebug and direct it at Linear.

When MallocDebug opens, it displays a window showing the path to the application and its command line parameters; if the parameters are still -AppleLanguages (fr), maybe you want to blank those out. Click **Launch**.

Now exercise Linear just enough that it does some allocations and releases. Create a couple of data sources and a few points. Allocate the points among the sources. Click **Compute**. Click **Graph**. Close the Graph window and the document window, and don't bother to save. Don't quit: MallocDebug drops its statistics when the target application quits!

We've now taken Linear through a cycle that should have created all the structures associated with a document and then released them: a full life cycle of a document. MallocDebug, meanwhile, has been recording every allocation of memory and the complete call stack at the time of the allocation. Switch over to MallocDebug; from the second pop-up, select **Leaks**. MallocDebug then examines every Malloc-allocated block in the application heap and makes note of every block that appears not to have any references. In a garbage-collected memory-management system, these blocks would be released.

Use the first pop-up to switch the stack-trace display to **Inverted** (see Figure 17.4). The inverted display lists the routines that made the allocations in the first column of the browser. In this case, 65.6K was allocated through one or more calls to MDNX-ZoneMalloc; 2.2K, through MDNXZoneCalloc. Tracing up from MDNXZoneCalloc, we come to an entry with a source file icon: +[DataPoint allDataPointsInContext:].

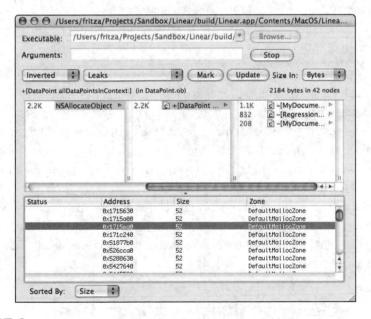

Figure 17.4 Leak analysis of Linear. MallocDebug launched Linear and recorded every allocation and release of memory blocks in the course of creating, filling, and closing a document. By selecting **Leaks** and the **Inverted** tree view, it's easy to find where Linear allocates blocks that end up not being referenced.

In the next column beyond that, we can see that `allDataPointsInContext:` was sent at different times from three different parts of Linear.

Below the browser is a listing of all the apparently leaked memory blocks. This run has 42 of them, each of 52 bytes. You can inspect a block by double-clicking it. It looks as though something is being allocated in Linear code that isn't being cleaned up. Let's have another look at +[DataPoint allDataPointsInContext:]:

```
+ (NSArray *) allDataPointsInContext:
                            (NSManagedObjectContext *) context
{
    NSFetchRequest *    request = [[NSFetchRequest alloc] init];
    [request setEntity: [NSEntityDescription entityForName:
                                        @"DataPoint"
                            inManagedObjectContext:
                                        context]];
    NSError *               error;
    NSArray *               retval;
    retval = [context executeFetchRequest: request
                            error: &error];
    return retval;
}
```

Note that we allocate an `NSFetchRequest` and never release it. It outlives its usefulness after it is sent in the `executeFetchRequest:error:` message. Adding `[request release]` between that message and the `return` statement fixes the leak.

But what about the 65.6K leak? By assiduously tracing up the stack for that allocation, we see that the trace never touches the code we wrote for Linear until it hits `main()`. This leak is initiated in the Cocoa framework. Looking at the block data, it appears to be a bitmap, probably the icon shown on the save/don't save sheet the document displayed when we closed it. It's possible that the pointer to the bitmap isn't lost but is held outside the heap. It may not be a problem; in any case, it isn't a problem we can solve.

17.5 The Release Build Configuration

So far, we have been working with Linear/Linéaire versions that were expressly built with our convenience as developers in mind. The application is built with no optimizations that would confuse the flow of control in a debugger and slow the progress of builds. The build products contain cross-references between addresses in the binary and lines of code. No attempt is made to analyze the code for unused routines that could be excluded from the product. With ZeroLink, the application isn't even portable to another machine!

This can't go on. We have to get Linear into releasable shape, which means changing all the developer-friendly build settings to settings that befit a finished product. Xcode makes such wholesale changes easy by collecting each set of options into *build configurations*.

For the gcc compilers and linker and for the Xcode packaging system, each configuration encompasses settings that are useful for a particular variant of a product build. The project templates provide three configurations for each target: Debug, Release, and Default. The Debug configuration contains the development-friendly settings we are used to; the Release configuration provides values for these settings that are more appropriate for a released product. The Default settings are used when the project is built with the xcodebuild command line tool, and no configuration is specified.

To examine the build configurations for a target, double-click the target's icon in the Groups & Files list, or select the target's icon and click the **Info** toolbar item or press **command-I**. Select the **Build** tab in the resulting Info window. The pop-up menu at the top of the panel allows you to select an existing configuration or to create one of your own. You can also set the list to display whatever configuration is current or a composite of all configurations, so that any change will affect them all. See Figure 17.5.

The build configuration list you see in the target Info window shows all the settings that apply to that target. The items that are shown in plain type are settings that are inherited from the default values for those settings. Items in boldface are settings that have been customized in the currently displayed configuration.

For string-valued settings, the empty string is a valid customization. This would be displayed as a boldface label next to an empty right-hand column. If you want the default value for such a setting, not simply a blank value, select the item, and press **Delete** so that the item reverts to plain type.

Switch the display from the **Debug** configuration to **Release** to see the difference: ZeroLink is removed from the build, as are all the debugging symbols. The optimization level is left to the default, which is for small, fast code.

> When writing a setting for a build configuration, you sometimes want to add to a default value rather than replace it completely. You can incorporate the default in your setting with the string $(value).

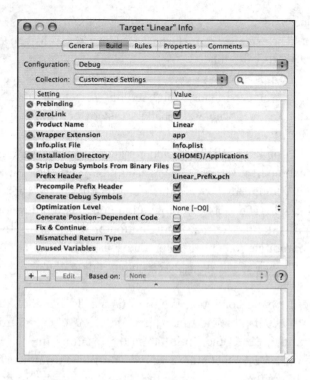

Figure 17.5 The Debug configuration as shown in the Info window for the Linear project. By selecting the **Customized Settings** collection, we can see exactly which settings this configuration overrides. Here, among other things, the application is set to **ZeroLink**, to maintain debugging information, and to enable **Fix & Continue** patching from the debugger.

Select the **Release** build configuration through the **Project** menu, and build Linear. Changing the configuration directs the build process to a different subdirectory of the project's build directory, so targets will be built for the Release configuration independently of whether they had been up-to-date for the Debug configuration. The result will be that a complete, self-contained version of Linear appears in the build/Release directory of the project directory.

17.6 Dead-Code Stripping

One last thing we can do for our application is to strip "dead code" from it. In the process of writing Linear, we saw that it is easy to write more functions for a data type, for completeness, than are used. Further, libraries include suites of functions that may be useful in some application, but it is rare that all are useful to any one application.

The static linker, ld, ordinarily pays no attention to unused code. If an object file—either alone or inside a library archive—is presented to the linking process and any symbol from the file is used, the whole contents of that file get added to the product. This will seem wasteful to CodeWarrior veterans, who are used to a linker that goes function by function, not file by file, but this is conservative practice under gcc. The object-file format used by the gcc tool chain can't guarantee absolutely correct linkage at less than the file level.

However, it is possible for ld to identify sections of code that never get used, assuming no assembly tricks are involved. The linker can slice object files into functions and remove the ones that aren't needed. In a large program that makes use of many static libraries, this can result in significant reductions in the size of the executable.

Dead-code stripping is available as a checkbox option in the build configurations. I recommend that you open the Release build configuration, type dead in the search field to isolate the setting, and check the box.

You can get stripping in Debug builds as well. For debugging work, dead-code stripping requires the -gfull flag to include the maximum level of debugging symbols and is incompatible with ZeroLink. My experience is that debugging is unacceptably slow with programs built with -gfull. For that reason, I regard dead-code stripping as a finishing touch, to be done in a Release configuration, with debugging symbols turned off and ZeroLink no longer an issue.

In my builds of Linear, the executable was 56,588 bytes without stripping and 56,356 stripped. Not a notable improvement, but Linear does not make heavy demands on static libraries.

17.7 xcodebuild

The final step in producing a distributable version of an Xcode target is taken from the command line. The xcodebuild command line tool embodies the Xcode build system in a form that mimics the well-known UNIX tool make, where .xcodeproj files take the place of makefiles.

When the invocation does not specify a configuration, xcodebuild chooses the configuration specified as default, which in template-generated targets is Default. We haven't seen this configuration before. It is basically the Release configuration, with additional installation processing done, including stripping symbols from the executable, which can save significant amounts of space.

You invoke xcodebuild from the project directory. Because we still have both the
Linear and the Linrg projects in that directory, we have to specify which project to
build from. The excerpted transcript shown here is edited for line width:

```
$ cd Linear
$ xcodebuild -project Linear.xcodeproj
== BUILDING NATIVE TARGET Statistics WITH CONFIGURATION Default =

PBXCp build/Default/Statistics.framework/.../Info.plist \
     build/Linear.build/Default/Statistics.build/Info.plist
    mkdir build/Default/Statistics.framework/Versions/A/Resources
    cd /Users/xcodeuser/Linear
    .../DevToolsCore.framework/.../pbxcp -exclude .DS_Store \
     -exclude CVS -exclude .svn -strip-debug-symbols \
     -resolve-src-symlinks \
     build/Linear.build/Default/Statistics.build/Info.plist \
     build/Default/Statistics.framework/Versions/A/Resources
.
.
.
=== BUILDING NATIVE TARGET Linear WITH CONFIGURATION Default ===
.
.
.
Touch build/Default/Linear.app
    mkdir /Users/fritza/Projects/Sandbox/Linear/build/Default
    cd /Users/fritza/Projects/Sandbox/Linear
    /usr/bin/touch build/Default/Linear.app

** BUILD SUCCEEDED **
$
```

The build proceeds, with high-level pseudooperations (PBXCp, Touch, Com-
pileC . . .), followed by the commands that implement them and any error or warning
messages that arise. In the end, our final Linear.app is placed in the Default subdirectory of the build directory. On my run, it's 184K in size, compared to 220K for the
result of the Release build.

17.8 Summary

This chapter began with some cleanup in the Nib file, followed by an improvement to our controller algorithm that incidentally added some English-language text to our application. We took stock of the places where human-readable text was to be found in Linear and found ways to provide alternative text for French localization. We checked our memory usage and fixed a leak. We learned how to institute dead-code stripping, for little gain in this frugally coded application.

PART II

Xcode Tasks

18

Navigating an Xcode Project

Part I of this book showed the use of Xcode in building a small project. We covered many features of the development environment, but the necessities of the task kept us from attaining much depth on any feature. In Part II, we look at Xcode's features in greater detail.

18.1 Editor Panes

In Xcode, practically everything that can move on the screen has an editing pane attached to it. The one in the project window lets you edit whatever you've selected in the Groups & Files list or the detail list. The one in the debugger window allows you to not merely see but also change the code you're executing. The one in the SCM status window lets you review versions and diffs. There are even windows that are only for editing text, with nothing in them but an editor pane.

The editor pane has a few features that we'd miss if we didn't stop to look at them. So let's do a quick review.

18.1.1 Jumps

Once the Code Sense index of a project is completed (see Section 18.1.2), you can jump to the definition of any symbol in the project or its included frameworks by holding down the **command** key and double-clicking the symbol. Multiple matches are possible: The same method may be defined in more than one class, or the characters you command-double-clicked may be the prefix for many different symbols. In that case, a pop-up appears, showing the possible matches, with badges indicating the type—method/member function, instance variable, #defined constant, and so on— and context of each symbol. (See Figure 18.1.) If there are more matches than will comfortably fit in a pop-up menu, a **Find More . . .** item appears at the bottom of the menu, displaying the remaining choices in the Project Find window.

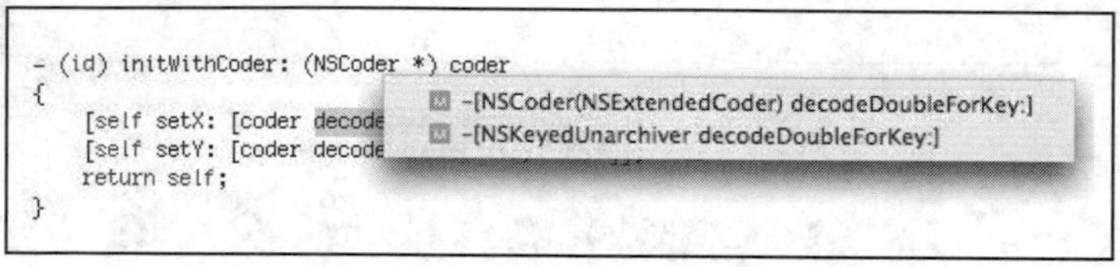

```
- (id) initWithCoder: (NSCoder *) coder
{
    [self setX: [coder decode          ☑ -[NSCoder(NSExtendedCoder) decodeDoubleForKey:]
    [self setY: [coder decode          ☑ -[NSKeyedUnarchiver decodeDoubleForKey:]
    return self;
}
```

Figure 18.1 The result of command-double-clicking `decodeDoubleForKey:`. Two classes define that method, so a pop-up menu appears, offering a choice of which definition to visit.

Recall from Section 14.3 the technique of typing in the name of the informal `NSTableDataSource` protocol and command-double-clicking on it to go immediately to the declarations of the methods of `NSTableDataSource`, which can conveniently be copied and taken back to our own source. Option-double-clicking a symbol or a partial symbol has the effect of opening the Documentation window and entering the selected characters in the API Search field in the toolbar.

18.1.2 Code Sense

Code Sense is Apple's name for the Xcode facilities that take advantage of indexing your project and its frameworks. Code Sense includes code completion, command-double-clicking, class browsing, class modeling, and the project symbol smart group.

Code completion is with you continually as you edit your code. When you type an identifier, Xcode will, after a brief pause, underline the word you are writing. This indicates that Code Sense has found in its index at least one symbol that has the same prefix as what you've already typed. If you press **option-escape** (Figure 18.2), a window will pop up, offering all the possible matches, highlighting the match adjudged "most likely." You can navigate this list by using the up- and down-arrow keys or narrow it by typing more of the symbol. Pressing **Return** accepts the current selection and enters it into the text. **Escape** closes the completion window with no effect.

Code Sense services rely on creating an index for a project the first time it is opened and maintaining the index as the project changes. This indexing is done on a background thread and in most cases does not impose a noticeable performance cost on Xcode. You can see what background tasks Xcode is performing by selecting **Window → Activity Viewer**. If you find that Xcode is not responsive enough and can live without the Code Sense services, you can turn indexing off by selecting the second panel (Code Sense) in the Preferences window and unchecking **Indexing: Enable for all projects**.

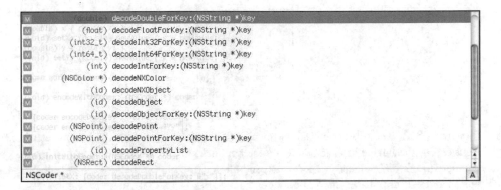

Figure 18.2 Code completion through Code Sense. When it determines that a word being typed could be completed with a known symbol, Xcode signals by underlining the word. Pressing **option-escape** causes a list of possible completions to appear, with the "most likely" completion highlighted. The arrow keys navigate among the choices; pressing **Return** enters the choice into the text. The **A** button at the lower-right corner of the completion window shows that the list is sorted alphabetically; clicking it changes it to π and sorts the list by probability of match.

The Code Sense panel also controls how code completion behaves. You can turn off the signaling of available completions, or you can have Xcode pop up candidate completions automatically after a short delay. You can also decide whether you want code completion to include placeholders for function and method arguments.

The Xcode text editor has a command for advancing the text selection to the next argument placeholder, although the default key-mapping set does not assign a key combination to make this function convenient. In the Key Bindings panel of the Preferences window, select the **Text Key Bindings** tab; in the list there, select **Code Sense Select Next Placeholder**. Double-click in the right-hand column, and type your preferred key combination; many users like to type `control-/`.

18.1.3 Navigation Bar

At the top of each editor pane is a series of pop-ups and buttons for navigating in and among files. The editor pane carries with it the concept of a navigation history, much like the history of a Web browser. You can go back and forth through this history or jump between documents in it.

Figure 18.3 The upper-right corner of an editor window, showing the buttons at the right end of the navigation bar. These are the bookmark menu, breakpoint-location menu, counterpart button, included-header menu, and file-locking button. Between the file-locking button and the scroll bar is the splitter button.

The first three controls in the navigation bar are for traversing the pane's history. The first two buttons are arrowheads representing a change to the previous or next file in the browsing sequence; you can hold the mouse button down on these to see a pop-up of files in the respective directions. **Command-option-left arrow** and **command-option-right arrow** are equivalent to these buttons. The third button is a pop-up menu of the full history of the pane, sorted alphabetically. Options at the bottom of the menu allow you to limit the size of the history list to the last 10, 20, or 40 files.

Next to the history pop-up is a pop-up for landmarks in the file. The pop-up allows you to jump to class, method, and function declarations; `#define`s and `typedef`s; function definitions; and markers set by `#pragma mark`. This menu is also active when displaying a class or a data model; the menu is filled with the names of the classes or entities in the diagram.

The remaining buttons stick to the right end of the navigation bar (Figure 18.3). The first is the bookmark menu, which lists all the bookmarks in the currently displayed file. Set a bookmark by pressing **command-option-down arrow** (or selecting **Find → Add to Bookmarks**) and typing the name for the new bookmark. Bookmarks are stored in the `.pbxuser`-suffixed file inside the project `.xcodeproj` package and aren't shared between users.

The breakpoint menu lists all the breakpoints set in the currently displayed source file. Next is the counterpart button. It is almost universal that for every implementation source file (`.m`, `.c`, `.cp`, or `.cpp`) in a C-family programming language, there is a header file of the same base name. Xcode calls such header-implementation file pairs "counterparts" and allows you to switch between them by clicking this button or by pressing **command-option-up arrow**. See also Section 18.1.4 for one more variant on this service.

An option-click on the counterpart button jumps to the *symbolic* counterpart of whatever is selected. If, for instance, you select the name of a class in a header file, option-clicking on the counterpart button will take you to the implementation of the class. Selecting a symbol, such as a function name or a constant, at its definition or use and option-clicking on the counterpart button will take you to its declaration.

Next comes the header menu. This menu lists every header included, directly or indirectly, in the current source file. If the current file is a header, the menu also lists every implementation file that includes it, directly or indirectly. Choosing an item in the menu focuses the editor on that file.

Last in line is the lock button. If you do not have write access to the displayed file, this button will show a locked padlock. On files to which you do have write access, you can click this button to prevent changes to the file; it will set the locked attribute of the file, so the condition persists and affects other applications.

Below the lock button is the pane splitter, a button showing a gray window with a horizontal line across it. Clicking this button divides the window into two independent editors, one above the other, on the same file. Each half has a splitter button and below it a button showing a gray window with no line across it. This button closes the pane it is attached to.

If you hold down the **option** key while clicking the split button, the split will be vertical instead of horizontal.

18.1.4 Editor Modes

Because different people have different styles of working with their development environments, Xcode tries to accommodate as many of the common choices as possible. One such preference is the number of editor windows the IDE opens for you. Some developers are used to working with a separate window for each source file, building up a stack of windows, much like having each file on a sheet of paper. Other developers find a multiplicity of windows cluttered and obstructive and instead want the editor window to know about all the files they are interested in and to be able to present each in the same view, as needed.

You can choose between these behaviors with the **Grouped/Ungrouped** button in the toolbar of separate editing windows (Figure 18.4). If the icon for the button shows a single window (**Grouped**), additional files will open in the same editor window. If the icon shows a stack of windows (**Ungrouped**), additional files will open in their own windows.

Figure 18.4 The **Grouped/Ungrouped** button in the toolbar of editor windows determines whether additional files will open in the same window (left) or each in its own (right).

In the case of ungrouped windows, there is an additional variant: Xcode allows you to switch quickly between implementation—.m, .c, or .cp, for instance—files and the associated header (.h) files. In the default Xcode key mappings, this is done with **command-option-up arrow**. A strict rule of a new window for every file would have such counterpart files appear in separate windows, but even developers who prefer many editor windows may make an exception in this case: It's very common to edit an implementation file in one half of a split editor and its header in the other. For this case, click **General** in the Preferences window and Select **Counterparts always load in same editor** if you want headers and implementation files to alternate in the same editor window, even though you generally want many editor windows.

18.2 Project Find Window

The Project Find window allows you to search for a string or a symbol in either your project or the frameworks it includes. This window consists of three panes. The bottom pane, as usual, is an editor pane. The middle pane contains the results of any searches you do. Each file containing a match for the search string is displayed with a disclosure triangle next to it; when the triangle is open, each match is shown in context. Selecting a match displays it in the editor pane. The top pane of the Project Find window allows you to specify the search you want to perform. See Figure 18.5

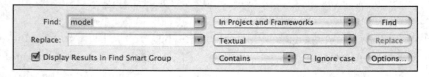

Figure 18.5 The Project Find window controls

The Find: and Replace: combo boxes are straightforward: type the text you mean to search for and, optionally, replace it with. The drop-down feature of the combo box allows you to browse recent find and replace strings.

There are three pop-up menus next to the text-entry boxes. The top menu allows you to specify what files to search: files already open, files selected in the Groups & Files list, files included in the project, and files supplied by frameworks the project uses. By clicking the **Options . . .** button, you can edit or add to these choices. You can define a set extending to open documents or open files; to selected files in a project, all files in a project, or all files in all open projects; files in projects or frameworks; files with names matching one of a list of regular expressions; or files in a list of files and folders.

The second pop-up determines whether the search is textual—the search string is searched for literally—regular-expression-based—the search string is interpreted as a pattern to be matched—or for a definition—the search string is looked up in the project index for declarations and implementations of that symbol.

The third pop-up specifies whether the search is for a simple match (**Textual**) or for a string that extends to a word boundary at either or both ends (**Starts with**, **Whole words**, **Ends with**). You can make the search case-insensitive (**Ignore case**).

Finally, you can click **Display Results in Find Smart Group**. This checkbox is misnamed, as every search you do will add the search to the **Find Results** group in the Groups & Files list, and selecting the search will redo the search and show you the fresh results. Checking this box will put the results of the search in the detail view, where you can narrow the results list further by use of the search field in the toolbar. For instance, you can search for "volume" in your project and then use the search field to narrow the list to lines that also contain the string max.

18.3 The Favorites Bar

The Xcode team heard from developers that the automatic groups at the end of the Groups & Files list were useful but rarely used because developers spend almost all their time among the files at the top of the list. The various smart groups are usually scrolled out of view. The favorites bar is Xcode 2's answer to that problem.

Add the favorites bar to your project window by selecting **View → Show Favorites Bar**. A gradient bar will appear in the project window, just below the toolbar. You can drag anything you want into the favorites bar. If the item is a file, clicking it will display it in the detail view and, if it's visible, the associated editor. If it's a group, holding the mouse button down will drop down a menu of all the items in that group.

The possibilities don't end with items from the Groups & Files list. Anything displayable in an Xcode editor window can go into the favorites bar. For instance, if you often refer to a page in the developer documentation, you can drag the icon from its title bar into the favorites bar.

18.4 Groups & Files List

The Groups & Files list at the left of the project window is at the root of all the work you do in Xcode. All access to project files and build settings starts in this list. A close look shows that it is more than a hierarchical file list.

18.4.1 The Project Group

The first "group" in the Groups & Files list is the **Project** group. Every file in your project appears somewhere in this group. I didn't say that the **Project** group includes every file that goes into building your product—though it does. The **Project** group also includes anything, anywhere, that you might want to search, copy, or otherwise refer to. It's *target membership* that identifies the files that are ingredients for a product.

An example: Cocoa applications link to Cocoa, an umbrella framework that includes the AppKit, Foundation, and CoreData frameworks but doesn't give ready access to the headers of those frameworks. So the Cocoa-application project template includes references to AppKit, Foundation, and CoreData, *without* linking to them. That gets them included when the project is indexed and searched. But of the four, only Cocoa has its target-member box checked.

Within the project group, you can have subgroups, identified by their disclosure triangles and their little yellow folder icons. You are free to use or ignore subgroups, as you like. Subgroups have nothing to do with disk organization or with how any of your targets are built. Subgroups are there for you to organize your files however you like.

For instance, most project templates have a Resources subgroup inside them and contain files that will end up in the product bundle's Resources directory. Moving a file out of the Resources subgroup doesn't change anything; the file will still be copied into the product's Resources directory. By the same token, moving a file into the Resources subgroup does nothing to your product; if you want it in your product's

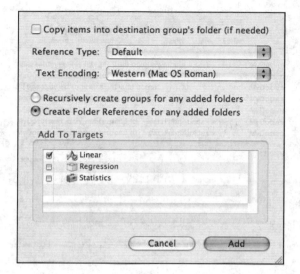

Figure 18.6 The add-to-project sheet, showing the option to add folders as live references to file directories. This would ensure that every build of the targets selected in the list at bottom is given an up-to-date set of files.

Resources directory, make sure that it shows up in the Copy Resources build phase of the product's target in the **Targets** group.

In two instances, the structure of a subgroup *does* represent something in the outside world. Both involve adding a directory rather than a file to the project. Suppose that we were to add a Linear option that would offer the user a choice of graphics to be drawn at each point of its graph view. We might have the Linear's Resources directory include a subdirectory containing an image file for each available graphic.

We get busy with our favorite art program and soon have a directory filled with a dozen .png files. We drag the folder from the Finder into the Groups & Files list or use **Project → Add to Project . . .** and select the directory. We are presented with the familiar add-to-project sheet, as shown in Figure 18.6. Look at the radio buttons in the middle. If you make the first choice, a new subgroup, with the same name as the directory and containing the same files, will be added to the project. Any subdirectories become subgroups of the new subgroup, and so on. So that is the first exception: You can add a directory to your project, and Xcode will start the added files off in your on-disk organization scheme.

The second choice, **Create Folder References for any added folders**, does something quite different. First, the new folder icon on the screen will be blue, not yellow. Second, Xcode will track the contents of that directory as they change. As you remove and add files in your repertoire of point markers, Xcode will automatically build your application with the correct set of files.

Those are the two ways that Xcode's Groups & Files list gets influenced by the file system world. Groups & Files can influence the file system in three ways.

1. If you add a file or a folder to your project, the checkbox at the top of the add-to-project sheet offers **Copy items into destination group's folder (if needed)**. This normally means that when you borrow a source file from one project directory, you can decide whether to copy it into the other or to use it in place.

2. You can rename any file or group in the project group by option-clicking it. That will make the name editable. Editing the name renames the file.

3. Deleting a file from the Groups & Files list could mean one of two things. First, you want to have the file out of the list, but do you also want to have it out of the file system? Xcode presents you with the option to delete only Xcode's reference or to delete the file itself as well.

18.4.2 The Targets Group

Next under the **Project** group is the **Targets** group. Inside this group is an entry for each target in the project. Selecting a target fills the detail view with every file included in that target. Double-clicking the target reveals an Info window for that target, which has the following tabs.

- **General** lets you name the target and designate other objects in the project—other targets or targets in included project files—that this target depends on. Such dependencies will be brought up-to-date before the target is built.

- **Build** is the repository for all the switches and shell symbols that control the building of the target.

- **Rules** instructs the build system which tool to use for each type of source file. You can add a source file type by clicking the + button and specifying a suffix for the type and a compiler or script to do the processing. You will rarely need to use this tab; the most common case is selecting **gcc 3.3** for cross-development.

- **Properties** provides a convenient user interface for editing the `Info.plist` of the target's product. Projects with more than one bundle target will have more than one `Info.plist`, in files distinguished by different prefixes; this panel will always edit the correct one.

- **Comments** allows you to enter comments for your benefit or for others. The detail list can be made to show comments, and you can then search on the comment column.

Clicking the disclosure triangle next to each target reveals the build phases that Xcode goes through to produce the target's product. Build phases, in turn, can be opened to reveal exactly which files participate in each phase. One way to add a file to a target is to drag its icon into the desired build phase of a target.

You can add a build phase to a target with one of the commands at **Project →
New Build Phase** or by control-clicking the target and selecting from **Add → New
Build Phase** in the contextual menu. The possible build phases are

- Copy Files, if you need to fill custom locations in your product bundle with custom contents: Use a Copy Files phase for each item to copy. The most common use for this phase is to place embedded frameworks in the Frameworks directory of application bundles. There can be as many Copy Files phases as there are files or directories to copy.

- Shell Script, to put arbitrary UNIX shell scripts anywhere in the build process. You can specify input and output files for the phase so that the build system can do dependency analysis on the inputs and products. You might use script phases for running testing frameworks, custom preprocessors, or documentation generators. There can be as many Shell Script phases as you need.

- Copy Headers, to move all headers marked public or private to Headers or PrivateHeaders, as each case may be.

- Copy Bundle Resources, the phase into which most noncode members of a target will fall. All the files in the Copy Bundle Resources phase are copied into the product's Resources directory. This phase is automatically a part of Cocoa and Carbon application targets.

- Compile Sources, the phase that analyzes the dependencies of source and object files and compiles any sources that are—or that include files that are—newer than their objects. This phase is part of virtually any kind of target.

- Compile AppleScripts, to compile AppleScripts in an AppleScript Studio application, yielding .scpt files in Resources/Scripts. Note that this phase does not execute AppleScripts; the Shell Script phase is the only way to insert custom behaviors in the build process.

- Link Binary With Libraries, a phase in any target that produces an executable. This phase contains any libraries and frameworks that are part of the target.

- Build Java Resources, for putting the files in it into the product `.jar` file for Java applications.

- Build Resource Manager Resources, for using the `Rez` resource compiler to compile `.r` files and copy `.rsrc` files into an application resource file.

18.4.3 The Executables Group

The **Executables** group contains references to every application or tool that you may run or debug while working on your project. The executable products of the project's targets are automatically added to this group; typically, that's all you'll need. However, you may add other executables with the command **Project → New Custom Executable**. You would do this, for instance, if your project built plug-ins to be hosted by a third-party application; you could set up the host application as a custom executable. With the custom executable set as the active executable for your project, running or debugging your plug-in is simply a matter of issuing the **Run** or **Debug** commands.

Double-clicking an executable's icon will run the executable. Selecting its icon and issuing **File → Get Info** (**command-I**) brings up an Info window with the following tabs:

- **General** allows you to designate the location of the executable, whether to use debug or profile variants of dynamic libraries (see Section 21.1), how standard I/O is to be handled for runs, and what the initial working directory for the executable will be. It's important to remember that no executable is guaranteed a particular working directory under Mac OS X.

- **Arguments** lets you edit one list that supplies command line arguments to the executable and another list that specifies key/value pairs for environment variables. Once added to a list, any element can be made active or inactive by clicking the checkbox next to it.

- **Debugging** allows you to specify the debugger to be used on the executable. This panel is valuable if you want to switch to `gdb` to debug Objective-C code used in an AppleScript application, for instance. A pop-up controls how standard I/O is handled for debugging sessions. The panel also sets up remote debugging, specifies whether to execute the executable immediately on starting the debugger and treat Carbon `Debugger()` and `DebugStr()` calls as debugger breaks, and specifies additional directories to search for source files.

- **Comments** allows you to add any comments you wish.

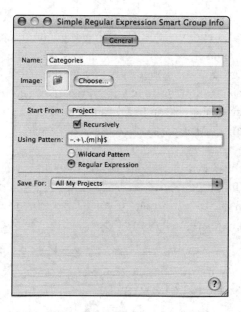

Figure 18.7 Creating a regular-expression smart group. This Info window appears when you issue the command **File → Select New Smart Group → Simple Regular Expression Smart Group**. You can name the new group, substitute your own icon for it, root its search anywhere in the Groups & Files hierarchy, and have it match file names either by regular expression or by "glob" wildcard patterns. Smart groups can be project-specific or available to all projects.

18.4.4 Smart Groups

The project group has a limitation. Any given file can appear in the list only once. This means that you must pick your classifications carefully; for example, your AirFlowView.m file can be in a **Views** group or an **Aerodynamics** group but not both.

Smart groups are a way for files to belong to additional groups, based on patterns in their names. For instance, AirFlowView.m could be tucked away in a manual **Aerodynamics** group but also be found in a **Views** smart group that includes all files matching the wildcard pattern *View*. Any new files with View in their names would automatically be added to the **Views** group.

For another instance, suppose that you've been sticking to the pattern of using hyphens only in the names of files that define Objective-C categories. You could then have a smart group that automatically includes header and implementation files for all your categories. Select **File → New Smart Group → Simple Regular Expression Smart Group** to create a smart group and open an Info window for configuring it (Figure 18.7).

All we need to do is give the group a name (**Categories**) and a regular expression ('`-.+\.(m|h)$`' for files ending with `.m` or `.h` and containing a hyphen), and close the window. The new smart group will appear at the end of the Groups & Files list.

Had we wanted a group that covered only, say, project resources, we could do this, as the configuration panel allows us to restrict the search to groups within the Groups & Files list. If it is very specialized and applicable to only one project, the smart group can be restricted to the current project; alternatively, it can be made available to all projects.

Smart groups appear last in the Groups & Files list, which makes them less accessible than they might otherwise be. You can move a smart group higher in the list but no higher than the **Targets** group. If you have the favorites bar active, you can drag a smart group into it, where the smart group will serve as a drop-down menu of its members.

18.4.5 Symbol Smart Group

The **Project Symbols** smart group is another feature that relies on the Code Sense index. This group is found near the bottom of the Groups & Files list, with a blue cube for an icon. Clicking it fills the detail view with a listing of every symbol—function, method, instance variable, constant, and so on—in your project. Symbols that have definitions—in implementation files—separate from declarations—in header files— will be listed twice. The list can be sorted by identifier, type, or location. Clicking a list item takes you to the definition or declaration that item represents. The list is searchable on any column, using the search field in the toolbar.

Control-clicking (or right-clicking) a **Project Symbols** item raises a contextual menu.

- **Reveal in Class Browser** opens the **Class Browser**, with the class list expanded to select the relevant class and, if the symbol is a member of the class, the member selected in the member list.

- **Find Symbol Name in Project** performs a textual **Project Find**, with the name of the selected symbol as the target. This will yield at least every reference to the symbol in your project.

- **Copy Declaration for Method/Function** puts the declaration for the function or method, as it might appear in a header, on the clipboard.

- **Copy Invocation for Method/Function** puts a use of the function or method on the clipboard. The parameters, including any object to which a method is attached, are marked with placeholder strings.

The Groups & Files list is configurable; control- (or right-) clicking in the list brings up a contextual menu that includes a **Preferences** submenu, allowing you to include or exclude any groups in the list. For instance, the **Breakpoints** list is not included, but you can add it to the Groups & Files list by checking it in the **Preferences** submenu.

18.5 Class Browser Window

By selecting **Project** → **Class Browser,** you can open a window that allows you to browse the headers of framework classes and the source of your own classes. The Class Browser window is anchored by a list of classes at the left side. Selecting a class from the class list fills the member list at top right with a list of all methods and instance variables; selecting one of these displays the selected item in the editor pane below.

If a method is declared in an interface, selecting it in the member list will always take you to the interface declaration. If it is not declared in the interface, selecting it will take you to the definition in the implementation file.

The anchor list of classes on the left is filtered according to the **Option Set** pop-up in the Class Browser window's toolbar. The standard option sets determine whether the class listing is flat or hierarchical by inheritance and whether the listing is of all classes or restricted to classes defined in the current project.

By clicking the **Configure Options** button, you can change these options or add option sets of your own. For instance, it is often easy to miss class features that are implemented by its superclass and not by the class itself. One of the options available is to include all inherited members in the member listing for a class.

Classes and methods from Apple-supplied frameworks, and for which there is online documentation, are marked with a small blue book icon. Clicking the icon will present the relevant documentation in the Class Browser window's editor space.

18.6 Class Modeler

When building the data model editor for Core Data, the Xcode team took care to make the graphical modeling framework as general as possible. The first added application is the class modeler tool. The easiest way to see a class model is to select some files in the Groups & Files list of the Project window and select the menu command **Design** → **Class Model** → **Quick Model**. The modeling tool analyzes the selected headers

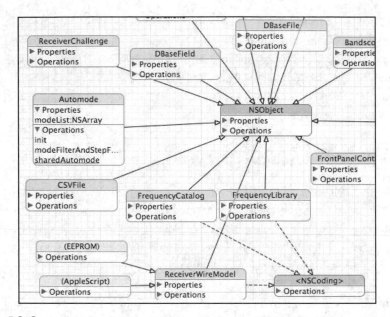

Figure 18.8 A part of a class model diagram, showing NSObject and some of the classes in a large project that derive directly from it. On the screen, classes are shown in boxes with blue title bars, categories with green, and protocols with red. Entities outside the immediate scope of the classes that were presented to the model, such as NSObject and NSCoding here, are shown with slightly darker title bars. Disclosure triangles control the visibility of class properties and operations; class Automode has both open in this view. The diagram was laid out with the **Force-Directed Layout** command, which results in a compact diagram with star-shaped class clusters.

and implementation files—Objective-C, C++, or Java—and produces an annotated diagram similar to the data model diagram from Chapter 15. See Figures 18.8 and 18.9.

As with the data model diagram, the class model diagram is supplemented by three panels at the top, displaying all the classes in the diagram, all the members—both properties and operations—of the selected classes, and a display of the properties of the selected members. Unlike the data model diagram, the class model diagram does not allow you to edit your class model by using the diagram or browser views.

Models may be *static* or *tracking*. A static model is a snapshot of the classes when they were presented for modeling; it documents particular classes at a particular moment. A tracking model observes the groups you designate when you select groups and files to include in the model; as files enter and leave the included groups, the classes they define enter and leave the model, too.

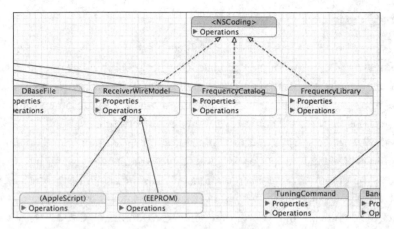

Figure 18.9 Part of the same class model, laid out hierarchically. Because class hierarchies, especially in Objective-C, tend to be flat and shallow, these diagrams often turn out to be one page tall and many wide.

A tracking model is available only through the **File** → **New File ...** (**command-N**) command. Select **Design** → **Class Model** from the New File Assistant, and you will be presented with a sheet that allows you to pick groups and files from your project. The sheet will also allow you to choose a static or a tracking model. Remember that a tracking model must include at least one group, or folder, icon. This model will be added to your project as a file with the .xcclassmodel extension.

The class model tool uses the Code Sense project-indexing facility as the source of its information. If you've turned Code Sense off or if the index isn't yet fully built, class model diagrams won't be available.

If the class model seems to be missing classes from a framework—perhaps you're using the Address Book framework and it doesn't show up in the model—be sure that the root header for the framework is #included somewhere in your source or headers. In our example, the following line should appear somewhere *in addition to* your prefix header:

```
#import <AddressBook/AddressBook.h>
```

Graphics from the modeling view can be exported to other programs. Select the objects you want to export, hold down the **option** key, and drag your selection into the Finder, where it will become a picture clipping, or the working area of your favorite graphics program.

18.7 Project Layout

Xcode is a tool for a diverse corps of developers, each with his or her own habits in managing the work of development, and using almost the full range of available screen sizes. Some developers like the orderly feel of a development environment that keeps all tasks in a single window; others are happiest when separate objects get separate representations on screen. There is every gradation between.

Xcode 2.1 reflects Apple's effort to accommodate as many development styles as possible. The default layout provides separate windows for each kind of task but showcases the Groups & Files and detail displays as the center of the project. An all-in-one format consolidates every operation into a single window. A condensed format sacrifices the detail view in favor of something more familiar to CodeWarrior veterans.

The format can be changed only when no project window is open. Set the format in **Preferences** (**Xcode** → **Preferences . . .** , or **command-,**), in the **General** (first) pane. Make your choice in the pop-up provided.

18.7.1 Default Layout

Your Xcode projects will have the default layout unless you decide otherwise. The Project window is anchored by the Groups & Files list on the left, which lists first all the files associated with the project, then all the project's targets, then all the associated executables, and then various automatically generated file groups. At the right of the window is a detail view, the contents of which are determined by the current selection in the Groups & Files list.

Clicking the **Editor** icon in the toolbar switches the right side of the window between all-editor and the detail view, possibly shared with the editor.

Build Results

This window is divided into a browser pane at top and an editor below. The browser consists of a list of the warnings and errors encountered in the course of building a target. Clicking an error or a warning will focus the editor on the place in your source code where the error was detected. At the bottom of the list are three buttons and one drop-down menu.

- The first button controls whether the list includes all the steps in the build or only the ones that generated warnings or errors.
- The second controls whether warnings are shown in the list.

- The third opens and closes a third pane in the window, between the browser and the editor, containing a transcript of the commands used to accomplish the build and the messages the underlying tools displayed in response.

- The menu determines, for this project only, whether the Build Results window will appear automatically and, if so, on what conditions; maybe you want to see it only if there are errors, for instance. The same settings, for *all* projects, can be made in the Preferences window.

The detailed build transcript can be a useful tool. If you aren't sure what flags are being passed to the compilers or if Xcode's interpretation of an error message isn't clear, refer to the transcript. The Build Results window is also useful in that it is the only window that, by default, contains pop-up menus selecting all three of the **Active Target**, **Active Executable**, and **Active Build Configuration**.

Run Log

The Run Log allows you to choose the active target and the active executable and to run the active executable. While the executable is running, the text area displays its standard output and error streams and accepts standard input.

The contents of the Run Log accumulate until they are cleared, either by the **Debug → Clear Logs** command or by your clicking the **X** button below the window's scroll bar.

SCM Results

Selecting **SCM → SCM Results** (**command-shift-V**) displays the SCM Results window. The window lists all the files in the project for which the SCM status is other than current. Selecting an editable item, such as a source file, in the list puts the contents of that file in the window's editor pane, which may be hidden; look for the dimple of the view splitter at the bottom of the window.

At the bottom of the scroll bar for the listing is a button with a representation of lines of text in it. Clicking this button switches the display to a transcript of Xcode's interactions with your chosen SCM system. The commands Xcode issued to the system will be shown in blue; the responses, in black.

18.7.2 All-in-One Layout

This layout does away with the great variety of specialist windows put up by the default layout. Instead, everything is done in the Project window, which has three

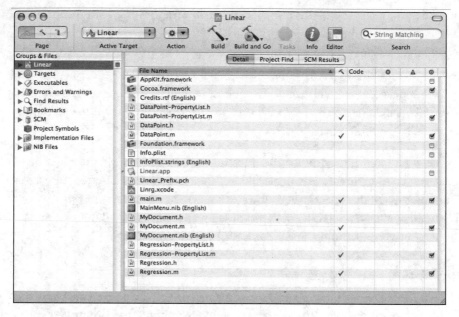

Figure 18.10 Unlike the default layout, the all-in-one project layout has a **Page** selector in the upper-left corner for switching among editing, building, and debugging functions, as well as tabs over the right-hand portion of the window for selecting services within a page.

pages for three phases in the project life cycle: editing, building, and debugging. See Figure 18.10.

Editing

The Editing page has three tabs: **Detail**, **Project Find**, and **SCM Results**. Selecting **Detail** gets you much the same window you have in the default layout. The only difference is that what were specialty windows in the default layout replace the detail view in the all-in-one. Pressing **command-shift-F**, for instance, does not bring up a separate Project Find window but switches the Project window to the **Project Find** tab.

Building

The Building page has two tabs: **Build** and **Run**. **Build** corresponds to the Build Results window in the default layout; **Run**, to the Run Log. As with the Build Results window, the toolbar for the Building page contains pop-ups allowing you to set the current target, executable, and build configuration. Buttons allow you to clean and build the current target and to run and debug the current executable.

Debugging

In the all-in-one layout, the debugger console is an additional pane at the bottom of the Debugger page. This cuts down on the precious vertical space available for other uses in the Debugger window but does relieve the common problem of losing the console in the stack of Xcode windows. That is the only difference from the separate Debugger window under the default layout.

18.7.3 Condensed Layout

The condensed layout (Figure 18.11) pares the Project window down to a subset of the Groups & Files list, a format familiar to CodeWarrior users. Which subset of Groups & Files is shown is controlled by three tabs at the top of the view: **Files**, **Targets**, and **Other**.

The **Files** tab is simply the first portion of the full Groups & Files list, the one dealing with the file system entities that are included in the project. Double-clicking an entry in the list brings up an editor window for that file.

The switch to the condensed layout leaves us with some settings that don't work well without the full Project window. Without the detail view, there is no way to

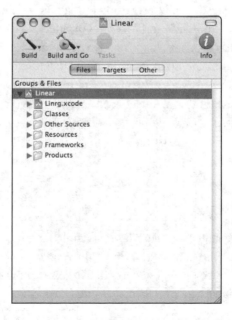

Figure 18.11 The condensed layout does away with the detail and editor portion of the Project window to provide an experience similar to the CodeWarrior IDE.

control what source files belong to a target. We can customize the Groups & Files view to make up for the loss. Control-click in the Groups & Files header, or select the **View** → **Groups & Files Columns** submenu, and select the **Target Membership** item. This adds a column of checkboxes to the list, allowing you to include or exclude files in the active target.

The **Targets** tab includes the **Targets** and **Executables** groups. The ability to open the build phases of a target and edit the files that go into them is analogous to the linkage view of a CodeWarrior project.

The **Other** tab covers all the automated groups—**Errors** and **Warnings**, **Find Results**, **Bookmarks**, **SCM**, **Project Symbols**, and the smart groups. If you left the Xcode defaults unchanged, the major notice you will have of errors and warnings after a build will be the status bar at the bottom of the Project window. By default, Xcode does not display a window listing errors after a build. You can summon the Build Results window by clicking one of the build-status icons in the status bar or by double-clicking the **Errors and Warnings** group icon.

Or, you can have the Build Results window open automatically. The Building (third) panel of the Preferences window allows you to set the conditions on which the Build Results window will open and close. For instance, if you like to have visible feedback when you start a build, change **Open during builds:** from **Never** to **Always**. If you don't want the window cluttering up your screen if it contains no news, you can change **Close after builds:** from **Never** to **On Success**.

Project Symbols is a dead loss in the condensed layout, relying on the detail view; there is no detail view in the condensed layout. Double-clicking **Project Symbols** opens a new Class Browser window, which is not the same thing at all.

If you do a **Project Find**, using the condensed layout, and check **Display Results in Find Smart Group**, Xcode will open an additional project window just to show a detail list. Double-clicking an existing find smart group will open the **Project Find** with the results of that search.

18.8 Summary

In this nuts-and-bolts chapter, we toured every visible feature in the main windows of Xcode. We covered the Project window, in all three layouts, and the Groups & Files list, which is at the heart of the Xcode workflow. We saw how editor windows work. We looked at the specialty windows: Project Find, Class Browser, and Class Modeler.

19

Xcode for CodeWarrior Veterans

Apple's announcement that Mac OS X would be transitioning to Intel chips came shortly after Metrowerks announced that it would no longer ship tools for development of Intel-based software with its popular CodeWarrior integrated development environment. As of late 2005, the next major revision to CodeWarrior is likely the last and will probably not produce binaries capable of running on Intel-based Macintoshes.

With this sad passing, the many programmers who made CodeWarrior their home are coming for the first time to Xcode. This chapter addresses Xcode from the point of view of the CodeWarrior veteran and explains how to make the Xcode experience less foreign.

19.1 Losses

Apple wouldn't start this chapter this way, but let's get the difficult parts out of the way. Turning away from CodeWarrior entails some losses for its users.

19.1.1 Speed

The big loss is in speed. The Metrowerks C++ compiler and linker fairly scream through code. Integrated tightly with the IDE, they can be kept preloaded and primed for action, wheread the gcc compiler and linker tools have to be reloaded and reinitialized with each source file. CodeWarrior's compiler is built, first and foremost—always granting accuracy—for fast compilation; other areas, such as code generation and standards compliance, have taken second place.

Apple has decided that it doesn't have to dive all the way into the compiler-writing business when GNU's gcc provides a compiler with most of the work done. The gcc compiler has been built to different priorities. Its code base is meant to be portable to many platforms, and the process is not receptive to fine-tuning for one machine. Increasingly, gcc emphasizes standards compliance and diagnostic warnings, which require analysis that would not be necessary in a sprint compilation. Reputedly, gcc has a good potential for code generation; the PowerPC generator hasn't fully lived up to the potential but is improving. Smarter code generation slows compilation. The gcc compiler is built as a harness for many different languages, including FORTRAN, Ada, and Java, not just the C family; generality slows compilation.

> Apple is an active developer of gcc. The Xcode gcc contains a number of Apple-specific extensions, and Apple feeds patches back to the gcc open-source project.

There are things you can do to alleviate the relative torpor of Xcode; see Chapter 22. The one habit that CodeWarrior veterans get into that probably causes the most trouble in Xcode is the use of long source files—on the order of tens of thousands of lines. With a lightning-fast compiler, the overhead of recompiling 30,000 lines just because you changed a few is not noticeable; with gcc, you might consider segregating your stable code base or using human-scaled source files in general. Also, the Xcode text editor, which is based on the Cocoa text system, bogs down on large files.

19.1.2 Syntax Coloring

Because Xcode is not integrated with its compilers, its syntax coloring is not nearly as good. CodeWarrior can use symbol tables from the compiler to identify a symbol as being a class name, a data member, a function, a macro, or whatever and color-code it accordingly. In Xcode, they're all black. Syntax coloring is limited to colorizing keywords, literals, and comments.

19.1.3 Debugging Templates

The support for debugging template classes is not as good in Xcode. According to Apple engineers, the gdb debugger is built on the assumption that a single line of code can be associated with only one block of machine-language instructions. It is in the nature of template code that each line of code generates a separate block of instructions for every instantiation of the template. Therefore, setting a breakpoint by clicking in the gutter next to a template function rarely works. The fix apparently will be difficult; in the meantime, the workaround seems to be to use the gdb console and issue an rbreak command:

```
(gdb) rbreak templateFunction
```

where *templateFunction* is a pattern for the function at which you wish to break. The parameter is interpreted as a regular expression, with `.*` for any additional text appended and prepended. If `Triangle` is a template class implementing a `draw` method, `Triangle.*draw` will specify all instantiations of `Triangle<T>::draw`; gdb will print a list of breakpoints set by `rbreak`, and you can issue a `delete` command specifying the numbers of the breakpoints you aren't interested in.

Also, you can set a symbolic breakpoint on a particular instantiation of a template method by opening the Breakpoints window (**Window** → **Tools** → **Breakpoints**) and entering the fully qualified name of that instantiation: `Triangle<double>::area`.

A similar situation arises in respect to C++ constructors and destructors; gcc may generate as many as three machine code implementations for every sourcecode implementation of these functions. Apparently, this is necessary to accommodate the semantics of the various ways a C++ object can be instantiated. Again, an `rbreak`, or a step-in from calling code, may be your best option.

19.1.4 RAD Tools

Xcode provides a class browser and a graphical class modeler, but these are look-but-don't-touch tools; you can't create or edit classes with them. Xcode does not come with any Java rapid application-development (RAD) tools, unless you are writing WebObjects applications. Interface Builder is an indispensable tool for Cocoa development and nearly so for Carbon. If you're sticking with PowerPlant, you can still use Constructor.

19.2 Make Yourself at Home

Xcode's designers have tried to make it accommodating to CodeWarrior veterans. The project layout, command keys, and build-results behavior can be customized so that most of your CodeWarrior muscle memory remains useful.

19.2.1 The Project Window

Start with Xcode running, without any project windows open. Select the **Xcode** → **Preferences . . .** menu item to open the Preferences window. In the first preference panel (**General**), select the **Condensed** layout; layouts can be selected only when no projects are open. Click **OK** or, at least, **Apply**. When the condensed layout is in effect, the Xcode project window loses its attached editor and searchable detail list and presents itself as a compact list of files much like the project window in CodeWarrior.

The condensed project window has three tabs. The **Files** tab is exactly analogous to the **Files** tab of a CodeWarrior project: It contains references and groups of references to files, which you can double-click to open in separate windows. The **Targets** tab combines the functions of the CodeWarrior **Targets** and **Link Order** tabs: The project's targets are contained in the **Targets** group, and each target contains the phases of its build process. Each build phase, in turn, includes the file references that participate in it; to the extent that order matters in a build phase, you can control it here.

In CodeWarrior, you're accustomed to selecting build settings by making a target the default target and opening a settings window. In the same way, Xcode provides three commands in the **Project** menu—**Edit Project Settings**, **Edit Active Target**, and **Edit Active Executable**—which will open Info windows for the relevant settings. You can edit the settings for any target or executable, active (default) or not, by double-clicking its entry in the **Targets** or **Executables** list. Project settings can be edited by double-clicking the top icon under the **Files** tab.

The segregation of settings into three Info windows, each with three to five tabs, may take some getting used to. In general, settings are placed at the project level when they must have project wide effect, such as build directories or SCM use, or when it would be a convenience to you to be able to make one setting apply to all the targets in the project; all the settings in the **Build** tab are like this. Executable settings deal solely with the launching of an application or tool from Xcode; this is where you set environment variables or command line parameters. Everything else can be set per target and appears in the target Info window.

A third tab, labeled **Other**, contains the "smart groups" that bring up the rear of the uncondensed Groups & Files list. The groups marked with purple folders are the user-defined smart groups; you can create new ones and specify glob or regular-expression patterns to select which of your project files appear in them. Your projectwide searches are listed under the **Find Results** group; double-click a search record to see a project search window with the current results of that search. If you have source code management active, the **SCM** group contains every project file whose status is other than current. The **Bookmarks** group lists your bookmarks.

Some of the members of the **Other** tab suffer from the condensed project layout. The **Errors and Warnings** group lists all source files for which compiler messages were noted; if the detail view provided by the other layouts were available, selecting an entry in this group would fill the detail list with the error messages, which would key the attached editor to the location of the error. The **Project Symbols** item loses most of all: Selecting it in the other layouts fills the detail list with a live-searchable roster of every symbol defined in your project, with each item taking you to its definition. In the condensed view, you can double-click the **Project Symbols** icon and get the Class Browser window, but it isn't the same thing at all.

As supplied, the **Targets** and **Other** tabs are one-column lists; the **Files** list adds columns to show needs-compilation status and counts of errors and warnings. By control- (or right-) clicking in the header of the Groups & Files list, you can select what columns to display. On multitarget projects, I like to add a column of target-membership checkboxes, and I drag the column so it is to the left of the file names. (Strict adherence to CodeWarrior style would put it on the right, but I find it easier to track on the left.) In the **Other** tab, I add the SCM column and put it on the left, so I can see the status of the files in the SCM smart group.

19.2.2 Key Mapping

Bring up the Preferences window again, and select the sixth panel, **Key Bindings**. At the top of the panel is a pop-up menu labeled **Key Binding Sets:**; select **Metrowerks Compatible** from the pop-up to bring you most of the way to the key bindings you're used to.

But not all the way. Xcode doesn't let you edit built-in key-binding sets, so you'll have to make a copy. Click **Duplicate . . .** , name your copy of the set—I admit, I can't improve on "Copy of Metrowerks Compatible"—and click **OK** to complete the duplication. Now you can make changes.

You build a project with **Make** (**command-M**). This is so ingrained in my habits that years of using the Xcode default key bindings have not prevented my pressing **command-M** to initiate builds. Well, even in the **Metrowerks Compatible** key set, **command-M** miniaturizes the front window.

In the **Menu Key Bindings** tab, open the **Build** list, and double-click the key combination assigned to **Build, command-option-K**. While the **Key** field is open, anything you type is captured as the new key binding, so press **command-M**. Xcode politely protests that **command-M** is already assigned to **Minimize** (Figure 19.1), but we know what we're doing, so click anywhere outside the key-binding field. This assigns **command-M** to **Build** and removes its assignment to **Minimize**.

There is no Xcode equivalent to the command to make the current selection the find string and find the next instance of it, assigned in the classic Mac OS tradition to **command-H**. Xcode, in obedience to the Mac OS X human-interface guidelines, assigns **command-H** to **Hide Xcode**. If you have a lot of muscle memory invested in the find-selection binding, you're going to be annoyed when Xcode disappears when

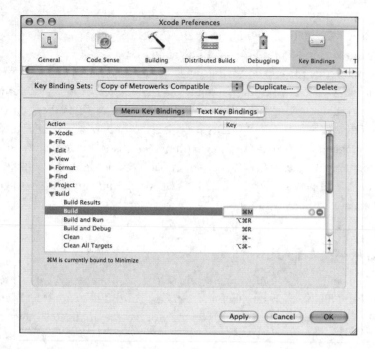

Figure 19.1 Remapping the **Build** command to **command-M**. We have not yet dealt with the previous assignment for **command-M**, **Minimize**, so a warning appears below the key-mapping list.

you try it. You can look at that as a learning experience, or you can remove the key binding from **Xcode → Hide Xcode**. As for finding the selected text, use **command-E, command-G** instead; it'll work in almost every Mac OS X application.

One feature that has drifted in the CodeWarrior world has been the command **Go to header/source file**, whereby you can, at a single keystroke, navigate to and from sourceFile.c to sourceFile.h. It was originally assigned to **command-tab**, but that was taken by the window server for application switching; then to **command-grave accent**, but that was taken by the window server for rotating among windows. In Xcode, even in the Metrowerks set, it's **command-option-up arrow**.

19.2.3 Build Behavior

Now turn to the third panel in the Preferences window, **Building**. CodeWarrior automatically saves all source files before compiling them; Xcode, by default, doesn't. At the lower-right of the panel is a pop-up menu labeled **For Unsaved Files:**. Set it to **Always Save**.

When it finds errors in a file during a build, CodeWarrior continues building the remaining files in the project. Xcode stops the build. CodeWarrior's approach gets more of the build done earlier and presents more errors at a time, whereas Xcode's minimizes the turnaround time between issuing a **build** command and correcting your code. It also saves the time taken up by its slower compiler when an error in a header file triggers redundant errors in several source files. To follow the CodeWarrior rule, check the box labeled **Continue building after errors**.

If errors or warnings are issued during a build, CodeWarrior opens a browser with the messages at the top and an editor at the bottom focused on the site of the selected error message. Xcode has an analogous window, the Build Results window, accessible by the command **Build → Build Results**. By default, Xcode doesn't show this window automatically; in the noncondensed project layouts, it would be mostly redundant to do so. With the Condensed project window, however, the Build Results window is your main access to errors and warnings. At the left of the **Building** panel is a group of two pop-up menus, labeled **Build Results Window:**. The best approximation to CodeWarrior's behavior is **Open during builds: On errors or warnings** and **Close after builds: On No Warnings**.

19.2.4 Window Behavior

In CodeWarrior, you are used to the one-document-one-window model of Macintosh applications. Each of your source files gets its own window, and you riffle through them like papers on a desktop. Xcode is a descendant of the NeXTStep tradition, which favors browsers and sees a multitude of windows as "clutter." Xcode therefore has a multitude of options whose goal is to keep you from opening additional windows. If you're looking for fidelity to the CodeWarrior experience, you'll want to turn all these options off.

The first of these options appears at the right end of the toolbar of every editor window: The **Grouped/Ungrouped** control (Figure 19.2) determines whether the

Figure 19.2 The **Grouped/Ungrouped** toolbar item that appears in editor windows. Xcode editor windows can edit more than one window at a time, holding the list of edited windows in a pop-up history menu. A window marked Ungrouped will not accept additional files; if an Ungrouped window is frontmost, opening a file for editing will open a new editor window.

next file you open for editing opens in its own editor window (**Ungrouped**) or in the front editor window (**Grouped**). A "grouped" editor window browses among a chain of files, using the history list in the pop-up menu just under the toolbar. If you are dedicated to the one-file-per-window model, click this icon so it shows **Ungrouped**. Then **command-option click** the toolbar widget in the title bar, or select **View** → **Customize Toolbar . . .** , and remove the item.

Another multiple-document-per-window feature is completely independent of the Grouped/Ungrouped preference, and you might consider leaving it on. This is **Open counterparts in same editor**, to be found in the first, **General**, pane of the Preferences window. When this option is in effect, switching between a source and its header file will be done in the same window, rather than opening a separate editor. My own experience is that I usually jump to counterpart files for quick reference to definitions or to deposit a prototype into a stub implementation. Keeping both files in the same workspace makes a lot of sense in such cases. Also, it's handy to be able to split a source file's window and switch one of the panes to the header.

19.3 Converting a CodeWarrior Project

CodeWarrior has a heritage of being a tool for developing applications for the classic Mac OS and is still the premier tool for producing single-file applications and plug-ins using Code-Fragment Manager (CFM) linkage. Mac OS X executables use the Mach-O executable format and except in very simple cases are delivered as package directories. Xcode is a tool that produces only Mach-O binaries and makes packages as a matter of course.

> If you have a product that must be a CFM binary, as some plug-ins still must be, CodeWarrior may still be your only option.

The first step in transitioning a CodeWarrior project, therefore, should be in making the changes necessary to convert your product to the appropriate package format and to produce the executable in Mach-O format. This can be done entirely in CodeWarrior, and it may be a good idea to make the transition in CodeWarrior so you can concentrate on the changes without having to deal with new tools at the same time.

This will also entail switching over to Mac OS X's versions of the standard C and C++ libraries. Add access paths for {OS X Volume}usr/include and {OS X

Volume}usr/lib. Remove any linkage to the Metrowerks Standard Libraries (MSL), and add /usr/lib/libSystem.dylib to the project.

Take the {Compiler}Mac OS Support tree out of your access paths, and replace any dependencies that leaves unfulfilled: Linking to Carbon.framework should take care of all of them for a conventional Mac OS project. Because you're using the system version of the support libraries, use the framework #include form <Carbon/Carbon.h> instead of manager-specific includes. Once you've got your project restabilized from these changes, you can swap in the gcc linker in CodeWarrior builds by selecting **Apple Mach-O PPC** for the linker in the Target Settings panel.

Because gcc is much, much stricter about syntax than CodeWarrior is, expect an onslaught of errors and warnings once you've switched over. You can reduce the pain by making CodeWarrior's compiler as strict as possible: Turn on all the warnings. If you're using C, enable the C99 dialect.

19.3.1 Importing the Project

In order to import a CodeWarrior project into Xcode, you need a runnable copy of CodeWarrior, at least version 8.3. Xcode does not build its project structure by reading the CodeWarrior files; the format of those files is not documented. Instead, Xcode discovers the project structure and settings through CodeWarrior's AppleScript interface. The process is fully automatic and requires no input once it's started.

Selecting **File → Import Project...** will bring up an Import Project Assistant. You'll first be asked whether you're importing a CodeWarrior project or a project from Project Builder for WebObjects. Select **Import CodeWarrior Project** and click the **Next** button. You will then be asked to identify the target CodeWarrior project, either by typing in the full path to the project or by clicking **Choose...** and finding it with a standard file-opening dialog. The assistant will offer to give the Xcode project the same base name as the CodeWarrior project, or you can enter a different name.

If your CodeWarrior project depended on the use of a global source tree that you intend to carry over to the Xcode project, you will want to check the box **Import "Global Source Trees" from CodeWarrior**. If your project includes subprojects, you can choose to have them converted as part of the import process; there is no option for giving them custom names.

When you're ready, click the **Finish** button, and the conversion will proceed.

19.3.2 Targets and Configurations

The typical CodeWarrior template for a new project envisions one kind of product—an application, a plug-in—per project and creates two targets to yield debugging and production versions of the product. An Xcode project can often encompass many kinds of products; one project might produce an application, a command line tool for prototyping, and two or three plug-ins. In that project, each product would correspond to one target. Xcode uses a separate mechanism, configurations, to produce variants of targets for debugging, testing, and release.

A configuration can be thought of as the set of all the options selected in the **Build** pane of the Info window you get by double-clicking the icon for a target (or by selecting **Project → Edit Active Target**). In that window is a long list of options to be passed to gcc, Rez, and the test of the Xcode build system. You can select which configuration list to view with the **Configuration:** pop-up at the top of the panel. You can select which configuration is in effect with the **Project → Set Active Build Configuration** menu or with the **Active Build Configuration** pop-up menu in the Build Results window. Targets built under different build configurations are built into separate subdirectories of the project's build directory.

Settings that have been changed at the target level in the displayed build configuration are displayed in boldface type. You can remove the setting—which exposes a lower-level setting and doesn't necessarily make the setting blank—by selecting its line in the **Build** list and pressing the **Delete** key.

I said, "at the target level" because build configurations come in two layers. What you see in the **Build** panel for a particular target are the settings in effect for that target. You can also set up a default configuration for all the targets in a project by making settings in the **Build** panel of the *project's* Info window. (Settings made in the project's Info window are shown in boldface there.) Target-level settings for a configuration override project-level settings, so you can set a general policy and then make exceptions.

If it's typical, your CodeWarrior project will have two targets for each product: one final and one for debugging. The imported project will have the same targets, and the project will have a single named configuration for imported settings. The variances in settings between the targets will show up as target-level settings for that configuration. There is no reason to change this arrangement right away. In the longer run, there are considerations for and against consolidating final and debug targets into single targets with Release and Debug configurations.

For Consolidating Targets

The case for making the switch is that if the debug version of a product is to be representative of the behavior of the final product, the two versions should be built from the same code base, with only compilation and build settings differing between them. In Xcode, a single target has the same set of source and resource files, regardless

Figure 19.3 Setting a preprocessor macro for a build configuration. We wanted to define a macro value just for debugging purposes. This can be done by editing the Debug build configuration and adding an item to the **Preprocessor Macros Not Used in Precompiled Headers** setting, as shown here. We use this setting instead of **Preprocessor Macros** so the Debug and Release build configurations can share a precompiled header.

of the configuration used to build it; nothing keeps separate targets in sync. Variants in code between versions can be achieved through defining preprocessor macros specially for Debug or Release configurations—look for the setting **Preprocessor Macros Not Used In Precompiled Headers** under the **Build** tab of the target Info window; see Figure 19.3.

Under CodeWarrior, you probably had separate precompiled-header files for the debug and final versions of your product. This is usually done in order to #define a preprocessor macro to enable debugging code. Under Xcode, you can save time by having a single precompiled header and using **Preprocessor Macros Not Used In Precompiled Headers** to take care of the macro definition.

Against Consolidating Targets

A case against consolidating versions into a single target would be made if your different versions were made up of different sets of files. You can finesse having to link against either a debug or a final version of a third-party library by putting them in different directories and supplying the appropriate library search path in the Debug and Release build configurations; sometimes, however, the differences are too great to be finessed. Two things made from two different file sets are two targets in Xcode.

If you decide to consolidate targets into configurations, start by opening the Info window for the project (double-click the top icon under the **Files** tab of the project window, or select **Project** → **Edit Project Settings**). In the **Configurations** tab, select the sole configuration transferred from CodeWarrior and click **Duplicate** twice. Name one of the new configurations Release and the other Debug. (Using the same name as Xcode uses in its templates helps if you ever embed projects in each other, because the configuration used for building a contained project is matched by name to the active configuration of the main project.)

Close the project Info window. Now select **File** → **New File . . .** to create an empty text file. You don't care where it's stored or what happens to it later; we're simply going to use it as a scratch pad to transfer the debug target's settings to the Debug configuration of the main target.

Click the **Targets** tab of the project window, open the **Targets** group, and double-click on the debug version of your target. Select the **Build** tab of the target's Info window. Make sure that the **Collection:** pop-up menu shows **Customized Settings**, because you are about to capture those settings. Click anywhere in the list, then press **command-A** to select the whole list. Hold down the mouse button anywhere in the list and drag into the empty text window; release. The text window should fill with the customized settings of the debug target.

Close this Info window. At this point, you are done with the imported debug target and can delete it, but you might want to wait until the rest of the task is safely done.

Double-click the imported final target, and select the **Build** tab in its Info window. Select **Debug** from the **Configuration:** pop-up menu and **All Settings** from the **Collection:** pop-up. Go through the list in the text file, and change the settings for the Debug configuration to match what you collected from the imported debug target.

We could have saved the text file as an .xcconfig file and used the pop-up at the bottom of the **Build** list to make the list be based on that file. This would have picked up the settings from the file automatically. The problem is that you are then committed to keeping the .xcconfig file around indefinitely; there is no way to copy settings-file settings permanently into Xcode target settings.

19.4 Traps in Conversion

The leading trap in converting from Metrowerks's compiler to gcc is the size of the bool Boolean type and the wchar_t "wide character" type. There is no standard for the storage of either type. Metrowerks uses one byte for bool and two for wchar_t; gcc uses four bytes for both on PowerPC.

If your code traverses arrays of these types bytewise, reads and writes them in binary format, or relies on how structures containing them pack, your code will break. The defense in the case of bool is to use an integer type of guaranteed size, as declared in stdint.h.

Another type to avoid is the long int. It is 32 bits long on code targeting every processor except the PowerPC G5, where it is 64 bits long.

If you have a static library target in CodeWarrior, make sure that its name is in the form lib*.a under Xcode. Xcode won't link against static libraries unless they are named according to the UNIX convention.

The Metrowerks preprocessor defines true, so you could use it to set macros that could be tested with #if directives. It's not set in gcc; use 1 instead.

The gcc compiler relies much less on #pragmas than the Metrowerks compiler does. For controlling properties of variables, such as alignment and packing, use the __attribute__ extension, as explained in **Specifying Attributes of Variables**, which you can find by doing a full-text search for gcc __attribute__ in the Documentation window. You can set compiler options on a per file basis by selecting the source file in the Groups & Files list, opening the Info window on the file (**command-I**), and selecting the **Build** tab; then type the desired flags into the large area provided. You can even set flags for several files at once by command-clicking to select the ones you want, opening the Info window, and editing the build settings. Whatever you enter will be applied to all selected files.

> Per file compiler flags are also per target: The flags you set for a file or set of files will have effect only for the target in effect at the time you set them. One way to be certain that you are setting the file-and-target combination you mean to set is to select the files from the Compile Sources phase of the relevant target and to execute **Get Info** on those.

If you need finer control than that—if you've been switching #pragmas back and forth in the course of a single file—you'll have to split the files in question according to what options you need.

The gcc tool does not provide preprocessor symbols for its compiler options. If, for instance, you've been relying on __RTTI_ENABLED to test whether C++ runtime typing is enabled, you'll have to make other arrangements, because that setting is not directly available to the preprocessor.

However, nearly every compiler flag has a shell variable associated with it, which you can discover by opening an Info window on the target, selecting the **Build** tab, and searching for the flag. The description at the bottom of the Info window will conclude with the flag and the associated shell variable. You can then use the **Preprocessor Macros** build setting to define a preprocessor setting for that value, such as RTTI_ENABLED=GCC_ENABLE_CPP_RTTI. Your symbol will then be #defined as YES or NO.

> Not all build settings have equivalent editors in the **Build** panel of the Target Info window or the **Styles** panel of the Project Info window. A complete list of Xcode's build settings can be found in the Build Settings release note, which you can see by selecting **Help → Show Build Settings Notes**. You can add a setting by clicking the + button in the **Build** or **Styles** panel and entering the name of the setting in the Setting column, and the value in the Value column. You can also use build-setting names as shell-script variables in Run Script build phases.

19.5 Exporting Symbols

19.5.1 #pragma export

One case in which it is simply not practical to set per file compiler flags to make up for the loss of CodeWarrior's #pragmas is #pragma export. When building a library in CodeWarrior, you can indicate that functions defined in a source file are to be visible outside a library by preceding them with #pragma export on. Functions can be kept private to the library—exportable to other files in the same library but not visible to clients of the library—by marking them with #pragma export off.

A library exports variables and entry points to make them available to users of the library; an application may export variables and entry points to make utility routines available to plug-ins. Exporting every symbol, however, is unnecessary and harmful to performance: Remember that the dynamic loader has to search all the components of an application for the definitions of unresolved symbols. The more symbol definitions are exported, the more there are to search, and the longer it will take to load the application. It therefore pays to export only the symbols that are on offer for others to link against.

By default, every application and library built with Xcode has almost all symbols exported. It's a good idea to take charge of the symbols an application exports. Start by applying the nm tool to the application executable or the library file:

```
$ cd build/Linear.app/Contents/MacOS
$ nm -g Linear
00000000 A .objc_category_name_DataPoint_PropertyList
00000000 A .objc_category_name_Regression_PropertyList
00000000 A .objc_class_name_DataPoint
00000000 A .objc_class_name_MyDocument
         U .objc_class_name_NSAlert
         U .objc_class_name_NSArray
 .
 .
 .
         U _objc_msgSend
         U _objc_msgSendSuper
0000c0c0 S _receive_samples
00008a2c T start
$
```

What we see is each symbol in the binary, tagged with a type identifier and, if the symbol is defined in the binary, an address. Had we not supplied the -g flag to nm, some of the type tags would be in lowercase, indicating that the symbol is not exported.

> I should add that we're doing all this with Linear compiled with the Release build configuration selected.

Our goal is to provide an external-symbols file for the use of the linker. The format of the file is one item per line, and every symbol in the file will be given external scope; everything else will be nonexternal. There's a catch: Externals defined by the runtime system have to be preserved as externals. These are common variables and routines that the application provides in its image and are shared through all the libraries the application loads.

So our strategy is to capture a list of every symbol defined in the application binary into a file and to remove from the file only the lines that name symbols that are defined in our code but that we do not want to export. We then save the file in the project directory and put the file's name in the **Exported Symbols File** setting of the **Build** panel of the application target's Info window.

There is no option for nm to restrict it to symbols defined in a binary, but situations like this are why there are pipelines in UNIX: Type

```
$ nm -g Linear | \
  ruby -ne \
  'if /^[0-9a-f]+.*\s(\S+)$/.match($_) then print $1,"\n" end' \
  > ../../../../symbols.exp
```

The first line produces our symbol table. The second sends the symbol table to a Ruby one-liner that extracts the symbol string from only those lines that have addresses on them. The resulting list goes to a file named symbols.exp, in the project directory, assuming that we're working with Linear in the build directory.

The symbols we want to remove turn out to be few:

```
.objc_category_name_DataPoint_PropertyList
.objc_category_name_Regression_PropertyList
.objc_class_name_DataPoint
.objc_class_name_MyDocument
.objc_class_name_Regression
```

These are string constants for the classes and categories we define. As no outside library or plug-in uses them, we can make them nonexternal.

You may remember that the Statistics framework makes use of methods implemented by MyDocument and be wondering why those methods—or any methods, for that matter—aren't public. The reason is that Objective-C methods aren't linked by address at build time or load time but are looked up, by the method signature, at the time the message is sent. The lookup process makes no use of the linkage symbol tables. If you ran nm Linear, without any options, you would see the method symbols, with the type t, the letter indicating that they are in the TEXT segment that code goes into, and the lowercase indicating that the symbols are not exported.

19.5.2 Another Way

If you are using gcc 4.0—and therefore are targeting Mac OS X 10.3.9 and later— you can control symbol exports from the source file. The __attribute__ compiler extension in gcc now includes a visibility attribute that you can attach to any external symbol. The form of the attribute for symbols that are to be exported is

```
__attribute__((visibility("default")))
```

The form of the attribute for symbols that are to be public within the library in which they appear but not exported beyond it is

```
__attribute__((visibility("hidden")))
```

Some examples are

```
int     moduleErrNo __attribute__((visibility("hidden")));

__attribute__((visibility("default")))
float   MyPublicFunction(double     inParam);
```

By default, all symbols have a visibility of "default", which makes sense. You can change this with the -fvisibility=hidden compiler flag. Use -fvisibility=default to make the default explicit.

19.6 Summary

I hope that experienced CodeWarrior users can make themselves more comfortable and productive with the hints provided in this chapter. We adjusted our expectations and then saw what we can do to customize Xcode so that it cooperates with the work habits of CodeWarrior veterans. We examined what is involved in moving a project from CodeWarrior to Xcode and how to minimize the mismatches from the transition. We gave extensive attention to the problem of controlling the export of symbols.

20

Xcode for make Veterans

This chapter is for experienced UNIX programmers who are accustomed to controlling application builds with a dependency manager, such as GNU make. As an integrated development environment, Xcode is at first glance far removed from the tools you are used to. But Xcode is not a tightly integrated tool set like Metrowerks's CodeWarrior. The editor, the build system, and some convenience services run as part of Xcode's process, but for preprocessing, compilation, assembly, and linkage, Xcode is a front end for gcc and other command line tools. You may feel that your builds have been sealed away from you in a black box; in this chapter, I hope to open the box for you a little.

A makefile is organized around a hierarchy of goals. Some goals, such as the frequently used clean or install targets, are abstract but most are files. Associated with each goal is a list of other goals that are antecedents—dependencies—of that goal and a script for turning the antecedents into something that satisfies the goal. Most commonly, the antecedents are input files for the programs that the script runs to produce a target file. The genius of make comes from the rule that if any target is more recently modified than all its antecedents, it is presumed to embody their current state, and it is not necessary to run the script to produce it again. The combination of a tree of dependencies and this pruning rule make make a powerful and efficient tool for automating such tasks as building software products.

The organizing unit of a makefile is the target-dependency-action group. But in the case of application development, this group is often stereotyped to the extent that you don't even have to specify it; make provides a default rule that looks like this:

```
%.o     :   %.c
    $(CC) -c $(CPPFLAGS) $(CFLAGS) -o $@ $<
```

325

So all the programmer need do is list all the constituent .o files in the project, and the built-in rule will produce the .o files as needed. Often, the task of maintaining a makefile becomes less one of maintaining dependencies than of keeping lists.

In the same way, Xcode makes dependency analysis a matter of list keeping by taking advantage of the fact that almost all projects are targeted at specific kinds of executable products, such as applications, libraries, tools, or plug-ins. Knowing how the build process ends, Xcode can do the right thing with the files that go into the project.

A file in the Xcode Groups & Files list is a member of three distinct lists.

1. By being in the Groups & Files list, the file is part of the project. This has nothing to do with whether it has any effect on any product of the project. It might, for instance, be a document you're keeping handy for reference or some notes you're taking.

2. A file may belong to zero or more *targets* in the project. A file is included in a target's file list because it is a part of that target's product, whether as a source file or as a resource to be copied literally into the product. When a file is added to a project, Xcode asks you which targets in the project should include the file. You can select what files belong to a target through checkboxes in the detail view or, optionally, in the Groups & Files list. You can select what targets a file belongs to with the **Targets** tab of the file's Info window.

3. What role a file plays in a target depends on what *phase* of the target the file belongs to. When a file is added to a target, Xcode assigns it to a build phase, based on the type of the file: Files with gcc-compilable suffixes get assigned to the Compile Sources phase; libraries, to the Link Binary With Libraries phase; Rez source and .rsrc files to the Build Resource Manager Resources Phase; and so on. (See Figure 20.1.) Files that don't fit anywhere else are put in the Copy Bundle Resources phase, for incorporation into the product's resource directory.

When you create a target, either in the process of creating an Xcode project or by adding a target to an existing project, you specify what type of product you want to produce, and you can't change that type except by making another target. The target type forms one anchor—the endpoint—in the Xcode build system's dependency analysis: It tells the build system what the product's desired structure—single file or package—is and how to link the executable.

The other anchor of the build system is the set of build-phase members for the target. The Compile Sources build phase, along with the sources you add to it, yield

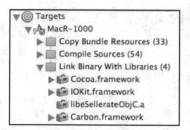

Figure 20.1 Build phases in a modest project. You gain access to build phases by opening the disclosure triangle next to the **Targets** group in the Groups & Files list and then opening the triangle for the target of interest. Each phase, in turn, contains the files that belong to it. Files can be added to a phase by dragging; removed, by selecting them and pressing **Delete**.

object files, which are the inputs to the executable-linkage phase implicit in your choice of target type. The various file-copying phases and the files you supply for them yield the copy commands needed to populate the auxiliary structure of an application.

20.1 Xcode Build Variables

The action for the default make rule for .c files parameterizes almost the entire action. The command for the C compiler and the set of flags to pass are left to the makefile variables CC, CPPFLAGS, and CFLAGS. You set these flags at the head of the file to suitable values, and all the compilations in your build comply.

Xcode relies similarly on variables to organize build options but at a much finer granularity. There is one variable for each of the most common settings. For instance, the variable GCC_ENABLE_CPP_RTTI controls whether gcc's -fno-rtti will be added to suppress generation of runtime type information. This variable is set by a checkbox in the **Build** tab of the Get Info window for the target.

In the Groups & Files list of any Xcode project, find the **Targets** group, and click the disclosure triangle next to it to open the group and reveal the contents. Double-click one of the targets inside. This should reveal the Get Info window for the target, as shown in Figure 20.2. Click the **Build** tab if it isn't already selected.

The list you see is a front end for most of the build variables Xcode maintains for this target. Click an item; the text area at the bottom of the Info window fills with text describing what that item does. In brackets, and usually at the end of the description, are the name of the build variable the item controls and what gcc option, if any, it

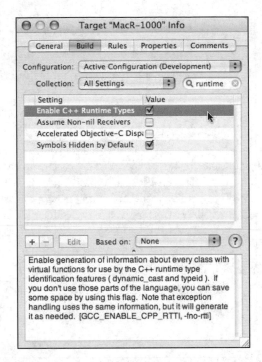

Figure 20.2 Finding a specific gcc option in a target's settings. Open the **Targets** group in the Groups & Files list, and double-click a target to open the Info window. The **Build** tab lists most of the settings for which Xcode maintains build variables.

affects. Both the label and the description are searchable: The list in Figure 20.2 was narrowed down to four entries by typing **runtime** into the search field at the top of the window.

20.2 Custom Build Rules

Xcode's build system can be extended to new file types and processing tools. The default rules in the build system match file extensions to product types and process any source files that are newer than the products. You can add a custom rule that instructs the build system to look for files whose names match a pattern and apply a shell command to such files. See Figure 20.3.

Create a rule by double-clicking a target icon in the Groups & Files list, selecting the **Rules** tab, and clicking the + button. At the top of the list, a "slot" will be added

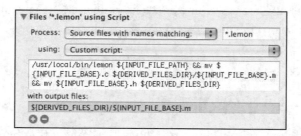

Figure 20.3 A custom build rule. This rule captures all target files that have the suffix .lemon, passes them to the lemon parser generator, and if that step succeeds, moves the product files to the project's derived-sources subdirectory. The rule specifies the form of the output file's path so the build system knows whether, and when, to trigger the rule.

that has two pop-up menus completing the sentence "Process . . . using . . . ." For a custom rule, you select **Source files with names matching:** and **Custom script:**. This will open a text field for the matching pattern, into which you will type the matching pattern—a glob pattern, such as *.lemon—and a second field for the single shell script line to process the matched file. Don't worry about the size of this field; it will grow vertically as you type. Remember also that you can chain shell commands with the && operator.

You may use any build variable you like in the shell command. Additionally, some variables are specific to custom rule invocations:

- INPUT_FILE_PATH, the full path to the source file (/Users/xcodeuser/MyProject/grammar.lemon)
- INPUT_FILE_DIR, the directory containing the source file (/Users/xcodeuser/MyProject)
- INPUT_FILE_NAME, the name of the source file (grammar.lemon)
- INPUT_FILE_BASE, the base, unsuffixed, name of the source file (grammar)

Apple recommends that intermediate files, such as the source files output by parser generators, be put into the directory named in the DERIVED_FILE_DIR variable. The build system is supposed to detect the type of such files and process them accordingly; however, as I write this, I find that the .m file I generated with the *.lemon rule shown in Figure 20.3 was copied to my application's resources directory instead of being compiled. If you're not satisfied with how your version of Xcode treats your intermediate files, make sure that they are sent to SRCROOT—the same directory as your project, which should be the working directory for the rule's command—and include them as regular source in your target. Thus, you'll have to generate one pass of the intermediate files by hand.

20.3 Run Script Build Phase

You can add arbitrary script actions to a build by adding a Run Script build phase. Select **Project** → **New Build Phase** → **New Shell Script Build Phase**, and you will be presented with an editor into which you can type commands in the scripting language of your choice (Figure 20.4).

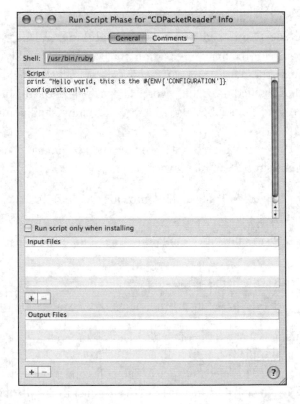

Figure 20.4   The Run Script build phase window. You can specify any language you could use in an executable script file. By adding files to the input and output files lists, you can have the Xcode build system run the script only when its products are out-of-date.

A Run Script phase can have specific files as inputs and outputs. If these files are present, they will be taken into account by Xcode's build system; if all the outputs are newer than all the inputs, the phase is skipped. If outputs are unspecified, the phase is always executed. The sequence in which a Run Script phase is executed is determined by the availability of its inputs and the need for its outputs.

When a Run Script build phase is executed, the script is copied to a temporary directory, and a series of `setenv` commands copy build variables into the environment. The script is then run, with your permissions, with the project directory current, with the input files passed in as parameters.

There are two caveats about build variables and Run Script phases. First, you can't change them: They are passed to your script by doing a `setenv` for each variable before the script is invoked. When the script finishes, those environment variables, along with any changes you might have made to them, go out of scope.

Second, you don't get all the build variables. Apple's documentation suggests that variables that set options specific to a single tool, such as the variables that begin with `GCC_`, are not exported to the Run Script environment. At present, such variables are exported, if they have been changed from their default values by the current build configuration. So if you have a script that sets up for code-coverage tests when the code-coverage flag (`GCC_GENERATE_TEST_COVERAGE_FILES`) is set, you will have to test whether that symbol is present in the environment—and know what its absence means—before using its value.

> A cautious user might take Apple's documentation to mean that the visibility of `GCC_` and similar variables is not guaranteed in future releases.

20.4 Under the Hood: A Simple Build

The Xcode build system—to repeat—is just a front end for `gcc` and other command line tools. Xcode's dependency analysis identifies what tasks need doing and issues high-level commands to accomplish those tasks. The high-level commands, in turn, map to shell commands, the execution of which Xcode monitors for warnings and errors.

The Build Results window, accessible through the **Build → Build Results** menu command, shows the progress of a build and a table of the results. By clicking the third icon to the bottom-left of the results list, you can open an additional panel in the

Build Results window; this panel contains a transcript of the build commands and the literal console output from the tools Xcode invokes.

In this section, we sample the build transcript of a Core Data–using program as it is built from a clean start for both PowerPC and Intel architectures. The transcript will be heavily edited for space and readability; the line breaks (\) and ellipses (. . .) don't appear in the original.

> **Native Build of Target "PktReader"**
> **using Build Configuration "Release"**

This build will use the Release configuration rather than the Debug configuration. The Debug configuration for this target does not take the extra time to build for both architectures, because ZeroLink would make the debug version runnable only on the build machine, which can run only the native-architecture version.

20.4.1 Copy Structural Files

The first thing that happens in a clean build is that `Info.plist` and `PkgInfo`, two files you may not have directly edited but that must be present in any application package, are copied from intermediate storage to their places in the application package. This step doesn't correspond to any build phase in the target but is performed when needed.

Here, we see the operation for `Info.plist`. Internally, Xcode denotes this step as a `PBXCp` high-level operation; this expands to the shell commands that create the destination directory, make the project directory current, and perform the copy. Project Builder-X `cp`, or `pbxcp`, is a private variant of the `cp` tool, offering options the regular command does not, such as the ability to exclude SCM directories from copy operations:

```
PBXCp build/Release/PktReader.app/Contents/Info.plist \
  build/PktReader.build/Release/PktReader.build/Info.plist

    mkdir build/Release/PktReader.app/Contents
    cd /Users/fritza/Projects/PktReader
    /.../pbxcp -exclude .DS_Store -exclude CVS -exclude .svn \
        -strip-debug-symbols -resolve-src-symlinks \
        build/PktReader.build/Release/PktReader.build/Info.plist \
        build/Release/PktReader.app/Contents
```

The build transcript shows the high-level commands flush left, with the commands that implement them indented in the lines that follow.

20.4.2 Copy Bundle Resources

The next series of high-level commands, CpResource, are issued in response to your explicit request, once for each file or directory in the Copy Bundle Resources phase. In this example, the file WeatherStation.plist gets copied into the application's Resources directory:

```
CpResource \
 PktReader.app/Contents/Resources/WeatherStation.plist \
 WeatherStation.plist

    mkdir build/Release/PktReader.app/Contents/Resources
    cd /Users/fritza/Projects/PktReader
    /.../pbxcp -exclude .DS_Store -exclude CVS -exclude .svn \
        -strip-debug-symbols -resolve-src-symlinks \
        WeatherStation.plist \
        build/Release/PktReader.app/Contents/Resources
```

20.4.3 Compile Sources

The build system then turns to producing executable binaries (C/C++/Objective-C). The first task is to produce a precompiled header for each architecture on which the binary is to be runnable. The process of building a universal binary is mostly the same as building stand-alone binaries for each architecture separately and then combining them into a "fat" binary file. Because we'll be compiling once for each of two architectures, we need two precompiled headers.

Precompiled headers are kept in a subdirectory of /Library/Caches. The high-level command ProcessPCH specifies what precompiled header file to create, from what prefix (.pch) file, using what dialect and which parser. The command maps to commands that ensure that the cache directory exists, an environment-variable setting, and an invocation of gcc:

```
ProcessPCH /Library/Caches/.../PktReader_Prefix.pch.gch \
 PktReader_Prefix.pch normal ppc objective-c \
 com.apple.compilers.gcc.4_0
```

```
    mkdir /Library/Caches/...
    cd /Users/fritza/Projects/PktReader
    setenv MACOSX_DEPLOYMENT_TARGET 10.4
    /usr/bin/gcc-4.0 -x objective-c-header -arch ppc -pipe \
        -Wno-trigraphs -fobjc-exceptions -fpascal-strings \
        -fasm-blocks -Os -Wreturn-type -Wunused-variable \
        -fmessage-length=0 -mtune=G5 -fvisibility=hidden \
        -Ibuild/PktReader.build/Release/.../PktReader.hmap \
        -mdynamic-no-pic -Fbuild/Release -Ibuild/Release/include \
        -Ibuild/PktReader.build/Release/.../DerivedSources \
        -isysroot /Developer/SDKs/MacOSX10.4u.sdk \
        -c PktReader_Prefix.pch \
        -o /Library/Caches/.../PktReader_Prefix.pch.gch

ProcessPCH /Library/Caches/.../PktReader_Prefix.pch.gch \
PktReader_Prefix.pch normal i386 objective-c \
com.apple.compilers.gcc.4_0

    mkdir /Library/Caches/...
    cd /Users/fritza/Projects/PktReader
    setenv MACOSX_DEPLOYMENT_TARGET 10.4
    /usr/bin/gcc-4.0 -x objective-c-header -arch i386 -pipe \
        -Wno-trigraphs -fobjc-exceptions -fpascal-strings \
        -fasm-blocks -Os -Wreturn-type -Wunused-variable \
        -fmessage-length=0 -fvisibility=hidden \
        -Ibuild/PktReader.build/Release/.../PktReader.hmap \
        -mdynamic-no-pic -Fbuild/Release -Ibuild/Release/include \
        -Ibuild/PktReader.build/Release/.../DerivedSources \
        -isysroot /Developer/SDKs/MacOSX10.4u.sdk \
        -c PktReader_Prefix.pch \
        -o /Library/Caches/.../PktReader_Prefix.pch.gch
```

Once the precompilation is done, Xcode's build system runs through every C-family source file in the Compile Sources build phase and compiles them for the first architecture:

```
CompileC build/.../ppc/PacketInterpreter.o PacketInterpreter.m \
    normal ppc objective-c com.apple.compilers.gcc.4_0
```

```
mkdir build/.../ppc
cd /Users/fritza/Projects/PktReader
setenv MACOSX_DEPLOYMENT_TARGET 10.4
/usr/bin/gcc-4.0 -x objective-c -arch ppc -pipe \
    -Wno-trigraphs -fobjc-exceptions -fpascal-strings \
    -fasm-blocks -Os -Wreturn-type -Wunused-variable \
    -fmessage-length=0 -mtune=G5 -fvisibility=hidden \
    -Ibuild/PktReader.build/Release/.../PktReader.hmap \
    -mdynamic-no-pic -Fbuild/Release -Ibuild/Release/include \
    -Ibuild/PktReader.build/Release/.../DerivedSources \
    -isysroot /Developer/SDKs/MacOSX10.4u.sdk \
    -include /Library/Caches/.../PktReader_Prefix.pch \
    -c PacketInterpreter.m \
    -o build/.../ppc/PacketInterpreter.o
```

PacketInterpreter.m: In function '-[PacketInterpreter
fillWeather]':
PacketInterpreter.m:59: warning: local declaration of 'origin'
hides instance variable

The high-level `CompileC` command divides into a `mkdir` for the intermediate-product directory for the current architecture, a `cd` to make sure that the project directory is current, a `setenv` to designate the target version of Mac OS X, and, finally, the invocation of gcc.

I chose as a representative sample a file that produced a warning. Xcode reads error and warning text directly from gcc's standard error stream and interprets it. In the build transcript, the standard error text is shown in a slanted font; the text of warnings and errors is collected and put into the list in the Build Results window, into the tooltips for the error-and-warning badges in the gutter next to the offending lines, and into the status bar when a badge is clicked.

Xcode is generally good at parsing gcc's error messages, but not every message passes intelligibly through to the IDE. Undefined and multiply defined symbols detected at link time, in particular, are reported in the IDE without the part of the message that says what the offending symbols are. If you're ever in doubt as to what an Xcode error message means, looking at the build transcript for gcc's exact output may clear things up.

20.4.4 Linkage (First Architecture)

```
Ld build/.../ppc/PktReader normal ppc

    mkdir build/.../ppc
    cd /Users/fritza/Projects/PktReader
    setenv MACOSX_DEPLOYMENT_TARGET 10.4
    /usr/bin/gcc-4.0 -o build/.../ppc/PktReader -Lbuild/Release \
        -Fbuild/Release \
        -filelist build/.../ppc/PktReader.LinkFileList \
        -framework Cocoa -framework IOKit -arch ppc \
        -isysroot /Developer/SDKs/MacOSX10.4u.sdk -Wl,\
        -syslibroot,/Developer/SDKs/MacOSX10.4u.sdk
```

The Ld high-level command links the compiled objects with the libraries and frameworks designated in the Link Binary With Libraries build phase. In this case, the -framework option is used to link the Cocoa and IOKit frameworks. The object files aren't listed to the gcc invocation but are drawn via a -filelist option from a file Xcode generates in the intermediate-products directory.

20.4.5 Compile Sources (Second Architecture)

Because this target is destined for both PowerPC and Intel architectures, the compilation and linkage phases have to be done all over again, the only differences being the -arch i386 option passed to gcc and the use of an i386 intermediate-products directory:

```
CompileC build/.../i386/PacketInterpreter.o PacketInterpreter.m \
  normal i386 objective-c com.apple.compilers.gcc.4_0

    mkdir build/.../i386
    cd /Users/fritza/Projects/PktReader
    setenv MACOSX_DEPLOYMENT_TARGET 10.4
    /usr/bin/gcc-4.0 -x objective-c -arch i386 -pipe \
        -Wno-trigraphs -fobjc-exceptions -fpascal-strings \
        -fasm-blocks -Os -Wreturn-type -Wunused-variable \
        -fmessage-length=0 -fvisibility=hidden \
        -Ibuild/PktReader.build/Release/.../PktReader.hmap \
        -mdynamic-no-pic -Fbuild/Release -Ibuild/Release/include \
```

```
-Ibuild/PktReader.build/Release/.../DerivedSources \
-isysroot /Developer/SDKs/MacOSX10.4u.sdk \
-include /Library/Caches/.../PktReader_Prefix.pch \
-c PacketInterpreter.m \
-o build/.../i386/PacketInterpreter.o
```

```
PacketInterpreter.m: In function '-[PacketInterpreter
                                            fillWeather]':
PacketInterpreter.m:59: warning: local declaration of 'origin'
                                    hides instance variable
```

20.4.6 Linkage (Second Architecture)

```
Ld build/.../i386/PktReader normal i386

    mkdir build/.../i386
    cd /Users/fritza/Projects/PktReader
    setenv MACOSX_DEPLOYMENT_TARGET 10.4
    /usr/bin/gcc-4.0 -o build/.../i386/PktReader \
        -Lbuild/Release -Fbuild/Release \
        -filelist build/.../i386/PktReader.LinkFileList \
        -framework Cocoa -framework IOKit -arch i386 \
        -isysroot /Developer/SDKs/MacOSX10.4u.sdk -Wl,\
        -syslibroot,/Developer/SDKs/MacOSX10.4u.sdk
```

20.4.7 Create Universal Binary

In the respective intermediate-products directories, the two linkage phases produced separate binary files, for Intel and PowerPC. The delivery format for binaries compatible with both architectures is a single file containing both versions of the binary. This is known to Apple marketing as a *universal binary*, and for historical purposes as a *fat binary*. The high-level command CreateUniversalBinary uses the lipo tool to assemble the binary in its final form and position in the application bundle:

```
CreateUniversalBinary \
  build/Release/PktReader.app/Contents/MacOS/PktReader \
  normal "ppc i386"
```

```
mkdir build/Release/PktReader.app/Contents/MacOS
cd /Users/fritza/Projects/PktReader
/usr/bin/lipo -create build/.../ppc/PktReader \
    build/.../i386/PktReader \
    -output \
    build/Release/PktReader.app/Contents/MacOS/PktReader
```

20.4.8 Compile Data Models

This application makes use of a Core Data managed-object model drawn from a
.xcdatamodel data model created in Xcode. Xcode data models are not directly usable
by Core Data but must be compiled into .mom managed-object model files. This is done
by the momc compiler embedded in Xcode's data-modeling plug-in.

Surprisingly, this is done twice, once for each architecture. In each case, the
resulting .mom file, with the same name, is copied to the same destination in the
application bundle.

The Xcode IDE lists .xcdatamodel files in the Compile Sources build phase:

```
DataModelCompile build/.../ppc/PktReader_DataModel.mom \
 PktReader_DataModel.xcdatamodel


    mkdir build/.../ppc
    cd /Users/fritza/Projects/PktReader
    /.../XDCoreDataModel.xdplugin/Contents/Resources/momc \
        PktReader_DataModel.xcdatamodel \
        build/.../ppc/PktReader_DataModel.mom


DataModelCompile build/.../i386/PktReader_DataModel.mom \
 PktReader_DataModel.xcdatamodel


    mkdir build/.../i386
    cd /Users/fritza/Projects/PktReader
    /.../XDCoreDataModel.xdplugin/Contents/Resources/momc \
        PktReader_DataModel.xcdatamodel \
        build/.../i386/PktReader_DataModel.mom


PBXCp PktReader.app/Contents/Resources/PktReader_DataModel.mom \
 build/.../ppc/PktReader_DataModel.mom
```

```
    mkdir build/Release/PktReader.app/Contents/Resources
    cd /Users/fritza/Projects/PktReader
    /.../pbxcp -exclude .DS_Store -exclude CVS \
        -strip-debug-symbols -resolve-src-symlinks \
        build/.../ppc/PktReader_DataModel.mom \
        build/Release/PktReader.app/Contents/Resources
```

```
  PBXCp PktReader.app/Contents/Resources/PktReader_DataModel.mom \
   build/.../i386/PktReader_DataModel.mom
```

```
    mkdir build/Release/PktReader.app/Contents/Resources
    cd /Users/fritza/Projects/PktReader
    /.../pbxcp -exclude .DS_Store -exclude CVS \
        -strip-debug-symbols -resolve-src-symlinks \
        build/.../i386/PktReader_DataModel.mom \
        build/Release/PktReader.app/Contents/Resources
```

20.4.9 Finishing Touch

Finally, the application package directory is touched to make its modification date match the end of the build process, which is what, intuitively, it ought to be:

```
  Touch build/Release/PktReader.app
```

```
    mkdir build/Release
    cd /Users/fritza/Projects/PktReader
    /usr/bin/touch build/Release/PktReader.app
```

20.5 The xcodebuild Tool

Sometimes there is no substitute for a command line tool. The UNIX command line presents a well-understood interface for scripting and controlling complex tools. Apple has provided a command line interface to the Xcode build system through the xcodebuild tool. Using xcodebuild is simple: Set the working directory to the directory containing an .xcodeproj project package, and invoke xcodebuild, specifying the project, target, configuration, and any build settings you wish to set. If only one

.xcodeproj package is in the directory, all these options can be defaulted by simply entering

    $ xcodebuild

That command will build the project's current target in its default configuration. Apple's intention is that xcodebuild have the same role in a nightly build or routine-release script that make would have.

In building a target, specify one of five actions for xcodebuild:

1. **build**, the default to build the specified target out of SRCROOT into SYMROOT/CON-FIGURATION. This is the same as the **Build** command in the Xcode application.

2. **clean**, to remove from SYMROOT the product and any intermediate files. This is the same as the **Clean** command in the Xcode application.

3. **install**, to build the specified target and install it at INSTALL_DIR (usually DSTROOT/INSTALL_PATH).

4. **installsrc**, to copy the project source to SRCROOT.

5. **installhdrs**, to copy headers to their installed location.

If more than one .xcodeproj package is in the current directory, you must specify which one you are interested in, with the option -project, followed by the name of the project. Not specifying a target is the same as supplying the -activetarget option; you can also specify -alltargets or -target, followed by the name of the target you want to build. It's a little different with configurations: The absence of a specification selects the default configuration; -activeconfiguration uses, as you would imagine, the active configuration for the selected project; and -configuration followed by a configuration name selects that configuration.

20.6 Settings Hierarchy

Build settings in Xcode can be set at any of four—or, in the case of xcodebuild, five—layers in a hierarchy. A setting may be made in

- A BSD environment variable
- A default, set for the Xcode application
- A configuration at the project level, if that configuration is active
- A configuration at the target level, if that configuration is active
- A command line parameter, if xcodebuild is doing the build

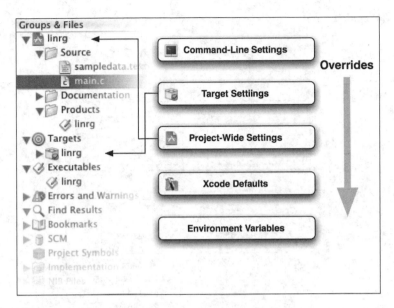

Figure 20.5 The hierarchy of build settings in Xcode and `xcodebuild`. A setting may be made at one or more of these layers, but the topmost setting in the hierarchy controls. Settings in higher layers may refer to settings from lower layers by the variable reference `$(VALUE)`. The top layer, command line settings, is present only in an `xcodebuild` invocation.

Settings in each layer override the settings from the ones below it, as shown in Figure 20.5.

For example, consider the build variables `ZERO_LINK` and `GCC_PREPROCESSOR_DEFINITIONS_NOT_USED_IN_PRECOMPS`. By default, `ZERO_LINK` is 0, and `GCC_PREPROCESSOR_DEFINITIONS_NOT_USED_IN_PRECOMPS` is empty. In Figure 20.6, `ZERO_LINK` defaults to `NO` in Xcode, and the Release configuration doesn't change that at either the project or the target levels. But the project setting for the Debug configuration sets `ZERO_LINK` to `YES`, and that is the value used when the Debug configuration is active. `GCC_PREPROCESSOR_DEFINITIONS_NOT_USED_IN_PRECOMPS` is empty so far as Xcode is concerned, and at the project level, the policy is to set `DEBUG_LEVEL` to 2 for Debug builds and to 0 for Release builds. But for this target only, the developer decides to set `DEBUG_LEVEL` to 1 for Release builds.

As a result, when the Debug configuration is selected, `ZERO_LINK` will be set to `YES`, and `GCC_PREPROCESSOR_DEFINITIONS_NOT_USED_IN_PRECOMPS` will be `DEBUG_LEVEL=2`. When the Release configuration is selected, `ZERO_LINK` will be `NO`, and `GCC_PREPROCESSOR_DEFINITIONS_NOT_USED_IN_PRECOMPS` will be `DEBUG_LEVEL=1`.

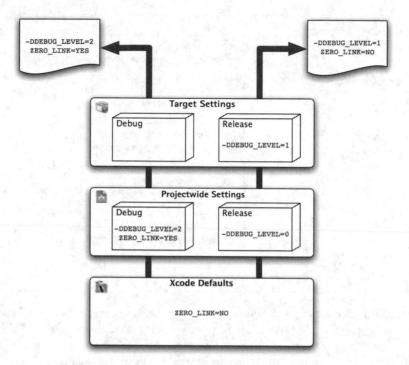

Figure 20.6 The build-settings hierarchy in action

20.7 Build Configurations

In a software development project, you typically don't want to use the same build settings for your day-to-day development as for releases of the product. In a development build, you'll want #define symbols that unmask debugging code, as well as compiler switches that suppress optimization and generate debugging symbols, but these settings would hurt performance and product size in a release build.

In a makefile, you'd take care of this need by drawing your compiler and linker flags from variables and setting the variables according to the intended use of the build. CFLAGS, for instance, might include -g -O0 for a working build and -Os for release.

In Xcode, you can organize groups of build-variable settings by purpose, using the build configuration feature. When a new Xcode project is created, it contains three configurations: Debug, for quick turnaround and easy debugging; Release, for optimal size and performance; and Default, which makes no changes, other than settings that name the product and identify its type, to the default values Xcode sets. The

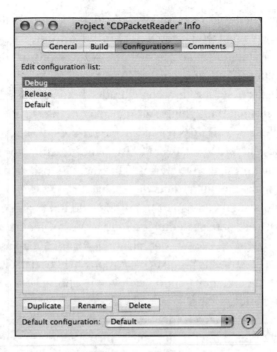

Figure 20.7 The project configuration list, showing the three standard configurations— Debug, Release, and Default—in an Xcode project. You can add configurations of your own by selecting a configuration you want to start from and clicking the **Duplicate** button. You can also delete or rename the selected configuration. The Default configuration, selected with the pop-up menu at the bottom of the window, is the configuration xcodebuild will use for builds for which you do not specify a configuration.

Default settings will yield an even more release-oriented product than the Release configuration, in that function symbols will be stripped, and the build product will be placed in an installation directory instead of the project's build subdirectory.

You can review the configurations in a project by double-clicking the project icon at the top of the Groups & Files list (or selecting **Project → Edit Project Settings**) and selecting the **Configurations** tab. See Figure 20.7.

When you edit the settings for a configuration using the **Build** tab of the project Info window, you are setting a policy for all the targets in your project. For instance, you might want **Fix & Continue** to be on for the Debug configuration and off for Release. You want this to be the case for everything you build with this project, so you double-click the project icon at the top of the Groups & Files list to open the project Info window and select the **Build** tab. With the **Configuration:** pop-up at the top of the window showing **Debug**, you check **Fix & Continue**; you switch the pop-up to the Release configuration, and make sure that **Fix & Continue** is unchecked.

Note that the **Fix & Continue** item label turns to boldface when you set it. When a window contributes a setting to a configuration, the setting's label is shown in boldface. This is an important point: An item may be blank or unchecked, but its label will be in boldface. This does not mean "no setting"! It means that this window affirmatively makes the setting blank or NO. To change a setting to "no setting," select the setting's line, and press the **Delete** key. The line will lose its boldfacing, and the value shown will be the default, or inherited, value.

Not every build setting can be left to projectwide policy; some must be set per target. The obvious cases are such things as the names of the targets' products, but it may be that you intend to use -O3 optimization, for instance, instead of -Os, for a library target. Open the **Targets** group in the Groups & Files list, and locate the target of interest. Double-click it, and an Info window will appear; it too will have a **Build** tab for you to alter build settings.

The **Build** panel of the target Info window is the place where you can see what settings will apply to that target in the selected configuration. Settings you make in the target window override the values inherited from the project level and below, but what you see in the target window is the final word.

At both the project and the target levels, you can select from the **Configuration:** pop-up menu which configuration your settings apply to. You can apply your settings to all configurations by selecting **All Configurations** in the pop-up.

20.8 Summary

This chapter covered Xcode as a build system like make that is a front end for command line tools that consume source files to replace out-of-date product files. We saw how to customize the build process by adding build rules and inserting shell-script build phases. We also discussed how build configurations can apply packages of build-time environment variables to a project.

21

More About Debugging

21.1 Debugging Techniques

We've been using the Debugger window since Chapter 2. Here are a few points that haven't been covered yet.

- The stack-trace and variable-list views of the Debugger window are at the top of the window. For many screens, vertical screen real estate is more valuable than horizontal screen real estate. **Debug → Toggle Debugger Layout** will make those panes appear at the left side of the window, allowing you to see more of the editor view.

- The Breakpoints window, available through **Window → Tools → Breakpoints** or the breakpoints toolbar icon, does more than display the breakpoints you set in the margins of your code. You can also set symbolic breakpoints in your code or in Apple-supplied libraries. For instance, it is often useful to click **New Symbolic Breakpoint** and type `-[NSException raise]` into the new entry. This sets a gdb "future break" (fb) so that the Debugger will get control whenever a Cocoa routine issues a diagnostic message. The prompt stoppage gives you a better chance at finding the problem. It's also helpful to add the debugger action po $r3 on PowerPC development machines when breaking on `-[NSException raise]`, as this will put a description of the exception into the gdb log. See Section 21.4.

- The Debugger Console allows you to type commands directly into the gdb session that underlies the Xcode debugger. It accumulates output from those commands, as well as output from your application's standard-output and standard-error pipes. (But for input, as well as regular access to standard output and standard error, use the Standard I/O Log.) This output accumulates indefinitely. If you want to clear it out, click the small **x** button at the bottom of the window's scroll bar, or choose

Debug → Clear Logs. If you always want logs to be cleared when you start a new debugging session, check **Automatically clear log** in the **General** (first) pane of the **Preferences** panel.

- Many of the system frameworks for Mac OS X have "debug" variants, which check the validity of arguments, log events, and include assertions for internal consistency. For instance, the Carbon framework contains the dynamic libraries Carbon (for regular use) and Carbon_debug. The dynamic loader has a simple rule for adding a suffix to the name of any library that gets loaded; simply set the environment variable DYLD_IMAGE_SUFFIX to the desired suffix. You can do this easily from within Xcode by opening the **Executables** group in the Groups & Files list and double-clicking the desired executable to open its Info window (or by selecting **Project → Edit Active Executable**). In the **General** tab of the Info window is a pop-up labeled **Use . . . suffix when loading frameworks**. Select **no**, **debug**, or **profile** from the pop-up menu. Be aware that many of the messages and breaks you will encounter will be strictly routine, especially the ones from the font services; be prepared to ignore a few breaks and continue from them.

- The Debugger variables view does not, by default, include any global variables, as an application may potentially have many of them, and probably only a handful are of interest at any given moment. Clicking the disclosure triangle next to the **Globals** label or selecting **Debug → Tools → Global Variables . . .** will open the Globals Browser. The left column of the browser lists every library comprising the application. Selecting a library lists in the table at right every global variable the library exports. Select the checkbox next to a global's name to include it in the Variables panel. Globals are always legal in the debugger's Expressions window (**Tools → Expressions . . .**).

- In addition to breakpoints, the Xcode debugger exposes gdb's ability to set watchpoints. A watchpoint is like a breakpoint but interrupts execution not when execution arrives at a particular place in the code but when the value of a variable changes. It often happens that a bug shows up as an inexplicable value in a variable, but you can't divine where in a complex or long execution it gets trashed. A watchpoint is the answer. To set a watchpoint, stop the program in the debugger at a point where the variable of concern is in scope. Select the variable in the Variables pane of the Debugger and select **Watch Variable** from either the contextual menu or the **Debug → Variables View** menu. A magnifying glass icon appears next to watched variables. Continue the program. The watchpoint will interrupt execution in two cases: if the value of the variable changes or if the watchpoint has to be removed because the variable has gone out of scope.

- If you use key-value observing (KVO) and don't override the `description` method of your observed classes, you'll find your observed objects described not as, for instance, `<MyObject...` but as `<NSKVONotifying_MyObject....` The KVO mechanism substitutes an ad hoc class when objects are observed. To see a list of what objects are observing an object, use the `gdb` command `po [myObject observationInfo]`.

- Suppose that you want to debug an application that doesn't run well in the Xcode environment—the classic example is a Terminal application that uses the `ncurses` library, which the debugger I/O window can't respond to. The trick is to launch the application in an environment it works well in and then attach the Xcode debugger to it. Open the **Executables** group in the Groups & Files list, select the application, open an Info window, and in the **Debugging** tab, uncheck **Start executable after starting debugger**. When you're ready to debug, start the debugger, and then launch the target application in its friendly environment. In the debugger's `gdb` console, type **attach** *applicationName*, and your debugging session is under way.

- The list at the left of the Breakpoints window is just another incarnation of the Groups & Files list but with only the **Breakpoints** group included. One Groups & Files command that may prove useful is **File → Group**, which will enclose the breakpoints you select in a subgroup of the **Breakpoints** list. Once you have a group of breakpoints, you can use a contextual menu (control- or right-click on the group) to enable or disable the whole group.

- Setting a breakpoint in a template function by clicking in the gutter next to the function's source code does not work reliably. The `gcc` tool is built on the assumption that a line of code is represented by a single block of machine instructions in the running program, and the whole point of templates is to have one block of code be instantiated as many different blocks of machine code. If you know which instantiation of a template function you want to break on, you can type the full name of the instantiation into the Breakpoints window—for example, **Shape<double>::area**. You may have to turn ZeroLink off to make this work properly. Or, you could set a regular-expression break by typing **rbreak** at the (gdb) prompt, followed by a regular expression matching the function(s) of interest: **Shape.*area**.

21.2 Printing Values

The Variables pane of the Xcode debugger is a nice presentation of program data, but it is limited by the table format it uses. Cocoa and Core Foundation container objects, for instance, are represented by their addresses in hexadecimal and a notation of how many objects they contain. Often, you want to know *what* they contain. The easiest way to do this is to control-click the variable in the table and select **Print Description to Console**. For Cocoa objects, this will write the result of the debugDescription method to standard error; for others, it writes to standard error the result of passing the value to CFShow().

The standard error stream is echoed to the Debugger Console, a separate window, except in the All-in-One layout, for interacting with the command line of the underlying gdb debugger. You make the console visible by clicking the **Console** button in the Debugger window's toolbar—you may have to widen the window to see it—or by selecting **Debug → Console Log**.

The gdb console gives you unlimited flexibility in accessing values in your application. You can print Cocoa objects with the print-object (po) command. Core Foundation and CF-compliant Carbon objects can be examined by calling CFShow() from the console:

```
(gdb) po item
<DataPoint: 0x3ed370> (entity: DataPoint; id: 0x3d7e50 <x-core...
    source = 0x3ce2f0 <x-coredata:///DataSource/t4FB5174A-2C60...
    x = 2005;
    y = 1330;
})
(gdb) call (void) CFShow(allPoints)
<CFArray 0x3f5ef0 [0xa0727150]>{type = immutable, count = 4, ...
    source = 0x3ce2f0 <x-coredata:///DataSource/t4FB5174A-2C60...
    x = 2003;
    y = 1330;
})
   1 : <DataPoint: 0x3ed370> (entity: DataPoint; id: 0x3d7e50...
  .
  .
  .
```

The call to CFShow() is an example of how gdb can execute, for its own use, code linked into an application.

Table 21.1   The gdb Format Codes for x and print

Code	Meaning
Format	
a	Address
c	Character
d	Decimal
f	Float
i	Instruction
o	Octal
s	String
t	Binary
u	Unsigned decimal
x	Hexadecimal
Size	
b	1 (byte)
h	2 (halfword)
w	4 (word)
g	8 (giant)

You can examine any address with the gdb x command, which takes the form x/*format address*, where format is a repeat count (1 if omitted), a format, and a size code. See Table 21.1. For instance, you can disassemble the next 20 machine instructions with the command x/20i $pc, where $pc denotes the CPU's program counter.

The print command, which may be abbreviated as p, allows you to print the result of any expression. The expression's syntax is that of the language in which the current file is written. You can use any variable in the current scope. You may specify most formats—using the format letter only, not the count or size parameter—by appending /*format* to the print command. You cannot print in formats s or i.

21.3 Custom Formatters

Some data types do not give up their secrets casually. Take as an example the Data-Point managed-object type from Chapter 15. The earlier version of DataPoint had x and y instance variables that could readily be inspected, but once we changed

DataPoint to a subclass of NSManagedObject, we eliminated the instance variables and made DataPoint into a black box.

Consider the method dataPointAtIndex:x:y:, in MyDocument.m:

```
- (void) dataPointAtIndex: (unsigned) index
                       x: (double *) outX
                       y: (double *) outY
{
    NSArray *      allPoints = [DataPoint allDataPointsInContext:
                                   [self managedObjectContext]];
    DataPoint *    item = [allPoints objectAtIndex: index];
    *outX = [item x];    // Line 4
    *outY = [item y];
}
```

Suppose that we are stopped at a breakpoint at the beginning of line 4. We have a new value for item and would like to know what it is. We have a choice of methods.

- We could try opening the disclosure triangle next to item's name in the Variable list. This yields us almost nothing, as the instance variables for an NSManagedObject reflect the task of storing and retrieving data, not the data itself.

- We could use gdb's print-object command po: po item. This is simple and produces in the debugger log a message that deals mostly with access particulars of the DataPoint and its DataSource reference but does include the x and y values of the point.

- We could control-click item's line in the Variable view and select **Print Description to Console** from the resulting pop-up menu. This is equivalent to typing **po item**.

- We could step over the next two lines and enter first **print *outX** and then **print *outY**, to see what the x and y values were. This certainly solves the problem in this case, but in the general sense, it's cheating: We won't always have convenient direct assignments of exactly the values we want to monitor. This method, and the two print-object methods, share another disadvantage, in that they don't make the x and y values continually accessible. You have to do something special to make them visible.

Data formatters were added to the Xcode Variables panel for exactly the purpose of providing continual, at-a-glance summaries of complex data structures. With the application stopped at a breakpoint at line 4 of dataPointAtIndex:x:y:, find item in the Variables panel. Double-click in the Summary column, and enter this:

(x = {(double)[$VAR x]} y = {(double)[$VAR y]})

When you press **Return** to end editing, the expression you entered is replaced with a string like (x = 1.0 y = 2.01). A data formatter consists of literal text in which are embedded expressions and references to values within data structures. In this case, the formatter pattern contains two expressions, set off with braces. $VAR takes the value of the variable itself, and in the first part of the formatter, we send the message [$VAR x]. We also indicate the return type (double) of the message, as gdb needs return types to be specified.

The formatter we use for DataPoint makes a call to methods of DataPoint. In fact, x and y, relying as they do on Core Data calls, are fairly complex operations. Be aware that you can use application code in your debugging data formatters. The good side of this is that you are free to do whatever you need to see what your data is. The bad side is that you make the debugger subject to the good behavior of the code you are debugging. If the data formatter calls application code that crashes, the least that will happen is that you'll be notified of an exception triggered inside gdb, and the Variables display will be degraded.

Determined debuggers and testers may introduce to their code functions and methods that exist solely to be called from the debugger console, to produce formatted output or reset objects to known states. Ambitious debuggers might even devise browser windows to be opened from debugger-console commands.

This problem becomes acute if the variable being examined hasn't been initialized yet. The uninitialized variable might contain values that trigger exceptions in the data formatter. To avoid this, you may have to declare and initialize the problem variable earlier, avoid single-stepping through code where the problem variable is uninitialized, or select **Debug** → **Variables View** → **Enable Data Formatters** to uncheck that menu item.

A data formatter "sticks" to its data type, not to the instance or data it was created for. By setting a data formatter for one DataPoint, we have set the Summary data column for the Xcode debugger wherever it finds a pointer to a DataPoint.

> If DataPoint still kept its x and y values in instance variables, there would have been no need to resort to expression substitutions. Members of structured data types can be referenced by path in custom-format strings by setting them off with %s, as in (x = %x% y = %y%). Such % substitutions can be followed with a colon and n, v, t, or s, to indicate that the substituted text should be what would appear in the Name, Value, Type, or Summary column if that element were displayed on its own line in the Variables display.

21.4 Breakpoint Commands

Sometimes, you need a breakpoint for information rather than as a place to stop execution. Suppose, for instance, that we were interested in what happens when the managed-object context changes. A method, storeChanged:, in Regression is called whenever a change is made to the context:

```
- (void) storeChanged: (NSNotification *) notice
{
    NSSet *     inserted = [[notice userInfo] objectForKey:
                                        NSInsertedObjectsKey];
    NSSet *     deleted = [[notice userInfo] objectForKey:
                                        NSDeletedObjectsKey];

    if ([inserted count] > 0 || [deleted count] > 0) {
        [self willChangeValueForKey: @"canCompute"];
        [self didChangeValueForKey: @"canCompute"];
    }
}
```

We'd like to see what gets inserted and deleted at each change notification, but we aren't interested in anything else. We can use the debugger's Breakpoints window to associate a series of commands with a breakpoint. Set a breakpoint at the if statement in storeChanged:, by which time inserted and deleted are set. Open the Breakpoints window, either from the button in the Debugger toolbar or the menu item **Debug →** **Breakpoints**.

The Breakpoints window shows a list of all the breakpoints set in the current project. It should be easy to find the one set in storeChanged:; open the disclosure triangle at the left end of its line in the table. A bubble appears, with a + button for you to add an action to the breakpoint.

You will add three actions:

1. A log action, which will print some text into the gdb log. Fill the text with **Breakpoint '%B' hit with insert/delete:**, and check the **Log** checkbox. You have a choice of having the log text written, spoken, or both.

2. A debugger command, printing the object value of the symbol inserted: po inserted. There is no need to check the **Log** box, as the command itself prints to the gdb transcript.

3. Another debugger command to print deleted: po deleted.

On the original, top line of the listing for this breakpoint, at the far right end, is a checkbox, under a column header with an arrowhead symbol in it. Checking this box will tell gdb not to stop at this breakpoint but to continue program execution after all commands are executed. We want to continue; check the box. See Figure 21.1.

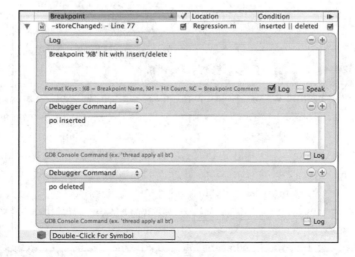

Figure 21.1   The Breakpoints list, with the breakpoint in -[Regression storeChanged:] expanded to show its actions. Clicking the + button at the right edge of the action list adds an action. The first action prints a label for the breakpoint occurrence, and the next two are gdb commands that output the objects inserted and deleted. The top line of the breakpoint listing shows the condition of the breakpoint—it fires only if inserted or deleted is not nil—and a checkbox to indicate that gdb is to continue after all the breakpoint actions have been done.

Now, as you use Linear, this sort of message appears in the gdb console, without otherwise interrupting the flow of the program:

```
Breakpoint '-storeChanged: - Line 77' hit with insert/delete :
<NSCFSet: 0x39b340> (<DataPoint: 0x3a0f60> (entity: DataPoint;
  id: 0x3a1980 <x-coredata:///DataPoint/tC7ADAA2C-54A1-4247-8089-
  759A3E1ADA5F> ; data: {source = nil; x = 0; y = 0; }))
Cannot access memory at address 0x0
Breakpoint '-storeChanged: - Line 77' hit with insert/delete :
Cannot access memory at address 0x0
Cannot access memory at address 0x0
```

The first pair reflects the addition of a newly initialized DataPoint to the managed-object context (with no deletions); the second, a change in an attribute of the data (no insertions or deletions).

An especially good application of command-and-continue breakpoints is in debugging handlers for continuous human-interface operations, such as drag-and-drop. You can have the debugger print out status information without stopping a drag in the middle.

You can remove breakpoint actions by pressing the – button on the action or by deleting the associated breakpoint.

21.5 Breakpoint Conditions

The breakpoint commands we set in the previous section were convenient, but you'll find that the breakpoint triggers every time a change is made to the managed-object context—four times for each DataPoint—three properties plus creation—and four times for each DataSource—three properties plus creation. After a while, we may decide that these breakpoint commands are generating too much noise from events in which there are no changes in context membership.

One solution might be to move the breakpoint to the line after the if test, but there is another. We can have gdb make a test of its own.

As before, we find the breakpoint in the list in the Breakpoints window. We are looking for the same breakpoint at -[Regression storeChanged:], and we want it to fire only when either inserted or deleted is not nil: inserted || deleted. Type this expression into the last text column of the table.

Conditions are stated in the same language as the file in which the breakpoint is set. We could also have made the condition

```
((int)[inserted count] > 0) || ((int)[deleted count] > 0)
```

In gdb, return types of methods and functions must be declared with casts, unless the return type is id for a method or void * for a function.

The first thing gdb will do when execution arrives at the if statement in store-Changed: will be to evaluate the condition. If it is true, the breakpoint actions are executed as before; otherwise, the program continues silently.

Of course, conditions work with breakpoints that have no associated commands, as well. You can remove the condition from a breakpoint by clearing the cell in the Condition column.

21.6 Lazy Symbol Loading

As you start debugging your application, you may look at the Breakpoints window and find a couple of breakpoints for which the **Enabled** checkbox is neither checked nor unchecked but has a minus sign (–) in it. This indicates that gdb understands you mean these breakpoints to be active but has yet to determine an address for the corresponding machine code. The reason for this is that gdb is set to load debugging symbols "lazily," waiting to resolve symbols that occur in not-yet-loaded object files until those files are loaded. The alternative is to examine every dynamic library and ZeroLinked module as gdb starts up, which takes a significant amount of time in a large application.

Unfortunately, this means that in some cases, symbols, such as breakpoint addresses, are not resolved when they are needed, as in time to break on entry to a function. If you find that a breakpoint you set is getting missed, particularly if it's in a plug-in or other shared library, you should tell gdb to load the relevant symbols earlier.

While the application is running under the debugger, open the Shared Libraries window (Figure 21.2) by selecting **Debug** → **Tools** → **Shared Libraries**.... This will list every loadable module in your application; if ZeroLink is on, there will be quite a lot of them. The table will show the name of every loadable module associated with the application, the address of that module, and how the symbols defined in that module are exported to gdb, both at start-up (Starting Level) and now that the application has run a while (Current Level).

The symbol levels are settable as pop-up menu items, offering choices of **Default**, **None**, **External**, and **All**. If a breakpoint is getting missed, locate the module in which the problem code occurs—you can use the search field to narrow the list down—and set the Starting Level for that module to **All**. This will ensure that all the

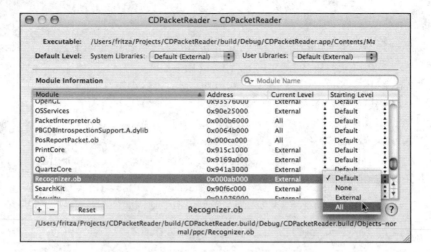

Figure 21.2 The Shared Libraries window from the Xcode debugger. All the loadable modules associated with the application being debugged are listed in this window, along with the initial and current levels of importation of symbols from those modules to gdb.

debugging information for that module will be loaded as soon as gdb starts debugging the application. To load all the symbols for a module for just the current session, select **All** in the Current Level column.

The two pop-ups at the top of the window determine what the Default setting means; this can be set separately for user and system libraries. By default, the Default policy is **External**, meaning that initially, only the symbols defined by a module as external are loaded by gdb.

Another approach to problems with lazy symbol loading is simply to turn the feature off. In the Preferences window, in the fifth pane, **Debugging**, you can uncheck **Load symbols lazily**. The performance penalty, for smaller projects, should not be great.

21.7 Zombies

The project Garden in the CD-ROM directory for this chapter contains a simple program for managing a very simple garden. The program contains a list of Gardens, each of which contains one prize Lily. You can plant new Lilys in a Garden, but that replaces any existing prize Lily. A Lily has a string to describe its variety and knows whether it has been gilded. `Lily` and `Garden` both implement the standard `description` method, which provides a string describing the recipient of the `description` message.

The `Garden` project defines in its Nib a window that contains a one-column table, in which we will list the prize `Lily` of each `Garden`. There is a button to add a new garden to the collection; the button makes sure that each garden gets a different variety of `Lily`, so we can tell them apart. There is a button that will gild the lily in the first garden. And, a button marked **Vandalize** sends the prize `Lily` object in the first garden a `release` message. As prize `Lily`s are held by only one reference—their respective `Garden`s—this will have the effect of returning the first `Lily`'s memory to free storage.

21.7.1 Released-Pointer Aliasing

Build `Garden` and run it under the debugger. Click the **Add Garden** button twice. The action method for that button does a `reloadData` on the table, so in the table, we immediately see

```
A Lily, calla, not gilded
A Lily, white, not gilded
```

Now click the **Vandalize** button. Here is the action method for that button:

```
- (IBAction) vandalize: (id) sender
{
    Garden *        garden = [allGardens objectAtIndex: 0];
    [[garden prizeLily] release];
}
```

This is a bug. The `Garden` at index 0 of `allGardens` still maintains a pointer to what it thinks is a `Lily`, but that pointer has been invalidated. The application is walking dead.

But it is still walking. You can move the window around. You can even try clicking **Add Garden** again. In some cases, depending on things you can't control, the list of `Garden`s changes to what you see in Figure 21.3. In this state, the application won't crash so long as you stay away from the **Vandalize** button but will simply display not the prize `Lily` of the first `Garden` but the description of the third `Garden`.

What happened? When `vandalize:` released the `prizeLily` object of the first member of `allGardens`, the storage for that `Lily`, and the address associated with it, were returned to free storage. That address became available for use by new objects.

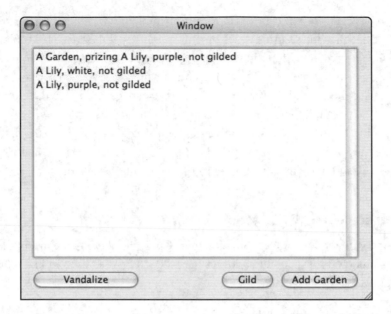

Figure 21.3 A memory-management bug that shows up as a behavioral error in a simple application. Clicking **Add Garden** twice added two lines of Lilys from the added Gardens to the list. **Vandalize** released the first of these Lilys, and a third **Add Garden** placed a new Garden at the same address as the old Lily.

Sure enough, when we allocated a new Garden by clicking **Add Garden**, the same address was used for the new instance of Garden.

The first Garden, in the meantime, has no clue that its prizeLily object has been deallocated and its storage given to something else. So far as it knows, prizeLily still points to an instance of Lily. When it comes time to supply content for the first line of the table, description gets sent to prizeLily of the first Garden. It happens that Garden also implements description, so the description of the replacement object, the third garden, appears in the table.

What happens if you try to send a message that Garden doesn't implement? The **Gild** button triggers this action handler:

```
- (IBAction) gildFirstLily: (id) sender
{
    Garden *         garden = [allGardens objectAtIndex: 0];
```

```
    [[garden prizeLily] gild];
    [gardenTable reloadData];
}
```

If you click the **Gild** button, nothing happens. But if you look in the Standard I/O Log or in the Debugger Console, you'll see the following message:

```
2005-03-25 16:04:58.854 Garden[1790] *** -[Garden gild]: selector
not recognized [self = 0x398b80]
```

This message is not mysterious to you, because you know what's going on: gildFirstLily: sends gild to an object that turns out to be a Garden, and Gardens don't implement gild. Usually, however, your bugs are not so deliberate. The first sign of trouble may be that nothing happens, and a message like this shows up in the standard error stream. When you see a selector-not-recognized message, especially for a strange class, suspect an overreleased object.

I said that when you clicked **Add Garden** after clicking **Vandalize**, the strange behavior we've been discussing *might* happen. What else might happen? Usually, what happens is that the application halts, and standard error contains the message "Program received signal EXC_BAD_ACCESS." If you are running the application under the debugger, you will see that execution stopped somewhere in the runtime library function objc_msgSend. The crash in objc_msgSend is another strong indicator of an overreleased object.

But the crashes and error messages are the good news. It's the first mode of failure—no crash, just subtly incorrect behavior—that's scary. What we badly need is a way to turn the subtle run-on bugs into identifiable bugs.

21.7.2 Zombies in Cocoa

Fortunately, there is such a way. Cocoa provides a mechanism that does not free released storage for reuse. Instead, the freed object is replaced by a *zombie* object that knows what kind of object was originally stored there. This facility is controlled by a switch called NSZombieEnabled. The switch is accessible by #importing Foundation/NSDebug.h into main.m and setting NSZombieEnabled= YES before anything else.

NSZombieEnabled is also accessible as an environment variable. Open the **Executables** group in the Groups & Files list, select the **Garden** application, and open the Info window. Select the **Arguments** tab, and click the + button under the lower list of environment variables. Set the name of the new environment variable to NSZombieEnabled and its value to YES.

Either way, here is what appears in the I/O log when we repeat the experiment of vandalizing a Garden and attempting to create a new one:

```
2005-03-25 18:15:04.928 Garden[1859] *** Selector 'description'
    sent to dealloced instance 0x361ff0 of class Lily.
Break at '-[_NSZombie methodSignatureForSelector:]' to debug.
```

This time, there's no ambiguity. The zombie object reports the message it was sent and what kind of object was overreleased. It doesn't matter what method is called—_NSZombie squawks at any method call. Further, we can open the Breakpoints window and set a symbolic breakpoint at -[_NSZombie methodSignatureForSelector:], and the debugger will break at any attempt to use the deallocated object.

Zombies are helpful in debugging a program, but they aren't perfect. Apple does not regard them as a primary feature of the operating system. The classes that are "toll-free bridged" between Cocoa and Core Foundation—the property list classes, attributed strings, streams, sets, character sets, timers, URLs, locales, calendars, and time zones—are not substituted with zombies.

Further, at least in early Mac OS X 10.4 versions, there is a bug that prevents zombies from working. Fortunately, a workaround restores the feature. Add the following two lines to the beginning of the main() function of your application:

```
[NSObject self];
[(id) objc_getClass("_NSZombie") self];
```

21.7.3 Zombies in Core Foundation

Core Foundation has a zombie facility of its own. Core Foundation objects can't dispatch messages, so a CF zombie cannot alert you in detail when one is used. The essentials, however, are the same: A deallocated zombie is never recycled and is "scribbled" with contents likely to crash, or at least be conspicuous in, the host program rapidly.

Core Foundation can scribble object memory on allocation or deallocation or both, and you can specify the byte with which to fill the scribbled area. You can specify whether the memory for freed objects is recycled for other objects and whether the scribbling at deallocation covers the block header.

You specify Core Foundation zombie behavior by setting the CFZombieLevel environment variable to the sum of the desired values shown in Table 21.2. For simple deallocation scribbling, then, you should set CFZombieLevel to 1.

Table 21.2 CFZombieLevel Flag Values

Value	Effect
0x00000001	Scribble on deallocation
0x00000002	Spare object header from deallocation scribbling
0x00000010	Never free deallocated CF blocks
0x00000080	Use bits 8–15 as scribble byte instead of 0xfc
0x0000nn00	Deallocation scribble byte (set bit 7 to use instead of 0xfc)
0x00010000	Scribble on allocation
0x00800000	Use bits 24–31 as scribble byte instead of 0xcf
0xnn000000	Allocation scribble byte (set bit 23 to use instead of 0xcf)

21.8 Summary

This chapter collected a number of techniques that didn't fit into the narrative of debugging Linrg or Linear but that I hope will bring you to a better feel for what is happening when you debug Mac OS X software. In addition to tips, we covered how to customize the display of variables in the debugger and how to tailor breakpoints to perform tasks when they trigger or trigger only on certain conditions.

We also covered the diagnosis of overreleased memory, which isn't strictly a matter of development tools but is a basic enough skill that I couldn't bear to leave it out.

Further Reading

This book can only introduce the deep and subtle art of debugging. The developer documentation installed with the Xcode tools includes the complete manual for gdb; do a full-text search for "Debugging with GDB" to find it.

Apple has also provided some helpful tech notes on debugging for Mac OS X.

- TN 2030 *GDB for* MacsBug *Veterans*:
  http://developer.apple.com/technotes/tn/tn2030.html
- TN 2032 *Getting Started with GDB*:
  http://developer.apple.com/technotes/tn/tn2032.html
- TN 2123 *CrashReporter*:
  http://developer.apple.com/technotes/tn2004/tn2123.html

- TN 2124, *MacOS X Debugging Magic*:
  `http://developer.apple.com/technotes/tn2004/tn2124.html`

The first two tech notes deal with using gdb under Project Builder, Xcode's predecessor, but the principles remain the same.

22

Xcode and Speed

One of the driving goals behind the development of Xcode has been to speed up the development cycle as much as possible. Some of what Apple has done to make Xcode faster comes for free: You don't have to do anything special when Apple shifts to a faster version of the gcc compiler package, for instance. Other strategies require your cooperation. This chapter covers them.

22.1 Precompiled Headers

Precompiled headers are a feature of almost every modern development system. The idea is that almost all implementation files rely on a large base of header files that they have in common and that don't often change. A naive strategy of simply reading the headers at the top of each implementation file would result in 90 percent or more of the lines of code processed for each file being parsed into identical symbol tables. Better to do that parsing once, cache the results, and pick up the process from there with each implementation file. A *precompiled header* is such a cache.

Xcode's precompiled-header support is done in two phases. First, you specify a *prefix file*, which encompasses all the identical content your implementation files will include. (There being a single prefix isn't a limitation, as it may contain #include or #import directives.) Xcode project templates set up new projects to have a prefix file named *projectName*_Prefix.pch, containing #includes of the umbrella frameworks associated with the project type. You can set the name of the prefix file by using the Prefix Header build setting in the Target Info window.

All implementation files in a project implicitly include the prefix file. It is prepended to them for compilation purposes, and any change to the prefix file forces a recompilation of all other files.

The second phase of precompiled-header support is the Precompile Prefix Header switch in the Target Info window. Setting this switch causes a precompiled version of the prefix header to be built whenever necessary. The compilation of the rest of the project will proceed from the state stored in the precompiled file rather than by reading in the prefix header file.

Typing **prefix** into the search field in the **Build** tab of the Target Info window will narrow the build-settings list to a very few items that include both the Prefix Header and Precompile Prefix Header settings.

Generating a precompiled header takes more time than a single reading of the constituent header files, so a project with very few implementation files may not see much improvement from using a precompiled header. If you manage to make regular changes to a file that goes into your prefix header, thus forcing a regular rebuild of the precompiled header and a complete rebuild of your project, you will lose time. Restrict the prefix header to those headers you are sure will rarely change over the lifetime of your project.

22.2 Predictive Compilation

Text editing is an undemanding task for a computer. The computer is idle for most of the time between keystrokes and cursor blinks. Xcode can fill this idle time by going through all the code you've changed since the last time you've compiled and compiling it—before you've asked for a build. Predictive compilation will even extend to the file you are actively editing.

Xcode does this compilation "on spec," because if you change anything it compiled this way, it has to throw the predictive compilation away. Often enough, however, you don't make any changes, and when you do ask for a build, substantial portions will have been done ahead of time.

By default, predictive compilation is off. Because it cranks up the CPU and hard drive, predictive compilation cannot be used while running on battery power. You can turn it on in the Building pane of the Preferences window, with the checkbox **Build Options: Use Predictive Compilation**.

Predictive compilation does make demands on a computer's resources, so if your Mac seems sluggish to you with it on, try turning it off. Also, earlier versions of Xcode would mistakenly report compilation errors based on versions of files that had been changed in recent editing sessions—a result of predictive compilation results hanging around after they became obsolete. Although these bugs seem to have been eliminated, try turning predictive compilation off if something similar arises in your work.

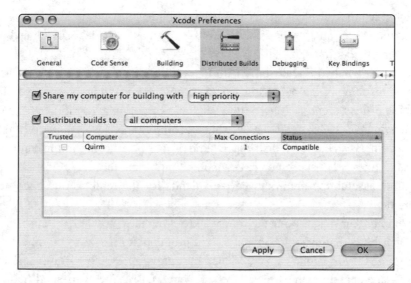

Figure 22.1   The **Distributed Builds** panel of the Xcode Preferences window. The upper checkbox makes this machine available to others for compiling modules. The lower checkbox makes this machine a host for distributed builds, either on every machine that advertises itself on the local Bonjour net as a `distcc` node or on only those listed machines you mark as trusted.

22.3 Distributed Builds

If you have a large project and more than one Macintosh at your disposal, you can see dramatically shorter build times with distributed builds. A Macintosh can volunteer idle time for distributed builds by opening the **Distributed Builds** panel of the Preferences window (Figure 22.1) and checking the first checkbox in the panel. Xcode processes on other computers or even the same computer can then send portions of their builds to the volunteer for compilation. The volunteer can choose to give the distributed-build background process low, medium, or high priority.

If you want to take advantage of distributed builds, check the second checkbox in the **Distributed Builds** panel of the Preferences window. The list below the checkbox will then fill with the names of all the local net's computers that are advertising via Bonjour (formerly Rendezvous) that they can take distributed builds. You can choose to distribute work to all comers or only to the machines you indicate in the list are trusted.

Each machine participating in a distributed build must be running the same architecture and the same versions of Mac OS X, gcc, and Xcode. Xcode need not be running on the distributed machines.

No matter what your **Distributed Builds** settings, some tasks are always done on the home machine of the build. In particular, the home machine builds precompiled headers and does preprocessing before sending out compilation units. Because the home machine has work to do that no other machine can, it is wisest not to enable the local machine as sharable for distributed builds. Distributed compilation can't benefit from more than about six remotes; beyond that point, the local machine is spending all its time assembling preprocessed compilands for the remotes and becomes the limiting factor.

Remember that distributing the source and getting the compiled objects back takes time. Distributed builds may be a net loss in productivity if you use it on a network of less than 100Mb/second capacity. This rules out wireless and 10Base-T networks.

If you are dealing with a firewall, be sure that it passes the distributed-build ports of 3632 and 7264.

22.4 ZeroLink

To summarize our discussion of ZeroLink from Section 4.5, a complex application will make hundreds or thousands of references among its modules and between its modules and the system frameworks. These references have to be resolved to "real" addresses of objects in memory, and the traditional strategy for resolving them is to end the application-build process with a linkage phase, in which every reference is matched to an object, and every link is stitched together. Linkage can take a lot of time, and one of the goals for Xcode was to reduce the time a programmer spends between calling for a build and starting to debug the program.

ZeroLink eliminates the separate linkage phase at the end of a build, leaving the task of mating objects to references to be done piecemeal, as each reference is used. Because the application would be running on a development machine, which is typically fast, and would be run by a developer studying the behavior of the program, the performance hit in linking at runtime is not noticeable. The gain in not having to link *everything* before the application can be run at all is quite noticeable.

You cannot distribute applications built with ZeroLink. ZeroLinked applications have to carry, for each unresolved symbol, information on where the corresponding object is to be sought. That information includes paths to object files inside the project's build-products directory. Obviously, the only person who has access to your project's build-products directory is you. For everyone else, the application will immediately quit after posting a ZeroLink error message to the System Console.

ZeroLink is a feature that relies on technology introduced with Mac OS X version 10.3. It isn't available to applications linked to an SDK for earlier versions of Mac OS X.

22.5 Project Indexing

As mentioned in Section 18.1.2, Xcode will devote a background thread to identifying and indexing all the symbols in your project and the frameworks it uses. On recent machines, with a moderately sized project and a reasonably paced typist, you will see no effect, other than having an index, from the indexing thread. In some cases, however, indexing may slow your machine down.

The drastic thing you can do about this is to turn indexing off. In the **Code Sense** pane of the Preferences window, clear the checkbox labeled **Indexing: Enable for all projects**. No indexing threads will then be started; nor will you be able to use the Class Browser, the Class Model, the Project Symbols smart group, Code Sense, or command-double-clicking to find symbol definitions.

The less drastic step is to reduce the amount of indexing that has to be done. In all but the very largest project, the lion's share of indexing is done in frameworks, and it makes sense to do that part of the indexing once, in advance, and have individual projects use these master indexes as bases for project indexes. The facility is formally known as *index templates*, and you have to build and enable them to make use of them.

You will find the necessary makings in /Developer/Extras/Xcode Index Templates/. There is a way to build and enable templates piecemeal and to control where they are stored, but for most purposes, it's good enough to build them all, store them in the /Library domain, and enable Xcode's use of them. Do this in the Terminal application by focusing on the templates directory and executing the command install_templates found there:

```
$ cd "/Developer/Extras/Xcode Index Templates"
$ sudo ./install_templates
Password:
$
```

More information about index templates, including details on manual installation, can be found in the read-me file in the Xcode Index Templates directory.

It sometimes happens that features that depend on indexing stop working or work unreliably. Code Sense, for instance, might not be delivering all the completions you think it ought to, given the context. It is possible that the project index has been corrupted. If you think that this may have happened, select **Edit Project Settings** in the **Project** menu (or double-click the **Project** icon at the top of the Groups & Files list), and click **Rebuild Code Sense Index** at the bottom of the Info window that results.

If a problem persists and you are using index templates, see whether turning index templates off and rebuilding the project index cures the problem. If so, rebuild the index templates before using them again.

22.6 Summary

This chapter addressed the vexing question of how to make Xcode faster. We reviewed all the technologies Apple offers to make the compile-link-test-edit turnaround as fast as possible. These technologies include the precompilation of headers that every development toolset offers; predictive compilation, which uses the idle time in the edit phase to get compilations done before they are requested; and ZeroLink, which obviates the link phase by delaying linkage until symbols are referenced at runtime. Portions of Xcode builds can be farmed out to other computers to compile in parallel; we showed how to set that up. Finally, we looked at project indexing, which underlies many convenience features of the IDE but does take up CPU time.

23

AppleScript Studio

Sometimes, a full-bore C or Objective-C application is too much effort for a task. AppleScript is a good alternative for many tasks, especially when applications expose a scriptable interface that can contribute to the work you want to do. However, the human interface you can summon up from AppleScript's Script Editor is pitifully thin—essentially a chain of dialog and alert boxes.

AppleScript Studio provides a middle ground, allowing you to construct a complete Cocoa application by using Interface Builder for the human interface and AppleScript for the logic of the application. To show how this is done, let's address ourselves to __MyCompanyName__, the default holder of all the copyrights in source files generated from Xcode templates. In Chapter 5, I mentioned that this string is held in an entry of the Xcode preferences, accessible through the `defaults` command line tool but not graphically. Let's change that.

23.1 An AppleScript Application

In Xcode, close out any open projects, and select **File → New Project . . .** (**command-shift-N**). At the top of the **Application** group is AppleScript Application, which is what we want. Click **Next**, and name the project MyCompanyName.

The template for AppleScript applications starts you out with three files:

1. `main.m`, which we could have left off this list because you won't be doing anything with it. I mention it here as a reminder that AppleScript applications are real stand-alone applications, with real, machine-language main entry points.

2. `MyCompanyName.applescript`, an AppleScript file that is empty but for a header comment.

3. `MainMenu.nib`, the basis of our user interface.

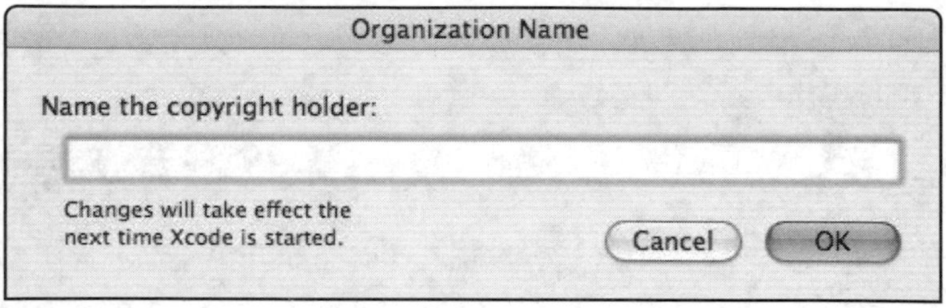

Figure 23.1 The desired human interface for MyCompanyName. The real work is done in the AppleScript (**command-8**) inspector for the window, the text field, and the buttons.

Double-click **MainMenu.nib**, which contains a menu bar and a blank window. Fill the window (see Figure 23.1). The window as shown has been set in its Attributes Inspector not to display the **Close, Minimize,** or **Zoom** buttons. The **Cancel** button is set to use the **Escape** key as an equivalent, and the **OK** button uses **Return**.

The human interface gets wired into AppleScript through the AppleScript inspector (**command-8**) for each element. Figure 23.2 shows the AppleScript Inspector for the window. Giving the window a name allows us to refer to it by name in scripts, so we call it `copyrightWindow`. Below the name is a list of various events that can transpire in the life of a window. Checking an event means that we intend to provide a handler for that event, written in AppleScript. So check **Nib** → **awake from nib**, and in the list below it, the name of the script **MyCompanyName.applescript**. We have just promised that `MyCompanyName.applescript` will contain a handler for `awake from nib`.

Likewise, turn the AppleScript Inspector on the **OK** button, name it `okButton`, and check its **Action** → **clicked** handler, again in `MyCompanyName.applescript`. Name the **Cancel** button `cancelButton`, and direct it, too, to `MyCompanyName.applescript`'s `clicked` handler. Finally, name the text field `copyrightField`.

Do one more thing, the purpose of which will become clear later. Switch to the **Classes** tab, select **NSObject**, and create a subclass named `AppDelegate`. Create `.m` and `.h` files for it (**command-option-F**), and instantiate it (**command-option-I**). Switch to the **Instances** tab. Control-drag a link from the **File's Owner** icon, which will be the NSApplication instance, to the `AppDelegate` instance, and connect it to the delegate outlet. We have just created an instance of a custom class to act as the application's delegate. This will come in handy.

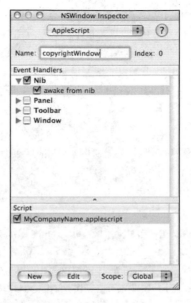

Figure 23.2 The AppleScript inspector (**command-8**) for the window of MyCompanyName. The window is given a name for easy reference, and boxes are checked to indicate that the window's **awake from nib** handler is to be found in MyCompanyName.applescript.

Save the Nib, and switch back to Xcode. Select **MyCompanyName.applescript** in the Groups & Files list. Hooking the controls to handlers in the script has added stubs for those handlers to the script:

```
-- MyCompanyName.applescript
-- MyCompanyName

--   Created by Xcode User on 3/28/05.
--   Copyright 2005 __MyCompanyName__. All rights reserved.

on clicked theObject
    (*Add your script here.*)
end clicked

on awake from nib theObject
    (*Add your script here.*)
end awake from nib
```

What happens first in the life of the application is that the window is loaded from MainMenu.nib, and the awake from nib handler is triggered. This is the first moment at which the user interface is all present and connected. We'd like to fill the text field, copyrightField, with the current value of the ORGANIZATIONNAME preference. We'll do this by executing a shell command that reads the default. On the terminal screen, it would look like this:

```
$ defaults read com.apple.Xcode PBXCustomTemplateMacroDefinitions
{ORGANIZATIONNAME = __MyCompanyName__; }
$
```

AppleScript provides a command, do shell script, that will execute a shell command for us and return the result. Now all we have to do is parse the result. We can probably get away with seeking past the equals sign and before the trailing characters to extract the value for ORGANIZATIONNAME, but there's always the possibility that Apple may generalize this setting to a dictionary of several template parameters. We want to be sure of extracting the correct value and of altering only ORGANIZATION-NAME when we're done.

And so we contemplate writing, in AppleScript, a recursive-descent parser for OpenStep-format property lists. Next, we wonder whether we have gone entirely nuts, because even if AppleScript doesn't make it easy to interpret property lists, Cocoa does. We can hand that part off to an Objective-C method so Cocoa can do what it does best; it will hand us back an AppleScript record object, from which we can easily extract the ORGANIZATIONNAME and save the rest for later reference.

Here is how all that translates into AppleScript:

```
property definitions : {}

on awake from nib theObject
    if theObject's name is "copyrightPanel" then
        local shellScript, scriptResult, holderName

        -- Construct the shell command
        set shellScript to ¬
                "defaults read com.apple.Xcode " & ¬
                "PBXCustomTemplateMacroDefinitions"
```

```
            try
                    -- Issue the shell command
                    set scriptResult to do shell script shellScript

                    -- Convert the result into an AppleScript record
                    set definitions to call method "parseOldPlist:" ¬
                                    with parameter scriptResult

                    -- Extract the org name from the record
                    set holderName to definitions's |ORGANIZATIONNAME|
            on error
                    -- Xcode 2.1 does not preset
                    -- PBXCustomTemplateMacroDefinitions.
                    -- If the defaults read fails, fill in the results
                    -- as if the read had succeeded.
                    set definitions to ¬
                            |ORGANIZATIONNAME|:"__MyCompanyName__"
                    set holderName to "__MyCompanyName__"
            end try

            -- Fill the field with the result
            tell text field "copyrightField" of theObject
                    set string value to holderName
            end tell
        end if
end awake from nib
```

Our use of `call method`, without specifying a recipient for the message, means that we'll have to implement the method in the application delegate. Fortunately, we created one in the Nib. Here is how you produce an AppleScript record (an `NSDictionary`) from the OpenStep-format string `defaults` handed us:

```
- (NSDictionary *) parseOldPlist: (NSString *) oldPlist
{
    // Turn string into byte stream
    NSData *        data = [oldPlist
                    dataUsingEncoding: NSUTF8StringEncoding];
    NSString *      error;
```

```
    //  Turn byte stream into NSDictionary
    return [NSPropertyListSerialization
                propertyListFromData: data
                    mutabilityOption: NSPropertyListImmutable
                        format: NULL
                    errorDescription: & error];
}
```

Our clicked handler will be called when either the **OK** or the **Cancel** button is clicked. In either case, we have to close the window; in the case of the **OK** button, we have to take the contents of the text field copyrightField, put it into plist form, and pass it to the defaults command line tool:

```
on clicked theObject
    if theObject's name is "okButton" then
        local newCopyName, defsAsPlist, shellScript

        -- Fetch the name that was entered
        set newCopyName to string value of ¬
            text field "copyrightField" of ¬
            window "copyrightPanel"

        -- Modify existing definitions so they include
        -- the new organization name
        set definitions to ¬
            {|ORGANIZATIONNAME|: newCopyName} & definitions

        -- Translate the definitions into OpenStep plist form
        set defsAsPlist to call method "writeOldPlist:" ¬
            with parameter definitions

        -- Set the default for Xcode
        set shellScript to "defaults write com.apple.Xcode " & ¬
            "PBXCustomTemplateMacroDefinitions '" & defsAsPlist ¬
            & "'"
        do shell script shellScript
    end if
```

```
        quit
    end clicked
```

Once again, we drop into Objective-C for string manipulation, this time to turn
an AppleScript record, an NSDictionary, into an NSString in the OpenStep plist
format. Unfortunately, NSPropertyListSerialization doesn't support this transformation, so we have to do it ourselves:

```
@interface NSString (HasWhitespace)
- (BOOL) hasWhitespace;
- (NSString *) whitespaceQuoted;
@end


@implementation NSString (HasWhitespace)

- (BOOL) hasWhitespace
{
    //  Return whether I contain any whitespace.
    NSCharacterSet *    wsSet =
                        [NSCharacterSet whitespaceCharacterSet];
    unsigned            i, iLimit = [self length];
    for (i = 0; i < iLimit; i++)
        if ([wsSet characterIsMember:
                        [self characterAtIndex: i]])
            return YES;
    return NO;
}


- (NSString *) whitespaceQuoted
{
    //  If I contain any whitespace return myself wrapped in
    //  double quotes; otherwise return myself.
    if ([self hasWhitespace])
        return [NSString stringWithFormat: @"\"%@\"", self];
    else
        return [[self retain] autorelease];
}

@end
```

```
@interface NSDictionary (OpenStepFormat)
- (NSString *) openStepFormat;
@end

@implementation NSDictionary (OpenStepFormat)

- (NSString *) openStepFormat
{
    //  Return myself formatted as an OpenStep-format
    //  property list string: Bounded in braces, separated by
    //  semicolons, pairs of strings (quoted if necessary)
    //  joined by the equals sign.
    NSMutableString *   retval =
                        [NSMutableString stringWithString: @"{"];
    NSEnumerator *      iter = [self keyEnumerator];
    NSString *          curr;

    while (curr = [iter nextObject]) {
        NSString *      key = [curr whitespaceQuoted];
        NSString *      value = [[self objectForKey: curr]
                                            whitespaceQuoted];
        [retval appendFormat: @"%@ = %@; ", key, value];
    }

    [retval appendString: @"}"];
    return retval;
}

@end

@implementation AppDelegate
- (NSDictionary *) parseOldPlist: (NSString *) oldPlist
{
    //  As before...
}
```

```
- (NSString *) writeOldPlist: (NSDictionary *) aRecord
{
    return [aRecord openStepFormat];
}


@end
```

23.2 Unit Testing

Debugging is available to AppleScript Studio applications as it is to Cocoa, Carbon, or BSD applications. The Xcode debugger controls a debugger that allows you to set breakpoints in your AppleScript handlers, single-step through them, and examine variables as they are set and accessed.

Further, you aren't limited to AppleScript debugging. The MyCompanyName application contains Objective-C code that one might want to inspect with a debugger before letting it loose. Open the **Executables** group of the Groups & Files list, and double-click on the **MyCompanyName** application icon there. The Info window for the executable includes a **Debugging** tab, in which you can switch the debugger you use for MyCompanyName from the AppleScript debugger to gdb. See Figure 23.3. You can't, however, switch debuggers while an application is running; you have to choose in advance.

If your instincts are good, just watching the data flow through the `AppDelegate` class a few times should feel like inadequate assurance that the code works. Especially for low-level transformations like the ones we're doing, the domain of possible inputs exceeds our patience for following their progress. If our instincts are especially good, we know that we ought to reaudit those inputs every time `AppDelegate` changes. We wish we had a computer to do this sort of thing for us.

This is why there are *unit tests*. A unit test isolates an element of an application and verifies that it behaves as it should. Ideally, every unit of every application should have tests written for it, and the tests should be repeated regularly to guard against newly introduced bugs. In practice, most programmers feel that they don't have the time or attention to step away from development, narrowly defined, to do testing.

Fortunately, unit testing can be added to the product-build life cycle without demanding more than the barest minimum attention from the programmer. All that is required is that code be written that exercises the unit and verifies the results. The unit framework takes care of administering the tests and reporting the results. We'll

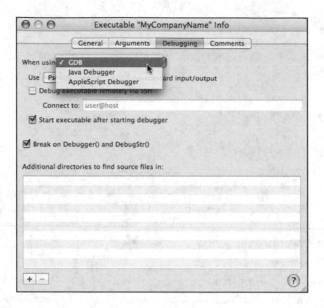

Figure 23.3 The Info window for the MyCompanyName executable. The **Debugging** tab gives a choice of the debugger to be used the next time the application is launched.

explore how one such framework can add to our confidence in the Objective-C portions of MyCompanyName.

Xcode 2.1 includes unit-testing frameworks for both Objective-C and C++ in its tool set. The project templates offer variants of most project types—alas, not AppleScript Studio projects—with testing built in, and there are new-file templates for adding test classes.

Users of Xcode 2.0 and earlier can obtain the same functionality for Objective-C by downloading the OCUnit framework from Sen:te in Switzerland: http://www.sente.ch/software/ocunit/. I recommend the version that installs at the root level. It is a disk image containing an installer archive, and the installation is rapid and painless.

23.2.1 Adding OCUnit

OCUnit, the framework Xcode uses for Objective-C unit tests, defines new-project templates that include unit-testing targets. MyCompanyName did not start with one of these templates, and as of late 2005, Xcode didn't have a test-enabled AppleScript application template, so this will be a good opportunity to see what is involved in adding tests and the test framework to an application.

You add OCUnit to a project's workflow by making the tests the product of a new target. Select **Project** → **New Target . . .** and the target type **Cocoa** → **Unit Test Bundle**. Name the new target UnitTests.

23.2.2 Test Cases

Now all we have to do is write our test cases. At its simplest, OCUnit iterates through every subclass of SenTestCase and runs every method in those subclasses with a selector that begins with test. To add a group of tests, we add a SenTestCase subclass.

Selecting **File** → **New File . . .**, we find the last entry in the list of Cocoa file templates: **Objective-C test case class**. Take this entry and make a subclass named StringTestCase with the unaltered header:

```
#import <SenTestingKit/SenTestingKit.h>

@interface StringTestCase : SenTestCase {

}

@end
```

Also make the following content for the implementation file, where our category methods for NSString are put through some simple exercises and the results checked:

```
#import "StringTestCase.h"
#import "AppDelegate.h"

@implementation StringTestCase

- (void) testHasWhitespace
{
    BOOL        result;

    NSLog(@"Entered testHasWhitespace");

    result = [@"NoSpacesHere" hasWhitespace];
```

```
    STAssertFalse(result, @"NoSpacesHere has no spaces");

    result = [@"Has space" hasWhitespace];
    STAssertTrue(result, @"Has space has a space");

    result = [@" Leading" hasWhitespace];
    STAssertTrue(result, @" Leading has whitespace");

    result = [@"Trailing " hasWhitespace];
    STAssertTrue(result, @"Trailing  has whitespace");

    result = [@"Tab\there" hasWhitespace];
    STAssertTrue(result, @"Tab\there has whitespace");
}

- (void) testQuotation
{
    BOOL IsQuoted(NSString * aString) {
        return ([aString length] > 1) &&
        ([aString characterAtIndex: 0] == '"') &&
        ([aString characterAtIndex: [aString length]-1] == '"');
    }

    NSString *      result;

    result = [@"anIdentifier" whitespaceQuoted];
    STAssertFalse(IsQuoted(result),
                @"Should not quote an identifier.");
    result = [@"Embedded space" whitespaceQuoted];
    STAssertTrue(IsQuoted(result),
                @"Should quote embedded space");
    result = [@"Embedded\ttab" whitespaceQuoted];
    STAssertTrue(IsQuoted(result),
                @"Should quote embedded tab");
    result = [@" LeadingSpace" whitespaceQuoted];
    STAssertTrue(IsQuoted(result),
                @"Should quote leading space");
    result = [@"TrailingSpace " whitespaceQuoted];
```

```
    STAssertTrue(IsQuoted(result),
                 @"Should quote trailing space");
}


@end
```

As you can see, unit testing is an accumulation of maddening little things that you assume to be true of the basic units of an application. When those maddening little things turn out not to be true, your assumptions often block you from seeing the bugs. Unit tests make sure that you can rely on the little things. Frequent tests tell you immediately when a change you make breaks your infrastructure.

The test methods won't have anything to test unless the UnitTests target includes the code for the NSString category we're exercising. That code comes from AppDelegate.m; add it to the UnitTests target by finding it in the Groups & Files list, opening its Info window, selecting the **Targets** tab, and making sure that **UnitTests** is checked in the target-membership list that is shown.

So now that some test cases are specified, what does testing consist of? It consists of building the test target. A shell-script build phase at the end of the target build process takes care of finding the tests, running them, and reporting the results. Here's what the StringTestCase tests add to the detailed build transcript:

```
Test Suite '/Users/xcodeuser/MyCompanyName/build/Debug/
                                  UnitTests.octest(Tests)'
    started at 2005-06-10 13:39:17 -0500
Test Suite 'StringTestCase' started at 2005-06-10 13:39:17 -0500
2005-06-10 13:39:17.900 otest[5961] Entered testHasWhitespace
Test Case '-[StringTestCase testHasWhitespace]' passed
    (0.003 seconds).
Test Case '-[StringTestCase testQuotation]' passed
    (0.000 seconds).
Test Suite 'StringTestCase' finished at 2005-06-10 13:39:17-0500.
Passed 2 tests, with 0 failures (0 unexpected) in 0.003
    (0.013) seconds

Test Suite '/Users/xcodeuser/MyCompanyName/build/Debug/
                                  UnitTests.octest(Tests)'
    finished at 2005-06-10 13:39:17 -0500.
Passed 2 tests, with 0 failures (0 unexpected) in 0.003
    (0.025) seconds
```

We can take this a step further and integrate testing with the process of building the application: Every time the application is built, we can check that the fundamentals are still sound. The principle is to exercise the code not as it sits in a testing rig but in the context in which it is linked into the application.

This is possible with Cocoa applications because Objective-C methods in a running application can be linked against as though the application were a library. The application can be run and the tests injected into it. The bundle finds the classes and methods it is to test in the running application instead of in modules linked to the bundle.

The first step is to make the UnitTests target dependent on the MyCompanyName application—the bundle can't run until the application is built. Double-click the **UnitTests** target; in the **General** tab, add the MyCompanyName target to the list of dependencies.

Next, *remove* AppDelegate.m from the UnitTests target. UnitTests will no longer be building the NSString category for itself but instead will draw it from MyCompany-Name.

We have to tell the gcc tool chain that UnitTests is to link dynamically against MyCompanyName. In the UnitTests target Info window, select the **Build** tab and **All Configurations** for the configuration, so anything we do will simultaneously set the values in all build configurations for this target. Change the Bundle Loader setting from blank to

```
$(BUILT_PRODUCTS_DIR)/MyCompanyName.app/Contents/MacOS/\
MyCompanyName
```

Further, we have to cue the unit-test script what application is the target for the test. The setting that does this is Test Host, and the value is the same as the one for Bundle Loader, so it's easiest just to set Test Host to $(BUNDLE_LOADER).

The final step is to turn off ZeroLink for all build configurations of MyCompany-Name. The method-injection mechanism used in running the tests does not work with ZeroLinked targets.

Select **UnitTests** as the active target, and click **Build**. Xcode's build system will first bring MyCompanyName up-to-date and then compile UnitTests' test class. As the last step in the build, the test is run, and because a host application is set, MyCompanyName is briefly run so that our test suite can attach to it and run the tests. When the test suite is done, MyCompanyName is terminated. Details of the testing appear in the detail panel of the Build Results window, as before.

23.2.3 Testing Options

OCUnit is far from the only choice you have for a testing framework. ObjCUnit (`http://oops.se/objcunit/`) and TestKit (`http://testkit.sourceforge.net/`) are frameworks that, like OCUnit, are based on the JUnit model of integrated testing. UnitKit (`http://unitkit.org/`) is a promising new entry that integrates tightly with Xcode and follows the philosophy that unit tests should not be incorporated into the product build. And, of course, for Java programming, there is JUnit itself (`http://www.junit.org/`).

23.3 Summary

This chapter introduced AppleScript Studio as a way to use Xcode to produce Cocoa-based applications, written in AppleScript. We saw that such applications can cross languages, dropping into Objective-C code where necessary. We used the Xcode debugger to step through both the AppleScript and the Objective-C portions of our applications.

No less important is the subject of unit testing, the practice of regularly challenging the elements of an application to verify their correct operation. We saw how to add a unit-test target to our AppleScript Studio project, write test cases, and verify the correctness of our Objective-C utility code.

A Large Project

Not every worthwhile software-source product is packaged as an Xcode project. The vast library of open-source software available for UNIX systems, such as Mac OS X, come as *tarballs*—archives packaged and compressed by the `tar` command line tool—to be built from the command line, using the `make` command.

The `make` tool—on Mac OS X it is GNU `make`—takes as its input a makefile, specifying how products in a project are to be built. The makefile specifies that some files, say, a `.o` file from a compilation, depend on others, such as the `.c` file of the same name, along with a set of `.h` files. On the strength of that information, `make` can detect whether a product's dependencies are newer than the product and, if so, can issue commands that bring the product up-to-date.

Xcode's native build system works the same way but does not usually need you to specify dependencies. It detects what files you put into a project, deduces what it is supposed to do with them—compile them, include them as resources, and so on—and determines what the intermediate products are and what additional files go into producing the intermediate products. From all of that, it produces dependency rules for the target and uses them to direct builds.

> The exception in which you do specify build dependencies to a native-build target is a Shell Script phase. When you add a Shell Script build phase, you can specify an input file and a product file.

If you have a source product that is organized around makefiles, you can still work within Xcode. Such projects are called *external build system* projects. Let's see what Xcode can and can't do for us with a moderately large product, Graphviz.

24.1 Graphviz

In mathematics, a *graph* is a group of nodes connected by edges. You can think of *nodes* as rooms in a maze and *edges* as the passages between them; or you can think of nodes as the boxes in an organization chart and the edges as the lines between them. Graphviz is a set of command line tools that turn text descriptions of graphs into diagrams. The Graphviz home page, http://www.graphviz.org/, provides much more information.

Glen Low has won two Apple Design awards for the Mac OS X Graphviz version (http://www.pixelglow.com/graphviz/). For illustration purposes, we'll be building the generic UNIX version. We'll be doing this purely as an exercise in technique. Generic Graphviz assumes the presence of libraries that are not by default installed on a Mac OS X system, and we won't be taking the time to assemble all the prerequisites for a fully working Graphviz. The project will take us far enough to illustrate some techniques; if you are interested in Graphviz as a tool, check out Glen's port.

First, obtain the Graphviz source, which can be found at http://www.graphviz .org/Download_source.php. The source archive will have the compound extension .tar.gz, meaning that it is a GNU-ZIP compressed tar archive. Download the archive to a place where you want the Graphviz project directory to be, or move it there after the download is complete.

24.2 Preparing the Project

Now for some work in the Terminal application. Before it can be taken over by Xcode, the Graphviz project has to be unpacked from its archive and configured to the tools and libraries available on your system. First, extract the archive; point the command interface at the directory that contains the archive, and invoke tar. The example here assumes that we're working with version 2.2 of Graphviz:

```
$ cd Projects
$ tar xzvf graphviz-2.2.tar.gz
graphviz-2.2/
graphviz-2.2/agraph/
graphviz-2.2/agraph/README
graphviz-2.2/agraph/aghdr.h
graphviz-2.2/agraph/agraph.h
```

```
graphviz-2.2/agraph/malloc.h
graphviz-2.2/agraph/vmstub.h
.
.
.
```

The options to tar (xzvf) told it to *extract* the contents after *unzipping* them from the named *file* and to be *verbose*, or print the name of each file. The verbosity isn't strictly necessary, but the extraction takes time, and it's nice to have something to show what's going on.

Next, the project has to be configured. If you point your command line interface at the newly created graphviz-2.2 directory and list the contents of the current directory, you'll find files named INSTALL and README and a script named configure. I can't promise that these files will be at the root of every open-source project you download, but you'll usually find them.

```
$ cd graphviz-2.2
$ ls
AUTHORS              config             graphviz.spec.in
COPYING             config.h.in        iffe
ChangeLog           config.h.old       lefty
Config.mk           configure          lneato
INSTALL             configure.ac       m4
.
.
.
README              dotty              tclhandle
.
.
.

$ cat README
Graphviz - Graph Drawing Programs from AT&T Research and
Lucent Bell Labs

See doc/build.html for prerequisites and detailed build notes.
$ open doc/build.html
$
```

The usual scenario is that if a project has a configure script, you must execute ./configure from the root of the project in order to adapt the project's makefiles and headers to the architecture, tool set, and library suite of your machine. The INSTALL file will usually contain annotations of any special flags or features this particular configure script accepts.

However, in this case, INSTALL appears to be unchanged from its generic content. Examining the README file shows that the build instructions are in graphviz-2.2/doc/build.html.

The build.html file confirms that Graphviz shares the same build-and-install recipe as almost every other open-source project (*do not* type this in):

```
./configure
make
make install
```

It also says that ./configure --help will show us all the available options, which are numerous. For the purposes of this tutorial, we'll take none of them.

So now we invoke ./configure. A glance at its voluminous output suggests why it is necessary:

```
$ ./configure
checking build system type... powerpc-apple-darwin8.0.0
checking host system type... powerpc-apple-darwin8.0.0
checking target system type... powerpc-apple-darwin8.0.0
checking for a BSD-compatible install... /usr/bin/install -c
checking whether build environment is sane... yes
checking for gawk... no
checking for mawk... no
checking for nawk... no
checking for awk... awk
checking whether make sets $(MAKE)... yes
checking for gcc... gcc
checking for C compiler default output file name... a.out
checking whether the C compiler works... yes
    .
    .
    .
$
```

During this process, the configuration script fails to find the header for the FreeType typographic library. As Graphviz relies on FreeType, not only for labeling but also for scaling objects, this will cripple our version of the package. In real life, we'd take the trouble to make up the gap—it involves installing X Window support and adding `--with_freetype=/usr/X11R6` to the parameters of `configure`—but we're doing this only for the exercise.

By the end of this process, all the makefiles in `graphviz-2.2` and its subdirectories will have been created and the header files adjusted to the peculiarities of your development environment. If all you cared about was obtaining Graphviz, the easiest thing would be simply to type `make` at the next command prompt and, assuming all went well, `sudo make install` at the command prompt after that.

But in our scenario, you want to bring Xcode into the picture. Maybe you want to modify Graphviz, or you think you'll have to edit its source for it to compile properly. Maybe you just want to study it. You need an interactive, integrated development environment. It's at this point in the life cycle—after configuration but before the first `make`—that Xcode can enter.

24.3 An External Build Project

From the **File** menu, select **New Project...**, and scroll down in the New Project Assistant to select the **External Build System** project type. Click the **Next** button and give the project a name, such as Graphviz. Be careful in choosing a directory for the project. It's easiest if the project directory is the same as the directory for the root makefile—in this case, the `graphviz-2.2` directory.

Next, add all the files in the `graphviz-2.2` directory to the Xcode project. The easiest way is to drag the project directory from the Finder to just below the project icon at the top of the Groups & Files list; or you can select **Project** → **Add to Project...**, and select the project directory. In either case, make sure that subdirectories will be included as groups, not as directory references. When the include is done, remember to remove `Graphviz.xcodeproj` and the build directory from inside the project list. The circular reference of a project to itself can't be healthy.

So, what can you do with this Xcode project? First, you can build it. Click the **Build** button in the toolbar. The build takes a few minutes and results in a couple

Figure 24.1 The Build Results window during the build of Graphviz. Clicking a warning in the upper panel does not bring the corresponding source code into the editor, owing to the nature of the build tree most external build systems use. Open the build details with the third button at the bottom of the upper panel to see the full error message and locate the problem code.

of dozen warnings but ultimately succeeds. As the build progresses, you can select **Build → Build Results** to open the Build Results window. Click the third button at the bottom of the upper panel to expose the detailed build listing. This will open a panel in the middle of the window (see Figure 24.1) that echoes each command issued by the makefiles as they do their work. If this panel is scrolled to the bottom, it tracks the new content as it is added.

Clicking an error or a warning in the upper panel highlights the corresponding message in the detailed build results but does not bring up a source listing as it would if this were a native-build project. The reason is that like most complex makefile-based projects, Graphviz has a separate makefile in each directory of the project. The master makefile at the root of the project directs make to the makefiles in the immediate subdirectories, and so on. This is a clever and economical arrangement, but Xcode cannot follow the thread of working-directory changes and so can't resolve the file references in the error messages.

This is why it's important to have the detail panel of the Build Results window open and to have all the project files loaded into the project. Consider these warnings:

```
compound.c: In function 'boxIntersect':
compound.c:51: warning: 'ipp$x' may be used uninitialized in this
function
```

In the Groups & Files listing, select the project icon at the top, so that all the files in the project appear in the detail view. Then type **compound.c** in the search field. The list swiftly narrows to the file you want. A click on the file's line summons the file, and you can use the function pop-up to find the boxIntersect() function. There you can see a point variable named ipp that might, in fact, go uninitialized—but only in cases in which, the documentation says, the function is not to be called. No problem here.

Use the function pop-up to scroll down to makeCompoundEdge(). Early on, we see the phrase

```
if (ED_spl(e)->size > 1) {
    agerr(AGWARN, "%s -> %s: spline size > 1 not supported\n",
        e->tail->name, e->head->name);
    return;
}
```

What's agerr()? Command-double-clicking on it takes us to an error-reporting function in lexer.c. What is AGWARN, and what are the other possible values for that parameter? Command-double-click: It's an enum of type agerrlevel_t, and the other defined values are AGERR, AGMAX, and AGPREV.

Command-double-clicking to find the definition of a symbol depends on the index Xcode builds of all projects. It won't work if indexing is turned off in the preferences or if it is still under way; select **Window** → **Activity Viewer** to see whether that is the case.

Incorporating every file from the Graphviz directory into our Xcode project is convenient but brings a lot of clutter to the Groups & Files list. If you've been accustomed to the relative ease of navigating the small Linear project, you may be feeling a little lost. This is where Smart Groups come into their own.

In Linear, which is built up from source files, the Groups & Files list is a fairly flat roster of implementation and header files. That isn't possible with a deep tree like the one we have in Graphviz. So let's create our own source roster.

Select **File** → **New Smart Group** → **Simple Regular Expression Smart Group**. In the Info window that appears, name the new group **Source Roster**. Have it search from `graphviz-2.2` recursively for the regular-expression pattern `\.(c|cpp|m|mm|h)$`, which means any file name ending with a period and one of the listed extensions. You need save the group only for this project.

Close the Info window and select the new **Smart Group**. Its members appear in the detail view in the top right-hand portion of the project window. You can narrow the list further by typing a search string into the search field above the list.

Try searching for `.cpp`. Control-click on any file in the list, and select **Reveal in Group Tree**. You have thus traced from a file name to the file's place in the organization of the project. Almost certainly, your `.cpp` file is part of the `dynagraph` subproject.

Select the `dynagraph` folder icon, and then select the **Design** → **Class Model** → **Quick Model** command. In a few seconds, you are rewarded with a diagram of the C++ classes in the `dynagraph` tool.

> As of late 2005, the C++ parser for the class modeler was not as strong as the Objective-C parser and apparently could not handle namespace- or class-qualified type identifiers properly. I expect this to be remedied shortly.

Now we're able to run the products of the build. Consulting the PDF manual pages included in the Graphviz package, we find that one of the products is the command line tool `neato`. Because it does not track the products of an external build, Xcode doesn't know what the executables are in this project, so we have to tell it. Select **Project** → **New Custom Executable**. Xcode brings up an assistant so you can name the executable and associate a file with it. Use the **Choose . . .** button to browse into the `dotneato` directory and select the `neato` executable.

Xcode then opens an Info window for you to adjust other parameters. I recommend setting the working directory to the `graphviz-2.2/graphs` directory, as this will make it much easier to access the sample data files.

In general, you can never be assured of what the working directory for an application will be on Mac OS X or any UNIX system. In this case, we have the option of setting it, and if we run an application from a shell process, that process will inherit the shell's working directory, but applications launched from the Finder start with a working directory path of /. Your applications, then, should rely only on well-known locations or prearranged paths, calculated locations from `CFBundle` and `NSBundle` or the Folder Manager, or explicit paths from application parameters or `NSOpenPanel` and its cousins.

Click the **Arguments** tab and add three arguments:

1. `-Tgif` to specify GIF output
2. `-o process.gif` for the name of the output file
3. `undirected/process.dot` for the input file

Now select **Run Executable** from the toolbar. The Run Log window appears and immediately gives the message

```
neato has exited due to signal 10 (SIGBUS).
```

It seems that we have some debugging to do.

24.4 Debugging a Custom Executable

Our debugging task is complicated by a peculiarity of the way Graphviz is built: It isn't fully linked until it is installed in its final locations. What looked like the `neato` tool was in fact a shell script that elaborately set up an environment to run the pieces of the tool in place.

So we bite the bullet and install Graphviz, as this will be the simplest way to gain access to it with `gdb` and the Xcode debugger. Go back to the Terminal application, make sure that your session is still pointed at the `graphviz-2.2` directory, and type **sudo make install** to assume the necessary privileges and install all the components:

```
$ sudo make install
Password:
```

```
Making install in cdt
test -z "/usr/local/lib/graphviz" ||
  /Users/xcode/Projects/graphviz-2.2/config/install-sh -d
    "/usr/local/lib/graphviz"
 /bin/sh ../libtool --mode=install /usr/bin/install -c
    'libcdt.la' '/usr/local/lib/graphviz/libcdt.la'
 .
 .
 .
```

This will take a minute or so. The next thing is to point the neato custom executable at the installed tool. (You can find the path to the tool by entering **which neato** at the command line.) Select **neato** under the **Executables** group, and press **command-I** to open the Info window; then use the **Choose...** button next to the **Executable Path:** field to bring up an open-file dialog. You will find neato at /usr/local/bin, which is a directory not usually shown in open-file dialogs. You can get there by typing **/usr/local/bin**; a panel will appear, to receive what you type; when you click the **Go** button, the dialog will display the desired directory. Find neato and select it.

There's one more snag, however. Select the **Debugging** tab, which specifies what debugger will be used for this executable and how it is to run. As this was written, Xcode would show the selected debugger as the **Java Debugger** and offer the **AppleScript Debugger** as an alternative. You need gdb, but because the original neato file selected for this executable was a text file, Xcode doesn't allow that choice. The only workaround is to delete this executable and create a new one pointed at the binary neato. That one will permit debugging with gdb.

At long last, we have an executable pointed at the binary neato, loading the process.dot file and outputting a GIF and ready for debugging. Select **Debug Executable** from the toolbar.

Once again, the bus error occurs, but this time, the debugger shows where it happens. It's in the one and only line of initDPI():

```
double _dpi;
void initDPI(graph_t * g)
{
    _dpi = GD_drawing(g)->dpi;
}
```

A quick command-double-click shows that GD_drawing() is a macro covering the u.drawing member of its pointer parameter; g shows up in the variable list. We open it, open u, and find that drawing is 0x0—NULL. A reference through NULL would certainly explain the bus error.

Next, we poke around a bit. Specifically, we look for where u.drawing gets initialized. A Project Find on u.drawing turns up nothing of interest; apparently, all access is through the GD_drawing macro. A Project Find on GD_drawing turns up a few places where it is set to NULL and one where it is set thus:

```
GD_drawing(g) = NEW(layout_t);
```

Looks like an initialization to me. This occurs in init_ugraph(). When I looked up the call stack, to see how initDPI() was called, I found this:

```
void graph_init(graph_t * g)
{
#if ENABLE_CODEGENS && !defined(HAVE_GD_FREETYPE)
    initDPI(g);
#endif
    /* initialize the graph */
    init_ugraph(g);
```

Aha! The call that relied on g's being fully initialized, initDPI(), comes *before* init_ugraph(), the call that initializes it. Reversing the order of the calls will cure the bus error, and a quick scan of the rest of init_ugraph() suggests that the delay in filling _dpi won't hurt:

```
void graph_init(graph_t * g)
{
    /* initialize the graph */
    init_ugraph(g);

#if ENABLE_CODEGENS && !defined(HAVE_GD_FREETYPE)
    initDPI(g);
#endif
```

Now to rebuild the project, which takes quite a bit less time, as it involves a change to only one file, and, alas, a return to the Terminal application to repeat the sudo make install. Return to Xcode and run the executable, which ends almost as soon as it is started, leaving a file, process.gif, in graphviz-2.2/graphs (Figure 24.2). If the configuration phase had found a typographic library, the nodes would be labeled polygons, but at least we have output.

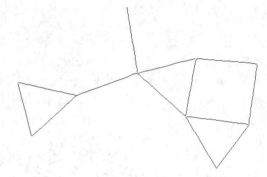

Figure 24.2 The first output of neato, from the process.dot example file. The absence of a typographic library makes the nodes small and unlabeled, but it's output.

24.5 Performance

Now for something meatier. We pick one of the largest example input files, graphs/directed/crazy.dot, and set neato to produce a GIF file from it. Giving it a first run, we find that it takes quite a bit of time—about 200 seconds on a 1.5GHz PowerBook G4—and produces an unreadable output file nearly 3MB in size.

It's natural to be curious about what's taking up all that time. Shark, the centerpiece of Apple's performance-measuring suite, can tell us. Shark is mainly a statistical profiler; it interrupts whatever the computer is doing, several thousand times a second, and records the active process, the call stack, and the program counter. Shark accumulates up to about 30 seconds' worth of data, after which it cross-references that data against debugging symbols to identify where applications are spending most of their time. When debugging symbols are available, the statistics are shown in the context of the source code, so you can see not only problem routines but also problem lines of code.

There are several ways to trigger Shark profiling on an application.

- While the application is running, run Shark, and click the **Start** button in the Shark control window.

- Have Shark running in the background. When you exercise a part of your application you want to measure, press the Shark hot-key combination. By default, this is **option-Escape**, but this conflicts with Code Sense in Xcode, so I recommend changing it to **command-Escape**.

- Start the target application from Xcode with the command **Debug → Launch using Performance Tool → Shark**.

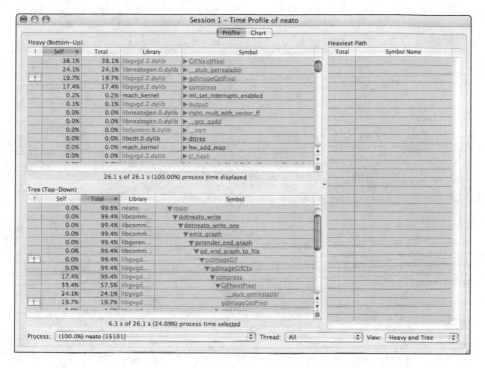

Figure 24.3 Shark's analysis of `neato`: 57.5 percent of the execution time was taken up inside `GIFNextPixel`, mostly in either `__stub_getrealaddr` or `gdImageGetPixel`

As we have our custom executable all set up for `neato` on `crazy.dot`, the last method is most convenient. Wait until the previous run of `neato` is done, and launch it again, using Shark. Shark displays a dialog box confirming the path to the tool, the command line parameters, and the working directory; these are correct, so click **OK**. After 30 seconds, Shark beeps and presents a window containing its analysis (Figure 24.3).

Shark offers two analyses of the statistics it takes. The first, called Heavy, analyzes in what routine the application's program counter was found to fall the most often. What piece of code was executed most commonly? In this analysis, the answer is `GIFNextPixel()`, from the `gvgd` library, where the PC was found in 38.7 percent of the samples. That one function took up nearly two-fifths of our execution time. Following it closely, at nearly a quarter of execution time, was `__stub_getrealaddr`.

The second analysis, called Tree, determines, given a function call, how much time was spent in the function itself and how much in each function it called. The tree starts at the starting symbol in the runtime system, the root function, which accounts

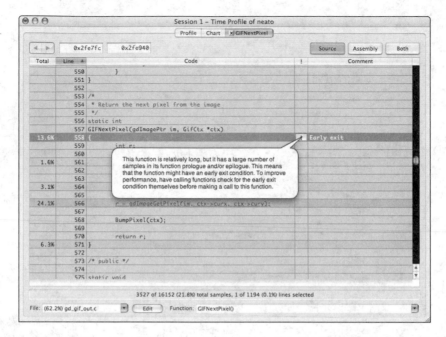

Figure 24.4 `GIFNextPixel()` as analyzed by Shark. The portion of the total sample time spent on each line of the function is shown at the left margin. Lines that took up more time are highlighted with denser colors. The big hot spot for the profiling session was at `gdImageGet-Pixel()`. The button with the exclamation point in it opens a suggestion for optimization; in this case, noting that the function is short enough that setup and teardown take up a significant portion of its execution time, so it might be a candidate for in-lining.

for 100 percent of the time, because although it spends little time in itself, its call to `main()` amounts to the whole run of the program.

Where the tree analysis gets interesting is in the first call to `compress()`, which took up 99.4 percent of the run in itself or calls it made. Some 18.3 percent was in itself. Most of the rest of the time—nearly three-fifths of the run—was inside `GIFNextPixel()`. Another good chunk of its time was spent in `gdImageGetPixel()`.

The signs are all pointing at `GIFNextPixel()` as a major bottleneck. What does it look like? Double-click on a line in one of the analyses containing the name of the function. Shark adds a tab to the analysis window, showing `GIFNextPixel()`, with line-by-line statistics on where it spent its time (Figure 24.4).

On the screen, the listing is shaded according to how "hot" each line is—the brighter the color, the more time was spent executing that line. About 20 percent of our run time was spent setting up and tearing down the function. Shark notices this and posts a button with an exclamation mark at the right margin; click it, and you'll see a balloon suggesting that it might be a good idea to in-line this function to save the overhead.

But the major portion of the time was spent in the line calling gdImageGetPixel(). This is mentioned as being a minor time sink in compress(), but the Shark analyses all pointed to __stub_getrealaddr as the call that sunk time in this function. Clicking the **Assembly** button clues us in: The call to gdImageGetPixel() is made through interlibrary glue provided by __stub_getrealaddr. There are a lot of pixels in a large graphic, and one can imagine that looking up a branch address for every pixel might take up some time.

What does gdImageGetPixel() consist of?

```
BGD_DECLARE(int) gdImageGetPixel (gdImagePtr im, int x, int y)
{
    if (gdImageBoundsSafeMacro (im, x, y))
      {
        if (im->trueColor)
        {
        return im->tpixels[y][x];
        }
        else
        {
        return im->pixels[y][x];
        }
        }
      else
        {
        return 0;
        }
}
```

After verifying that gdImageBoundsSafeMacro is in fact a macro, we conclude that this code is on the high end of trivial. If it can be in-lined and put into a header as a static function, it can save interlibrary calling overhead everywhere it is used. So we #define a preprocessor symbol GD_IGP_INLINE, and #if it is 1, include in gd.h the definition of the gcImageBoundsSafeMacro macro and gdImageGetPixel() as a static inline int function.

Rebuild, reinstall, and run against `crazy.dot` again. Before, our `neato` took about 202 seconds to run. Now, it takes 92 seconds. Doubling the speed of the program is not a bad reward for a few minutes' work.

The lesson here is *not* that you should in-line every function. Overall, that would be a bad idea, because the size of your application would grow dramatically, and other things being equal on Mac OS X, a program built to be *smaller* is more responsive than one built blindly to be "faster." Blind optimization that results in using more memory grows your code beyond the processor cache and makes virtual memory faults more likely.

The lesson, instead, is to *measure* your code. The most efficient use for your optimization skills is to concentrate them on the things that slow down your application.

24.6 A Better Way to Include Files

In Section 24.3, we filled the Groups & Files list for the Graphviz project by brute force by dragging the project root directory into the list, thus including every file and directory in the tree, whether it was source code or not. If you had put the drag off until after the first build, the included files would even include the `.o` object files produced by the build, which makes no practical sense at all.

There is a better way. Xcode has an extensive AppleScript dictionary that encompasses enough to build a source code tree in the Groups & Files list. Our goal here is a script that will take the front project in Xcode and fill its list with source files from the project directory and all its subdirectories. Such an application, with no human interface at all, doesn't need AppleScript Studio; indeed, I find AppleScript's Script Editor a better tool for experimenting with scriptable applications.

Make no mistake: Writing a new AppleScript is an experimental process. You'll be marrying components and applications with scriptable interfaces written to varying standards in both specifications and quality. For example, almost all of AppleScript is built around the HFS file system model, in which absolute file paths begin with the volume name and separators are colons (:). In the Xcode Project Suite for AppleScript, *project* objects have a *project directory* property. It is reported as a string, formatted as a POSIX path—rooted at a mount point and separated by slashes. To be useful anywhere else in AppleScript, this string has to be converted. It may take some experimentation to find that the conversion is

```
tell application "Xcode"
    set pDirect to the project directory of project 1
    set pDirect to ((POSIX file pDirect) as file) as string
end tell
```

24.6.1 The Script

As with most good AppleScript interfaces, Xcode's interface centers on classes that describe elements of the Model layer of its design. The application is presented as a hierarchy of containers with the *application* at the top, containing *projects* and *windows*. A *project*, in turn, contains *targets*, *executables*, *groups*, and *file references*. Because the Xcode object model defines the objects we want to manipulate—we want to add file-reference and group objects to a project container—there is no need for a special AppleScript command for importing and filtering directory trees. Everything can be done with the make command from the workhorse Standard Suite.

The make command is used twice in our script. When it first enters a new directory, the TraverseDirectory handler has two pieces of information: the name of the new directory (dirName) and a reference to the group representing the new directory's parent (currContainer). The command, simplified, is

```
tell currContainer
    make new group
        with properties {name:dirName,
                         path:dirName,
                         path type:group relative}
end tell
```

Two different hierarchies are being maintained here. In the hierarchy of the Groups & Files view, currContainer is being told to contain a new group and to use the contents of dirName as the label. Separately, these groups represent a hierarchy in the file system. In that hierarchy, we set the new group to have a path consisting of the contents of dirName, relative to the path of currContainer, its parent group.

The great advantage of the group-relative path type is that so long as the group hierarchy matches the file hierarchy, the paths for groups and file references match the names of directories and files. If the path type had been project relative, we'd have to accumulate the directories traversed from the project directory into the path. And, if the path type had been absolute, which is rarely a good idea, the path would have to trace down through to the root of the file system. Avoiding directory references also allows us to avoid translation between Xcode's reliance on POSIX-style paths and the HFS-style paths generated by the rest of AppleScript:

```
property pDirect : ""

property sourceSuffixes : {".h", ".c", ".m", ".cp", ".cpp",
                           ".M", ".mm"}
```

```
on IsSourceFile(fileName)
    repeat with suffix in sourceSuffixes
        if fileName ends with suffix then return true
    end repeat
    return false
end IsSourceFile

on CatenateFileElements(root, path, leaf)
    set retval to root
    if path is not "" then
        set retval to retval & ":" & path
    end if
    if leaf is not "" then
        set retval to retval & ":" & leaf
    end if
    return retval
end CatenateFileElements

on TraverseDirectory(parentPath, dirName, currContainer)
    tell application "Xcode"
        -- Make relativePath the cumulative relative path
        --  from the project root directory
        if parentPath is "" then
            set relativePath to dirName
        else
            set relativePath to
                my CatenateFileElements(parentPath, dirName, "")
        end if
        tell project 1
            -- Make dirGroup refer to the group we're filling.
            if currContainer is "" then
                -- The root group if we're starting out.
                set dirGroup to root group
            else
                -- A new group if this is a deeper directory.
                tell currContainer
                    set dirGroup to make new group
```

```
                with properties {name:dirName,
                                 path:dirName,
                                 path type:group relative}
        end tell
    end if

    try
        -- Fill contentList with the names of the
        -- contents of the current directory.
        set longPath to
            my CatenateFileElements(pDirect, parentPath,
                                    dirName)
        set contentList to list folder longPath

        repeat with itemName in contentList
            -- With each file in the current directory:
            set fileInfo to
                info for file (longPath & ":" & itemName)
            if not alias of fileInfo then
                if folder of fileInfo and
                        not package folder of fileInfo then
                    -- Go down into the directories.
                    my TraverseDirectory(relativePath,
                                         itemName,
                                         dirGroup)
                else if my IsSourceFile(itemName) then
                    -- Add source files to the group.
                    tell dirGroup
                        make new file reference
                            with properties
                                {name:itemName,
                                 path:itemName,
                                 path type:group relative}
                    end tell
                end if
            end if
        end repeat
```

```
            end try
        end tell
    end tell
end TraverseDirectory

tell application "Xcode"
    set pDirect to the project directory of project 1
    set pDirect to ((POSIX file pDirect) as file) as string
    set pDirect to (characters 1 through
                ((length of pDirect) - 1) of pDirect) as string
    my TraverseDirectory("", "", "")
end tell
```

The script takes nearly 6 minutes to cull Graphviz 2.2 on my 1.5GHz PowerBook G4.

24.6.2 Building the Project Index

When it's done, click in the **Project Symbols** smart group; the list is empty. Perhaps the project needs to be reindexed. Select the project icon at the top of the Groups & Files list and double-click to open the project's Info window. At the bottom of the window, click the button for rebuilding the project index. Wait a little bit; the **Project Symbols** smart group is still empty. In fact, if you choose **Window → Activity Viewer**, you find that rebuilding the index takes no time at all. The newly added files are not being indexed.

Why? Select one of the source files and open an info window (**command-I**) on it. You find an **Include in Index** checkbox, but it's disabled. It appears beneath a **File Type** pop-up menu, which is set for the most generic type possible, **file**. If you change the file type to something more congruous, such as sourcecode.c.c or sourcecode.c.h, the file becomes indexable.

We won't have to set each file's type individually. The file-type property is not exposed to AppleScript, but it's easy to set manually. Make sure that the detail view is visible in the project window, and select the project icon. Click in the detail view to activate it, and press **command-A** to select all the files. Get an info window by pressing **command-I**; an info window opens for the multiple selection. For **File Type**, select **Default for File** at the top of the pop-up menu. Then make sure that **Include in Index** is checked. Now you can reindex the project and get results.

24.6.3 Compromising with AppleScript

After running the script, you may notice that although the Groups & Files list is much trimmer than it was when you simply dragged into it, it could be trimmer still. Many of the Graphviz subdirectories didn't contain any source files and show up in the Groups & Files list as empty. Can we not trim these while building the list?

We could make a start on this by setting a flag named didAddItem to false at the beginning of TraverseDirectory and setting it true if a file or a subgroup ever gets added to the group. If the flag is still false at the end of TraverseDirectory, we can tell Xcode to delete the group created on that pass. Although this solution misses groups that include only empty subgroups, it would be a start.

As of Xcode 2.1 and AppleScript 1.10.3, this doesn't work. Adding the following phrase after the try block causes the script to stop the first time the delete is executed:

```
if (not didAddItem) and (currContainer is not "") then
    tell dirGroup to delete
end if
```

No error is shown. Looking at the Console application in /Applications/Utilities shows that Xcode logged an error that class PBXProject is not key/value coding compliant for the key allGroups. So it is off to http://bugreporter.apple.com/ to report the problem, which perhaps will be resolved by the time you read this. The enduring point is this: You have to experiment with AppleScript. Not everything in the application script terminologies sees its way through to functionality. You have to script what the applications will do, not what they promise.

24.7 Summary

This chapter used, and arguably abused, the excellent Graphviz project as a backdrop for exploring the issues that arise in building large projects with Xcode. These include using external build systems (make), debugging custom executables, and taking advantage of the Shark external profiler. We also used AppleScript to make life with a large source tree more livable.

25

Closing Snippets

25.1 Miscellaneous Traps

- Case-insensitive file names: HFS+, the recommended file system for Mac OS X, is case preserving—files will get names in the same case as you provide—but case insensitive: Xcode.txt, XCODE.TXT, and xcode.txt all refer to the same file. Most other UNIX variants are case sensitive, so if you import code, be on the lookout for the assumption that, say, the following two lines refer to different files:

  ```
  #include "polishStrings.h"
  #include "PolishStrings.h"
  ```

  By the same token, make sure that your code uses file names with consistent letter casing. Even if you don't expect to port your work, HFS+ isn't the only file system a Macintosh application sees, and a case-sensitive version of HFS+ does exist.

- Library links: It is common practice in UNIX programming to provide the latest version of a library—say, libFoo.2.3.2.dylib—in a library directory and then provide symbolic links (libFoo.2.dylib and libFoo.dylib) to that file. When they link, programmers can specify the library generically through one of the symbolic links and be assured that the symbolic link will take the application to the right library, no matter what version is current on a user's machine.

  This seems like a trivial practice to follow in Xcode: You want to link to a generic version 2 libFoo, so you select **Project → Add to Project...**, type **/usr/lib**, and select the link libFoo.2.dylib. But **NSOpenPanel**, which implements the file-selection dialog, resolves links before returning them to the calling application. Xcode gets the path to libFoo.2.3.2.dylib, and your application will refuse to launch if exactly that library is not available.

  The solution is to drag the symbolic link directly into the Groups & Files list. In the Finder, expose /usr/lib by pressing **command-shift-G** and typing **/usr/lib**; locate the desired symbolic link. Drag it into the Groups & Files list in Xcode; in the resulting add-to-project sheet, specify the targets the `.dylib` is to join, and do not copy the file into your project folder. Make sure that the `.dylib` appears in the Link Binary With Libraries phases of the relevant targets.

- The `.pbxuser` file: The `.xcodeproj` project document is a package directory containing four files, of which only one, *projectname*`.pbxproj` contains information critical to the structure of the project. The remaining files store the state of the project as last set by a particular user. The *username*`.mode`*N* files record the tiniest details of all, such as window and split-bar positions and contents of history lists.

  The *username*`.pbxuser` file encompasses nontrivial matters, such as the placement of bookmarks, breakpoint specifications, custom executables, and parameters for executables. Sharing a project file will not transmit these settings to the other party. Depending on your taste, you may or may not think that these are important things to preserve; decide for yourself whether `.pbxuser` files belong in SCM.

  If a `default.pbxuser` file is present in a project package and no user-specific `.pbxuser` file is there, the settings in the default file will be used.

- Header ambiguity: Xcode is sometimes perverse in picking header files. C programmers are accustomed to the convention that files named in quotes in an `#include` directive are sought in a "local" directory tree, whereas files in angle brackets are supposed to be sought in a "system" header tree. Xcode doesn't do this. It searches the project paths first in both cases. If you have, say, `String.h` in your project directory, that file will be used to satisfy `#include <string.h>`, at least on the case-insensitive HFS+ file system.

  If you find that you have been bitten by this peculiarity, you can turn it off. Add the setting `USE_SEPARATE_HEADERMAPS` to the applicable target build configurations, and set it to `YES`. The setting applies only to `gcc` 4.0 and later; for earlier versions of `gcc`, set `USE_HEADERMAP` to `NO`.

- Intrinsic libraries: Different UNIX systems have different requirements for the libraries that must be linked into a program in order to make it runnable. If you are porting an application to Xcode, be sure *not* to include `libc`, `libstdc++`, or `libgcc` in the list of files to link against; `gcc` will link against `libc`—in fact, `libSystem`—and `libgcc` automatically. Additionally, if you use the g++ front end for compiling C++, which Xcode does, `libstdc++` is automatically linked.

  Note that `gcc` 4.0 relies on a dynamic `libstdc++`, which is available only on Mac OS X 10.3.9 and 10.4. If you are targeting a C++ application at earlier versions, you'll have to use `gcc` 3.3.

25.2 Miscellaneous Tips

- Window sizes: In Xcode, when you open a new editor window it opens to a size and screen position set in the Xcode defaults. To change the default, size and position a window to suit you, select **Defaults...** in the **Window** menu. A sheet will drop from the front window, asking whether you want to make its layout the default for all windows of its type. Click **Make Layout Default** to set the new default.

- Multiple-target info: If you select more than one item in the Groups & Files list, you can click the **Info** button in the toolbar or press **command-I**, and a single Info window will appear that applies to *all* the selected items. We used this feature in Section 24.6.2 to select every .c file in the project and mark them all as C source.

    You can perform the same trick with multiple targets; suppose that you have many targets in a project and decide that you want the Release builds of them all to optimize their instruction scheduling for the G4 processor. Command-click to select each target, and then bring up an Info window, which will apply to all of them. Select the **Build** pane and the **Release** build style, and seek out the **Instruction Scheduling** setting. Change this to **PowerPC G4**, and all selected targets will be set.

- Sharing precompiled headers: Xcode 2.1 introduces the idea of caching precompiled headers, on the theory that if sharing header compilation within a project is good, sharing it across projects is even better. Precompilation results are held in /Library/Caches/com.apple.Xcode.*n*, where *n* is the ID number of the user doing the precompilation. Xcode tries to keep a cache directory pruned down to 1GB in size, while keeping any file that was used in the past 24 hours. These retention parameters can be changed by using the defaults tool and the keys BuildSystemCacheSizeInMegabytes and BuildSystemMinimumRemovalAgeInHours.

    The sharing of precompiled headers makes it important to avoid putting project- or build-specific predefined symbols into prefix files, if at all possible. Ordinarily, this would put us in a quandary because the predefined-symbol switch for gcc, -D, applies to precompilations as well as source compilations; adding such a setting changes the precompiled file and restricts its usefulness to the scope of the definition.

    Fortunately, an alternative way to define a symbol does not affect precompiled headers. The setting **Preprocessor Macros Not Used In Precompiled Headers** allows you to define symbols "downstream" from the precompilation of the headers, so the precompiled header file remains generic and shareable. See Figure 25.1.

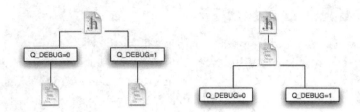

Figure 25.1 Setting a global preprocessor symbol (left) changes the environment in which the prefix header is compiled, so a different precompiled header has to be generated each time the symbol is changed. If the symbol is defined in **Preprocessor Macros Not Used In Precompiled Headers** (right), a single precompiled header serves all cases, as the symbol is injected into the environment "downstream" from the precompilation.

- Parameters for `Info.plist`: This file is crucial in any bundled target, and Xcode handles it specially. You are already familiar with the way the project templates populate the file with default values and how the **Properties** tab of the target Info window serves as an editor for common `Info.plist` entries.

    As of Xcode 2.1, you can use the `gcc` C preprocessor on your `Info.plist` file. You can `#define` and use macros to build values in the file. The obvious uses might be in repeatedly used strings, such as the reverse-domain-name prefix for bundle and UTI identifiers and for version numbers. Search on "Info" in the target **Build** settings list for the switch that enables preprocessing and for settings that allow you to predefine macros and set other preprocessor options.

    Also, any of the build system's settings can be embedded in `Info.plist` by using the `$(SETTING_NAME)` reference style. Or, you can substitute `$(PRODUCT_NAME)` for all instances of your product's name, so that one change to the build settings will propagate automatically. Using `$(EXECUTABLE_NAME)` may be safer for the `CFExecutableName` key.

- Single build directory: Prior to Xcode 2.1, all builds, regardless of build style—the predecessor of build configurations—yielded a product in the `build` subdirectory of the project directory. Both intermediate and final products were commingled, and the only way to ensure that a product was all-release or all-debug was to clean targets every time the build style changed.

    Xcode 2.1 changed all this. The `build` subdirectory and its intermediates subdirectory now contain one directory for each build style. Results of builds are kept segregated, so build dependencies don't get crossed between configurations, and there is much less need to build from clean targets.

Some developers, however, prefer the unitary build directory. This can be restored by setting the Xcode application preference `UsePerConfigurationBuild-Locations` to `NO`:

```
$ defaults write com.apple.xcode \
                UsePerConfigurationBuildLocations NO
```

This is a per user preference. There is no way to attach it to a project or to restrict it to a single project.

- More build settings: Some build settings are read-only, reflecting the state of the build or derived values from other settings. Some settings exist but don't have a graphical interface; there are more settings than there are entries in the target Build Info panel. A complete list can be seen by selecting **Help** → **Show Build Settings Notes**. You can use any of the settings as variables to build values for the Build panel or `Info.plist`, and you can set the "unlisted" but writable ones if you need to by adding a row to the Build list. Build settings are also available to Shell Script phases as environment variables.

  One setting that isn't mentioned is `$(VALUE)`. Targets inherit build settings from the project, which in turn inherits settings from Xcode's defaults. Sometimes, you want to add to, not replace, an inherited setting. Use `$(VALUE)` to include the inherited value in your setting.

- More preferences: Not every useful preference in Xcode is accessible through the graphical interface; some have to be set through the `defaults` command line tool. Select **Help** → **Show Expert Preferences Notes** for a list.

- Folder references: In Section 24.3, when we selected a folder to add to our project, we wanted to add each particular file in the folder to the project. But sometimes, adding a folder to a project means adding the folder itself to the project. Suppose that you were building an educational program about presidents of the United States and wanted the `Resources` directory of the application to include a subdirectory containing a picture of each president. Your intention is that the application include that directory and whatever it may contain—as new administrations or replacement portraits come in—not the particular files.

  In such a case, when you drag the portrait folder into the Groups & Files list, you select **Create Folder References for any added folders** in the sheet that appears. The folder you dragged in will appear in the list in the same blue color as folders in the Finder, not in the yellow of Xcode's file-grouping folders. The folder reference can then be dragged into the Copy Bundle Resources build phase;

the folder and its contents, whatever they might be at build time, will be copied into the product's Resources directory.

- Moving views in Interface Builder: The normal consequence of dragging a view in Interface Builder is that the view slides to where you drag it but does not change its position in the view hierarchy. Suppose that you had a window containing an NSBox and an NSSlider. Dragging the slider toward the box would make the two views overlap but would not put the slider into the box. Both would still be immediate subviews of the window's content view.

  One way to place the slider in the box might be to select it and then select **Cut (command-X)** from the window, double-click in the box to select its interior, and **Paste (command-V)** the slider in. The problem is that you may already have set a target and action for the slider or bound it to an NSController. Such connections are lost when a control is removed from the view hierarchy.

  The better way is to hold the mouse button down on the slider for a few seconds. The slider will develop a deep shadow around it, indicating that it has been "lifted off" the view it had been in. When you drag the browser into the box in this condition and drop it there, the slider is put inside the box. This click-and-hold strategy will temporarily take views out of the hierarchy without damaging their connections.

- Enclosing views in Interface Builder: Suppose that you are working in Interface Builder on a group of controls enclosed in another view, such as an NSBox. You turn your attention from arranging the controls inside the box to moving or resizing the box itself. Chances are, your first effort is a fumble, because once you've selected something inside a container in Interface Builder, you can't grab hold of the container itself.

  The intuitive, if clumsy, solution is to select something else outside the NSBox and then select the box. There's a shortcut: Pressing the **Escape** key will select the container of the currently selected view.

- Code optimization: The optimization-setting flag for gcc goes in a progression from -O0 (none at all) to -O3 (everything). The temptation, when driving for the sleekest, whizziest application, is to turn the knob up full and let the optimizer fly. And yet the standard Release setting for optimization in Xcode is -Os—optimize for *size*. What's going on?

  The problem is that -O3 optimization can dramatically increase the size of the generated code: gcc will autonomously convert function calls to in-line code, so that the content of those functions will be repeated, perhaps many times, throughout the application. It will turn counted for loops into series of n iterations of the loop body, one after the other, because it's quicker to run straight through four copies of the same code than to keep a counter, test it against four, and conditionally branch.

All these optimizations are ingenious, but they can be short-sighted. Modern processors are dramatically faster than the main memory buses that serve them; waiting for loads of data or program instructions can stall a processor for a substantial proportion of time. Therefore, limited amounts of very fast cache memory are put between the processor and RAM, to make the instruction stream available at a pace that keeps up with the CPU. But cache sizes are limited. An application that has been doubled in size throughout by unrolling and in-lining everywhere will overrun the cache and hit RAM to fetch instructions at least twice as often. In the usual case, "faster" code runs slower than smaller code.

This isn't true in every case. As we saw in Section 24.5, your code will have hot spots where in-lining and even loop unrolling will yield substantial performance gains. You simply have to run your application and measure it to see where the hot spots are. You can set -O3 optimization for a single source file by opening an Info window on it, selecting the **Build** tab, and typing the flag into the window.

- Quicker text editing: Xcode Users have reported that when they have many editor windows open, text editing and global searching become sluggish. Oddly enough, much of the lost performance can be regained by hiding the status bars at the bottom of editor windows. With an editor window frontmost, select **View → Hide Status Bar**; close all editor windows. From then on, all editor windows will open without status bars. Search and build results will still be summarized in the status bars that remain in the Project, Project Find, Build Results, and other specialized windows.

25.3 Documentation

The Apple Developer Connection Reference Library encompasses comprehensive documentation of all the supported technologies of Mac OS X, including sample code, release notes, and technical notes. The complete library is freely accessible through the Web at http://developer.apple.com/referencelibrary/. Most of the library is also installed with Xcode at /Developer/ADC Reference Library. Xcode provides a specialized ADC library browser that you can summon with the command **Help → Documentation**.

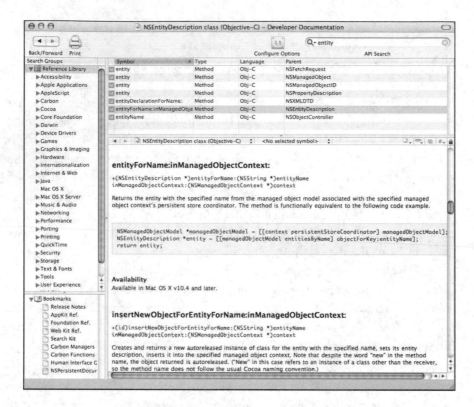

Figure 25.2 The Xcode Documentation window. When the search field at top is set to **API Search**, typing in the field performs an immediate search of the entire Mac OS X API set, showing the applicable language and context—for instance, owning class—for each entry. Selecting an entry displays its documentation in the browser pane. Searches can be restricted in scope by selecting the section of the ADC Library of interest in the list at the left.

25.3.1 The Documentation Window

The Documentation window (Figure 25.2) follows the familiar iTunes layout: a list of categories appears at the left of the window, which drives a detail list at the top of the main portion. In the usual case, this detail list shows the name of every documented symbol that falls under the selected category of the Mac OS X documentation. You can narrow the contents of the detail portion by typing a string into the search field at upper right. Selecting an entry in the detail list displays the corresponding document.

Not every API set is useful to every developer. If you are a Cocoa programmer, you are probably interested in Cocoa's Objective-C API or its Java API but not in

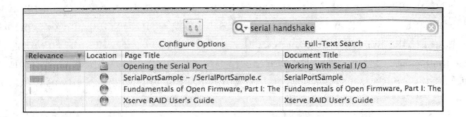

Figure 25.3 A full-text search for "serial handshake" in the Documentation window. Unlike the API search, the full-text search waits for you to press **Return** before offering results. Results are presented with bars indicating the relevance of the match between the search and the found document. In this case, the results were narrowed even further by selecting the **Hardware** category in the **Search Groups** list. On the screen, the blue globes in the second, third, and fourth lines indicate that these documents are available only on-line.

both. As installed, the results of most of your searches for Cocoa symbols will turn up results for your language of choice, interleaved with results for the language you didn't choose. To remedy this, click the **Configure Options** toolbar button to obtain a list of languages to be included in API searches. Uncheck **Objective-C** or **Java**, as suits your needs, and click **OK**.

The window lends itself to less-directed browsing as well. Selecting any topic in the list at the left of the window presents an index page of subtopics, with brief descriptions of the technologies they cover. Selecting one of these brings up a page listing the articles collected for that topic and subtopic. Most of these articles are available as additional pages that are viewable in the Documentation window, but specialized content, such as sample code and technical notes, will be referred to your Web browser for retrieval from Apple's server.

The search field has a second mode. You can select **Full-Text Search** from the pop-up menu at the field's magnifying glass icon, and enter keywords to be found anywhere in the ADC Library. The index that Xcode uses does not cover only the portion of the library that is on your hard drive; articles that are available only on line, labeled with the blue globe icon, will also be offered in the results. See Figure 25.3.

As with the API search, selecting a section of the library in the list at the left of the Documentation window restricts the search to that part. If you type a phrase into the full-text search field, each word will be sought in the index separately and the resulting matches ranked by relevance. Relevance searches can be sloppy—a document can appear surprisingly high in the results list but completely lack one of the terms you are looking for. Sometimes, you want to say that you really do want a word to be

present in the document. You can make a term mandatory by preceding it with a +
character. Preceding a term with a − indicates that you wish to exclude any documents
containing that term. You can indicate that a phrase is to appear literally in order by
enclosing it in quotes. So if you were interested in a summary of power-management
issues but found discussions of heat dissipation tedious, you might specify as follows:

```
"power management" +overview -heat
```

Even more finesse in full-text queries can be had with Boolean operators. Search
terms can be joined by | for "or," and & for "and," grouped by parentheses, and negated
with !. On our query, a variant that accepts articles about power management or energy
management might be

```
("power management" | "energy management") & overview & !heat
```

25.3.2 Documentation Updates

Apple is continually revising its documentation, adding articles and making revisions
as Mac OS X features mature. New and revised documents come out in a steady
stream, on which you can keep posted by following the RSS feed at

```
feed://developer.apple.com/rss/referencelibrary.rss
```

Additionally, Xcode can check with Apple's servers and download revised editions
of the ADC Reference Library when these become available, which is expected to be
monthly. Using the **Documentation** panel of the Preferences window, you can make
Xcode check for updates at once or have it make automatic checks every day, week,
or month.

When a reference library update becomes available, Xcode will present you with
an alert asking whether you wish to download it. If you accept, Xcode will refer your
browser to a page at developer.apple.com asking for your ID and password with the
Apple Developer Connection. ADC membership, for access to the updates, is free.

When the ID and password are taken care of, the download begins. The result
is a Mac OS X installer package, which you may have to find and open yourself.
Installation should require no more than an administrator password, to authorize
a change to the /Developer directory. There is no need to quit Xcode. Once the
installation is finished, Xcode will notify you that it must reset itself to the root of
the documentation tree, because the documentation has changed. You can browse,
search, and read the new documentation immediately.

Installing Xcode

With every copy of Mac OS X and on every new Macintosh, Xcode is provided free

- As a compressed archive on the hard drives of new Macintoshes. Look in /Applications/Installers and Demos for a disk-image (.dmg) file named Xcode Tools. Double-click this file, and it will appear in the Finder as a removable disk containing the Xcode installation package.

- As an installable package on Mac OS X installation DVDs. Look for a folder named Xcode Tools.

- In an additional CD-ROM in Mac OS X installation CD-ROM sets.

- As a free download from http://connect.apple.com for members of the Apple Developer Connection.

Find the XcodeTools.mpkg installation package and double-click on it to start the installation. The Mac OS X installer will open with its familiar window showing the progress of the installation. Click the **Continue** button to acknowledge the welcome message, and then read the license agreement. You will have to click the **Agree** button before you can proceed with the installation. Next, the installer will ask whether it's OK to "run a program" before installing. This is normal and benign. Click **Continue**.

At this point, the Apple installer offers you a choice of installation locations, but you don't really have a choice: Xcode and the associated tools have to be installed on the start-up volume of your computer. Click **Continue** to acknowledge this.

The installer will now offer you Easy Install, with no options presented. As it never hurts to see exactly what you're getting yourself into, click the **Customize** button to display the available subpackages and see which are selected. You'll notice the following things.

- The default installation offers to install more than one version of gcc, the compiler behind the Xcode tools. Why would you need more than one? The reason is that although the latest version—version 4 as this was written—takes advantage of developments in Apple hardware and generally produces better code, version 3.3 produces code that conforms to certain specifications for Mac OS X kernel extensions and is compatible with Mac OS X versions 10.3.8 and earlier. Also, some developers may have a policy that treats recompiling existing software with a major revision to the compiler as a major revision to the software itself, requiring extensive testing and validation. Having older compilers available lets them choose when to bear that cost.

- One thing that may not be checked is a package called CHUD Tools, a suite of applications for measuring the efficiency and behavior of the code you write. Check this item. No matter what your previous experience with profiling and performance measurement was, on Mac OS X it's different: These tools make detailed, easy-to-understand analyses of your code's behavior available to you for almost no effort on your part, and you are almost guaranteed a noticeable improvement in the quality of your product.

- Another thing that is not checked is a group of cross-development kits. *Cross-development* means using one computer system to develop software for another. The other computer systems in this case are all Mac OS X, in particular, the last revisions of versions 10.2, 10.3, and 10.4 of Mac OS X. Mac users seem to upgrade their operating systems fairly cheerfully, but a developer hoping for the greatest possible market may want to ensure that software runs on earlier versions of the OS. Apple continually introduces new APIs and libraries. It's easy to write code intended to run on, say, version 10.2 and inadvertently use features, or even constants, that are available only on later versions. The cross-development kits install complete header and library directories for earlier Mac OS X versions. If you use a 10.3 feature in a project intended for 10.2, you'll get compilation and linkage errors to warn you away. Unless you are sure that you will *never* distribute one of your programs to someone with an older system, I recommend checking this item.

- Another thing not checked is the documentation for the Java Development Kit that Xcode uses for Java programming. These are the Sun Java API documents for J2SE, and many Java programmers already have a copy of them, online or in a book, that they prefer to use. If you don't already have access to these documents and have the space to spare, check this item. Finding the resulting pages can be a little tricky; they're on your disk at `/Developer/ADC Reference Library/Java/Reference/1.4.2/`—the version number will, of course, advance with time—with separate subdirectories for the standard API and Apple extensions.

Once you've made your choices, click the **Continue** button. Because the installation will be making changes to the common area of your hard disk, the installer will now ask for the user name and password of an administrator of the computer. Provide these, and click **OK**.

Now you can sit back and watch the progress bar inch across your screen. Depending on the computer and the options you've chosen, the installation could take from 5 to 20 minutes. If all goes well, the installer will inform you that the Xcode Tools were successfully installed, and you can click the **Quit** button to leave the installer.

A.1 Apple Developer Connection

The most current version of Apple's developer tools, including Xcode, is always available for free download through the Apple Developer Connection (ADC), Apple's user group for developers, which can be found on the Web at `http://developer.apple.com/`. The ADC contains current documentation in the form of manuals, technical notes, release notes, sample code, and Q-and-A documents for all current, and most past, Apple technologies.

Additionally, the Apple Developer Connection has a membership component that handles licensing and nondisclosure between Apple and its members. Basic and student memberships in ADC are free to anyone over 18. Paid memberships, beginning at $500 a year in the United States as of late 2005, allow access to prerelease "seed" versions of Apple software, discounts on Apple system purchases, two free accesses to personal help from Apple's Developer Technical Support, and free copies of major releases of Mac OS X as they are released. If you need the services bundled with a paid ADC subscription, the subscription fee easily pays for itself.

Even the free online ADC membership will give you access to the most current developer tools. If you aren't already a member, direct your Web browser to `http://connect.apple.com/`. Click the button labeled **Join Now**.

First, you will be presented with an agreement acknowledging Apple's rights in its intellectual property, limiting its liability, and defining the relationship you are about to enter with it. If this is all acceptable to you, click the **Agree** button.

Next comes the setup for your online account with ADC. Enter your real name and create an Apple ID; if you have an existing online relationship with Apple—through .Mac, consumer support, or the iTunes music store, for instance—you should use the same ID. Enter a password. Next, provide some contact information, at least including a full mailing address. You will then be asked some marketing questions about your areas of work and interest.

The process may end at a page offering to sell you a Select- or Premier-level membership. Don't worry—you're done! You have already completed the sign-up process for the free online membership in ADC.

From here, you can download the current Xcode tool set, about 960MB in late 2005. In the past, Apple offered the option of purchasing a CD-ROM with the lastest Xcode tools at a nominal fee. This practice seems to have ended now that Xcode has grown larger than the capacity of a CD. If you don't have access to a broadband Internet connection, your options are to borrow a friend's connection, or stick with the Xcode that came with your Mac OS X distribution media.

A.1.1 Downloading from ADC

To one side of the page is a menu that includes **Downloads** as a choice. Select it, and then select the subitem **Developer Tools** when it appears. The tool-related releases will be listed, newest first, so the first item, named **Xcode Tools**, is the one you want. Be sure to read the descriptions of the later items—the ones appearing above **Xcode Tools** in the list—as they may include important patches to the full release.

Click on the link for the Xcode Tools disk image. Your browser should begin a download automatically. The resulting file will be in MacBinary format. Depending on your browser and its settings, this may be automatically converted to a .dmg (disk-image) file and the disk image mounted; or you may have to use Stuffit Expander, available at http://www.stuffit.com/, to do the expansion yourself.

Once the disk image is mounted, you will find an Xcode Tools.mpkg icon inside and can proceed as with any other delivery method. Disk images can be ejected by dragging them to the trash or clicking the eject symbol that appears next to them in the Finder windows. Disk images can be ejected only when every file inside them has been closed.

A.2 Setting up the Dock

If you're going to be using the Xcode tools extensively, as I hope you will, in following along with the examples in this book, you will find that there are three applications— Xcode itself, Interface Builder, and the Terminal application—that you will be using frequently, but none of them are in the /Applications folder. The first two are installed in /Developer/Applications, and the third is in /Applications/Utilities. They are therefore much less handy to you than are, say, the calculator or TextEdit.

I put all three in my dock, and you should consider doing the same. Simply find the applications and drag their icons into any part of the dock to the left, or above, the hairline. Or, if the application is already running, choose **Keep in Dock** from its dock icon's menu.

Some Build Variables

You can see all the build variables that are available to Run Script build phases by creating a phase that consists only of the command env. You'll find that there are more than 250 variables. Here's a list of the more useful ones. For purposes of example, assume that user "xcodeuser" is making a debug build of an application named MyApp out of a project named MyProject on a PowerPC; the project uses the 10.4 Universal SDK. See Figure B.1.

A comprehensive list of the build variables can be found in the Xcode **Help** menu under **Show Build Settings Notes**. This appendix lists the highlights of the available build variables.

Some of these settings have no corresponding interface in the **Build** panels of the Info windows. You can set these—if they are not read-only—by clicking the + button at the bottom of the **Build** panel and entering the name of the build setting in the left column and the value in the right. Boolean values are kept as YES and NO.

B.1 Useful Build Variables

PROJECT_NAME, the name of the project file, without extension (MyProject).

PROJECT_DIR, the directory that contains the project file (/Users/xcodeuser/ MyProject).

PROJECT_FILE_PATH, the full path to the project file (/Users/xcodeuser/MyProject/ MyProject.xcodeproj).

ACTION, the task the build system is carrying out, corresponding to the action parameter for xcodebuild (build).

CONFIGURATION, the name of the selected build configuration (Debug).

PACKAGE_TYPE, the kind of product to be built. Apple documents the possible values to be EXECUTABLE (a single file, not an .app bundle), DYLIB (a single .dylib file),

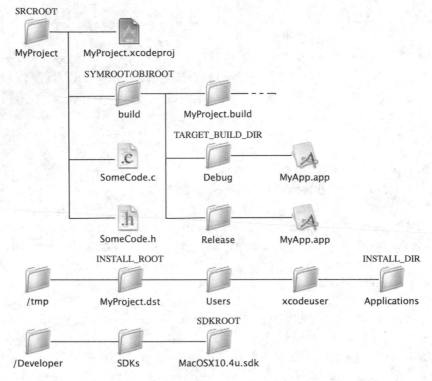

Figure B.1 Layout of the MyProject/MyApp project used as an example for the build variables listed here

WRAPPER, FRAMEWORK_WRAPPER, JAR_FILE, ZIP_FILE, and JAVA_CLASS_FOLDER, but indications are that they will be switching to UTIs for this setting. The thing to do is to use a Run Script build phase in your project one time to echo the value of this setting, so you'll know what to test for (com.apple.package-type.wrapper.application).

OBJROOT, the folder containing, perhaps indirectly, the intermediate products, such as object files, of the build (/Users/xcodeuser/MyProject/build).

SDKROOT, the root of the tree in which to search for system headers and libraries. When no SDK is selected, SDKROOT is set to / (/Developer/SDKs/MacOSX10.4u.sdk).

SRCROOT, the folder containing the source code for the project, usually the project document's directory (/Users/xcodeuser/MyProject).

SYMROOT, the container for folders that receive symbol-rich, meaning not yet stripped, versions of the product (/Users/xcodeuser/MyProject/build).

BUILT_PRODUCTS_DIR, the full path to the directory that receives either every product of the project or, if the products are scattered, symbolslinks to every product. A script can therefore depend on reaching all the products through this path. By default, $(SYMROOT)/$(CONFIGURATION) (/Users/xcodeuser/MyProject/build/Debug).

TARGET_BUILD_DIR, the directory into which the product of the current target is built; the installation location in an install build. Otherwise, the CONFIGURATION subdirectory of the SYMROOT directory (/Users/xcodeuser/MyProject/build/Debug).

TARGET_NAME, the name of the active target. Note that the target usually has the same name as the product, but this is not necessarily the case. For instance, a separate target for running unit tests might yield the same product as the principal target of a project but have another name, such as MyApp (testing). (MyApp).

CONTENTS_FOLDER_PATH, the path, within the target build directory, that contains the structural directories of a bundle product (MyApp.app/Contents).

EXECUTABLE_FOLDER_PATH, the path, in a bundle target in the target build directory, into which the product's executable file is to be built. Not to be confused with EXECUTABLES_FOLDER_PATH, which points to a directory named Executables in the Contents directory (MyApp.app/Contents/MacOS).

FRAMEWORKS_FOLDER_PATH, the path, in a bundle target in the target build directory, that contains frameworks used by the product. There are variables for other possible bundle directories; see the Xcode documentation for more (MyApp.app/Contents/Frameworks).

UNLOCALIZED_RESOURCES_FOLDER_PATH, the directory, within a bundle product in the target build directory, that receives file resources (MyApp.app/Contents/Resources).

DERIVED_FILE_DIR, the directory that receives intermediate source files generated in the course of a build, such as the sources generated by the bison parser generator. This variable is paralleled, presumably for historical reasons, by DERIVED_FILES_DIR; my guess is that the singular version is preferred. If you have a more general need for a place to put a temporary file, consult the Xcode documentation for PROJECT_TEMP_DIR or TARGET_TEMP_DIR (/Users/xcodeuser/MyProject/build/MyProject.build/Debug/MyApp.build/DerivedSources).

`OBJECT_FILE_DIR_normal`, the directory containing subdirectories, one per architecture, containing compiled object files, for the "normal" variant of the product. The other possible variants are debug and profile; variants of dynamic libraries can be chosen at load time by setting the `DYLD_IMAGE_SUFFIX` environment variable (`/Users/xcodeuser/MyProject.build/MyProject.build/Debug/MyApp.build/ Objects-normal`).

`ARCHS`, the architectures, as a space-separated list, for which the product is to be built (`ppc`).

`NATIVE_ARCH`, the architecture on which the current build is taking place (`ppc`).

`VALID_ARCHS`, the possible values that could go into the `ARCHS` list. The list encompasses all the architectures for which OpenStep has historically been available; in practice, only the `ppc` options and `i386`, plus G3, G4, and G5, are available (`m68k i386 sparc hppa ppc ppc7400 ppc970 ppc64`).

`GCC_VERSION`, the `gcc` compiler version to use. This is generally selected in the **Rules** tab of the target Info window, but setting it in a configuration in the **Build** tab will override it. If the **Rules** setting selects the "system version" of the compiler, this variable will be empty; if you need the version in that case, try parsing the output of the `gcc_select` tool. As of Xcode version 2.2, you can set `GCC_VERSION` per architecture (`GCC_VERSION_ppc` and `GCC_VERSION_i386`) (empty).

`GCC_PREPROCESSOR_DEFINITIONS`, a space-separated list of symbols to be `#defined` in all compilations. Items of the form *symbol=value* assign values to the symbols. Symbols defined in this way will be incorporated in precompiled headers. Related is `GCC_PREPROCESSOR_DEFINITIONS_NOT_USED_IN_PRECOMPILED_HEADERS`, which specifies symbols defined in every compilation but not incorporated in precompiled headers. This allows you to share precompiled headers between build configurations, with variants in global definitions taken as options in the respective configurations.

`OTHER_CFLAGS`, the catchall variable that receives the `gcc` options that do not have their own build variables for C compilation. It's easy to put in this variable an option that contradicts a setting made in the **Build** tab of the Info panels, with unpredictable results. Therefore, it's a good idea to type a flag into the **Build** list's search field, to see whether a direct setting is available. There is also an `OTHER_CPLUSPLUSFLAGS` variable. For linker flags, the equivalent is `OTHER_LDFLAGS` (empty).

OTHER_CFLAGS_normal, to specify OTHER_CFLAGS only for the "normal" variant of a dynamic library; debug and profile variants are also possible. For linker flags, the equivalent is OTHER_LDFLAGS_normal_ppc, where the order is variant and then architecture, and either can be omitted. If you are stuck with single-architecture libraries, you can link a fat target by specifying the PowerPC version in a -1 option in OTHER_LDFLAGS_ppc; the Intel version, in OTHER_LDFLAGS_i386 (empty).

PER_ARCH_CFLAGS_ppc, applied only to PowerPC builds; the most useful other architecture suffixes are ppc64 and i386; similarly PER_ARCH_CPLUSPLUSFLAGS_ppc (empty).

WARNING_CFLAGS, a string of options setting warning options for all gcc compilations. Apple is trying to provide fine-grained control of warnings through checkboxes in the **Build** panels, so check to be sure that there isn't a checkbox for your warning before putting it into this variable. The equivalent for the linker is WARNING_LDFLAGS (empty).

HEADER_SEARCH_PATHS, a space-delimited list of paths to directories gcc is to search for headers, in addition to standard locations, such as /usr/include. If you add your own paths, carry the default paths through by putting $(VALUE) at the beginning or end of your list. If the headers in question are in frameworks, set FRAMEWORK_SEARCH_PATHS instead. SDKROOT is prepended to the paths of system headers and frameworks (/Users/xcodeuser/MyProject/build/Debug/include).

LIBRARY_SEARCH_PATHS, a space-delimited list of paths to directories the linker is to search for libraries. If set, SDKROOT is prepended to the paths of system libraries. Developers sometimes are given libraries in production and debug forms, as binaries, with no source; they'd like to use one version of the library in Debug builds and the other in Release builds. A solution is to put the two library versions in separate directories and specify different LIBRARY_SEARCH_PATHs for the two build configurations (/Users/xcodeuser/MyProject/build/Debug).

USE_HEADERMAP, If set to NO, Xcode follows the more expected practice of searching only project directories for quoted include files, at the expense of some performance. (In Xcode, gcc treats angle-bracket #includes the same as it treats quoted ones: It searches the project header directories for the named header and then the system directories.) In Xcode 2.1 and later, USE_SEPARATE_HEADERMAPS is the preferred solution.

USE_SEPARATE_HEADERMAPS, available beginning in Xcode 2.1. In Xcode, gcc treats angle-bracket #includes the same as it treats quoted ones: It searches the project header directories for the named header and then the system directories. If your project has headers with the same names as system headers, such as string.h and you have been relying on angle brackets to make the distinction, set this option to YES. Angle-bracket #includes will then be searched for in system directories first (empty).

MACOSX_DEPLOYMENT_TARGET, the minimum version of Mac OS X on which the product can run; symbols in the SDK from later versions of the OS are weak-linked (10.4).

INFOPLIST_FILE, the name of the file that will be the source for the bundle's Info. plist file, if the product of this target is a bundle. This is not necessarily Info.plist, as a project with more than one target will use one project directory to specify more than one Info.plist file (Info.plist).

INFOPLIST_PREPROCESS, if YES, preprocesses the INFOPLIST_FILE, using the gcc preprocessor for C. You can specify a prefix file with INFOPLIST_PREFIX_HEADER and set symbols with INFOPLIST_PREPROCESSOR_DEFINITIONS (NO).

DEPLOYMENT_POSTPROCESSING, indicating whether the build system is to strip symbols from the product, install it to INSTALL_DIR, and set its ownership and permissions (YES). The install build action sets this option, or you could set it yourself in one of your configurations (NO).

INSTALL_PATH, the intended directory that would receive the installed product. Installation is done by the Default configuration (/Users/xcodeuser/Applications).

INSTALL_ROOT, the path to prepend to the INSTALL_PATH to hold the installation tree—install builds do not, by default, install directly to the "live" installation destinations (/tmp/MyProject.dst).

INSTALL_DIR, the full path of the directory to receive the product. Obtained by concatenating $(INSTALL_ROOT)/$(INSTALL_PATH) (/tmp/MyProject.dst/Users/xcodeuser/Applications).

INSTALL_OWNER, the owner of the MyApp.app product, when installation is done (xcodeuser).

INSTALL_GROUP, the group for the MyApp.app product, when installation is done (xcodeuser).

INSTALL_MODE_FLAG, the permissions for the installed MyApp.app product (a-w, a+rX).

LIBRARY_STYLE, set to STATIC, DYNAMIC, or BUNDLE, as the case may be, for a library product project type.

ZERO_LINK, indicating whether ZeroLink linkage is enabled (YES).

EXECUTABLE_NAME, the name of the product, net of any prefixes or suffixes made necessary by its file type (MyApp).

EXECUTABLE_PATH, the path, within TARGET_BUILD_DIR, to the executable binary (MyApp.app/Contents/MacOS/MyApp).

EXECUTABLE_PREFIX, the prefix needed for the product's file name to conform to the product type. If this were a static library target, for instance, this variable would be lib.

EXECUTABLE_SUFFIX, the suffix needed for the product's file name to conform to the product type. If this were a static library target, for instance, this variable would be .a.

B.2 Splitting Build Variables

Some build variables have variant forms that override the principal variable's setting for an architecture. For instance, selecting an SDK in the **General** tab of the project Info window sets the SDKROOT build variable to the path corresponding to the selected SDK. When you build a universal binary, you are forced to select the 10.4u SDK, because that's the only SDK with a library set that includes stubs for Intel libraries. This also has the effect of setting MACOSX_DEPLOYMENT_TARGET to 10.4, so the application will not run on systems earlier than Tiger.

However, it's often desirable from a marketing standpoint to support PowerPC users running versions of Mac OS X earlier than 10.4. Fortunately, MACOSX_DEPLOYMENT_TARGET is among the variables that can be split by target architecture. In every configuration that will build a PowerPC binary (Debug and Release if you're running PowerPC; Release only if you've got an Intel Mac), add a new variable to the build list, MACOSX_DEPLOYMENT_TARGET_ppc, and set it to 10.3. This sets—for PowerPC builds only—weak-linking of Tiger-only features and enables the application to run on Mac OS X 10.3. See Figure B.2.

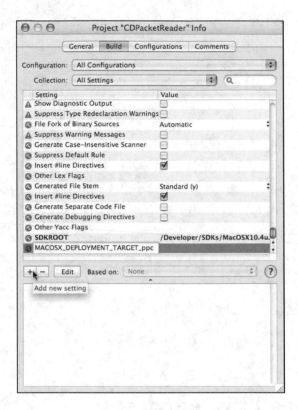

Figure B.2 Adding a PowerPC-specific build setting. In the **Build** tab of the Project Info window, select all configurations in the **Configurations:** pop-up, and click the + button to add a new build variable, named MACOSX_DEPLOYMENT_TARGET_ppc. This allows for different linkage and minimum-OS requirements between PowerPC and Intel processors.

B.3 Source Trees

A source tree provides a particular kind of build variable, a path to a directory or to the root directory of a tree with a known structure. The path can be a location to receive build results or provide access to a system of libraries and headers. When used to build source paths, a source tree provides a reliable shorthand for packages that do not belong in the directory tree of any one project.

For example, I use the eSellerate libraries in my projects. I define a source tree for the eSellerate libraries by opening the Preferences window, selecting the **Source Trees** panel, and clicking the + button to add an entry. I choose **ESELLERATE_DIR** for the setting name and **eSellerate Directory** for the display name, and I type the full path name for the root of the eSellerate SDK into the path column.

Now, whenever I add a file reference to my project, I will have the option of making the reference **Relative to eSellerate Directory**. If the reference is to a header or a library, a search path relative to $(ESELLERATE_DIR) will be added to the invocations of gcc. If I take the project to other computers or if I share it with other users, ESELLERATE_DIR has to be defined as a source tree for those users on those machines, but I don't have to care about the details of the path.

Search trees are global—they span projects—but are per user.

Glossary

absolute reference. The entire path name of a file. Files are added to Xcode projects by reference.

action. Along with target, one of the two external properties of controls, settable in Interface Builder. A control will store as its action the selector of a method it will send to a particular target—or to the responder chain—when the control is activated.

active target. The target in a project to which all project-level commands, such as **Build**, **Build and Debug**, or **Set Active Build Configuration**, are applied. When using the detail view to check and uncheck files as members of a target, make sure that the target you mean to be editing is the active target.

agent application. A Mac OS X application that may present a user interface if necessary but otherwise has no presence in the dock; for example, the `loginwindow` application. An agent application has the key `LSUIElement` set to 1 in `Info.plist`.

arranged objects. The content array of an `NSArrayController`, after sorting and filtering.

breakpoint. In program code, a fixed location at which execution is to be halted intentionally for display in a debugger. You can set unconditional breakpoints in Xcode by clicking in the margin to the left of the editor text at the line where you want to stop. The breakpoint is marked by a dark blue arrowhead.

build configuration. A group of settings encompassing the option set for building a target. Build configurations are defined at the target level, in the **Build** pane of the Info window. Default values for similarly named configurations in a project can be set in the **Build** pane of the project file's Info window. When editing the settings for a target, you can tell that a setting overrides the default if Xcode draws the title of the setting in boldface. Xcode defines three configurations—Debug, Release, and Default—for every native project; you may define additional configurations as needed.

bundle. A structured directory tree in which the executables and resources of a product are packaged as a single entity. Applications and library frameworks are the commonest examples of bundles.

compiler. The computer program that transforms source into machine-executable code. Strictly speaking, the output of a compiler is an object file, which requires linking before it can be executed, but one may speak loosely of the entire source-to-executable process as "compilation."

correlation coefficient. In statistics, a measure of how well a liniear regression fits the data from which it was derived. A perfect fit would be $+1$ or -1, depending on whether the line slopes upward or down; 0 indicates no fit at all. The square of the correlation coefficient is the proportion of the variation in y explained by linear dependence on x.

cross-development. In general, the development of software for a kind of computer other than the one on which the development is done. In Xcode, this refers to using the SDKs for noncurrent versions of Mac OS X to develop backward-compatible applications.

dependency. In the current or another Xcode project, a target that must be brought up-to-date before the current target is built. Add dependencies by double-clicking the current target in the Groups & Files list, and clicking the + button under the **Direct Dependencies** list. A project must be included in the current project for its targets to be available as dependencies.

dynamic loading. The practice of bringing external libraries needed for execution of a program into the program's memory when the program is run. This makes it possible for many programs to share a common library out of a single file and to load such a library into shared, read-only memory.

edge. In a graph, a link between two nodes. If the graph represented a maze, the edges would represent passages or doorways between rooms.

entity. In Core Data, a particular kind of aggregate of stored data, analogous to a class or structure in general programming.

external build system. Any method other than Xcode's own for determining what source files need to be recompiled in order to produce a current version of a target's product. Typically, the external system is make.

First Responder. The first NSResponder to which events are offered for handling. If the First Responder does not handle the offered event, it is shopped up the responder chain until a handler is found. The status of First Responder corresponds roughly with keyboard focus in a Mac OS X application. Interface Builder offers a placeholder icon for the First Responder in its Nib windows, to serve as a target for commands directed at the responder chain; at the implementation level, the target value is NULL.

framework. A bundle that encompasses a dynamically loadable library, its public headers, and, possibly, other resources in a single directory tree. Frameworks are versioned bundles.

graph. In mathematics, a system of nodes joined by edges. If a graph represented a map, the nodes would be the individual territories, and the edges the boundaries between each pair of territories.

import. To transfer the files of a module to the repository of a SCM system.

index templates. Indexes of the symbols in system frameworks, prepared in advance to save time in indexing new projects.

informal protocol. In Objective-C, a suite of methods that an object may expect another to implement but that is not set forth in a protocol. Informal protocols are frequently used in the delegate design pattern, in which delegate objects may be of any class but are expected to respond to certain messages. Informal protocols are often declared as categories on class `NSObject`.

linear regression. The statistical derivation of a straight line that most nearly fits a series of x, y points.

linking. The process by which a linkage editor examines a group of object files and libraries and attempts to resolve all the unknown symbols required for the execution of a program.

makefile. The usual name for the principal input file to the `make` utility and hence the name for any such file. A makefile specifies what components go into the production of a target, such as an application to be built, as a dependency network; `make` determines what components are newer than the things they produce and applies rules from the makefile to bring the products up-to-date. `Make` is the most commonly used build system in the UNIX world. Xcode uses its own build system but can use `make` as an external build system.

message invocation. The only new expression type added to C by Objective-C, consisting of a reference to an object, followed by a message selector and its parameters, all enclosed in brackets. Messages are dynamically dispatched, meaning that they are matched to implementation code at runtime; if an object does not implement a message it was sent, it is a runtime, not a compile-time, error.

metadata. Information about a file and its contents, made accessible without having to be privy to the format of the file.

modern bundle. The structure used for all bundles except for frameworks (see **versioned bundle**). A modern bundle immediately contains a `Contents` directory, which in turn contains an `Info.plist` file specifying version, copyright, and configuration information.

module. A group of files under control by CVS.

NaN. (Not a Number) A special flag value for floating-point numbers to indicate that the number is the result of an undefined operation, such as division of 0 by 0 or the square root of a negative number. Any operation on a NaN results in another NaN, so the flag value "poisons" any calculation it participates in.

Nib. A file—a package—produced by Interface Builder, consisting of an archive of Cocoa objects or Carbon interface specifications.

node. In a graph, a distinct position or state. If the graph represented a maze, the rooms in the maze would be nodes.

object file. The product of a compiler, whereby the logic of the source code has been transformed into machine-executable form but within which symbols may not be resolved, because they are not all defined in the file being compiled. Resolving such unknown symbols is the process of linking.

package. A directory tree that the Finder presents to the user as though it were a single file. Common examples include application bundles and compound documents, such as RTFDs.

prebinding. In a dynamic library, the practice of designating an address at which the library is to load. In an application, the practice of linking against prebound libraries, so that the addresses of all dynamically loaded symbols will be known in advance. Before Mac OS X 10.3.4, prebinding significantly reduced the time it took applications to start up. It is deprecated for applications intended to run on 10.3.4 or later.

precompiled header. The state of a compiler after it has parsed the included files that all the sources in the project have in common, saved so it need not be recompiled for each source file. In Xcode, the only option is to precompile the prefix file.

prefix file. A file to be prepended as though by an `#include` to the compilation of every source file in the project. Typically, this file would itself `#include` large and rarely changed headers, such as umbrella frameworks. Almost always, this file is made into a precompiled header.

product. The file, package, or bundle that is produced when a target is built.

project. The largest unit of work in Xcode. A project consists of a set of files—source code, resource, and reference—executables, targets, and settings. The project is embodied on disk in the project file, a package with the extension `.xcodeproj` and within Xcode by the project window.

project file. The on-disk embodiment of an Xcode project, containing the file lists, targets, settings, and user interface state. This is a package document with the `.xcodeproj` extension.

property list. A data structure embodying a number, string, date, data block, or Boolean; or an array or string-indexed dictionary of those objects or of other arrays or dictionaries. Also, a file, often with suffix `.plist`, that stores property list data. The format is used throughout Mac OS X whenever a simple, flexible data structure is needed.

protocol. In Objective-C, a suite of methods that a class may promise to implement. The compiler will post an error if the class does not implement all the methods of the protocol. An object pointer type of `id <ProtocolName>` specifies an object of any type implementing the `ProtocolName` protocol.

regression line. In an x, y plot, the straight line that represents the nearest fit to a series of data points.

repository. In an SCM system, the central file structure or network-based server that stores and manages the files.

resource. A nonexecutable component of a software product, especially when considered as a parameter to an application. Examples include strings, lookup tables, images, UI layouts, and sounds.

resource file. In Carbon, a file structured with a simple type-and-identifier index for ready retrieval of application parameters, such as strings, dialog layouts, pictures, and sounds.

responder chain. The linked series of `NSResponders`, beginning with the First Responder, proceeding through the enclosing `NSViews` to the `NSWindow` and its delegate—often, a subclass of `NSDocument`—and ending at the `NSApplication` instance and its delegate. A way of specifying an anonymous and context-dependent way of determining which commands are available at any moment and what objects handle them.

SCM system (software configuration management system). A library or database for storing successive revisions of the files that make up a software or other product. SCM has the advantages of centralized storage and backup, easier coordination among members of a project team, and ready retrieval of past revisions of a product.

source code. The human-written, and, it is hoped, human-readable artifact from which executable code is derived. Usually, source code takes the form of a text file in a programming language: C++, C, Objective-C, or Java.

static model. A class-model diagram that applies to a fixed set of class files at a fixed time. This is the only type of diagram available from the **Design** → **Class Model** menu.

symbol. A name by which something in a program—some executable code, a variable, a class—is identified and distinguished from other things.

symbol table. A dictionary associating entities, such as variables, classes, methods, and functions, with names. Libraries and other object files contain such tables to advertise what symbols they define and what symbols they need to have resolved.

tag. A set of revisions of the files that constitute a module, identifying the revisions that make up a particular version of a product.

target. Within an Xcode project, a group of source code and resource files and settings that produce a particular product. The target settings are where the general build settings for the target are made. Also, along with action, one of the two external properties of controls, settable in Interface Builder. When the control is activated, it sends the stored action message to the object designated as its target.

tracking model. A class-model diagram that monitors a group or groups in the Groups & Files list and dynamically updates the model diagram as files are added to or removed from those groups. Tracking models are available only from the New File Assistant.

umbrella framework. A framework that contains other frameworks. For example, the Cocoa framework includes the Foundation, AppKit, and CoreData frameworks. Apple does not support the making of umbrella frameworks by anyone but Apple.

unit test. A regularly made trial of the workings of the elementary parts of a program to verify that those parts behave as expected. Automated unit testing is relatively easy under dynamic languages, such as Java and Objective-C.

universal binary. A single file in the Mach-O executable format, containing machine code for both PowerPC and Intel processors. In an ancestor version of Mac OS X, these were referred to as "fat binaries" but such labeling was adjudged distasteful.

update. Under an SCM system, to load the latest revisions of the files under control from the repository into the working directory.

versioned bundle. The structure of framework-library bundles, which may expose more than one version of the headers and executable of the framework. The format relies extensively on links for easy access to the current version. See also **modern bundle**.

watchpoint. A directive that the debugger interrupt execution of an application when the value of a variable changes.

weak link. To reference an external symbol so that an error is not raised if the linker cannot provide a definition. Unresolved weak-linked symbols take the value NULL. Weak-linking is used in cross-development, so that an application that can run on an earlier version of the operating system can link against features available in later versions and test at runtime to see whether those features are available.

ZeroLink. The Xcode feature that speeds up development builds of applications by omitting most linking before launching an application. Only the routines needed to start the application running are linked and loaded, and any other code is discovered, loaded, and linked only as it is called. ZeroLinked applications are bound tightly to the object file set on the development machine and are not portable to other computers.

Index

Develop Full-Feature Mac OS X Applications with Cocoa

Cocoa® Programming for Mac® OS X, Second Edition

Aaron Hillegass

0-321-21314-9

The highly acclaimed introduction to Cocoa—recommended most by experienced Mac OS X developers—now updated and expanded!

To help programmers develop applications for Mac OS X, Apple is now giving away XCode, Interface Builder, and the Cocoa frameworks—the tools used to create Safari, GarageBand, Mail, and the iApps. *Cocoa® Programming for Mac® OS X, Second Edition,* will give you a complete understanding of how to use these tremendously powerful tools and frameworks to write full-featured applications for the Mac.

Guiding programmers through the key features of Cocoa, this book emphasizes design patterns that enable you to predict the behavior of classes you have never used before. Written in a tutorial format, it takes you step-by-step through the creation of six applications and an Interface Builder palette. Each project introduces several new ideas, and as each concept or technique is discussed, the author, drawing on his own extensive experience, shows you the right way to use it.

Praise for the First Edition

"Reading this book is the absolute best way to learn how to harness the power of this amazing technology."
    – ANDREW STONE, President, Stone Design, www.stone.com

"Make sure this is the first one you pick up. It's the best book for a beginning Cocoa programmer."
    – From the review on HyperJeff.net&

"I love this book. The descriptions are clear, the examples logical. Everything a programmer needs to get up to speed on Cocoa."
    – DAVE MARK, Editor, *MacTech Magazine*

For more information about this title please visit www.awprofessional.com/title/0321213149.

THIS BOOK IS SAFARI ENABLED

INCLUDES FREE 45-DAY ACCESS TO THE ONLINE EDITION

The Safari® Enabled icon on the cover of your favorite technology book means the book is available through Safari Bookshelf. When you buy this book, you get free access to the online edition for 45 days.

Safari Bookshelf is an electronic reference library that lets you easily search thousands of technical books, find code samples, download chapters, and access technical information whenever and wherever you need it.

TO GAIN 45-DAY SAFARI ENABLED ACCESS TO THIS BOOK:

● Go to **http://www.awprofessional.com/safarienabled**

● Complete the brief registration form

● Enter the coupon code found in the front of this book on the "Copyright" page

If you have difficulty registering on Safari Bookshelf or accessing the online edition, please e-mail customer-service@safaribooksonline.com.

informIT

YOUR GUIDE TO IT REFERENCE

Articles

Keep your edge with thousands of free articles, in-depth features, interviews, and IT reference recommendations – all written by experts you know and trust.

Online Books

Answers in an instant from **InformIT Online Book's** 600+ fully searchable on line books. For a limited time, you can get your first 14 days **free**.

Safari
POWERED BY
TECH BOOKS ONLINE

Catalog

Review online sample chapters, author biographies and customer rankings and choose exactly the right book from a selection of over 5,000 titles.

CD-ROM Warranty

Addison-Wesley Professional warrants the enclosed CD-ROM to be free of defects in materials and faulty workmanship under normal use for a period of ninety days after purchase (when purchased new). If a defect is discovered in the CD-ROM during this warranty period, a replacement CD-ROM can be obtained at no charge by sending the defective CD-ROM, postage prepaid, with proof of purchase to:

Disc Exchange
Addison-Wesley Professional
Pearson Technology Group
75 Arlington Street, Suite 300
Boston, MA 02116
Email: AWPro@aw.com

Addison-Wesley Professional makes no warranty or representation, either expressed or implied, with respect to this software, its quality, performance, merchantability, or fitness for a particular purpose. In no event will Addison-Wesley Professional, its distributors, or dealers be liable for direct, indirect, special, incidental, or consequential damages arising out of the use or inability to use the software. The exclusion of implied warranties is not permitted in some states. Therefore, the above exclusion may not apply to you. This warranty provides you with specific legal rights. There may be other rights that you may have that vary from state to state. The contents of this CD-ROM are intended for personal use only.

More information and updates are available at:

http://www.awprofessional.com/